Challenges to Democracy in Latin America and the Caribbean:

Evidence from the AmericasBarometer 2006-07

Mitchell A. Seligson, Ph.D., Editor

The publication of this report was made possible thanks to the support of the Democracy and Governance program of United States Agency for International Development. The opinions expressed herein do not necessarily reflect the views of the United States Agency for International Development.

March, 2008

CONTENT

Preface

The United States Agency for International Development (USAID) takes pride in its support of the Latin American Public Opinion Project (LAPOP) democracy and governance surveys in Latin America and the Caribbean over the past two decades. LAPOP findings have been a crucial tool to USAID missions in diagnosing the nature of the democratic challenge; sparking policy dialogue and debate within Latin American countries; monitoring on-going USAID programs; and evaluating and measuring USAID performance in supporting democracy and good governance in the region. The reports have often served as the "voice" of citizens on the quality of democracy. We hope that this 2006-2007 study also proves to be useful to policy-makers, democracy advocates, donors and practitioners.

The decision to undertake democracy surveys in Latin America and the Caribbean emerged from the USAID country missions, where field democracy officers have increasingly depended on them as a management and policy tool. The depth and breadth of the questionnaire allows us to look beyond simple questions and examine complex relationships related to gender, ethnicity, geography, economic well-being, and other conditions, and delve deeply into specific practices and cultures to identify where our assistance might be most fruitful in promoting democracy. The surveys represent a unique USAID resource, as a comparative, consistent, and high quality source of information over time. USAID is grateful for the leadership of Dr. Mitchell Seligson at Vanderbilt University, his outstanding Latin American graduate students from throughout the hemisphere and the participation and expertise of the many regional academic and expert institutions that have been involved in this project.

Two recent trends in these surveys have made them even more useful. One is the addition of more countries to the survey base, using a core of common questions, which allows valid comparisons across systems and over time. The second, and even more important, is the introduction of geographically or project-based "over-sampling" in some of the countries where USAID has democracy programs. The result is a new capability for USAID missions to examine the impact of their programs in statistically valid ways by comparing the "before and after" of our work, and also comparing changes in the areas where we have programs to changes in areas where we do not have them. These methodologies should provide one of the most rigorous tests of program effectiveness of donor interventions in any field.

Promoting democracy and good governance is a US government foreign policy priority, and our investment of both effort and money is a substantial one. Democratic development is a relatively new field of development, however, and our knowledge of basic political relationships and the impact of donor assistance is still at an early phase. It is critical that we be able to determine which programs work and under what circumstances they work best, learning from our experience and constantly improving our programs. To meet this challenge, USAID has undertaken a new initiative, the Strategic and Operational Research Agenda, (SORA). With the assistance of the National Academy of Sciences. SORA has already incorporated the insights of numerous experts in political science and research methodology into our work. The LAPOP democracy surveys are a critical component of this evaluation effort. We hope their findings will

stimulate a dialogue among governments, NGOs, scholars and the public that will help, in the long run, to solidify democracy in Latin America.

Dr. Margaret Sarles
Division Chief, Strategic Planning and Research
Office of Democracy and Governance
U.S. Agency for International Development

Foreword

The AmericasBarometer, 2006-2007: Background to the Study

By Mitchell A. Seligson
Centennial Professor of Political Science
and Director, the Latin American Public Opinion Project (LAPOP)
Vanderbilt University

I am very pleased to introduce to you the 2006-2007 round of the **AmericasBarometer** series of surveys, one of the many and growing activities of the Latin American Public Opinion Project (LAPOP). That project, initiated over two decades ago, is hosted by Vanderbilt University. LAPOP began with the study of democratic values in one country, Costa Rica, at a time when much of the rest of Latin America was caught in the grip of repressive regimes that widely prohibited studies of public opinion (and systematically violated human rights and civil liberties). Today, fortunately, such studies can be carried out openly and freely in virtually all countries in the region. The **AmericasBarometer** is an effort by LAPOP to measure democratic values and behaviors in the Americas using national probability samples of voting-age adults. The first effort was in 2004, when eleven countries were included, and all of those studies are already available on the LAPOP web site. The present study reflects LAPOP's most extensive effort to date, incorporating 20 countries. For the first time, through the generosity of a grant from the Center for the Americas, it was possible to include the United States and Canada. The United States Agency for International Development (USAID) provided the core funding to enable to study to incorporate much of Latin America and the Caribbean, so that in 2006-2007, as of this writing, the following countries have been included: Mexico, Guatemala, El Salvador, Honduras, Nicaragua, Costa Rica, Panama, Colombia, Peru, Chile, Dominican Republic, Haiti and Jamaica). The U.S and Canada were also included, with the support of the Center for the Americas. Brazil and Uruguay were added too late to be included in this volume. The sample and questionnaire designs for all studies were uniform, allowing direct comparisons among them, as well as detailed analysis within each country. The 2006-2007 series involves a total of publications, one for each of the countries, authored by the country teams, and a summary study, written by the author of this Foreword, member of the LAPOP team at Vanderbilt and other collaborators.

We embarked on the 2006-2007 **AmericasBarometer** in the hope that the results would be of interest and of policy relevance to citizens, NGOs, academics, governments and the international donor community. Our hope is that the study could not only be used to help advance the democratization agenda, it would also serve the academic community which has been engaged in a quest to determine which values are the ones most likely to promote stable democracy. For that reason, we agreed on a common core of questions to include in our survey. The United Nations Development Programme (UNDP) provided a generous grant to LAPOP t bring together the leading scholars in the field in May, 2006, in order to help determine the best questions to incorporate into what was becoming the "UNDP Democracy Support Index." The scholars who attended that meeting prepared papers that were presented and critiqued at the

Vanderbilt workshop, and helped provide both a theoretical and empirical justification for the decisions taken. All of those papers are available on the LAPOP web site.

The UNDP-sponsored event was then followed by a meeting of the country teams in Heredia, Costa Rica, in May, 2006. Key democracy officers from USAID were present at the meeting, as well as staffers from LAPOP at Vanderbilt. With the background of the 2004 series and the UNDP workshop input, it became fairly easy for the teams to agree to common core questionnaire. The common core allows us to examine, for each nation and across nations, such issues as political legitimacy, political tolerance, support for stable democracy, civil society participation and social capital, the rule of law, participation in and evaluations of local government, crime victimization, corruption victimization, and voting behavior. Each country study contains an analysis of these important areas of democratic values and behaviors. In some cases we find striking similarities from country-to-country, whereas in other cases we find sharp contrasts.

A common sample design was crucial for the success of the effort. Prior to coming to Costa Rica, the author of this chapter prepared for each team the guidelines for the construction of a multi-stage, stratified area probability sample with a target N of 1,500. In the Costa Rica meeting each team met with Dr. Polibio Córdova, President of CEDATOS, Ecuador, and region-wide expert in sample design, trained under Leslie Kish at the University of Michigan. Refinements in the sample designs were made at that meeting and later reviewed by Dr. Córdova. Detailed descriptions of the sample are contained in annexes in each country publication.

The Costa Rica meeting was also a time for the teams to agree on a common framework for analysis. We did not want to impose rigidities on each team, since we recognized from the outset that each country had its own unique circumstances, and what was very important for one country (e.g., crime, voting abstention) might be largely irrelevant for another. But, we did want each of the teams to be able to make direct comparisons to the results in the other countries. For that reason, we agreed on a common method for index construction. We used the standard of an Alpha reliability coefficient of greater than .6, with a preference for .7, as the minimum level needed for a set of items to be called a scale. The only variation in that rule was when we were using "count variables," to construct an *index* (as opposed to a *scale*) in which we merely wanted to know, for example, how many times an individual participated in a certain form of activity. In fact, most of our reliabilities were well above .7, many reaching above .8. We also encouraged all teams to use factor analysis to establish the dimensionality of their scales. Another common rule, applied to all of the data sets, was in the treatment of missing data. In order to maximize sample N without unreasonably distorting the response patterns, we substituted the mean score of the individual respondent's choice for any scale or index in which there were missing data, but only when the missing data comprised less than half of all the responses for that individual.

Another agreement we struck in Costa Rica was that each major section of the studies would be made accessible to the layman reader, meaning that there would be heavy use of bivariate and tri-variate graphs. But we also agreed that those graphs would always follow a multivariate analysis (either OLS or logistic regression), so that the technically informed reader could be assured that the individual variables in the graphs were indeed significant predictors of the dependent variable being studied. We also agreed on a common graphical format (using chart templates prepared by LAPOP for SPSS 14). Finally, a common "informed consent" form was prepared, and approval for research on human subjects was granted by the Vanderbilt University Institutional Review Board (IRB). All senior investigators in the project studied the human subjects protection materials utilized by Vanderbilt and took and passed the certifying test. All publicly available data for this project are deeidentified, thus protecting the right of anonymity guaranteed to each respondent. The informed consent form appears in the questionnaire appendix of each study.

A concern from the outset was minimization of error and maximization of the quality of the database. We did this in several ways. First, we agreed on a common coding scheme for all of the closed-ended questions. Second, our partners at the Universidad de Costa Rica prepared a common set of data entry formats, including careful range checks, using the U.S. Census Bureau's CSPro software. Third, all data files were entered in their respective countries, and verified, after which the files were sent to LAPOP at Vanderbilt review. At that point, a random list of 100 questionnaire identification numbers was sent back to each team, who were then asked to ship those 100 surveys via express courier LAPOP for auditing. This audit consisted of two steps, the first involved comparing the responses written on the questionnaire during the interview with the responses as entered by the coding teams. The second step involved comparing the coded responses to the data base itself. If a significant number of errors was encountered through this process, the entire data base had to be reentered and the process of auditing was repeated on the new data base. Fortunately, in very few cases did that happen in the 2006-2007 **AmericasBarometer**. Finally, the data sets were merged by our expert, Dominique Zéphyr into one uniform multi-nation file, and copies were sent to all teams so that they could carry out comparative analysis on the entire file.

An additional technological innovation in the 2006-2007 round is that we used handheld computers (Personal Digital Assistants, or PDAs) to collect the data in five of the countries. Our partners at the Universidad de Costa Rica developed the program, EQCollector and formatted it for use in the 2006-2007 survey. We found this method of recording the survey responses extremely efficient, resulting in higher quality data with fewer errors than with the paper-and-pencil method. In addition, the cost and time of data entry was eliminated entirely. Our plan is to expand the use of PDAs in future rounds of LAPOP surveys.

The fieldwork for the surveys was carried out only after the questionnaire were pretested extensively in each country. In many cases we were able to send LAPOP staffers to the countries that were new to the AmericasBarometer to assist in the pretests. Suggestions from each country were then transmitted to LAPOP at Vanderbilt and revisions were made. In most countries this meant now fewer than 20 version revisions. The common standard was to finalize the questionnaire on version 23. The result was a highly polished instrument, with common questions but with appropriate customization of vocabulary for country-specific needs. In the case of countries with significant indigenous-speaking population, the questionnaires were translated into those languages (e.g., Quechua and Aymara in Bolivia). We also developed versions in English for the English-speaking Caribbean and for Atlantic coastal America, as well as a French Creole version for use in Haiti and a Portuguese version for Brazil. In the end, we had versions in ten different languages. All of those questionnaires form part of the

www.lapopsurveys.org_web site and can be consulted there or in the appendixes for each country study.

Country teams then proceeded to analyze their data sets and write their studies. When the drafts were ready, the next step in our effort to maximize quality of the overall project was for the teams to meet again in plenary session, this time in Santo Domingo de Santo Domingo, Costa Rica. In preparation for that meeting, held in November June 2004, teams of researchers were assigned to present themes emerging from the studies. For example, one team made a presentation on corruption and democracy, whereas another discussed the rule of law. These presentations, delivered in PowerPoint, were then critiqued by a small team of our most highly qualified methodologists, and then the entire group of researchers and USAID democracy staffers discussed the results. That process was repeated over a two-day period. It was an exciting time, seeing our findings up there "in black and white," but it was also a time for us to learn more about the close ties between data, theory and method.   After the Costa Rica meeting ended, the draft studies were read by the LAPOP team at Vanderbilt and returned to the authors for corrections. Revised studies were then submitted and they were each read and edited by Mitchell Seligson, the scientific coordinator of the project., read and critiqued each draft study. Those studies were then returned to the country teams for final correction and editing, and were sent to USAID democracy officers for their critiques. What you have before you, then, is the product of the intensive labor of scores of highly motivated researchers, sample design experts, field supervisors, interviewers, data entry clerks, and, of course, the over 27,000 respondents to our survey. Our efforts will not have been in vain if the results presented here are utilized by policy makers, citizens and academics alike to help strengthen democracy in Latin America.

Acknowledgements

The study was made possible by the generous support of the United States Agency for International Development (USAID). Margaret Sarles, Chief of Strategic Planning and Research in the Office of Democracy and Governance of USAID, assisted by Eric Kite, Maria Barrón and Elizabeth Ramirez in the Latin American Bureau, secured the funding and made possible the entire project thanks to their unceasing support. All of the participants in the study are grateful to them.   At Vanderbilt University, the study would not have been possible without the generosity, collaboration and hard work of many individuals. Vanderbilt's Dean of Arts and Science, Richard MacCarty provided financial support for many critical aspects of the research.   Nicholas S. Zeppos, Provost and Vice Chancellor for Academic Affairs generously offered LAPOP a suite of offices and conference space, and had it entirely reconditioned and equipped for the project. Vera Kutzinski, Director of the Center for the Americas has strongly supported the project administratively and financially, and contributed key funding to enable the inclusion of the United States and Canada in this round of the AmericasBarometer. Her administrative assistant, Janelle Lees made lots of things happen efficiently. Neal Tate, Chair of the Department of Political Science at Vanderbilt has been a strong supporter of the project since its inception at Vanderbilt and facilitated its integration with the busy schedule of the Department. Tonya Mills, Grants Administrator and Patrick D. Green, Associate Director, Division of Sponsored Research, Vanderbilt University performed heroically in managing the countless contract and financial details of the project. In a study as complex as this, literally dozens of contracts had to be signed and hundreds of invoices paid. They deserve my special appreciation for their efforts.

At LAPOP Central, the burden of the project fell on Pierre Martin Dominique Zéphyr, our LAPOP Research Coordinator and Data Analyst. Dominique worked tirelessly, almost always seven days a week, on virtually every aspect of the studies, from their design through their implementation and analysis. He also had central responsibility for preparing the training material for the teams for the data analysis and for handling the data audits and merging of the data bases. Dominique also served as Regional coordinator of the Caribbean countries, and personally did the pretesting and interviewer training in each of them. Finally, he worked as co-collaborator on the Haiti study. Julio Carrión of the University of Delaware served as Regional Coordinator for Mexico, Central America and the Andes. He managed this while also serving as co-collaborator of the Peru study. The members of the LAPOP graduate research team were involved in every aspect of the studies, from questionnaire design, data audits and overall quality control. I would like to thank them all: María Fernanda Boidi, Abby Córdova Guillén, José Miguel Cruz, Juan Carlos Donoso, Jorge Daniel Montalvo, Daniel Moreno Morales, Diana Orces, and Vivian Schwarz-Blum. Their Ph.D. programs at Vanderbilt are being supported by USAID, the Vanderbilt University Center for Latin American and Iberian Studies and the Department of Political Science. My colleague Jon Hiskey participated in our weekly meetings on the surveys, adding his own important expertise and encouragement. Our web master, María Clara Bertini, made sure that our efforts were transparent, and has done an outstanding job managing the ever-growing web page of LAPOP and the AmericasBarometer. Héctor Lardé and Roberto Ortiz were responsible for cover design and text formatting, and did so with great attention to detail.

Critical to the project's success was the cooperation of the many individuals and institutions in the countries studied who worked tirelessly to meet what at times seemed impossible deadlines. Their names, countries and affiliations are listed below:

Country	Researchers
Summary Report	Prof. Mitchell Seligson, Director of LAPOP, and Centennial Professor of Political Science, Vanderbilt University (project director)
Mexico and Central America Group	
Mexico	●Dr. Kenneth M. Coleman, Senior Research Analyst and Study Director of Market Strategies, Inc. ●Pablo Parás García, President of DATA Opinión Pública y Mercados
Guatemala	●Dr. Dinorah Azpuru, Senior Associate at ASIES in Guatemala and Assistant Professor of Political Science at Wichita State University in the U.S.
El Salvador	●Dr. Ricardo Córdova (Salvadoran national), President of FundaUngo, El Salvador ●Prof. Miguel Cruz, Director of IUDOP (Public Opinion Institute) at the Universidad Centroamericana (UCA)
Honduras	●Prof. Miguel Cruz, Director of IUDOP (Public Opinion Institute) at the Universidad Centroamericana (UCA) ●José Rene Argueta, Ph.D. candidate, University of Pittsburgh
Nicaragua	●Prof. Manuel Ortega-Hegg, Director of the Centro de Análisis Socio-Cultural (CASC) at the Universidad Centroamericana (UCA), Managua, Nicaragua ●Marcelina Castillo Venerio, Centro de Análisis Socio-cultural (CASC), Universidad Centroamericana. (UCA)
Costa Rica	●Dr. Luis Rosero, Director of Centro Centroamericano de Población (CCP, and Professor at the Universidad de Costa Rica. ●Jorge Vargas, Sub-Director of the Estado de la Nación project, United Nations
Panama	●Dr. Orlando Pérez, Associate Professor of Political Science at Central Michigan University

Country	Researchers
Andean/Southern Cone Group	
Colombia	•Prof. Juan Carlos Rodríguez-Raga, Professor at the Universidad de los Andes
Ecuador	•Dr. Mitchell Seligson, Director of LAPOP, and Centennial Professor of Political Science, Vanderbilt University •Juan Carlos Donoso, Ph.D. student, Vanderbilt University •Daniel Moreno, Ph.D. student, Vanderbilt Universtity •Diana Orcés, Ph.D. student, Vanderbilt University •Vivian Schwarz-Blum, Ph.D student, Vanderbilt University
Peru	•Dr. Julio Carrión (Peruvian national) Associate Professor at the University of Delaware in the US, and Researcher at the Instituto de Estudios Peruanos •Patricia Zárate Ardela, Researcher at the Instituto de Estudios Peruanos
Bolivia	•Dr. Mitchell Seligson Director of LAPOP, and Centennial Professor of Political Science, Vanderbilt University •Abby B. Córdova, Ph.D. student, Vanderbilt University •Juan Carlos Donoso, Ph.D. student, Vanderbilt University •Daniel Moreno, Ph.D. student, Vanderbilt Universtity •Diana Orcés, Ph.D. student, Vanderbilt University •Vivian Schwarz-Blum, Ph.D. student, Vanderbilt University
Paraguay	•Manuel Orrego, CIRD, Paraguay
Chile	• Juan Pablo Luna, Instituto de Ciencia Política, Pontificia Universidad Católica de Chile
Uruguay	•María Fernanda Boidi, Ph.D. student, Vanderbilt University •Dr. María del Rosario Queirolo, Professor of Political Science at the Universidad de Montevideo
Brazil	• Denise Pavia, Universidade Federal de Goiás, Goiás, Brazil • Simon Bohn, York University • Rachael Meneguello, Brazil, Diretora do Centro de Estudos de Opinião Pública (CESOP) and Professor of Political Science, University of Campinas, Brazil • David Samules, University of Minnesota • Luicio Renno, University of Arizona
Caribbean Group	
Dominican Republic	•Dr. Jana Morgan Kelly Assistant Professor of Political Science at the University of Tennessee in the US •Dr. Rosario Espinal, Professor of Sociology Science at Temple University in the US
Guyana	• Dr. Mark Bynoe, Director, School of Earth and Environmental Sciences, University of Guyana •Ms. Talia Choy, Lecturer, Department of Government and International Affairs, University of Guyana.
Haiti	•Dominique Zephyr, Research Coordinator of LAPOP, Vanderbilt University • Yves François Pierre, Groupe de Recherche en Sciences Sociales (GRESS)
Jamaica	•Ian Boxill, Professor of Comparative Sociology, Department of Sociology, Psychology and Social Work, UWI, Mona. •Roy Russell, Lecturer in statistics, Department of Sociology, Psychology and Social Work, UWI, Mona. •Arlene Bailey, Information Sytems specialist, Department of Sociology, Psychology and Social Work, UWI, Mona. •Balford Lewis, Lecturer in research methods, Department of Sociology, Psychology and Social Work, UWI, Mona. •LLoyd Waller, Lecturer in research methods, Department of Government, UWI, Mona

Finally, we wish to thank the more than 30,000 individuals in these countries who took time away from their busy lives to answer our questions. Without their cooperation, this study would have been impossible.

Nashville, Tennessee, March, 2008

Overview

By Margaret Sarles and Mitchell A. Seligson

There is much to celebrate in the strengthening of democratic practices and institutions in Latin America. Once ruled almost entirely by dictators, countries in the region are now ruled almost entirely by democrats. Elections have emerged as the established norm for deciding "who rules," replacing the frequent and irregular transfers of power via military and executive coups of the past. Indeed, even the most charismatic leaders who espouse radical change seem committed to free and fair elections as the path to legitimate leadership. With greater access to power through elections, even the radical left is using the political system to come to power, rather than using violence. The holdouts, such as the protracted guerrilla movement in Colombia, or the nearly half-century long socialist dictatorship in Cuba, seem like anachronistic, isolated anomalies in a region committed to electoral politics. Similarly, democratic trends are evident outside of electoral politics. Civil society organizations and independent business groups grow and prosper; political parties take their turns in and out of power; an increasingly independent and feisty press uncovers malfeasance, and local officials assert more independence from the center. State-sanctioned human rights violations, so frequent in the recent past, are now the exception to the rule. On the governance side, Latin American democracies have been able to put together political coalitions to successfully tackle a number of important policy issues, providing macroeconomic stability, increased investment, increased access to education and health, and a number have made impressive gains in fighting poverty. Democracy seems to have become, to use Adam Przeworski's classic terminology, "the only game in town."

Yet, continued progress in the direction of democratic consolidation and higher quality democracies is certainly not a foregone conclusion, as the results of Freedom House's 2007 "Freedom in World" survey demonstrates. The report notes an overall decline in the state of freedom worldwide, and a growing pushback against democracy by authoritarian governments, including Venezuela. Even in the relatively consolidated democracies of Mexico, Argentina, and Brazil, "freedom scores" declined last year. While competitive electoral politics continue to thrive, and the institutionalization of electoral institutions is indeed a significant hallmark of progress, other democratic institutions show worrisome signs of weakness in the region. Continuing government corruption scandals illustrate the weakness of accountability and rule of law, as do high crime rates. Furthermore, after being democratically elected, a number of presidents are pushing the boundaries of executive power to new extremes, making every effort to amass greater and greater power at the expense of representative institutions fundamental to liberal democracy. Political parties in many countries remain weak. The rule of law is fragile in many countries, while local governments are starved for resources. Ethnic-based parties are on the rise in some countries, suggesting increasing sectarianism.

What are we to make of this mixture of trends, both positive and negative? At the macro-level, the patterns are not clear. At best, they show that democratic consolidation is not a linear process, providing evidence of democratization as a somewhat lumpy process, with some aspects proceeding well, while others seem frustratingly intractable. It is not clear whether a negative change in a particular year, in a particular country, is a real set-back to democracy, part of an

underlying movement away from liberal democracy, or whether we are simply seeing an unsteady, back and forth process that may in fact be compatible with long-term democratic consolidation. To understand Latin American democracies, we need to go below the macro level. We need more and better data. And we need to undertake a more fine-grained analysis that permits detailed comparisons among specific aspects of democratic change in the region.

It is the purpose of this regional volume to begin such a comparative, detailed analysis of democratic processes in Latin America and the Caribbean, to provide a different kind of lens through which to analyze and make judgments on the state of democracy in the region.

This research is based on the AmericasBarometer democracy surveys undertaken in 22 countries in 2006 and 2007, involving more than 34,000 in-depth, face-to-face interviews with citizens in the region. The AmericasBarometer data reveal what citizens do, think, and feel in terms of democracy, as well as information on personal attributes, allowing detailed analysis available through no other source. For nearly all of the countries, detailed country case studies have been written based on the surveys, covering themes such as democratic legitimacy, corruption, crime and violence, and citizen participation.[1] For some countries, there are multiple surveys, stretching back ten years or more. As they are published, the country survey studies often receive great publicity, and their results are debated and discussed in the national press and among people interested in politics, contributing to the overall dialogue on the state of democracy and democratic reforms.

This regional report is a companion to the country studies. It brings together some of the most important findings from the surveys, but focuses on the region as a whole. The articles cover topics critical to democratic development and sustainability in the region, and should broadly contribute to the ongoing discourse on democracy and governance reform in policy and development communities.

We have chosen to focus on a single, important theme: the challenges to democracy in Latin America and the Caribbean. Even focused this way, we have nonetheless had to be selective in choosing a limited number of topics. We selected them on the basis of 1) our evaluation of their importance to the processes of democratic development; 2) their salience within Latin America as important political topics; and 3) how well survey research can deal with the topic. Obviously, there are many aspects of institutional development, macro-political change, and leadership that require analysis beyond survey research that are important for understanding democratic development in Latin America. And, conversely, there are certain themes for which surveys provide excellent, and sometimes the only, robust empirical evidence. We have naturally emphasized those themes in this report.

---

[1] The country reports are available on the Latin American Public Opinion Project website in pdf format. (see www.LapopSurveys.org). The data sets for each country are also available world-wide, free, for on-line analysis through the above website. We welcome and encourage other scholars to use the data freely, both to test the findings presented here and to undertake their own research. Given the sheer quantity of data available, this volume, as well as the country monographs, can only begin to scratch the surface in uncovering interesting findings on democracy.

The articles in this volume cover a broad spectrum of approaches to democracy, but present a unified set of analyses in many ways. All link democratic theory to some aspect of the survey data, and all suggest the broad policy concern that lies behind the topic. Most deal with some aspect of the questions of who supports democracy, what kind of democracy, and under what conditions do they support it. Some search for broad findings, while others dig more deeply into a particular relationship that has implications for democratic sustainability. Many of them combine survey data with macro, structural variables, using complex regression analysis that allow us to assess the relative importance of individual attitudes and behaviors compared to country-level characteristics such as a country's wealth. As a group, they show how much can be learned from surveys that goes beyond easy characterizations of the region's democratic culture. In fact, many of them present findings that directly contradict what has passed for the "common wisdom" about Latin American democracies.

Careful readers will note that there is not total agreement on all points among the authors. In part, this reflects the fact that authors have often chosen different, but related, concepts and measurements to examine a basic relationship, and the findings themselves therefore will differ. In part, however, it reflects the imperfect state of democratic theory itself, in which there is still great debate over the significance of unresponsive political parties, or people's willingness to consider political options other than democracy as a political system. We have not made an effort to have all the authors conform to a single definition of democratic stability or change, and in fact welcome the diverse interpretations that they bring to their work.

These articles as a whole move the debate on democratization away from the tendency of policy wonks to declare the region's progress in black or white terms, or to provide facile characterizations of an entire hemisphere. While the aggregation of country level data to a regional level surely leads to some loss of nuance, the authors are careful to limit their generalization, or provide country level comparisons, when appropriate. Overall, these region-based analyses provide the kind of comparative evidence that has been lacking, in the debate on democratization.

The Challenges

The first challenge to democracy we address is one of the most worrisome to analysts focusing on the contemporary state of democratization in Latin America: the willingness of many Latin Americans to grant, and even encourage, their newly elected Presidents to disregard the normal checks and balances of a modern democracy and assume semi-authoritarian powers. Creeping presidentialism in Latin America was noted by Guillermo O'Donnell in his classic paper on "delegative democracy" in 1995, and the tendency seems, if anything, to have grown stronger in the thirteen years since the article was published (O'Donnell 1995). At times it has been the a president himself who has sought widened powers, expanding the use of "decree laws," for example, that can be enacted with limited legislative input, or none at all. Many presidents have also successfully lobbied for Constitutional changes allowing them to stay in power beyond their original limits. But it would be a mistake to think that presidents in these relatively new democracies are taking on these powers without citizen approval. Such changes, in fact, are usually very popular. It appears that many citizens want to have their free and fair

elections, but that once elected, they feel comfortable with giving their presidents extraordinary powers.

Many researchers have seen this political/cultural characteristic as an indication of the emergence of electoral authoritarianism, or a contemporary form of democratic populism, characterized by virtually unchecked executives, supported by mass movements who see the opposition and competitive party politics as a threat, rather than as a necessary condition for liberal democracy to prosper. Is this an important characteristic of democratic culture in Latin America? If so, does it represent a limit to the institutionalization of democratic practices in the region?

It is precisely this phenomenon that Mitchell A. Seligson explores in the first article in this report: the extent to which citizens support executive dominance, and are willing to abandon many of the checks and balances required in a sustainable democratic state. Seligson looks at electoral authoritarianism in terms of the left/right political ideology of citizens. He finds those identifying as "left" "are more skeptical and mistrustful of political institutions, less inclined to believe that democracy is better than other systems, and more favorable to a strong leader. If Latin America is "turning left," as a number of recent elections seem to demonstrate, this might be a cause for great concern. It would indicate an electorate less and less committed to a democratic political system.

Yet, Seligson's analysis of context provides a much more nuanced picture. First, he finds that even with the small increases in leftist orientation that seem to have taken place, Latin American citizens remain slightly to the "right" ideologically, compared to other regions of the world. More importantly, however, he is able to determine important limitations that most citizens, even those on the left, want to impose on the power of an elected leader. He notes that even as they greatly distrust political parties, most citizens nonetheless consider them essential to democracy: they do not want to abandon them or other political institutions. And even while those surveyed are impatient with the slow pace of economic reform, there are indeed important limits to the "populist" measures they will support to get there.

In Chapter II, Julio Carrión then examines a more theoretical, but equally important question for those interested in the state of democracy in Latin America: What kind of democracy do people have in mind when they say they "support democracy?" How deep and consistent is their commitment? What kind of people most and least support democracy?

Carrión's approach is methodologically path-breaking, particularly in the Latin American context. His analysis is based on open-ended questions asking people to define what they mean by democracy. These questions, developed by AfroBarometer, and administered in numerous African countries over time, allow us for the first time to get a good sense of citizens' understanding of democracy in Latin America, and even to compare Latin American and African countries. It should come as no surprise that mass publics do not agree on a single definition of democracy, since even experts disagree on its meaning. Carrión applies sophisticated modeling techniques, making it possible to control for a series of variables that have often hidden the real relationships between support for democracy and other attributes, uncovering somewhat startling relationships.

While Carrión finds that a majority of Latin Americans hold a view of democracy that embraces freedom and liberty, he also demonstrates that a significant percentage refer to government services and benefits or economic progress as part of their definition. Perhaps even more troubling is the number of respondents who seem to have no idea what the term means. This in itself represents a democratic challenge.

Like Seligson, Carrión finds that people who most embrace a liberal definition of democracy have certain characteristics: they support democracy as a system to a greater extent, and are likely to be older, to be male, to be wealthier, to live outside of rural areas, and to have greater political knowledge. Controlling for these attributes, Carrión finds that the often-discussed relationship between "social trust" and support for democracy disappears completely. In addition, and again in contradiction to much of the prevailing analysis, he finds that "whether a person has been a victim of crime does not make him or her less likely to support democracy." This suggests that a policy priority on lowering crime rates may not have the effect on increasing support for democracy, at least in general terms, which some reformers had hoped for. On the other hand, those who are most upset at government corruption and those negative about the national economy are indeed more inclined to support non-democratic political alternatives.

In Chapter III, María Fernanda Boidi tackles one of the most debated and least understood institutional aspects of democratization in the region: the state of political parties. Political parties are essential for a modern democratic political system to function, but are often characterized as "weak" in Latin America, and mistrusted by citizens. In fact, while surveys have shown that political parties are the least trusted political institutions world-wide, Latin American parties have the dubious honor of being least trusted even within this sorry group. What does this mean for democracy?

Boidi's contribution to this discussion lies first in the presentation of new data. She has amassed data from the surveys by country on party identification, participation in partisan activities, trust in political parties, and other party-related behavior voting, that has never before been analyzed. Her chapter illustrates the richness of the survey data as it relates to political parties, and should spur other party researchers to pursue it further. She sets out to explain why Latin Americans have such low trust in parties, developing a multiple regression model that includes variables based on many of the most frequently cited reasons for low trust, including perceived government ability to combat corruption, crime, and poverty, and to reduce unemployment. Her preliminary analyses indicate that these factors seem to have almost no explanatory power.

Like other contributors to this volume, Boidi is struck by what appear to be inconsistencies in citizens' views of politics and democracy. She notes that not only is trust in parties low, voters do not use parties as an "information shortcut" for voting choices: only one-fifth of the respondents choose a presidential candidate based on his or her party, with wide variations by country. She concludes that "political parties are failing to provide meaningful alternatives for leading the government; as a consequence, they do not fulfill their representational task." Yet, she also finds that citizens reject having a democracy without parties, and that there is a close relationship between ideology and party vote, with people who identify

more as "rightist" voting more for "rightist" parties, and the reverse, as Seligson also showed from a somewhat different perspective. Boidi's analysis offers intriguing evidence that Latin American political parties are not merely vehicles for personal ambition for leaders, nor "patrimonial" parties kept alive only through distribution of jobs and personal linkages, but are also based in genuine policy and ideological differences.

An even more basic challenge to the sustainability of democracy than political parties is the low level of "system support" than many Latin Americans express towards their new democracies. For democracies to remain stable, citizens must express at least minimal levels of support for their political system. Democracies that are not supported by their citizens are vulnerable to instability and even breakdown. This problem is explored in Chapter IV by Vivian Schwarz-Blum.

Schwarz-Blum reiterates an important initial point: In highly industrialized countries, "system support" for democracy is relatively high (even if it has declined in recent years), and basically unaffected by a country's poor economic performance or even by a citizen's own economic situation. Unfortunately, in Latin America, she finds that this is not the case. Schwarz-Blum uses as a definition of "system support" an index composed of five questions created by LAPOP that probes whether or not the respondent is proud of his/her political system, whether trials are fair, whether political institutions should be respected, whether basic rights are safe-guarded, and whether the political system should be supported. This, she argues, is a more demanding measure of support than the question of whether citizens support democracy as "better than the alternatives" used in other articles in the report. By this measure, Canada and the US stand at the highest end of the 19 countries studied, with about two-thirds of respondents supporting their democratic systems, with Ecuador and Paraguay at the other end, with less than 40 percent system support. These findings lead to a concern for the democratic sustainability among the countries at the low end of the scale.

In an interesting contrast to Boidi's findings that economic performance does not affect trust in *parties*, Schwarz-Blum finds that good economic performance does, in fact, increase more *general support* for a country's political system. Latin American citizens dissatisfied with their country's economic performance, or who perceive their own economic situation negatively, support their democracies less. Understanding this linkage of democracy support to economic progress contributes to a much wider contemporary discussion on the relationship of economic performance to democratic sustainability, particularly during the early years of a new democracy, and illustrates the potential for survey data to analyze it. Her results place some of the burden of democratic success squarely on the shoulders of those who manage national economies, including national political leaders, central banks, parties and policy makers.

Historically, political power in Latin America has been excessively centralized at the national level, and, within the national government, in the executive branch, making authoritarian political rule easier and more likely. Seligson addressed one major aspect of this challenge to democracy in his discussion of executive dominance in Chapter I, revealing some continuation of citizen support for "electoral authoritarianism" even a generation after new democratic systems were constituted, although with important limitations. Daniel Montalvo addresses the other side of over-centralization in Chapter V, carefully examining the decentralization of power from of the national arena into municipal governments. Is decentralization one of the solutions to developing sustainable democracies?

Montalvo's work is one of the few empirical studies that apply survey data to this important problem. Decentralization has been promoted as a permanent impediment to the re-imposition of authoritarian rule, as the growth of independent, sub-national power centers potentially restricts the powers of national government. It promises to place citizens closer to the governments that influence their daily lives, and to provide wider access to and greater opportunities for citizen participation in government, as well as government knowledge of and sensitivity to local voters' needs. Over the past generation, country after country has instituted direct elections for mayors and municipal authorities; the final democratic government to do so was Costa Rica, with direct mayoral elections first taking place in 2002. Yet we know little about whether citizens in fact feel that this promise for better democracy and improved governance has been realized.

Montalvo, in fact, finds some divergence between the grand hopes for decentralization and its support among citizens in Latin America. Overall, people's trust in local government is about the same as in national governments. However, this obscures great variation within the region, with citizens in some countries trusting much more in local government, and preferring that services be provided locally, while in other countries just the reverse is true. The research sets out a typology of states, based on differential levels of trust at the national and local levels. It then probes into the historical events that have led to these differences, illustrating how survey data can complement and strengthen more traditional forms of country-level research. Jamaica's positive experience with local government plans, Ecuador's poor track record with stable national governments – these and other unique country experiences help explain wide country differences. These findings suggests that there are differential opportunities for decentralization as a means of promoting democracy across Latin America, and that programs directed at increasing decentralization need to consider the beliefs and attitudes of citizens in each country if they are to reach their goals. The evidence in this chapter shows that it is not a silver bullet.

In Chapter VI, Rosario Queirolo returns to two themes discussed in other papers in the report: the relationship of economic performance to voting patterns, and whether the rise of the left observed in voting patterns represents a threat to democracy. She tests her hypotheses using slightly different data in the surveys, however, which both illustrates the multiple approaches possible using the survey data and also shows that the findings of the researchers will vary to some degree depending on the survey questions chosen. Queirolo tests competing economic theories that have been advanced to explain why Latin Americans have elected leftist Presidents in a number of countries. She concludes that the move to leftist government is not driven by fatigue with the market reforms of the "Washington Consensus," nor by ideology of the left, but rather by the failure of government – whatever its ideological stripe – to improve economic performance. Latin American voters have been more driven by economic outcomes than by ideology, she concludes. Voters choose parties that have not been "tainted" by being in office.

As she re-focuses us on the question of whether the left poses a "danger to democracy," she brings a different set of survey instruments to bear, using scales developed by LAPOP to measure political tolerance and support for basic liberties, in addition to the frequently used

question of whether a respondent agrees with the proposition that "Democracy may have its problems, but it is better than any other form of government." Her findings diverge in provocative ways from those of Seligson, however. While both find that the right has higher levels of support for a democratic political system than the left, Queirolo reports that leftists score higher in terms of political tolerance and support for civil liberties, while rightists are less inclined to support any use of force to overthrow a government. She concludes that the left poses no danger to democratization in Latin America: leftists are using the democratic political system rather than rejecting it, and they support beliefs consistent with a democratic culture.

Abby Córdova Guillén turns to another challenge to democracy – the often-cited lack of a "social capital" in Latin America that, according to experts like Robert Putnam and Larry Diamond, is necessary for democracy to be sustained. This is a complex topic, and Córdova Guillén offers important insights on Latin American democratic culture in Chapter VII. Does Latin America have the social capital needed to sustain democracy? Guillén compares Latin American countries to the consolidated democracies of the US and Canada, looking at the two components of social capital, interpersonal trust and civic participation. As expected, she finds that levels of social trust in the US and Canada are higher than in Latin American countries. In contrast, however, civic participation rates vary greatly, led by some countries, like Haiti, with very low levels of social trust. On the whole, the evidence shows that it is trust, rather than participation, with the more important relationship to democratic development and social capital.

Córdova Guillén then examines the sources of social trust to determine how enduring or, conversely, how malleable, social trust is as a societal value. If, as some have argued, it is deeply rooted in the history and religion of the region, and resistant to change, then we can expect that many Latin American countries will have great difficulty in sustaining democracy. Conversely, if the concept is rooted in structural or individual factors amenable to change, then it is more likely that if these factors are changed, a more democratic culture could take root.

She uses a hierarchical linear regression model to analyze individual and country contextual factors together, controlling for age, gender, schooling levels, and crime victimization, all possible explanations of differences between Latin America and the US and Canada scores on social trust. She concludes finally that it is not individual differences, but economic country-level factors that best explain trust levels. Like other researchers, she finds that the wealthier a country, the higher the level of social trust. However, she finds this potentially positive relationship between development and social trust undercut by another factor: economic inequality. The greater the inequality, the less impact that economic growth has on social trust. In other words, for social trust to increase, it is not enough to focus on economic development: there must also be a focus on improving economic equality. This conclusion on the primacy of economics to explain social trust is also important because economic development, and even, income distribution, are "malleable;" they are not individual traits resistant to change. Social trust can be changed.

To what degree does ethnicity pose a challenge to the consolidation of democracy in the region? Daniel Moreno addresses this challenge in Chapter VIII. In many Latin American countries, indigenous people and minorities have historically faced brutal discrimination, denied access to political and social power. The new democracies have been more inclusive, offering

political leadership opportunities for the first time to many such groups. But given Latin American history, do traditionally excluded groups truly feel part of the new political system? Are they willing to play the democratic political game? Will countries divide on the basis of ethnicity?

Moreno introduces the concept of a "sense of national integration," a combination of pride in country, and a belief that one's country holds a set of common values. He argues persuasively that this positive sense of country and political community is essential for consolidating democracy. He then asks the question whether people from traditionally excluded groups have the same sense of nationhood, the same sense of pride and common values, as the rest of the population. Given historical patterns of political and social exclusion of minorities, do they represent an "unintegrated," more alienated group within the polity?

His analysis finds the answer is no, with a very few exceptions. He shows that a very high percentage of all citizens across the hemisphere feel pride in their countries and that minorities express the same level of pride as their fellow citizens, except in four countries, Canada, Honduras, Peru and Panama. When he turns to the question of "sharing common values," however, some differences appear. People who describe themselves as ethnic minorities are less persuaded that there are commonly shared values, a concern because those who believe there are common values among citizens are also more politically tolerant. Like other researchers in this report, he notes how important individual attributes are for explaining differences, with older people feeling more national pride than younger ones, and women having a stronger sense of national common values than men. Overall, the story is a positive one. Ethnic identity seems to have no effect on the strength of the bond between citizens and the political community.

This research, as Moreno himself notes, only scratches the surface of what can be learned about ethnicity and democracy from the survey data. Studies of voting patterns and political behavior, in addition to political and practices, should in the future give us a better understanding of whether the new democracies will be able to integrate all citizens fully into politics and society.

Democratic political systems provide a means for all citizens to participate in politics, protecting even unpopular groups from the potential tyranny of the majority, with free speech and access to political power. Do the political cultures of Latin American countries support this very basic principle of democracy? Diana Orcés's analysis of this question in Chapter IX should lead to serious concern among democratic reformers.

Orcés uses a very basic definition of "political tolerance" developed by Seligson that asks respondents if they support the right of groups they don't agree with to vote, to demonstrate peacefully, to run for office, and to make political speeches. Each of these is a protected right in a democracy. Yet, many, and often most, citizens in Latin American countries do not agree that opposition groups should have these rights. Even in the consolidated democracies of the US and Canada, fully 20 percent of respondents are willing to deny opponents these rights. Most countries in Latin America and the Caribbean have about 40 percent who do not agree, and in four countries– Bolivia, Honduras, Ecuador, and Panama– a majority of citizens do not agree.

There are important differences in levels of tolerance among countries, with the data providing some support for the argument that the British and French colonial experiences might have provided a firmer base than Spanish colonialism for developing tolerance. But as she explores the roots of political tolerance, Orcés finds one factor above all others that explain differences in tolerance: the individuals' level of education. Those with a secondary education are much more likely to be politically tolerant, and those with a higher education even more so. She finds other factors also at play: Women on the whole are less politically tolerant than men, urbanites are more tolerant than those who live in rural areas. But higher education is by far the strongest attribute of those who support basic rights for groups they dislike. These differences are important to understand from a policy perspective, as they help guide efforts to develop a more democratic culture.

Does crime undermine democratic sustainability? The LAPOP survey analyses have led the way in identifying high crime victimization rates as a major challenge to democracy in Latin America. Particularly in Guatemala, El Salvador and Honduras, citizens in repeated surveys have said they would support a military coup d'état more to bring down crime. Some Central American countries have among the highest crime rates in the world. As crime has soared and youth gangs expanded, democratic reformers have struggled with how high a priority to place on lowering crime rates as a means of improving the quality and sustainability of democracy.

José Miguel Cruz's findings in Chapter X may change the way reformers look at the relationship of crime to democracy. Cruz looks at three different crime-related independent variables: whether an individual has been a crime victim; whether he/she feels insecure due to crime; and how he/she assesses government performance in combating crime. (It should be noted that this is the only article that focuses on a specific government performance measure, although the surveys include questions on government performance in combating poverty and corruption, and is interesting for that reason alone). He also looks at a broader array of democracy indicators as dependent variables: not only system support, but rejection of authoritarianism, and whether the police should be allowed to ignore the law in combating crime.

The results are startling. Based on a comparison of Central American countries, Cruz finds that "crime victimization" may not have the importance we have often given it, as a risk factor for democracy. Assessment of the government's performance, not actual crime victimization, and not even perception of insecurity, turns out to be the most significant crime-related independent variable: he notes that "personal victimization loses its powers of prediction in countries where it had previously appeared to be of importance," in Honduras and Nicaragua. It is institutional performance that is the key.

There is a complex relationship between victimization, perceptions of insecurity, and perceptions of institutional performance that needs greater exploration. His work also brings out some intriguing relationships between assessment of performance and people's willingness to let the police violate the law, and other non-democratic attitudes. Further research on this topic is likely to improve our ability to develop reforms to fight crime in a better way, which strengthens the foundations of a democratic culture rather than potentially undermining it.

In Chapter XI, Dominique Zephyr addresses the challenge that governmental corruption poses to democratic stability in the region. Democracy analysts often refer to "crime and corruption" as a double-barreled shotgun that weakens the new democracies and turns citizens away from them. As Zephyr quotes a former president of the Organization of American Studies: "Corruption is a terrible cancer that threatens the legitimacy of institutions and the rule of law."

Zephyr uses the empirical data on corruption developed by Mitch Seligson with the LAPOP surveys over the past decade, and expands the analysis to include many more countries. In general, analysts have needed to rely on Transparency International's Corruption Perception Index as the best measure available of a country's corruption levels, and it is still the only world-wide measure available. Within Latin America, however, the AmericasBarometer now makes available a series of questions to determine whether a citizen has had to pay a bribe, and to whom. This "corruption victimization" index moves us away from perceptions and "contagion effects," towards a much harder and more reliable measure of corruption. Using the LAPOP data, then, do the high corruption levels in many Latin American countries undermine democracy?

Zephyr notes that previous studies using TI data found no evidence that corruption affected citizens' opinions of democracy as a form of government. Using the LAPOP corruption victimization data, however, a different picture emerges. In fact, citizens who are forced to pay a bribe have less support for democracy as a system, trust government less, and view their democratic governments as less legitimate than people who have not have to pay a bribe. Wealthier, older people are more likely to have to pay bribes – people who in general are greater supporters of their democratic governments and of democracy in general. Corruption levels vary greatly by country, and within country, by the "source" of corruption – police systems, health ministries, local government, etc. As with many of the topics in this report, Zephyr's work raises a whole series of subsidiary questions for future research that would be useful not only for analysts but for practical policy-makers who need to focus their resources on where the problem resides.

In the final chapter, Juan Carlos Donoso looks at the challenge of rule of law in the region. "Rule of law" means many things to many people, and no single set of empirical data can capture its multi-dimensionality. But Donoso rightly identifies the need to shed whatever light is possible on a part of democracy that all bemoan as weak, in which donors have put great amounts of funding, and which suffers from lack of valid and reliable measurement.

This chapter brings together some very interesting and cutting-edge measures of rule of law for the first time. To capture whether the judiciary is independent, Donoso adopts a measure developed from the State Department's Annual Human Rights report. This State Department report has assumed rather remarkable credibility over the past decade or more, and political scientists are increasingly constructing measurable variables from its annual country essays on rule of law and human rights. He analyzes the autonomy of the judiciary in terms of people's support for democracy, their level of social trust, and adds some specific questions on whether citizens believe that trials are fair, that they can trust the police and trust the Supreme Court.

He arrives at some generally discouraging conclusions. The Supreme Court is one of the least trusted institutions in Latin America, although there are great differences among countries.

In fact, even controlling for alternative explanations, there is an "independent country effect" in rule of law. In Ecuador, where the Supreme Court has been the football in a no-holds-barred political struggle for years, citizens have lower trust in the Court than similar citizens elsewhere in the region. Most individual characteristics are not important, except for education and whether a person has been victimized by corruption or crime. These have a corrosive effect on trust in rule of law institutions.

Donoso makes a compelling case that attitudes towards rule of law are crucial for sustaining a democracy. In countries where the rule of law is more entrenched, citizens seem to recognize this, have greater trust in institutions, and more support for democracy. When citizens have less trust in rule of law institutions, they tend to agree with non-democratic statements such as "Judges get in the way of our presidents and they should be ignored."

Conclusions

These chapters provide much food for thought in how to understand democratic culture, and its importance for sustaining the new democracies of Latin America. They cover topics often not addressed in the literature, and make use of rich data that increase our knowledge of democracy below the surface of current events, crises, and elections. This is a detailed, nuanced micro-level look at democracy in the Americas. The findings present a complex mosaic, suggesting that "democracy" itself is a complex phenomenon, all too often simplified by a single index or number. The data behind these chapters in fact pose a challenge to democratic theorists: our information may be out-running our political constructs. Furthermore, policy makers and developmentalists will find in the information provided here conclusions that may challenge the conventional ways reformers have focused on democratic development. We look forward to widening the discussion on Latin America's path of democratic reform.

References

Huntington, Samuel P. *Political Order in Changing Societies*. New Haven: Yale University Press, 1968.
O'Donnell, Guillermo. "Delegative Democracy." *Journal of Democracy* 5, no. 1 (1995): 55-69.

Part I. Challenges to the Institutional Infrastructure of Democracy

I. The Rise of Populism and the Left: Challenge to Democratic Consolidation?[1]

Mitchell A. Seligson[*]

Abstract

What are we to make of the recent dramatic rise of the left in power and the resurrection of populism in Latin America? Do the trends reflect little more than a pendular shift in "mood" among voters, or are there more profound implications for democratic development? This paper examines citizens' political orientation, showing that over the last two years, there has been a slight movement "to the left," which is reflected at the ballot box. Furthermore, those with a more leftist orientation are more skeptical and less supportive of traditional political institutions and democratic values, and more willing to support a non-elected political leader. While levels of political tolerance, a critical democratic value, are about the same across the ideological spectrum, on most measures, those with on the right are firmer in their support for checks and balances on executive power and less willing to grant unlimited powers to a President. The variance across the countries is the region is high, however, and it is not clear whether these relationships will endure. However, the willingness of citizens to grant their Presidents extraordinary power should remain a concern to those committed to democratic consolidation.

A growing number of countries in Latin America now have elected Presidents from leftist or center-left political parties, more than at any time in history. In South America, leftist-oriented Presidents now lead most countries, including every large one: Argentina, Bolivia, Brazil, Chile, Ecuador, Guyana, Peru, Uruguay, and Venezuela, with the possibility of a leftist victory in Paraguay next year. While most of the Presidents of these countries publically express a commitment to democratic values, some are pressing the limits of executive dominance acceptable in a democracy, and may have gone beyond it. Venezuela's Hugo Chavez, who attempted a military coup in 1992, and, has now been popularly elected in two elections, has openly challenged the principles of liberal democracy, controlling the courts and the legislature, openly espousing single-party rule, and embracing Castro' Cuba as a political model. Two more recent additions to the left, Bolivia's Evo Morales, who took office in 2006, and Ecuador's Rafael Correa who began his presidency in early 2007, are, in various ways, also challenging the checks-and-balances system of liberal democracy, supporting Constitutional reforms to enhance their powers.

---

[1] An earlier draft of this paper was presented at Brigham Young University, March 15, 2007, and a shorter, somewhat different version was published in the *Journal of Democracy*, "The Rise of the Left and Populism in Latin America," volume 18, No. 3 (July, 2007), pp. 81-95. I would like to thank the Kirk Hawkins and Darren Hawkins of BYU for their comments, as well as the suggestions made by many at LAPOP, especially José Miguel Cruz and John Booth.

[*] Centennial Professor of Political Science and Director, Latin American Public Opinion Project, Vanderbilt University.

Of course, it is not only leftist Presidents who have been intrigued by the possibility of developing greater power at the expense of other institutions. Many across the ideological spectrum continue to make use of decree laws that by-pass the legislature, and, many, regardless of ideology, have considered Constitutional amendments that would allow them to extend their Presidencies. Nonetheless, the recent efforts of leftist leaders particularly in Venezuela, Ecuador, and Bolivia to widen Presidential power so that they are essentially no countervailing checks and balances, and the support they received from their fellow citizens to do so, is a concern for those concerned with the consolidation of representative democracy and democratic practices in the region.

The concern with populist political leadership is not limited to those already in power. Other potential leaders whose commitment to political pluralism may be in doubt wait in the wings. Some have lost elections in the recent past. Coup-plotter former Lieutenant Colonel Ollante Humala won a plurality of the votes in the 2006 first round Peruvian elections, but was defeated in the run-off. The leftist Presidential candidate in Mexico was defeated by the narrowest of margins in the 2006 elections, and since then has refused to accept the legitimacy of the electoral process. In Paraguay, the decades-long hegemony of the Colorado Party is being challenged by suspended Roman Catholic bishop Msgr. Fernando Lugo who espouses a mixture of leftist and populist rhetoric. The legitimacy of representative democracy, at least, seems called into question by many leaders and potential leaders.

But, like the tango, it takes "two" for the dance to work. And it is the other side of the partnership that concerns us here: the beliefs and practices of the citizens who are electing those Presidents. Presidents are expanding their powers not only because they "can," as other institutions are weak, but because many of their citizens are supporting this expansion, sometimes loudly and insistently. There appears to be within the region a growing level of citizen support for increased Presidential power, at the expense of other branches of government, and increased support for the dismantling of checks and balance critical to a democratic political system. This phenomenon has been noted for some time, most notably by Guillermo O'Donnell, and his term "delegative democracy," in which citizens grant their newly elected Presidents extraordinary powers (O'Donnell 1995).

It is not hard to find concrete examples of citizens' urging Presidents to take strong, unilateral measures, ignoring courts and legislatures. When President Fujimori closed down the Congress completely in 1992, insisting that its members were corrupt and many were tied to a violent revolutionary movement, Sendero Luminoso, strong majorities of Peruvian citizens supported his actions (Seligson and Carrión 2002; Carrión and Zárate 2007). In Venezuela, large majorities of voters have repeatedly reelected President Chavez, even though he has neutered the legislature and the courts.

There is a long tradition of populists leaders in Latin America, emerging first in Brazil in the 1930s with the government of Getúlio Vargas of Brazil and in Argentina in the 1940s with the rule of Juan Domingo Perón. Other key populist figures include Lázaro Cárdenas (Mexico), Jorge Gaitán (Colombia) and José Velasco Ibarra (Ecuador). While the brand of populism Vargas and Perón espoused was rooted in the right, drawing inspiration from Mussolini and European fascism, there also have been populist leaders of the left, such as Juan Velasco Alvarado's

4

military dictatorship in Peru from 1968-1975. The term "populism" is sometimes confused merely with charismatic, personalistic leaders who appeal to a trans-class base (Taggart 2000). The unifying characteristic of populist governments is not their left-right orientation. Rather, it is a core belief that the institutions of classical liberal democracy, especially the legislature and the courts, are anachronistic, inefficient and inconsistent with their own interpretation of the "will of the people."[2] Populist leaders propose instead to listen to "the people" and to personally carry out their will, while isolating the "rejectionists" usually running roughshod over fundamental democratic guarantees of civil liberties, especially free expression and the right to due process.[3]

Are citizens willing to forego the institutions of liberal democracy, and imbue their elected leaders with unchecked power, returning to an earlier epoch of authoritarianism? Are those who favor greater executive dominance more on the "left," coinciding with the rise of leftist Presidents? If so, does this pose a threat to further democratic development in the region? Do the trends reflect little more than a pendular shift in "mood" Stimson (1998; 2004) found periodically occurs in the U.S., or are they a sea change, that might ultimately represent a threat to democratic consolidation?

The 2006-2007 AmericasBarometer surveys allows us, for the first time, to analyze these questions in a unique way that goes beyond general impressions. We will first examine citizen ideology, defined in terms of their self-identification with the political left or right, and then examine whether Latin American voters actually use their "political orientation" as the basis of their vote. We will also see whether their orientation is linked to their support of democratic values, including institutional checks-and-balances and political tolerance.

Second, we will examine in more detail the characteristics of those who seem to hold democratic values in low regard. Who are they as a group, and how do they differ from those who value democratic values? Finally, based on this analysis, we will look at whether political orientation, as well as those who do not esteem democratic values, are likely to pose a threat to further democratic consolidation in the region.

The Political Orientation of Latin Americans is Important to Democracy

How far "left" are Latin American and Caribbean citizens, and is there a trend toward the left? To the surprise of many, it turns out that ideologically they are actually slightly to the *right* of most respondents world-wide. We are able to say this because for many years, beginning with the Eurobarometer and the early World Values Surveys (WVS), public opinion questionnaires around the world have included a 10-point left-right ideology scale, with a score of 1 selected by those who self-define themselves on the far left of the political spectrum, and a score of 10 by

---

[2] In this sense, Weyland (2001 14) best formally defines populism as: "a political strategy through which a personalistic leader seeks or exercises government power based on direct, unmediated uninstitutionalized support from large numbers of mostly unorganized followers. This direct, quasi-personal relationship bypasses established intermediary organizations or deinstitutionalizes and subordinates them to the leader's personal will."

[3] Among the classic works exploring the elements of the populist tradition are Conniff (1999) and Malloy (1977). For a modern take, see Roberts (forthcoming) .

those who place themselves on the far right. The arithmetic mid-point on this scale would be 5.5, but since whole numbers are accepted as the only possible choices, focus group studies show that 5 is nearly universally viewed as the neutral (neither left nor right) point by respondents.[4] It turns out that most countries hover near the center of the scale, although there are exceptions, with, for example Belarus in 1990 averaging 3.88 while Bangladesh in 2000 averaged 7.56. The average score for the world, however, was 5.56 for the pooled WVS data of 84 countries, incorporating over 267,000 interviews for all nations from the entire series from 1981 to 2004. This indicates a slight right-bias world-wide.[5] Unfortunately, the coverage of Latin America and the Caribbean in the WVS has been limited, but of the four countries included in the most recent round (2000-01) the following average values are observed: Chile, 5.22; Mexico, 6.55; Peru, 5.69; and Venezuela 6.32. In sum, world-wide, and in the limited set of countries from Latin America using the WVS, on a 1-10 scale, averages are just slightly right of center.

The AmericasBarometer data for 2006-07, which included 20 countries in the region, finds that the regional average is 5.71, very close to the world average reported above, although slightly more to the *right*.[6] Overall, therefore, the data reveal that the citizens of Latin American countries have a slightly "right" political orientation.

Over time, however, The AmericasBarometer data also show a shift to the left over the past two years, as we can see by comparing the 2004 surveys with the 2006-2007 surveys in the countries that were surveyed both years. In 2004, the mean was 6.17; by 2006-2007, the mean had dropped to 5.71. Most countries moved to the left, six of them significantly; one significantly moved to the right, with the rest statistically unchanged. Thus, a slight "shift to the left" has indeed occurred, and the trend is region-wide, but the magnitude of the shift is small and the center of gravity still remains somewhat to the right. Moreover, longer-term trend data would need to be examined before we could be confident that the move to the left in Latin America is more than a transitory change.

Political Orientation Matters: People Vote their Beliefs

The question of whether Latin Americans vote on the basis of their political orientation is an important one. In terms of the topic of this paper, whether the turn to the left presages a decrease in support for democratic consolidation, we must link "orientation" to actual support for

---

[4] A scale ranging from 0-10 would have provided a true neutral point, but the AmericasBarometer conforms to world-wide standard of 1-10.

[5] The WVS has expanded its range of countries over the years, moving from a concentration on advanced industrial democracies to one that now includes many countries from the developing world. Looking exclusively at the 70 countries surveyed since 1999, the mean ideology score is 5.58, nearly identical to the entire series since 1981, indicating no world-wide shift in the post Cold War epoch. World-wide, non-response on this question is typically higher than on other survey items. The WVS mean is based upon 193,531 individuals who responded to the ideology question on at least one wave of the WVS. In the AmericasBarometer, approximately 20% non-response was encountered, which is typical for many surveys.

[6] This comparison includes a subset of 10 countries from 2004 that were also surveyed with the identical survey item in 2006.

the left in elections. For ideology to matter politically, it needs to translate into behavior consistent with that orientation. If it does not, then there is little reason to be concerned about the significance of shifts in ideological orientation. Since the survey not only included questions on ideology but on party preference, we can analyze this relationship, and further examine results by looking at social class, employment, and other factors that might cause societal "cleavages."

However, the question of whether voters chose their leaders on the basis of political orientation is important for other reasons. Within the study of political parties in Latin America, researchers have grappled with this over time. Some have argued that most parties are highly personalistic, and that voters choose their Presidents on the basis of their "personal" feelings about him/her, rather than on the basis of the left/right orientation of the party from which he/she is running (Gunther, Montero and Linz 2002). There is another long-standing literature on the "patrimonial" party, that argues most people support a party based on their personal "clientelist" linkages to the leadership, rather than on ideology and political beliefs (Linz 2000). These competing explanations cannot be fully tested in this research, but we can explore in depth the questions related to political ideology.

The survey research reveals not only the political orientation of voters, but also what party they supported in the elections, and their personal characteristics (age, gender, income, region, etc.) This allows us to get the most detailed empirical basis on the relationship of orientation to vote, and the characteristics of the voters by party and political orientation.

In terms of poetical orientation, the data show that ideological dispositions along the classic left-right continuum do indeed have a meaningful impact on how people vote. People with more leftist orientations vote more for political parties on the left, and people with more rightist orientations vote for parties on the right. However, the effect of ideology is different in each country, as the party systems vary greatly. In more established democracies with consolidate party systems, "left" and "right" parties are not very far apart ideologically, and their voters are, similarly, drawn to the center, while in systems with deeper cleavages, the party vote reveals a great polarization among the electorate.

This variation across countries can be illustrated through comparisons of some of the countries in the sample of AmericasBarometer data. First, consider the case of Costa Rica, compared to Nicaragua and El Salvador. In Costa Rica, Latin America's most consolidated democracy, ideological differences among the principal political parties around a left/right continuum are minimal. In contrast, Nicaraguan parties show a significant ideological split and parties in El Salvador are the most polarized of the three. In Figures I-1 and I-2 the mean ideology score of those who supported particular presidential candidates are indicated with a small circle.[7] In Costa Rica, the average ideology score on the left-right scale in 2006-2007 was 5.9, and as can be seen in Figure I-1. All of the candidates who received a significant number of votes in the election lined up very closely to that mean. (The greatest deviation was only .6 of a point, and that was for voters supporting the Libertarian Party, at the very fringe of the Costa Rican political spectrum.) The traditional right-of-center party, the PUSC, coincides precisely

---

[7] The 95% confidence interval around that mean is shown by a horizontally placed "I" in the figures, such that the larger the number of respondents who selected that candidate in the survey, the narrower the confidence interval.

with the national mean, whereas supporters of the traditionally left-of-center PLN, averaged 6.3, slightly to the *right* of the national mean. These findings, incidentally, dramatically illustrate the electoral realignment taking place in that country (Lehoucq 2006), as the PLN, the party of the Nobel Peace Prize winner Oscar Arias, actually received support from voters slightly to the right of the "traditional" center-right party. But the larger point is to note the very narrow range of ideological difference in Latin America's oldest and most stable democracy. Even though the electoral scene has been marked with declining voter participation and evidence of declining support for the system (Seligson 2002b), Costa Rica remains at the top of all of the countries in the region in terms of political legitimacy, and, as these results show, the ideological disagreements are very limited (Booth and Seligson 2005).

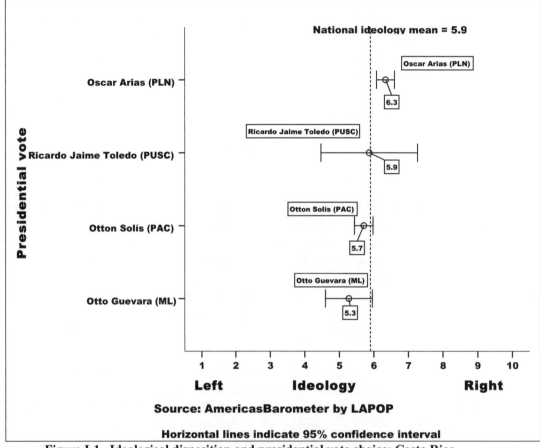

Figure I-1. Ideological disposition and presidential vote choice: Costa Rica

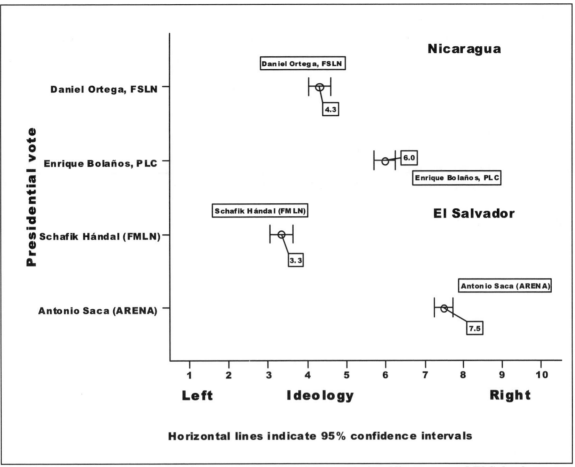

Figure I-2. Ideological disposition and presidential vote choice: Nicaragua and El Salvador

Consider now the more divided picture in two of Costa Rica's neighbors in Central America, Nicaragua and El Salvador, depicted in Figure I-2. In Nicaragua, supporters of Sandinista candidate Daniel Ortega are, as would be expected, considerably to the left of those who supported Enrique Bolaños of the PLC. More importantly, however, the ideological gap between left and right in Nicaragua, looking at the political orientation of the voters, is far wider than in Costa Rica. In Nicaragua, therefore, partisanship is more determined by political orientation than in Costa Rica, and there is much greater polarization of the political system within the party system. This phenomenon is even more acute in El Salvador, where the ideological distance is far greater still. Supporters of (the now deceased) Schafik Hándal of the FMLN, the leftist party that emerged from the guerilla organizations of the civil war of that broke out in the 1980s, averaged 3.3 on the scale, much more to the left than their "left" counterparts in Costa Rica, compared to the 7.5 for supporters of Antonio Saca, head of the rightist ARENA party that has won the presidency in every election since democracy was restored to that country.

Chile offers a final interesting case, with party and voters very closely aligned. As shown in Figure I-3, the winning presidential candidate, socialist Michelle Bachellet, attracted voters who were closest to the national ideological mean. Far to her left was Tomás Hirsch, who espoused a more radical program during the campaign, but won only a small portion of the votes (thus explaining the wide confidence interval around the mean of the survey respondents who say

that they voted for that party). The rightist candidate, Joquín Levin, attracted voters who were ideologically furthest to the right, while the center-right Sebastián Piñera, who lost in the run-off election held in January 2006, was supported by voters that the AmericasBarometer data show were not as far right. In short, the voters in Chile hold ideologies that map perfectly onto the spectrum of candidates from which they had to choose.

There are three key conclusions to draw from this review of ideology in Latin America and the Caribbean. First, the median voter is slightly to the right of world opinion, even as more "leftist" Presidents are elected in the region. Second, within that "slightly rightist" orientation, voters moved somewhat toward the left, even in the brief span of years analyzed here 2004-2006. Third, political orientation is an important determinant of voter preference in Latin America, with its impact varying sharply by country.

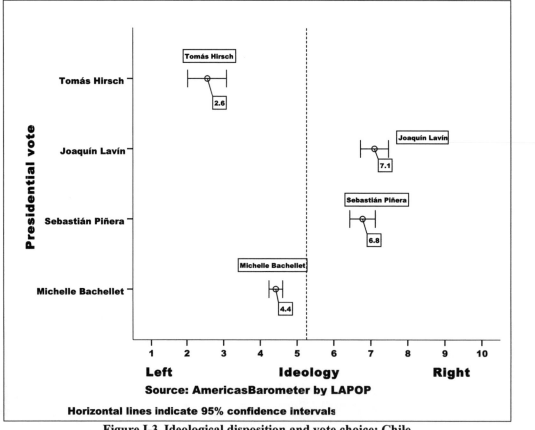

Figure I-3. Ideological disposition and vote choice: Chile

Leftists are Less Likely to Favor some Core Democracy Values

Beyond the ballot box, the AmericasBarometer data show that ideology matters for the far deeper and ultimately more profound issue of support for democracy. People who self-define as more leftist tend to view their political systems as less legitimate and are less likely to favor democracy as a political system less than do others. In some ways this is a very surprising finding. Many of the leftists now in power came into politics fighting repressive regimes. In

many countries it was leftists who led the creation of new, more democratic constitutions and fought for free and fair elections. An entire generation of leftists led the fight for democracy.

Yet, it is also true that historically, in the Latin American region as a whole, the institutional trappings of democracy – courts, legislatures, local governments – have been controlled by a small elite for its own benefit. The political systems of Latin America supported economic policies that led to some of the highest income inequality in the world. It might not be surprising that citizens wary of corrupt legislatures and non-transparent governments become highly skeptical of "institutional" solutions to democracy. Their institutions have not served them well.

How did we arrive at this conclusion that citizens who are more "leftists" are also less likely to favor democratic values? This section will first analyze overall support for democratic values. It will then link it to the left/right political orientation of citizens. Finally, it will add a new dimension, a set of questions designed specifically to probe at support for executive dominance, looking at both overall findings and breaking the findings down by political orientation.

We used a number of methods. First, we developed a scale based on a question often used to measure democratic support in contemporary democracy surveys, drawn from the work in post-communist Europe of Mishler and Rose (1999 81-82), which has become known as the "Churchill" question. Respondents are asked, on a 1-7 scale, whether they agree or not with the statement: "Even though democracy has many problems, it is better than any other form of government." The scale was converted to the more familiar 1-10 range to match the second item. This second item involved the use of a composite index to measure legitimacy. This index is based upon the classic conceptualization of Lipset (Lipset 1959b) and Easton (Easton 1975).[8] It is comprised of five items that seek to tap the extent to which citizens trust their political system. Both of these measures led to the same conclusion, as shown in Figure I-4: the more leftist the respondent's political orientation, the lower his belief that democracy is "better than any other form of government" and the. These results are for the AmericasBarometer sample as a whole; in one country, however, Chile, the pattern is reversed.

This is a disturbing finding, when coupled with the growing leftist political orientation of citizens, and the salience of it in determining what Presidential candidate to support. For the region as a whole, the finding that citizens of the Americas on the left are less likely to prefer democracy than those on the right suggest that the movement to the left may represent a move away from democratic values, while the legitimacy scale suggest that more citizens will question the right of a democratic regime to govern.

In the AmericasBarometer survey respondents were also asked: "There are people who say that what we need is a strong leader who does not have to be elected via the ballot. Others say that even though things don't work, electoral democracy, that is, the popular vote, is always the best." Overall in the region, in 2006 only 14,6% percent or respondents preferred a strong

---

[8] This is measured by a 5-item series, each scored on a 1-7 and then transformed into a 1-10 index. Details can be found in (Seligson 2002a; Booth and Seligson 2005; Seligson 2006).

leader, a very encouraging sign for democracy. Yet, in 11 of the 15 countries where this question was asked, a those who preferred a "strong leader" were more likely to be further to the left than those who preferred electoral democracy. Only in Guatemala, Chile and the Dominican Republic does the left more heavily support electoral democracy than the right, and reject a strong leader. In Mexico, it was a tie.

However, by another standard measure of democratic values in the surveys, political tolerance, this difference between left and right disappears, or, in some cases, has the reverse tendency. In most countries, the left and right are equally tolerant. In three countries, Mexico, Guatemala, and Chile, the left is more tolerant than the right. Interestingly, in prior studies of Latin America conducted by LAPOP, the left has often been found to be more tolerant than the right. The questions used to measure tolerance have centered on the willingness of respondents to grant to opposition minorities basic civil liberties, such as the right to vote, run for office, protest and enjoy free speech. It is possible that because the left is in power now in much of region, that they have become *less* tolerant of the right, now out of power. This hypothesis, however, would require considerable effort to test and prove, a subject beyond the scope of this short chapter.

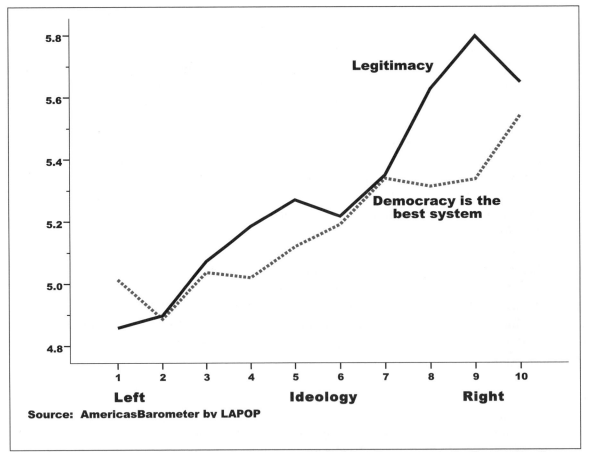

Figure I-4. Impact of ideology on legitimacy and belief that democracy is the "best system"

In sum, the left and right in Latin America about equally support one important democratic value: political tolerance. However, they are sharply divided on whether democracy is the best system of government, and in their willingness to support a non-elected leader, with the left more inclined to favor a non-elected leader, and showing much greater skepticism for democracy as a political system. Given at least a slight move to the left over the past two years (although overall still generally "rightist"), and the increasing number of political systems headed by leftists parties, if this trend continues, more and more Latin Americans may opt for non-democratic alternatives when given the opportunity. There is great variance among countries, however.

Latin Americans are not Ready to Jettison Democratic Institutions

While there are important differences between the left and right in their support of checks on executive power, it is important to put this in context, looking at overall patterns of support within the region. We have already noted the fact that in comparison with the rest of the world Latin Americans remain slightly to the right of the mean on the left/right continuum of political orientation. In this section, we will examine attitudes towards specific political institutions, to better gauge where Latin Americans are likely to put their trust. We will also examine other characteristics of Latin Americans, to see whether other traits, seem related to their support of democratic institutions and checks and balances, or to put it another way, whether there are certain groups of people more inclined to jettison these institutions.

Is there evidence that citizens of Latin America and the Caribbean would prefer populist-style governments rather than liberal democracies? One way to measure this is to look at trust in institutions. Nearly all surveys of Latin America and the Caribbean have found that citizens hold legislatures and judiciaries in low regard. An examination of the AmericasBarometer data confirms that picture. Respondents were read a long list of institutions and asked how much they trust each one. Converted to the familiar 0-100 scale, the Catholic Church[9] always scores at the top, with a mean of 68 for the region as a whole. At the very bottom were political parties, with a trust score of half that of the Church (35). The justice system averaged 44; the legislature and supreme court, 45; and the police, 46. The armed forces, in contrast, scored second highest at 60, trailing the Church by only 8 points. In sum, of the state institutions covered in the surveys, only the armed forces averaged on the positive end of the 0-100 continuum, while the key representative institutions of liberal democracy were allon the low end.

How low are these scores compared to other countries in the world? The WVS, using a slightly different measurement scale, allows us to roughly compare these scores to countries outside the region. In the WVS around the world, the same pattern of trust prevails. An examination of the WVS rank-order of the church, the military, the police, parties, the legislature and the judiciary shows that the lowest average trust score for all countries world-wide is for parties, followed by the legislature and then the justice system. In that sense, then, Latin America conforms precisely to the international pattern. The AmericasBarometer findings provides even more interesting comparisons, as it includes the United States and Canada in the data set, allowing us to compare the Latin American and Caribbean results with identically worded and

---

[9] In all countries except Jamaica and Guyana, respondents were asked about the "Catholic Church," whereas in those two countries they were asked about "the Church."

scaled questions for the U.S. and Canada. Confidence in parties is low in Canada (49.1) and the U.S. (42.9), but even so, in comparative terms Canada ranks higher than any country in the region, while the U.S. ranks fourth. Only three other countries average above 40 on the 100-point scale, and two, Paraguay and Ecuador average below 30. When it comes to the courts and the supreme court, the gap between Canada and the U.S., on the one hand, with Latin America on the other is greater. Canada scores 71.3 and the U.S. 67.1 for the supreme court, while all of the countries in Latin America and the Caribbean scoring below 60 and half of them below 50. At the very low end are Haiti (31.4), Paraguay (30.2) and Ecuador (24.7). For the system of justice, the pattern is the same, with the U.S. and Canada the only counties to score above 60, and the tail end being comprised of Peru (32.6) Paraguay (31.0) and Ecuador (28.0). It is of note that Uruguay, among the best established democracy in the region, is the country closest to the U.S. and Canada on this question, scoring 55.6, followed by Costa Rica (52.9), the oldest established democracy in the region.

Given these low scores for the traditional institutions of liberal democracy, one might expect populist sentiment to be high and citizens readily willing to jettison them. Yet, this is not an accurate reading of the survey evidence. Despite the low support for parties, when asked one of the standard items included in many democracy surveys: "In your opinion, can there be democracy without political parties?" the AmericasBarometer 2006-2007 finds only a minority, 43%, of them agreeing. This is not uniformly true, however. In Ecuador, j 50.5% of respondents agreed, while in Haiti 62.2% agreed that there can be democracy without parties. It is difficult to determine if this is good news or bad; while in most countries a majority rejects the notion that there can be democracy without parties, yet a strong minority accepts it. It is important to dig a bit deeper to better interpret the implications of these findings for the proclivity of Latin Americans to accept populist rule.

To gain further insight into the appeals of populism, LAPOP developed a new set of items for the 2006-2007 AmericasBarometer round specifically designed to gauge the extent to which citizens are willing to dispense with parties, legislative and judicial institutions, ceding power to the executive. This provides the most compelling data to date on attitudes towards representative institutions. Five items were constructed that formed a single dimension (using factor analysis) when the data were analyzed. One item, for example, read: "With which of these two opinions do you agree more: 1) For the progress of the country, its is necessary that our presidents limit the voice and vote of the opposition parties; 2) There is no reason that would justify that our presidents limit the voice and vote of the opposition parties, even if they hold back the progress of the country."[10] An overall scale of "support for populism" was created, in which it was found

---

[10] The other items in the series (with appropriate wording change for parlimentary vs. presidential systems) are:
POP2: 1. The Congress hinders the work of our presidents/prime ministers, and should be ignored 2. Even when it hinders the work of the president/prime minister, our presidents/prime ministers shold not bypass the Congress.
POP3: 1. Judges frequently hinder the work of our presidents/prime ministers, and they should be ignored. 2. Even when judges sometimes hinder the work of our presidents/prime ministers, their decisions should always be obeyed.
POP4: 1. Our presidents/prime ministers should have the necessary power so that they can act in the national interest. 2. The power of our presidents/prime ministers should be limited so that they do not endanger our liberties.
POP5: 1. Our presidents/prime ministers should do what the people want even when laws prevent them from doing so. 2. Our presidents/prime ministers should obey the laws even when the people don't want them to.

that one-third (32.6%) of the respondents for the sample as a whole refused to accept any populist measure, and only 15.9% of the respondents would support more than two of the five populist measures. Yet, 47.6% of the respondents in the pooled data set were willing to accept two of the five measures, and 63.4% were willing to accept at least one such measure. By this accounting, then, while only a small minority of citizens in Latin America and the Caribbean favor a wide variety of measure to strengthening of the presidency at the expense of representative, liberal democratic institutions, a substantial majority would accept at least some reductions in the principle of separation of powers.

What of the minority that rejects liberal democracy on our Populism questions? In democracies, minorities can be important, especially if they are concentrated in a homogeneous sector of the population. In elections, for example, minorities with a unified position can achieve electoral victory when the opposition is divided. Minorities also can carry great weight in the street, should they decide to embark upon demonstrations, civil disobedience or engage in terrorism. It is important to know, therefore where minority support for populist rule is strong in Latin American and Caribbean area.

The results of our analysis echo the findings in the classical work by Seymour Lipset (1959a), who expounded on the concept of "working class authoritarianism" that is, it is the working class, rather than the elite, who exhibit more authoritarian tendencies.

Consistent with Lipset's work, regression analysis on the pooled data finds that populist sentiment is significantly higher among the poorer and less well educated.[11] The Lipset-confirming results are depicted in Figures I-5 and I-6. A surprising finding, however, is that even when controlled for wealth and education, the *younger* the age of the respondent, the more likely s/he would be to support populist measures. This comes as a surprise to many, since it has long been assumed that older people are "set in their ways" and therefore more likely to support a government that controls dissenters. In fact, it is the youth of Latin America and the Caribbean who are more likely to support populist measures. One needs to probe the data more deeply for an explanation of these findings, but it is the case that many older citizens of the region personally experienced the dictatorial military regimes that predominated in the 1970s. That experience may have helped "immunize" them against the appeals of populist rule. They have been there; they know the costs. The young, in contrast, know only the contemporary democratic period, which has been filled with bitter disappointments for many; economic growth in much of Latin America and the Caribbean has been modest, but more than that, it largely has not "trickled down" to the poor. Moreover, it may well be that the young are the most susceptible to populist appeals, while older citizens are more jaded, having seen politicians of all stripes come and go, they may be resistant to the latest fad. Perhaps it is not surprising, therefore, that Chile and Haiti are the two countries that show the strongest impact of age on rejection of populists.

The public opinion data presented here, therefore should not come as a surprise. The implications of these results are potentially sobering; as the youth of today grow to become the

---

[11] Analysis of individual country data, not reported here, finds variation in these regression patterns. Extensive studies on each of the AmericasBarometer countries can be downloaded at www.lapopsurveys.org.

majority of voters, the findings here suggest increasing susceptibility of populist appeals.[12] Of course, as the young age, they may become more conservative and less willing to accept such appeals, but in fact, the populist questions are not focused on a liberal/conservative dimension, but instead are tapping into populist vs. democratic notions of governance. For those, one could have expected that it would be the youth who would be less inclined to accept anti-democratic measures.

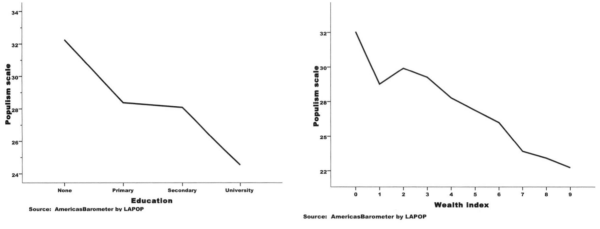

Figure I-5. Impact of education on support for populism

Figure I-6. Impact of wealth on support for populism

Conclusions: Political Institutions and Values Remain Important

The survey data presented here do indeed suggest that more "leftist oriented" voters are somewhat more likely to jettison the political checks and balances needed in a democracy, and to grant their elected executives too much power, leaving the door open for some form of "electoral authoritarianism." Given the rise of leftist Presidents, supported by these voters, there is ample reason to be watchful. Many of the moderate leftist Presidents and their cadres may be completely committed to and respectful of democratic institutions. This analysis has shown, however, that at least some of their partisan supporters are less so.

Yet, there is at this point no immediate threat that the increasing support of the left will pose a challenge to the consolidation of democracy.   In fact, this research has uncovered some underlying dynamics that are positive in terms of democratic institution-building.   First, supporters on the left remain in the political system and use the vote, rather than violence, to make their political concerns felt. Second, the political parties in a number of countries are at least mildly programmatic, reflecting the left/right continuum of the voters. Third, while there is

---

[12] An obvious alternative explanation is that as the youth age they will come to resemble the older population and thefore will be equally resistant to populist appeals. Unfortunately, the panel data to unpack age vs. cohort effects do not exist (Firebaugh 1997).

little trust in most representative political institutions, citizens would like to keep them – even political parties, which are at the bottom on the heap on trust measures.

Yet, the data point to some overall trends that merit careful attention. The ideological center of gravity in Latin America is, by world standards, slightly to the right, yet it attitudes are moving to the left. Ideological cleavages in Latin America, long after the end of the Cold War, in some countries still line up along a distinct left-right dimension, and voters support parties consistent with their ideological orientations. The gap between left and right is very narrow, however, in other countries (e.g., Costa Rica) but strikingly wide in other countries (e.g. Nicaragua, El Salvador and Chile). Being on the left in Latin America and the Caribbean has implications beyond the ballot box; for the region as a whole, those on the left are far less likely to believe that their political system is legitimate and are less likely to believe that despite all its flaws, democracy is still the best system. Moreover, in a number of countries, the left is more likely to support strong leaders who do not need to be elected via the ballot. A second, related, trend is the rise of populist figures and governments, especially in South America. This trend emerges, no doubt, from the very low level of trust that many citizens hold of key institutions of liberal democracy, especially parties, the courts and the legislature. In some countries, such as Ecuador, trust in these institutions is at extremely low levels. This should come as no surprise given the events in Ecuador over the past decade, in which a succession of democratically elected presidents have been forced to leave office, while the executive has eviscerated any notion of judicial independence. While demands for across-the-board measures that would essentially create dictatorial rule is still very much a minoritarian sentiment for the region as a whole, close to two-thirds of respondents in the region would accept at least some reduction in the institutional autonomy of the courts, the legislature and opposition parties. Support for those measure that would result in what Diamond has called a "hollowing out" of democracy (Diamond 1999), is closely associated, in the region as a whole, with the poor, the less-well educated and the young.

Finally, there are other long-term trends of increasing inclusion at work as well, that may work to strengthen support of democracy. It may well be that these findings are related to a change in the long-term pattern of historical exclusion of the poor and ethnic minorities in the region. The survey data for Bolivia, for example, show that soon after Evo Morales, whose roots are in the indigenous community, was elected president of that country, the gap between indigenous and non-indigenous support for democracy disappeared. Thus, the lower support for democracy among those on the left could well shift as governments take power that are more responsive to the demands of the excluded populations.

References

Booth, John A., and Mitchell A. Seligson. "Political Legitimacy and Participation in Costa Rica: Evidence of Arena Shopping." *Political Research Quarterly* 59, no. 4 (2005): 537-50.

Carrión, Julio F., and Patricia Zárate. *The Political Culture of Democracy in Perú: 2006*. Edited by Mitchell A. Seligson. Lima: Instituto de Estudios Peruanos, 2007.

Conniff, Michael L., ed. *Populism in Latin America*. Tuscaloosa: University of Alabama Press, 1999.

Diamond, Larry. *Developing Democracy: Toward Consolidation*. Baltimore: Johns Hopkins University Press, 1999.

Easton, David. "A Re-Assessment of the Concept of Political Support." *British Journal of Political Science* 5 (1975): 435-57.

Firebaugh, Glenn. *Analyzing Repeated Surveys*. Thousand Oaks, Calif.: Sage Publications, 1997.

Gunther, Richard, Josâe R. Montero, and Juan J. Linz. *Political parties : old concepts and new challenges*. Oxford ; New York: Oxford University Press, 2002.

Lehoucq, Fabrice. "Costa Rica: Paradise in Doubt." *Journal of Democracy* 16, no. 3 (2006): 140-54.

Linz, Juan. "Democratic Political Parties: Recognizing Contradictory Principles and Perceptions." *Scandinavian Political Studies* 23, no. 3 (2000): 252-64.

Lipset, Seymour Martin. "Democracy and Working-Class Authoritarianism." *American Sociological Review* 24 (1959a): 482-502.

———. "Some Social Requisites of Democracy: Economic Development and Political Legitimacy." *American Political Science Review* 53 (1959b): 65-105.

Malloy, J. M. *Authoritarianism and Corporatism in Latin America*. Pittsburgh: University of Pittsburgh Press, 1977.

Mishler, William, and Richard Rose. "Five Years After the Fall: Trajectories of Support for Democracy in Post-Communist Europe." In *Critical Citizens: Global Support for Democratic Governance*, edited by Pippa Norris, 78-99. Oxford: Oxford University Press, 1999.

O'Donnell, Guillermo. "Delegative Democracy." *Journal of Democracy* 5, no. 1 (1995): 55-69.

Roberts, Kenneth M. *Changing Course: Parties, Populism, and Political Representation in Latin America's Neoliberal Era*. Cambridge: Cambridget University Press, forthcoming.

Seligson, Mitchell A. "The Impact of Corruption on Regime Legitimacy: A Comparative Study of Four Latin American Countries." *Journal of Politics* 64 (2002a): 408-33.

———. "Trouble in Paradise: The Impact of the Erosion of System Support in Costa Rica, 1978-1999." *Latin American Research Review* 37, no. 1 (2002b): 160-85.

———. "The Measurement and Impact of Corruption Victimization: Survey Evidence from Latin America." *World Development* 34, no. 2 (2006): 381-404.

Seligson, Mitchell A., and Julio Carrión. "Political Support, Political Skepticism and Political Stability in New Democracies: An Empirical Examination of Mass Support for Coups D'Etat in Peru." *Comparative Political Studies* 35, no. 1 (2002): 58-82.

Stimson, James A. *Public Opinion in America : Moods, Cycles, and Swings*. 2nd ed, *Transforming American politics*. Boulder, Colo: Westview Press, 1998.

———. *Tides of consent : How Public Opinion Shapes American Politics*. New York: Cambridge University Press, 2004.

Taggart, Paul A. *Populism, Concepts in the Social Sciences*. Buckingham [England] ;
    Philadelphia: Open University Press, 2000.
Weyland, Kurt. "Clarifying a Contested Concept: Populism in the Study of Latin American
    Politics." *Comparative Politics* 34, no. 1 (2001): 1-22.

II. Illiberal Democracy and Normative Democracy: How is Democracy Defined in the Americas?

Julio F. Carrión*

Abstract

How do Latin Americans define democracy? Following a methodology developed by the AfroBarometer, this paper finds that the majority of them do so in normative terms, and that those who do so are more likely to endorse it than those who define it in instrumental or negative terms. But I also find that the effect of defintional differences is not very strong. The data show that the majority of Latin Americans endorse democracy, but that there are important cross-national variations. Moreover, the study finds that this support is rather shallow. Many of the self-declared democrats hold views that are inimical to democratic rule, such as endorsement of military coups or willingness to support illiberal exercises of political power. I find that depending on the question, as few as 18 percent and as many as 47 percent of self-declared democrats are ready to justify a military coup. I also find that a quarter of those who endorse democracy have no problem agreeing with the statement that presidents should limit the voice and vote of the opposition if "it is necessary for the progress of this country." These findings thus suggest very careful analysis is called for when using approaches to measuring democracy based on respondent definitions of it.

An important milestone in the analysis of public attitudes towards democracy was the publication by the United Nations Development Programme (UNDP) of *Democracia en América Latina* (PNUD-PRODDAL 2004). Th UNDP report offers a gloomy assessment of Latin Americans' commitment to democracy. Although it finds that a majority of the respondents support democracy as an ideal form of government, it argues that this support is shallow. According to the study (PNUD-PRODDAL 2004, 132), a significant segment of the public is willing to sacrifice a democratic form government in exchange for real socioeconomic progress. The UNDP report (PNUD-PRODDAL 2004, 134) classifies 43 percent of Latin Americans as "democrats" and 26 percent of them as "non-democrats." The UNDP identifies a category for those who are "ambivalent," that is, have contradictory views about democracy: they choose democracy as their preferred system of government but are also willing to support authoritarian or "delegative" acts "when circumstances merit it." According to this report (PNUD-PRODDAL 2004, 137), what differentiates democrats from those who are ambivalent is their attitude toward the tension between democracy and economic development: "democrats" are not willing to sacrifice the former for the latter whereas the "ambivalents" are.

Based on the UNDP study, it appears that the commitment to democracy among many Latin Americans is, to use the term developed by Bratton and Mattes (2001a), merely

---

* Associate Professor at the University of Delaware in the US and Researcher at the Instituto de Estudios Peruanos.

instrumental. That is, people support democracy because of the material benefits expected from it and not because of the normative values that democracy embodies. In their study of public attitudes toward democracy in Africa, Bratton and Mattes (2001a) confront this issue of the "instrumental versus normative" foundations of support for democracy head on, and find contradictory evidence. On the one hand, they report (2001a, 473) that "[t]he fact that African survey respondents support democracy while being far from content with its concrete achievements suggests a measure of intrinsic support for the democratic regime form that supersedes instrumental considerations." On the other hand, they also argue (idem) that "the general public in African countries thinks instrumentally: in other words, support for democracy hinges critically upon popular approval of government achievements."

Echoing this ambivalence about the foundations of the support for democracy, Bratton and Mattes (2001b, 118-119) write in another article that "in at least five of our six countries [in Africa], popular support for democracy has a strong instrumental component. Citizens extend support to a democratic regime in good part because they are satisfied with its performance in delivering desired good and services. Yet 21 percent of all survey respondents…say that they support democracy in principle even though they are dissatisfied with the performance of their own regime. These citizens value democracy intrinsically, that is, not merely as a means of delivering development but as an end in itself." A more recent study (Mattes and Bratton 2007), confirms that support for democracy in Africa is driven by both normative concerns and instrumental considerations.

Two conclusions can be drawn from the AfroBarometer results. First, when we lear than that the majority of people support democracy in Latin America, we should conclude that this finding is not the end of the analysis but the beginning of it. What kind of democracy do people have in mind when they say they support democracy? What important cross-national variations in these definitions and in the levels of support for democracy can be found in Latin America? How deep and consistent is the commitment to democracy? What are the factors that foster a stronger commitment to democracy? The second point to be made is that we do not need to ask whether support for democracy in Latin America is driven by normative commitments *or* instrumental considerations. Clearly, it is driven by both. What we need to do is "unpack" the idea of instrumental support. For instance, do people accept democracy because they like the incumbent, or perceive an improvement in their economic condition, or because they trust their political institutions? Is it the perception of personal threat that drives their attitudes towards regimes, or is it people's satisfaction with the way democracy is working in general?

In the following pages I address these questions. I start the analysis by examining people's conceptualizations of democracy. Then I examine how these conceptualizations relate to support for democracy. After that, I examine the depth of democratic commitments, exploring mass support for liberal and illiberal forms of democracy. I propose a more robust way to measure attitudinal support for democracy. I conclude the analysis by identifying the factors associated with support for liberal democracy. A summary section ends the chapter.

Mass Conceptualizations of Democracy

Before proceeding with the analysis of the conceptualizations of democracy among the public, it is important to examine first the overall degree of support for democracy in the region. We measure this with the item that asks respondents if they prefer a democracy, a dictatorship or are indifferent as to regime-type preference. For the entire Latin American and Caribbean sample, 67.1 percent prefer democracy while 14.0 percent support an authoritarian government, and 11.4 percent are indifferent (an additional 8.4 percent does not answer the question). When those who don't answer the question are removed from the calculation, support for democracy rises to 73 percent in Latin America and the Caribbean.

In some countries, however, people are quite reluctant or unable to declare a regime preference. In Guatemala almost 20 percent of the respondents refuse to answer the question. In Mexico, Colombia, and Nicaragua, ten percent or more of the respondents are in similar situation (Haiti is a borderline case, with 9.6 percent declining the answer the question). One could hypothesize that these countries have large rural and/or poorly educated populations that do not have the sophistication of expression to answer a question like this. This, however, does not explain why refusal rates are much lower in countries such as Bolivia, Ecuador, or Honduras, which also have large rural and poorly educated populations. Perhaps support for democracy is related to the ability to define it, as Mattes and Bratton (2007) argue. This section explores this hypothesis.

The 2006-2007 AmericasBarometer questionnaire asked the following open-ended question: "In a few words, what is the meaning of democracy for you?" Respondents could provide up to three different definitions. They were then asked to specify (if they mentioned more than one definition) which of their definitions was the most important. Table II.1 reports the summary of the multiple answers given to this question (the table does not include respondents from Canada and the United States). Three quarters of Latin American and Caribbean respondents were able provide a definition of democracy. Interestingly, this is almost the exact proportion of respondents who could provide a definition of democracy in a study of six African nations in 1999-2000 (Bratton and Mattes 2001b, 108). In Canada, in contrast, only 15.5% could not provide any response, while in the U.S. it was only 8.5%. Among the different meanings assigned to democracy, the single most frequent was "freedom of expression" (18.9 percent) followed by "liberty" (10.4 percent).

Before grouping these varied definitions into more parsimonious clusters it is necessary to examine cross-national variations in the ability to provide any definition of democracy. To analyze cross-national variations, I collapse the information provided in Table II.1 into two groups. The first group is composed of all the respondents who provided a definition of democracy, even if it had a negative connotation. The other group was composed of all of those who could not assign a meaning to the term. Figure II.1 gives the distribution of this variable ("ability to define democracy") in the countries in which this question was asked in 2006-2007.

Table II-1. Mass Conceptualizations of Democracy, 2006-2007

	Frequency	Percent	Valid Percent
It does not have any meaning	6958	22.3	24.7
Liberty (without specifying what type)	3237	10.4	11.5
Economic liberty	457	1.5	1.6
Liberty of expression	5907	18.9	20.9
Liberty of movement	427	1.4	1.5
Liberty, lack of	165	.5	.6
Being independent	563	1.8	2.0
Well being, economic progress, growth	587	1.9	2.1
Lack of well being, no economic progress	106	.3	.4
Capitalism	35	.1	.1
Free trade, free business	128	.4	.5
Employment, more opportunities of	400	1.3	1.4
Lack of employment	210	.7	.7
Right to choose eaders	991	3.2	3.5
Elections, voting	493	1.6	1.7
Free elections	451	1.4	1.6
Fraudulent elections	20	.1	.1
Equality (without specifying)	1181	3.8	4.2
Economic equality, or equality of classes	303	1.0	1.1
Gender equality	189	.6	.7
Equality before the law	283	.9	1.0
Racial or ethnic equality	119	.4	.4
Equality, Lack of, inequality	103	.3	.4
Limitations of participation	68	.2	.2
Participation (without specifying what type)	572	1.8	2.0
Participation of minorities	82	.3	.3
Power of the people	574	1.8	2.0
Human rights, respect rights	963	3.1	3.4
Disorder, lack of justice, corruption	322	1.0	1.1
Justice	310	1.0	1.1
Obey the law, less corruption	219	.7	.8
Non military government	82	.3	.3
Live in peace, without war	830	2.7	2.9
War, invasions	21	.1	.1
Other answer	854	2.7	3.0
Total	28210	90.4	100.0
Missing	3000	9.6	
Total	31209	100.0	

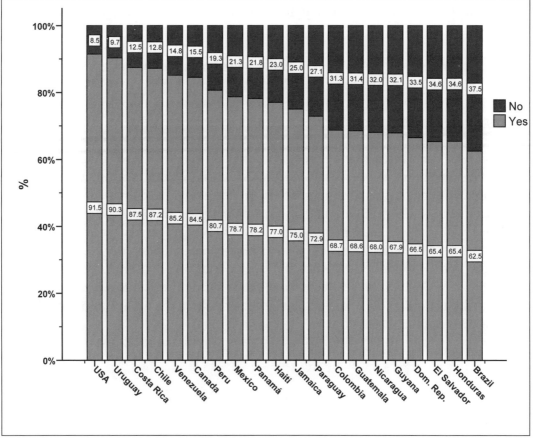

Figure II-1. Ability to Define Democracy

Figure II.1 shows two clusters, one in which 80 percent or more of the respondents can provide a definition of democracy (Peru, Canada, Chile, Costa Rica, Uruguay, Venezuela, and the United States), and another where less than 70 percent of the interviewees can do so (Colombia, Guatemala, Nicaragua, Dominican Republic, El Salvador, Guyana, Brazil, and Honduras). In the first group, with the exception of Peru, we have countries with a strong tradition of democratic rule (despite the 1973-1990 interregnum in Chile, and recent events in Venezuela). The second group, with the exception of Colombia and Guyana, is composed by Central American countries.

Bratton and Mattes (2001b, 117) argue that "individuals who cannot define democracy are much less attached to it as a preferred form of regime." The overall evidence from the Americas seems to support this view. When the entire pooled data (without including respondents from the United States and Canada) are analyzed, the ability to define democracy is found to increase support for it,[1] and the effect is moderately strong. For instance, 65 percent of those who cannot provide a definition of democracy are quite willing to say that they prefer it

---

[1] For purposes of this analysis, non-support for democracy is defined as those who did not choose the option "democracy is always preferable." Those who did not answer the question on support for democracy were removed from the analysis.

over authoritarianism.[2] Among those who can define it, support for democracy rises to 75 percent. The difference is 10 percent points and although statistically significant, it is not overwhelming.

In some countries in the Americas, however, the impact of the ability to define democracy on its support is quite strong (Figure II.2). In the advanced democracies, we see a very strong correlation between the ability to define democracy and support for it. In the United States, for instance, those who can provide a definition of democracy were twice as likely to support it as those who cannot define it. In Canada, the difference in the levels of support for democracy between those who can define it and those who can't is about 30 percentage points. In Latin America and the Caribbean, we also find that some countries exhibit a strong correlation between the ability to define democracy and support for it. In Uruguay the difference is 32 points. In Peru support for democracy is 19 percent points higher among those who can offer a definition than it is among those who cannot. In Paraguay the difference is 27 percent points; in Colombia the difference is 15 points. In other countries, such as Guatemala, Honduras, Panama, the Dominican Republic, Haiti, Jamaica, and Costa Rica there is no statistically significant difference in the levels of support for democracy between those who can define it and those who cannot. No pattern is immediately clear to explain why in some countries the ability to define democracy is so intertwined with its level of support.

---

[2] Support for democracy is measured by agreement with the following option: "Democracy is preferable to any other form of government." Support for authoritarianism is measure by agreement with the following: "Under some circumstances an authoritarian government can be preferable to a democratic one." Regime indiference is measured by agreement with the following: "For people like us, a democratic regime is the same as a non-democratic one."

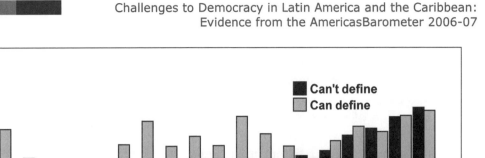

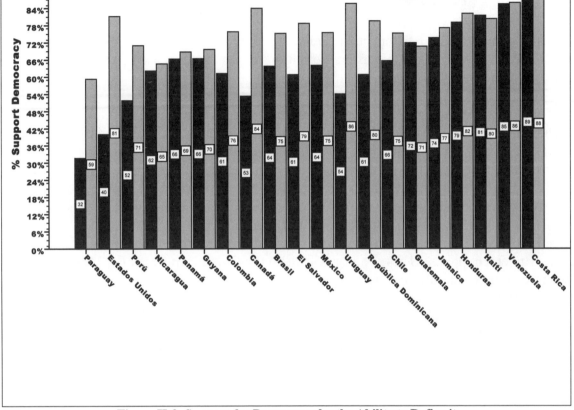

Figure II-2. Support for Democracy by the Ability to Define it

I nowreturn to the definitions of democracy listed in Table II.1. These can be grouped in more parsimonious ways to facilitate analysis. The question is what categories to use? Democracy is a concept with multiple meanings that is the product of more than 2,500 years of history (Dahl 1989; Dunn 2005; Held 1996; Touraine 1997). There are many ways to classify the multiplicity of its definitions. One is to group all the possible definitions into the traditional meanings associated with democracy: liberty, equality, protection against arbitrary rule, and participation. This is the strategy that, in general terms, was initially adopted by C. B. Macpherson (1977) and later developed by Held (1996). Another way is to follow Dahl's (1956) insight, and define democracy in either procedural or substantive terms.

Yet another way of approaching this task is to define democracy based on the source of rationality underscoring the belief (Bratton and Mattes 2001a; Mattes and Bratton 2007; Sarsfield 2003; Sarsfield and Echegaray 2006; Sarsfield and Carrión 2006). One could hold a given belief, in this case democracy, because it is associated with certain values that are considered to be desirable (i.e., liberty, equality, justice). Alternatively, one could hold that belief because it produces certain goods or utilities (i.e., economic progress, development). In the first case, the commitment to democracy is normative because it is based on an axiomatic rationality; in the

second case, it is instrumental because it is based on a means/end rationality. Democracy can also be defined, from this perspective, in pejorative or negative terms, because it "produces" an undesirable outcome (i.e., civil war, violence, disorder). And, of course, people could have no conceptualization of democracy at all (an "empty" definition). This is the classificatory strategy that it will be followed here because it builds on Bratton and Mattes's successful and pathbreaking analyses of African public opinion. Table II.2 lists the definitions presented in Table II.1 and how they relate to our four definitions of democracy based on the rationality of the belief.

We can now examine if the way people define democracy is related to its support. The data show that those who define democracy in normative terms are only slightly more likely to support it than those who define it in instrumental terms (77.2 and 71.9 percent, respectively). The most important difference in the levels of support for democracy is found between those who define it in negative terms and those who conceptualize it in normative terms: 64.4 percent and 77.6 percent, respectively (Figure II.3; data from the U.S. and Canada are not included in this figure). In only a handful of countries, the difference in the level of support for democracy between those who define it in normative terms and those who define it in instrumental terms exceeds 10 percent points. These countries include the Dominican Republic, Mexico, and Chile. In seven countries, the differences between those who see democracy in normative ways and those who define it instrumentally are less than 5 percent points. Thus, while one can perceive an association between certain definitions of democracy and support for it, one can conclude with a certain degree of confidence that support for democracy in Latin America is not primarily determined by the way people define it but rather by the ability to define it (in either positive or negative ways).

Table II-2. Conceptualizations of Democracy Based on the Rationality of the Belief

Normative	Instrumental	Empty	Pejorative
-Liberty (without specifying what type)	-Free trade, free business	-It doesn't have any meaning	-Lack of liberty
-Liberty of expression, voting, choice and human rights	-Economic liberty	-Other answer	-Lack of well being, no economic progress
-Liberty of movement	-Well being, economic progress, growth	-DK/NA	-Lack of employment
-Liberty, lack of	-Capitalism		-Fraudulent elections
-Right to choose leaders	-Employment, more opportunities of		-Lack of equality, inequality
-Elections, voting			-Limitations of participation
-Free elections			-Disorder, lack of justice, corruption
-Equality (without specifying)			-War, invasions
-Economic equality, equality of classes			
-Gender equality			
-Equality before the laws			
-Racial or ethnic equality			
-Participation (without specifying which type)			
-Participation of minorities			
-Power of the people			
-Respect for human rights			
-Justice			
-Obey the law, less corruption			
-Non-military government			
-Live in peace, without war			

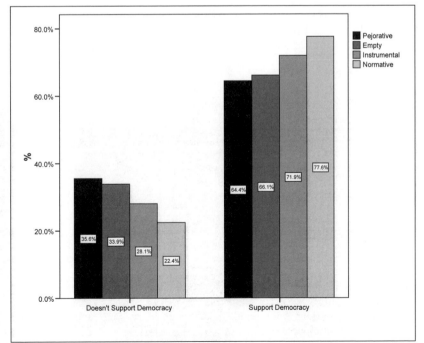

Figure II-3. Conceptualizations of and Support for Democracy

How Consistent is the Support for Democracy?

It should be said from the outset that an expressed preference for democracy does not inoculate the Latin American public from embracing illiberal or even outright authoritarian alternatives. The inconsistencies of mass preferences for democracy are not a novel finding. In a pioneering and classic study, James Prothro and Charles Grigg (1960) found that people who manifest support for democracy in the abstract do not always endorse democratic choice in more concrete domains. What we need to ask is, then, how deep or consistent is expressed support for democracy, and what factors make people more consistently supportive of democracy? To answer this question I will, first, explore the extent to which self-professed democrats[3] also endorse authoritarian and illiberal choices. In the next section I explore what factors are associated with preference for liberal forms of democratic rule.

A traditional threat to democracy in Latin America has been the sudden overthrow of civilian governments by a military coup. One would expect that those who endorse democracy over authoritarianism would be less inclined to support a potential coup d'état. This is indeed the case. Figure II.4 reports the mean scores of support for military coups by regime preference. As expected, the strongest support for military coups is found among those who declare a preference for an authoritarian regime and the lowest is reported among those who declare a preference for democracy. But the important point of this figure is that a sizable portion of self-professed democrats are ready to support military coups under some circumstances.[4] For instance, 17 percent of those who endorse democracy declare that a military coup to confront high unemployment would be justified. Similarly, and more worrisome, 45 percent of self-declared democrats would justify a military coup to fight delinquency. In a similar vein, 40 percent of those who endorse democracy would justify a military coup to fight excessive corruption. Clearly, determining the proportion of people who endorse democracy as an ideal form of government is a necessary first step in our efforts to examine the diffusion of democratic attitudes in the region. But the data just presented also suggest that to determine how deep democratic attitudes are in the region, we need to look beyond the formal endorsement of democracy as an ideal form of government.

---

[3] Those who choose the option "Democracy is preferable to any other form of government" in the question described in footnote 2 are considered "self-professed democrats" here.

[4] Our survey asked a series of questions, including whether a military coup will be justified under a series of circumstances: to confront high unemployment, to control social protest, to stop delinquency, to fight inflation, and to fight corruption. For each positive answer, a score of one was assigned. The resulting index was then transformed so it would range from zero (no support for coups under any circumstances) to 100 (support under all circumstances).

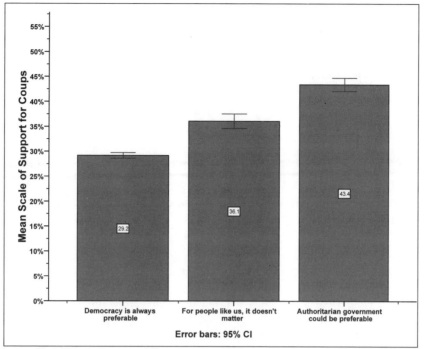

Figure II-4. Mean Scores of Support for Military Coups by Regime Preference

Today, the authoritarianism that Latin America faces is different from the traditional military coup. In a disturbing development, some Latin American democracies seem to have been at least partially undermined by elected presidents who use their considerable popular support to erode the precarious democratic foundations of their respective nations. This situation is a manifestation of a larger trend of democratic devaluation in the developing world, a phenomenon characterized by Diamond (1999) as "the globalization of hollow democracy." While externally maintaining formal democratic institutions, many elected governments systematically engage in anti-democratic behaviors aimed at the elimination of credible challenges to their rule. The emergence and growth of these regimes have led some observers to characterize them as electoral or competitive authoritarianism (Carrión 2006; Diamond 2002; Levitsky and Way 2002; Schedler 2006). Democratic reversals in Latin America are more likely to come today from publics who elect and reelect overbearing presidents bent on aggrandizing their own powers at the expense of the legislature and the courts than from traditional military coups.

Until recently, former President Alberto Fujimori of Peru was the best example of this emerging authoritarianism, but the 2000 reelection of coup-plotter Hugo Chávez in Venezuela along with subsequent developments there suggest the establishment of another electoral authoritarian regime in the region. Recent political crises in Bolivia and Ecuador have at their root the fears of the opposition that a similar path may be engulfing their countries, as presidents use their popularity to undermine existing (and very unpopular) legislatures. In extreme cases, elected presidents have openly assumed dictatorial powers, as was the case in Peru in April of 1992 and in Guatemala in May of 1993 (an attempt that was eventually defeated). Evidently no single reason can explain why the presidential authoritarian takeover was successful in Peru and

not in Guatemala, but popular support/opposition was certainly an important factor in these diverging outcomes. Whereas Fujimori's self-coup generated significant public approval in Peru (Conaghan 1995; Carrión 2006), Serrano's similar action was rejected outright in Guatemala (Cameron 1998, 133). This discrepancy highlights the risks of mass support for civilian forms of authoritarianism. As the PNUD-PRODDAL report concludes (2004, 137), "democracies become vulnerable when, among other factors, authoritarian political forces find in citizens' attitudes a fertile ground to act."

For this reason, the AmericasBarometer 2006-2007 probes potential mass support for illiberal acts against the legislatures, the courts, the opposition, and the laws in general by elected chief executives. In order to do that, the 2006-2007 questionnaire developed a new series, asking the following questions:

I am going to read several pairs of statements. Taking into account the current situation of this country, I would like you to tell me with which of the following two statements you agree with the most?
POP1. [Read the options] 1. It is necessary for the progress of this country that our presidents/prime ministers limit the voice and vote of opposition parties [or, on the contrary] 2. Even if they slow the progress of this country, our presidents should not limit the voice and vote of opposition parties.
POP2. [Read the options] 1. The Congress hinders the work of our presidents/prime ministers, and should be ignored [or, on the contrary] 2. Even when it hinders the work of the president/prime minister, our presidents/prime ministers should not bypass the Congress.
POP3. [Read the options] 1. Judges frequently hinder the work of our presidents/prime ministers, and they should be ignored. [or, on the contrary] 2. Even when judges sometimes hinder the work of our presidents/prime ministers, their decisions should always be obeyed.
POP4. [Read the options] 1. Our presidents/prime ministers should have the necessary power so that they can act in the national interest. [or, on the contrary] 2. The power of our presidents/prime ministers should be limited so that they do not endanger our liberties
POP5. [Read the options] 1. Our presidents/prime ministers should do what the people want even when laws prevent them from doing so. [or, on the contrary] 2. Our presidents/prime ministers should obey the laws even when the people don't want them to.

It is encouraging to report that in all five questions, the liberal answer (presidents should follow the law) prevailed over the illiberal response. Without including those who did not volunteer an answer, 72 percent declared that presidents should not limit the opposition, 80 percent asserted that they should not bypass the Congress, 80 percent demanded that they obey judges, 59 percent wanted their powers to be limited, and 70 percent thought that they should obey the laws.[5]

---

[5] All these five questions were added in a summary index of support for liberal rule. When a respondent answered four of these questions, the average value of these questions was imputed to the missing fifth answer. This was done in an effort to keep as many valid cases as possible. To facilitate the analysis, each question was numerically transformed so that the resulting index will have a range from 0 to 100. Values below 50 indicate low support for liberal rule, and consequently values at or above 50 indicate high support for liberal rule. For the entire sample, 82

Despite these encouraging figures, it is also clear that many self-professed democrats chose the illiberal response in these questions. For instance, 25 percent of those who chose democracy as the ideal form of government selected the illiberal answer in question POP1. In POP4, 41 percent of self-professed democrats chose the illiberal answer. This, of course, raises the issue of how deep or consistent is their democratic commitment.

One way to measure support for democracy in a more robust fashion is to combine regime preferences with attitudes about how political authority should be exercised. If we take regime preferences,[6] collapsing the three choices into two, one for the democratic choice and the other for those who prefer authoritarianism (or are indifferent) and combine them with the index of support for liberal rule (dichotomizing the index into low and high support) we obtain the following theoretical situations (Table II.3).

Table II-3. Conceptual Relationship between Regime Preference and Constraints on Political Authority

Constraints on political authority	Regime Preference	
	Democracy	*Non Democracy*
Liberal rule	Liberal democracy	Liberal authoritarianism
Illiberal rule	Illiberal democracy	Illiberal authoritarianism

The optimal choice for the consolidation of a healthy democracy is the combination of attitudes that favor democratic rule with constraints on the power of presidents or prime ministers to exert their political power. Those who exhibit such a combination of preferences are labeled here "liberal democrats." I will center the analysis on them. All the other choices are sub-optimal for the prospects of democratic rule, but the worst possible combination is the one that pairs preference for authoritarian forms of government (or indifference between them) with support for the illiberal exercise of executive power.

The distribution of these attitudes for the entire sample is shown in Table II.4. While 73 percent of the respondents favor democracy (this figure excludes those who do not answer the question), 61 percent of all respondents can be labeled as liberal democrats, that is, they support democracy *and* constraints on the exercise of political power. It is encouraging to find that only 7 percent of those interviewed in 2006-2007 favor the worst possible combination of support for illiberal rule and preference for non democracy.

---

percent of the respondents have values at or above 50 in the scale. These questions were not asked in Bolivia and Ecuador.

[6] Measured by the responses to the following question: With which of these phrases are you most in agreement? Democracy is preferable to any other form of government; under some circumstances an authoritarian government can be preferable to a democratic one; for people like us, a democratic regime is the same as a non-democratic one.

Table II-4. Support for Liberal Democracy and Illiberal Democracy

		Support for Democracy		
		Democrats	**Non Democrats**	**Total**
Constraints on power	Liberal Rule	60.6%	18.9%	79.5%
	Illiberal Rule	13.6%	6.9%	20.5%
Total		74.2%	25.8%	100.0%

Is this a valid or useful classification? One way to validate it is by using it to predict certain attitudes that are related to support or rejection of democratic values. If the classification has validity, it should help us predict, for instance, levels of political tolerance, with liberal democrats being more tolerant that illiberal non democrats. Similarly, if this is a valid classification it should be able to differentiate between those who endorse social authoritarian values from those who do not, with liberal democrats being less socially authoritarian than illiberal authoritarians.[7] Figures II.5 and II.6 display the means of political tolerance and authoritarian values for each our four "regime x authority" groups. In each case, the results are in the expected direction and, more importantly, they are monotonic, meaning than liberal democrats are more tolerant and less socially authoritarian than illiberal democrats, and in turn illiberal democrats are more tolerant and less conservative than liberal authoritarians, with the illiberal authoritarians ranking last in both attitudes.

---

[7] It should be noted that the questions utilized to measure social authoritarianism do not have a political content. They ask whether the respondent agrees with the following statements: "a very effective way of correcting employees' mistakes is to criticize them in front of other employees;" "the person who contributes the most money to the home is the one who should have the final word in household decisions;" "at school, children should ask questions only when the teacher allows it;" "when children behave badly, parents are justified in occasionally giving them a spanking."

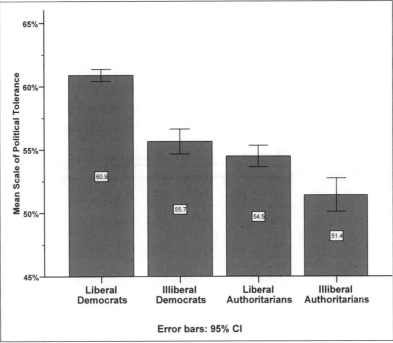

**Figure II-5. Political Tolerance by Regime Preference and Support
for Liberal Rule**

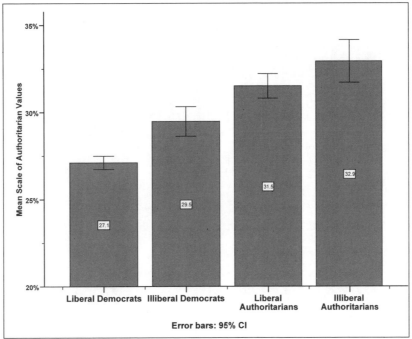

**Figure II-6. Social Authoritarianism by Regime Preference and
Support for Liberal Rule**

As expected, there is important cross-national variation in the distribution of liberal democrats (Figure II.7). Countries with strong democratic traditions, such as Costa Rica and Uruguay, and those with strong parliamentary histories, such as Jamaica, report the highest number of liberal democrats. Honduras, Venezuela, the Dominican Republic, Guyana, and Chile follow. On the other hand, Haiti, that has the third highest percentage of people declaring a preference democracy over authoritarianism, falls to next to last place when we qualify preference for democracy with support for liberal rule. Paraguay exhibits the lowest levels of attitudinal support for liberal democracy. Guatemala, Brazil, Nicaragua, and Peru, all countries with spotty democratic records, follow Paraguay and Haiti as having the lowest percentages of liberal democrats.

To have a better understanding of the factors that help discriminate between liberal democrats and those who have other regime/authority preferences it is necessary to go beyond national differences. It is imperative to explore the personal characteristics of each of these groups. This is what it is done in the next section.

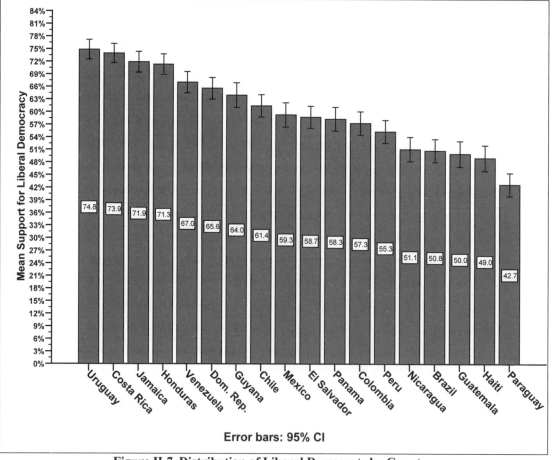

Figure II-7. Distribution of Liberal Democrats by Country

Who Is More Likely to Embrace Liberal Democracy?

An attitude, such as support for the liberal exercise of democracy, cannot have just one single factor determining it. Attitudes are influenced by personal characteristics, such as gender, education, and place of residence, as well as formative life experiences, personality traits and other attitudes such as, in this particular case, evaluations of the political system. It is useful to distinguish all these different influences when trying to determine their impact on support for liberal democracy. Thus, I develop five models that explain membership in the "liberal democracy" cell as opposed to those who fall in the "illiberal democracy" cell or the "authoritarian" cells (to simplify the statistical analysis and the discussion, liberal and illiberal authoritarians are aggregated into a single category).

The first model includes sociodemographic characteristics: gender, age, education, material wealth (a way to measure socioeconomic status), residence in rural or urban areas, and whether the respondent grew up in a rural area or in a town or city. In addition to these factors, I include two variables associated with interest in and knowledge of politics.[8] This is our baseline model.

The second model includes, in addition to the previous variables, a series of questions associated with Putnam's work on social capital (Putnam 1993) and Inglehart's (1977; 1988) theory that general satisfaction with one's life is associated with stronger democratic attitudes. The core of the social capital theory is that a stronger associational life and trust in others foster the development of democratic values. Accordingly, I include a scale of participation in civil society organizations, a question probing the respondent's level of interpersonal trust, and another inquiring about the respondent's level of satisfaction with his or her life.

The third model tries to determine whether perceptions of personal or economic threat affect our redefined regime choices. The underlying theory is that threat perception increases a person's propensity to support authoritarian alternatives (Altemeyer 1996; Fromm 1941; Stenner 2005). The longing for security and predictability is thought to be a psychological mechanism that leads people with an elevated threat perception to endorse authoritarianism. To measure the sense of personal security I employ three variables. The first question asks the respondent to assess how safe she feels in her neighborhood. The second question probes whether the respondent has been a victim of a crime in the previous year. The last variable is an index of the total number of corruption acts that the respondent experienced in the year previous to the survey. To measure economic insecurity, two standard questions are utilized: the respondent's retrospective assessment of both his or her personal situation and the country's. The assumption is that those who have negative views of their personal or the country's economic situation will

---

[8] Interest in politics is measured by the answer to two questions: a) "How much interest do you have in politics: a lot, some, little or none;" b) "How frequently do you watch the news on TV: every day, one or twice a week, rarely, or never?" The responses were recoded so they would go from low to high interest. Political knowledge was measured by a scale that added the correct answers to five questions of general political knowledge (see battery of "GI" items in the questionnaire). Political knowledge has been found to be an important predictor of many political attitudes (Althaus 2003; Delli Carpini and Keeter 1996; Grofman 1995).

have a lower sense of economic security than those who have a more positive evaluation of the economy.

While the previous model centers on threat perceptions, the fourth model focuses its attention on evaluations of political performance. As Bratton and Mattes (2001a; 2007) argue, there is evidence that support for democracy is partially driven by assessments of how well the political system is functioning. The impact of two types of political assessments, one that is specifically related to the incumbent's performance and the other that is more generally related to the performance of the political system is explored. In the latter case, three variables are used: a scale of system support, a scale of trust in political institutions, and a question that measures the respondent's satisfaction "with the way in which democracy functions" in his or her country.

Finally, the fifth model adds to all the previously mentioned influences two variables that measure ideology (on the traditional left-right scale) and a scale of social authoritarian values (which, as I mentioned before, it is not "contaminated" with political content). Following the work of Altemeyer on conventionalism (1996), I hypothesize that those who are on the socially authoritarian side the spectrum (displaying support for patriarchal and authoritarian conventions) are more likely to support authoritarian forms of government.

The table reporting the full results for the five models is attached at the end of the chapter. Table I-5 summarizes the results in a non-technical fashion, providing the sign of the relationship for only those predictors that turn out to be statistically significant. Predictors that are not significant are noted as "ns." The reference category in the table is those who support authoritarianism (whether in its liberal or illiberal variants).

To analyze the results, I will compare, first, the factors that differentiate those who support liberal democracy from those who endorse authoritarian forms of government. After that, I will analyze the differences between those who support illiberal forms of democracy versus those who endorse authoritarianism.

The summary table suggests that three sociodemographic factors are consistent predictors of support for liberal democracy. Older citizens are more likely to be classified as liberal democrats (based on their answers to the questions on regime preference and how executive power should be exercised) than younger voters (Figure II-8). This finding is entirely understandable but nonetheless troublesome. Older citizens grew up in a period when many Latin American countries were experiencing military rule. They probably remember well the abuses associated with these regimes and the citizens' efforts to dislodge them from power. Younger citizens, on the other hand, were socialized in a different environment. They never experienced regimes other than the often weak and troubled democratic governments that characterize a good part of the region; therefore they lack the comparative reference afforded to those who had lived under authoritarian regimes. Not surprisingly, the association between age and regime choice is very consistent and remains significant even when variables associated with political performance and democratic values are introduced in the analysis.

In three of the five models gender emerges as a statistical significant predictor, with men more likely than women to endorse liberal democracy than authoritarianism. Similarly, the data

38

lend general support to the idea that greater possession of material goods enhances democratic predispositions.

The evidence also shows that liberal democrats, in comparison to authoritarians, are more educated and more likely to have spent their formative years in towns or cities than authoritarians. These findings are consistent with what one would expect, as both education and early socialization in urban areas are thought to be related with stronger democratic preferences.

Table II-4. Predictor Variables of Support for Liberal and Illiberal Democracy (Summary)

Predictor Variables	Baseline Model	Social Capital	Threat Perception	Political Performance	Values
I. Liberal Democrats					
Age in years	+	+	+	+	+
Gender (0=Women)	ns	+	+	+	ns
Education in years	+	+	+	+	+
Material wealth	+	+	+	+	ns
Hometown (0=countryside)	+	+	+	+	+
Hometown (0=city)	ns	ns	ns	ns	ns
Place of residence (0=rural areas)	ns	ns	ns	ns	ns
Watch news on TV	ns	ns	ns	ns	ns
Interest in politics	ns	ns	ns	ns	ns
Political knowledge	+	+	+	+	+
Associational life		ns	ns	ns	ns
Interpersonal trust		+	+	+	ns
Life satisfaction		+	+	ns	ns
Feels safe in his/her neighborhood			ns	ns	ns
Has been a victim of crime (0=No)			ns	ns	ns
Index of corruption victimization			-	-	-
Retrospective eval. of personal economic situation			ns	ns	ns
Retrospective eval. of country's economic situation			-	-	-
Presidential approval				ns	ns
System support				+	ns
Trust in political institutions				ns	ns
Satisfaction with the way democracy works				+	+
Ideology					ns
Scale of authoritarian values					-
Scale of political tolerance					+
II. Illiberal Democrats					
Age in years	+	+	+	+	+
Gender (0=Women)	ns	ns	ns	ns	ns
Education in years	ns	ns	ns	ns	ns
Material wealth	ns	ns	ns	ns	ns

Hometown (0=countryside)	ns	ns	ns	ns	ns
Hometown (0=city)	ns	ns	ns	ns	ns
Place of residence (0=rural areas)	ns	-	-	-	-
Watch news on TV	ns	ns	ns	ns	ns
Interest in politics	ns	ns	ns	ns	ns
Political knowledge	+	+	+	+	+
Associational life		ns	ns	ns	ns
Interpersonal trust		ns	ns	ns	ns
Life satisfaction		+	+	ns	ns
Feels safe in his/her neighborhood			ns	ns	ns
Has been a victim of crime (0=No)			ns	ns	ns
Index of corruption victimization			-	ns	ns
Retrospective eval. of personal economic situation			ns	ns	ns
Retrospective eval. of country's economic situation			-	-	-
Presidential approval				-	-
System support				ns	ns
Trust in political institutions				ns	ns
Satisfaction with the way democracy works				+	+
Ideology					ns
Scale of authoritarian values					-
Scale of political tolerance					ns

Reference category: Authoritarians; ns=not significant. Variables not included in the model are shaded.

Neither TV news watching nor interest in politics increases the likelihood of choosing liberal forms of democracy over authoritarian governance. On the other hand, and consistent with our previous finding about the role of education, having higher levels of political knowledge is associated with a greater likelihood of belonging in the liberal democracy cell.

Turning to variables associated with the social capital approach, the data show very mixed support for the view that interpersonal trust or membership in civil society organizations strengthen commitment to democratic values. When included along with the variables that constitute our baseline model, both interpersonal trust and associational life emerge as significant predictors of membership in the liberal democracy group. They are also significant when they are included in the perception of threat model. However, when political performance, ideology, political tolerance, and social authoritarianism variables are taken into account, the effect of social capital variables disappears. A similar pattern can be detected when the impact of life satisfaction on support for liberal democracy is analyzed. The impact is positive and significant when it is first introduced, but when performance and other attitudinal variables are included, its influence vanishes.

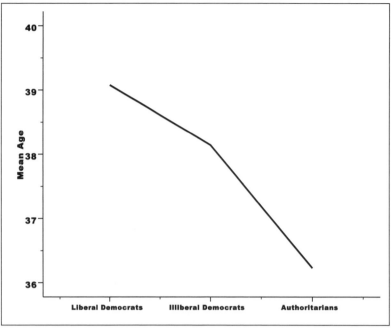

Figure II-8. Regime Preference/Support for Liberal Rule by Age

There is also mixed support for the thesis that elevated levels of threat perception depress support for liberal forms of democracy. Whether a person has been victim of a crime does not make him or her less likely to support democracy. Nor is the sense of personal insecurity associated with regime preferences. This is relatively good news because it implies that the increase in crime that the region is experiencing is not affecting, at least not yet, attitudes towards liberal democracy. On the other hand, I do find that greater personal experience with corruption and negative evaluations of the national economy diminish the likelihood that a respondent will prefer liberal democracy over authoritarianism. People who believe that the country's economic is worse today than it was in the previous are less likely to support liberal democracy and more likely to embrace authoritarianism (Figure II-9). This effect does not disappear when political performance and other attitudinal variables are included in the analysis.

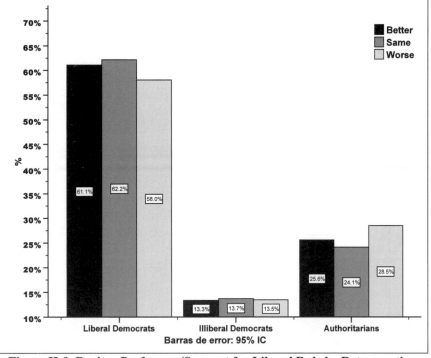

**Figure II-9. Regime Preference/Support for Liberal Rule by Retrospective
Evaluations of the Country's economy**

Model 4 examines how important are assessments of the political system, trust in political institutions, presidential approval and general satisfaction with the way democracy is working in the support for liberal democracy. The results indicate that preference for liberal democracy is not affected by assessments of the incumbent performance or trust in political institutions. Similarly, while system support emerges as a positive, significant predictor in one model, its effect vanishes when ideology, political tolerance, and the scale of authoritarian attitudes are included in the analysis. Of the political performance variables, only one exhibit a consistent influence on regime choice, namely satisfaction with the way democracy is working: a generalized sense that democracy is not functioning properly makes people more likely to support authoritarianism (Figure II-10).

Finally, while we fail to find a relationship between ideology (measured on a left-right scale) and our redefined regime categories, we do find that rejection of social authoritarian values increase support for liberal democracy.

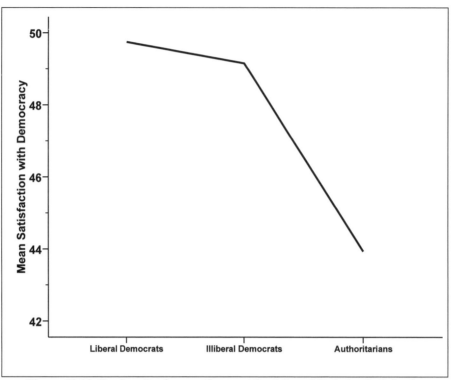

**Figure II-10. Regime Preference/Support for Liberal Rule by Satisfaction
with the way Democracy is Working**

Turning our attention to the differences between liberal and illiberal democrats, the following can be said. First of all, many of the factors that help us discriminate between liberal democrats and authoritarians help us also discriminate between illiberal democrats and authoritarians. As the summary table suggests, older citizens with levels of political knowledge higher than the average, who have positive assessments of the country's economy, generally satisfied with the way democracy works, and who are also politically tolerant and less inclined to support social authoritarianism are more likely to endorse democracy in illiberal variants than to support authoritarianism.

However, some of the factors that make people choose liberal democracy as opposed to authoritarianism do not help us distinguish between those who prefer illiberal forms of democracy and authoritarianism. For instance, while having early socialization experiences in towns or cities as opposed to rural areas lead people to endorse liberal democracy, these socialization experiences do not help us distinguish between illiberal democrats and authoritarians. In similar vein, while people with more material possessions are more likely to choose liberal democracy as opposed to authoritarianism, economic wealth does not help us discriminate between authoritarians and illiberal democrats. This means that authoritarians and illiberal democrats tend to have similar early socialization and economic wealth backgrounds.

On the other hand, there are two variables that are significant predictors of membership in the group of illiberal democrats as opposed to authoritarians. The first is the area of current residence, with illiberal democrats being more likely to live in cities than authoritarians are. The

second variable is presidential approval. Those who are unsatisfied with the job of the president are more inclined to support authoritarianism than to endorse illiberal forms of democracy. Those who approve of the job the president or the prime minister is doing are more likely to endorse democracy but in its illiberal variant. This makes sense because illiberal democrats are the ones willing to grant extraordinary powers to presidents or prime ministers. Liberal democrats, on the other hand, may or may not support the president. Whether they do or do not has no bearing on their disposition to prefer one type of rule over other.

Concluding Remarks

I find that the majority of Latin Americans define democracy in normative terms, and that those who do so are more likely to endorse it than those who define it in instrumental or negative terms. But I also find that the effect is not very strong. The data show that the majority of Latin Americans endorse democracy, but that there are important cross-national variations. Moreover, the study finds that this support is rather shallow. Many of the self-declared democrats hold views that are inimical to democratic rule, such as endorsement of military coups or willingness to support illiberal exercises of political power. I find that depending on the question, as few as 17 percent and as many as 45 percent of self-declared democrats are ready to justify a military coup. I also find that a quarter of those who endorse democracy have no problem agreeing with the statement that presidents should limit the voice and vote of the opposition if "it is necessary for the progress of this country."

Given these inconsistencies, I proposed a typology that seeks to provide a more robust conceptualization of support for democratic rule. I did so by combining regime preferences (for democracy or authoritarianism) with attitudes about how political power should be exercised (with constraints or without constraints). Liberal democrats, in this conceptualization, are those who support democracy in principle and are unwilling to grant unchecked powers to presidents or prime ministers. Illiberal democrats are those that while preferring democracy are also willing to endorse the illiberal exercise of power. Liberal and illiberal authoritarians are, for purposes of this article, grouped into a single category. While 73 percent of the respondents declare a preference for democracy over other regimes, the analysis conducted in this chapter shows that only 61 percent of all respondents could be classified as liberal democrats. The latter figure probably provides a more realistic picture of the extent of attitudinal support for democracy than the former. Even then, and as the subsequent analysis makes clear, some liberal democrats are not completely exempted from the temptation of endorsing some authoritarian positions.

To identify who are those more likely to be classified as liberal democrats, a series of models were developed. The main findings are that endorsement of liberal democracy is driven by both instrumental and normative considerations. On the utilitarian side, the data show that positive evaluations of the country's economy and general satisfaction with the way democracy is working increase support for liberal forms of democratic rule. On the normative side, the data show that greater levels of political tolerance and low predispositions to social authoritarianism increase support for liberal democracy. In addition to these utilitarian and normative considerations, certain demographic characteristics such as age and material wealth, as well as political information, affect the degree of support for liberal democracy, with older, more affluent

and more politically informed citizens being more likely to prefer liberal democracy than authoritarianism.

The general conclusion of this chapter is that mass support for democracy is not as high or robust as one would expect or hope. On the other hand, it is clear than a majority of Latin Americans look with sympathy on the liberal exercise of democratic rule. Even if this support is at times inconsistent, it provides a core from which stronger and more consistent democratic attitudes could be encouraged.

References

Altemeyer, Bob. *Enemies of Freedom: Understanding Right-Wing Authoritarianism.* San Francisco: Jossey-Bass, 1988.

———. *The Authoritarian Specter.* Cambridge: Harvard University Press, 1996.

Althaus, Scott L. *Collective Preferences in Democratic Politics: Opinion Surveys and the Will of the People.* Cambridge: Cambridge University Press, 2003.

Bratton, Michael and Robert Mattes. "Support for Democracy in Africa: Intrinsic or Instrumental". *British Journal of Political Science.* Vol. 31, No. 3 (2001a): 447-474.

———. "Africans' Surprising Universalism." *Journal of Democracy* 12 (1) (2001b): 107-121.

Cameron, Maxwell. "Self-Coups: Peru, Guatemala, Russia." *Journal of Democracy* 9 (1) (1998).

Carrión, Julio F. "Conclusion: The Rise and Fall of Electoral Authoritarianism in Peru". In *The Fujimori Legacy: The Rise of Electoral Authoritarianism in Peru,* ed. Julio F. Carrión, University Park: Pennsylvania State University Press, 2006.

Conaghan, Catherine M. *Fujimori's Peru: Deception in the Public Sphere.* Pittsburgh: University of Pittsburgh Press, 2005.

Dahl, Robert. *A Preface to Democratic Theory.* Chicago and London: The University of Chicago Press, (1956).

———. *Democracy and its Critics.* New Haven: Yale University Press, 1989.

Delli Carpini, Michael X. and Scott Keeter. *What American Know About Politics and Why it Matters.* New Haven: Yale University Press, 1996.

Diamond, Larry. *Developing Democracy: Toward Consolidation.* Baltimore and London: The Johns Hopkins University Press, 1999.

———. "Thinking about Hybrid Regimes." *Journal of Democracy* 13 (2) (2002).

Fromm, Eric. *Escape From Freedom.* New York: Holt, Rinehart and Winston, 1941.

Grofman, Bernard (editor). *Information, Participation, and Choice.* Ann Arbor: University of Michigan Press, 1995.

Held, David. *Models of Democracy. Second Edition.* Stanford: Stanford University Press, (1996).

Inglehart, Ronald. *The Silent Revolution.* Princeton: Princeton University Press, 1977.

———. "The Renaissance of Political Culture." *American Political Science Review.* Vol. 82 (1988): 1203-1230.

Lakoff, Sanford. *Democracy: History, Theory, Practice.* Boulder: Westview Press, (1996).

Levitsky, Steven, and Lucan A. Way. "The Rise of Competitive of Authoritarianism." *Journal of Democracy* 13 (2) (2002).

Macpherson, C.B. *The Life and Times of Liberal Democracy.* Oxford: Oxford University Press, 1977.

Mattes, Robert and Michael Bratton. "Learning about Democracy in Africa: Awareness, Performance, and Experience." *American Journal of Political Science* 51 (1) (2007): 192-217.

PNUD-PRODDAL. *La democracia en América Latina: Hacia una democracia de ciudadanos y ciudadanas*. Lima: PNUD, 2004.

Prothro, James W. and Charles M. Grigg. "Fundamental Principles of Democracy: Bases of Agreement and Disagreement." *Journal of Politics* 22 (2) (1960): 276-294.

Putnam, Robert. *Making Democracy Work*. Princeton: Princeton University Press, 1993.

Sarsfield, Rodolfo. ¿*La no-elección de Dorian Gray o la decisión de Ulises? Racionalidad y determinación en la preferencia por democracia en América Latina*. México: FLACSO. Ph.D Dissertation, 2003.

Sarsfield, Rodolfo and Julio F. Carrión. *The Different Paths to Authoritarianism: Rationality and Irrationality in Regime Preferences*. Annual Meeting of the World Association of Public Opinion Research, WAPOR. May 16-18, Montreal, Canada, 2006.

Sarsfield, Rodolfo and Fabian Echegaray. "Opening the Black Box. How Satisfaction with Democracy and its Perceived Efficacy Affect Regime Preference in Latin America." *International Journal of Public Opinion Research*, Vol. 18 (2006): 153-173.

Schedler, Andreas (editor). *Electoral Authoritarianism: The Dynamics of Unfree Competition*. Boulder and London: Lynne Rienner Pub, 2006.

Stenner, Karen. *The Authoritarian Dynamic*. New York: Cambridge University Press, 2005.

Touraine, Alain. *What is Democracy*. Boulder, Westview Press, 1997.

Appendix. Modeling Support for Liberal Democracy

Table II-6. Predictors of Support for Liberal Democracy

Predictor Variables	Baseline Model	Social Capital	Threat Perception	Political Performance	Values
I. Liberal Democrats					
Constant	-1.498 (.765)*	-11.875 (1.240)**	-12.218 (1.265)**	-11.918 (1.292)**	-9.554 (1.437)**
Age in years	.014 (.001)**	.014 (.001)**	.014 (.001)**	.015 (.001)**	.016 (.002)**
Gender (0=Women)	.062 (.034)	.080 (.036)*	.076 (.037)*	.076 (.039)*	.070 (.042)
Education in years	.032 (.005)**	.037 (.005)**	.038 (.005)**	.039 (.006)**	.030 (.006)**
Material wealth	.057 (.011)**	.026 (.011)*	.028 (.012)*	.024 (012)*	.020 (.013)
Hometown (0=countryside)	.199 (.048)**	.192 (.051)**	.178 (.052)**	.187 (.054)**	.205 (.059)**
Hometown (0=city)	.022 (.048)	.065 (.051)	.071 (.052)	.101 (.053)	.084 (.058)
Place of residence (0=rural areas)	.022 (.043)	-.051 (.046)	-.038 (.047)	-.030 (.050)	-.031 (.055)
Watch news on TV	-.019 (.019)	-.009 (.021)	-.014 (.021)	-.012 (.022)	-.005 (.024)
Interest in politics	.012 (.018)	.001 (.019)	-.002 (.020)	-.002 (.021)	-.007 (.022)
Political knowledge	.194 (.014)**	.113 (.016)**	.112 (.017)**	.110 (.017)**	.078 (.019)**
Associational life		-.083 (.087)	-.038 (.089)	-.107 (.093)	.075 (.101)
Interpersonal trust		.086 (.020)**	.066 (.021)*	.047 (.022)*	.031 (.024)
Life satisfaction		.070 (.024)*	.056 (.025)*	.030 (.026)	.027 (.028)
Feels safe in his/her neighborhood			.001 (.001)	.001 (.001)	.001 (.001)
Has been a victim of crime (0=No)			.057 (.049)	.029 (.050)	.043 (.055)
Index of corruption victimization			-.088 (.024)**	-.066 (.026)*	-.058 (.029)*

Predictor Variables	Baseline Model	Social Capital	Threat Perception	Political Performance	Values
Retrospective evaluation of personal economic situation			-.014 (.030)	.029 (.031)	.028 (.033)
Retrospective evaluation of country's economic situation			-.137 (.030)**	-.133 (.032)**	-.154 (.035)**
Presidential approval				.046 (.024)	.035 (.027)
System support				.003 (.001)*	.002 (.001)
Trust in political institutions				-.001 (.001)	-.001 (.001)
Satisfaction with the way democracy works				.005 (.001)**	.005 (.001)**
Ideology					.011 (.008)
Scale of authoritarian values					-.010 (.001)**
Scale of political tolerance					.009 (.001)**
II. Illiberal Democrats					
Constant	-3.017 (1.112)*	-12.966 (1.605)**	-13.689 (1.319)**	-14.099 (1.667)**	-11.590 (1.855)**
Age in years	.010 (.002)**	.011 (.002)**	.011 (.002)**	.012 (.002)**	.013 (.002)**
Gender (0=Women)	-.003 (.049)	.049 (.052)	.057 (.053)	.052 (.055)	.034 (.060)
Education in years	.004 (.008)	.006 (.008)	.006 (.008)	.007 (.008)	.000 (.009)
Material wealth	.025 (.016)	.004 (.017)	-.006 (.017)	-.008 (.018)	-.005 (.019)
Hometown (0=countryside)	.103 (.067)	.110 (.071)	.101 (.072)	.090 (.075)	.102 (.082)
Hometown (0=city)	-.091 (.068)	-.077 (.071)	-.055 (.072)	-.049 (.075)	-.065 (.080)
Place of residence (0=rural areas)	-.087 (.062)	-.186 (.066)*	-.182 (.068)*	-.160 (.071)*	-.173 (.078)*
Watch news on TV	-.018 (.028)	-.008 (.029)	-.018 (.030)	-.018 (.031)	-.016 (.034)
Interest in politics	.044 (.026)	.040 (.027)	.033 (.028)	.015 (.029)	.014 (.032)
Political knowledge	.152	.087	.087	.091	.060

Predictor Variables	Baseline Model	Social Capital	Threat Perception	Political Performance	Values
	(.020)**	(.023)**	(.024)**	(.024)**	(.027)*
Associational life		-.008	.034	.037	.123
		(.123)	(.126)	(.132)	(.142)
Interpersonal trust		.046	.012	-.003	-0.012
		(.028)	(.030)	(.031)	(.034)
Life satisfaction		.123	.084	.045	.058
		(.034)**	(.035)*	(.037)	(.040)
Feels safe in his/her neighborhood			.002	.001	.001
			(.001)	(.001)	(.001)
Has been a victim of crime (0=No)			.095	.057	.040
			(.070)	(.072)	(.077)
Index of corruption victimization			-.078	-.069	-.055
			(.034)*	(.036)	(.040)
Retrospective evaluation of personal economic situation			-.008	.020	.018
			(.043)	(.044)	(.047)
Retrospective evaluation of country's economic situation			-.254	-.213	-.215
			(.043)**	(.045)**	(.049)**
Presidential approval				-.147	-.118
				(.038)**	(.042)*
System support				.000	.002
				(.002)	(.002)
Trust in political institutions				-.002	-.003
				(.002)	(.002)
Satisfaction with the way democracy works				.006	.005
				(.001)**	(.001)**
Ideology					.000
					(.012)
Scale of authoritarian values					-.008
					(.001)**
Scale of political tolerance					.002
					(.001)
Pseudo R square	.082	.083	.087	.092	.111
-2 log likelihood	36008.5	32736.6	31749.4	29721.6	25196.6

Reference category: Authoritarians
Entries are multinomial logistic regression coefficients. Corresponding standard errors are between parenthesis.
*p ≤ .05; **p ≤ .001. Country effects are omitted to save space.

III. "Throw them All Out"? Attitudes towards Political Parties in the Americas[1]

María Fernanda Boidi [2]

Abstract

Political parties are the intermediate structures between society and government in representative democracies. When the links between citizens and parties are weak, the fundamental intermediary role is not in place, and as a result, society and government are not connected. This seems to be the case in Latin America, where citizens trust political parties very little, and where other links between citizens and parties such as voting for political parties, identifying with a party, and participation in party activities are also generally weak Notwithstanding this discouraging outlook, in most countries in the region there is still a reservoir of support for political parties. Overall, the belief in the need to have parties in order for there to be democracy surpasses (in some cases by a wide margin) the levels of trust in political parties. Most Latin Americans believe that parties are necessary for democracy, ranging from 33 percent in Haiti to 66 percent in Uruguay) This suggests that contempt for parties is related to the context: it would be the way that parties currently operate, rather than rejection of them as an institution, which distances citizens from political parties.

In 1942, referring to the American party system, Schattschneider stated that modern democracy is unthinkable without political parties (1942:1). Contemporary democracies continue to be "unthinkable" without political parties because democracies have been designed in such a way that parties are the "intermediary structure between society and government" (Sartori 1976: iv). If the links between citizens and parties are exceedingly weak (as the available data suggest is the case in many Latin American countries) the basic intermediary task is not being fulfilled, and as a result society and government are not connected.

One of the clearest examples, not only of the breach between citizens and political parties, but also of the rejection of the party as an institution of political mediation is the "throw them all out" protest carried out in Argentina in 2001, when people poured out into the streets to literally "oust" their rulers chanting "Throw them all out, not a single one stays." The

[1] The "Americas" refers to the 22 countries included in the 2006-07 round of the LAPOP AmericasBarometer: Bolivia, Brasil, Canada, Chile, Colombia, Costa Rica, Ecuador, the United States, El Salvador, Guatemala, Guyana, Honduras, Haiti, Jamaica, Mexico, Nicaragua, Panama, Paraguay, Peru, Dominican Republic, Uruguay and Venezuela. This round of interviews was made possible thanks to the support from USAID. When all the available data allow, the analysis covers all 22 countries. The central discussion on trust in political parties is limited to the countries of Latin America and the Caribbean.

[2] This article has benefited from my conversations on the topic with Florence Faucher-King and Jonathan Hiskey. Mitchell Seligson carefully read preliminary versions and contributed valuable comments; my thanks to all three. The final product, of course, is my sole responsibility. I wrote this chapter during academic year 2006-2007, while I was studying in the Ph.D program in Political Science at Vanderbilt University. I would like to thank for the financial support received from the Department of Political Science as well as from the Center for the Americas. Likewise, extensive thanks go to the office of the Provost at Vanderbilt University.

protests that culminated with then president Fernando de la Rua stepping down, was begun by groups of unemployed workers who rejected the government's economic policies. They were subsequently joined by middle class citizens all across the country, turning a local protest into a national mass protest (Bonnet s.d.; Dinerstein 2003; Giarraca 2002).

Notwithstanding its origins and unique motivations, the demand to "throw them all out" is an expression of citizen rejection of representative democracy's central institutions, which is very much a part of the region-wide interest in populist governments discussed in the chapter in this volume by Mitchell Seligson. In this regard, the Argentine crisis is not exceptional. González (2006:8) has tallied nine "severe political crises" involving institutional weakening or rupture in six other countries in Latin America to date since 2000 (Paraguay 2000, Peru 2000, Venezuela 2003, Bolivia 2003 and 2005, Ecuador 2000 and 2005, and Nicaragua 2005). If the clamor to "throw them all out" is a protest against the whole system, a demand to start over, the outrage is directed at the institutions of representative democracy, and in this regard, the targets of the complaint are none other than the political parties as the agents in charge of organizing, channeling, and representing interests in the public sphere.

The parties themselves recognize that they are part of the problem. In their study on Central American political parties, Achard and González found that 64 percent of the politicians interviewed, and 80 percent of the non-political observers interviewed, considered that political parties were not performing well in the region. Among the reasons that respondents gave for this poor performance were patrimonial and corrupt practices, the existence of oligarchic party structures, and the lack of internal democracy (Achard and González 2004:83). On another front, Córdova Macías (2004) pointed out that among the causes of the crisis of political parties in Latin America are their lack of transparency and their inability or unwillingness to carry out campaign promises and citizens' demands.

The level of trust in political parties is the central theme of this chapter. Previous research has demonstrated that a low level of trust in political parties is detrimental to the process of democratic consolidation in several ways, as described in the main section of this paper, *"Why trust in political parties matters."* This chapter begins with a brief description of citizen-parties linkages in the Americas, which is followed for the main section on trust in political parties. The chapter concludes with a discussion of the implications that low levels of trust in political parties have for the process of consolidating democracy in the region.

Weak Citizen-party Linkages in the Americas

The relationship among citizens and parties can be analyzed from several perspectives. Citizens can be members of party organizations or participate in activities organized by parties, such as public meetings, caravans or rallies. Ultimately, citizens vote for a political party, in what constitutes for many their sole act of political participation (Campbell et al. 1960). At the level of attitudes, aside from the aforementioned trust, individuals may or may not identify themselves with a given political party, and they also have their own ideas regarding the role of parties in democracy. These behaviors and attitudes, particularly when considered as a

whole, provide a map of the citizen-party linkages in each of the countries. This chapter's aims is to outline that map.

Table III- 1. Citizen-party linkages in the Americas

	Vote in presidential election % (a)	Vote in legislative election % (b)	Difference presidential/ Legislative vote	Party identification % (c)	Attend Meetings Mean (d)	Convince others (total respondents) Mean (e)	Convince others (only identifiers) Mean (f)	Work for the party (total respondents) % (g)	Work for the party (only identifiers) % (h)
Mexico	71.3	58.1	13.2	49.2	0.2	0.4	0.6	7.4	9.7
Guatemala	56.5	41.1	15.4	14.7	0.1	0.4	0.7	3.8	14.2
El Salvador	67.9	65.6	2.3	31.3	0.1	0.4	0.7	8.3	15.6
Honduras	82.5	70.3	12.2	44.2	0.2	0.5	0.7	19.9	27.3
Nicaragua	61.2	46.8	14.4	49.8	0.3	0.5	0.6	10.9	16.8
Costa Rica	70.8	92.7	-21.9	36.2	0.1	0.6	0.8	11.2	19.6
Panama	79.5	51.0	28.5	20.8	0.2	0.9	1.2	12.8	26.6
Colombia	60.2	46.5	13.7	28.6	0.2	0.4	0.7	11.7	25.2
Ecuador	83.8				0.1	0.5		9.3	
Bolivia	90.9				0.2	0.6			
Peru	91.8	91.8	0	29.9	0.3	0.7	1.0	8.0	15.4
Paraguay	67.6				0.2	0.5		12.1	
Chile	70.8	66.4	4.4	25.6	0.1	0.6	0.9	3.8	9.2
Uruguay	88.9			53.3	0.2	0.6	0.8	15.2	21.6
Brazil	84.1			34.1	0.1	0.7	0.9	14.0	23.8
Venezuela	76.8	29.8	47	32.5	0.3	0.7	1.0	13.2	26.8
Dominican Rep.	80.3	77.2	3.1	60.4	0.5	1.0	1.2	20.0	27.3
Haiti	78.0	72.5	5.5	37.9	0.4	0.5	0.7	15.4	23.7
Jamaica	48.0	33.1	14.9	47.1	0.3	0.6	0.9	6.8	12.9
Guyana	78.1	56.8	21.3	19.5	0.3	0.8	1.1	10.1	22.5
Canada	84.0			50.7	0.2				
United States	89.3			62.2	0.2				
Total Americas	74.8	59.2		37.1	0.2	0.6	0.9	11.3	20.01

a. Percentage of respondents who answered "yes" to question vb2 Did you vote in the previous presidential election? b. Percentage of respondents that answered "yes" to question vb6. Did you vote for a deputy in the last elections? c. Percentage of respondents that answered "yes" to question vb10. Do you currently identify with a political party? d. Average of attendance to party meetings or political movements (0. Never, 1. Once or twice a year, 2. Once or twice a month, 3. Once a week). Created based on recodification of the original values for question cp 13. Do you attend meetings of a political party or political movement? e. Average of how often respondents said they have attempted to convince others to vote for a party or candidate (0. Never, 1. Rarely, 2. Sometimes, 3. Frequently). Created based on recodification of original values of question pp 1. How frequently have you tried to convince others to vote for a party or candidate? Calculated for the total of respondents who answered the question. f. Average of how often respondents said that they have attempted to convince others to vote for a party or candidate (0. Never, 1. Rarely, 2. Sometimes, 3. Frequently). Created based on modification of original values of question pp 1. How often have you tried to convince others to vote for a party or candidate? Calculated only for those identified with a political party. g. Percentage of respondents that answered "yes" to question pp 2. There are people who work for some party or candidate during election campaigns. Did you work for any candidate or political party during the last presidential elections? Calculated for the total of respondents who answered the question. h. Percentage of respondents who answered "yes" to question pp2.There are people who work for some party or candidate during election campaigns. Did you work for any candidate or political party during the last presidential elections? Calculated only for those who identify with a political party.

The study in comparative perspective of behaviors such as voting for political parties or membership in party organizations is problematic in that variations among countries could be determined to a great extent by characteristics that are specific to the electoral systems and the incentive structures in each country. Actually, the proportion of citizens that become

involved in political parties differed greatly from country to country (Table III-1). Thus, participation through voting for parties in presidential elections can be as low as 48 percent, as seen in Jamaica or over 90 percent as in Bolivia and Peru.[3]

An even greater gap between countries is found in participation in legislative elections; participation ranges from 33 percent in Jamaica to over 90 percent in Costa Rica and Peru. According to Mainwaring and Scully (1995:5, 9), the difference between the proportion of votes in presidential and legislative elections is an indicator of how much political parties have penetrated society. When political parties are the central actors in shaping preferences in society, the differences in voting for both types of elections should be minimal given that citizens' votes would be more frequently based on party distinctions in each instance. According to this indicator (whose results per country are presented in the third column of Table III-1), parties would be less entrenched in Panama, Guyana, and Costa Rica, where the differences in the proportion of voters in one and the other elections is greater. However, it is worth mentioning that this indicator needs to be pondered in light of each country's electoral regulations. Whether voting is mandatory or not, and the enforcement or not of the sanctions, as well as the concurrence in time of presidential and legislative elections are all factors that may also affect the differences in the proportion of voters in each kind of election.

Party identification in its classic conception, according to the Michigan model, is a psychological attachment to a political party which can occur without a formal link such as membership, with the party. It is an affective orientation that persists through time though not necessarily associated with consistently voting for the party that is the object of identification (Campbell et al. 1960: 121-123). Party identification is a central link between citizens and parties. Low levels of party identification suggest that political parties are incapable of establishing medium and long-term links with citizens. The weakness in these links can be due to the existence of a fluid party system in which parties appear and disappear between elections, the inability of "old" and "stable" parties to inspire long-term loyalty, or to new citizen values that are not reflected by the political parties and consequently do not inspire belonging (Dalton 2006, Dalton and Wattenberg 2000). Whatever the reason, a low level of identification with parties is an indicator of the weakness of the links between citizens and political parties. A little over one third (37.1 percent) of citizens of the countries studied identify with a political party (Table III-1). In this respect, variations between countries are also significant; the proportion of citizens that identify with a party can be as low as 15 percent in Guatemala, or as high as 60 percentage points, as in the United States and the Dominican Republic. Other activities through which citizens connect to parties, such as attending party rallies or participating in campaigns (also presented in Table III-1) are even less frequent among the citizens of the Americas, although there are per-country variations in this case as well.

---

[3] The figures corresponding to participation in presidential and legislative elections show higher rates of participation than those officially registered by country. This is a frequent problem in public opinion research and it is related to the desirability effect. Social desirability refers to the need for presenting oneself in the most favourable light possible (Turangeau and Rasinski 2000:5). Given that the act of voting is valued positively in the democratic context of the region, some respondents could have been tempted to answer that they had voted in the previous elections, when in reality they had not. Nevertheless, this effect does not obnubilate the important differences among countries.

Prominent among the functions that political parties are typically expected to carry out are channelling interests and demands, and the promotion of participation in elections by reducing the cost of information at the time of voting (Mainwaring and Scully 1995: 23). Political parties in Latin America and the Caribbean do not seem to be performing these tasks effectively. When respondents were asked about their most important consideration when choosing a president based on party, the candidate or the government program, the least mentioned reason was the candidate's political party (19 percent)[4], and the most frequent reason in all countries was "the government plan" (54 percent in the aggregate). That the majority of citizens cast their vote for president based on the government program does not *per se* imply a weakness in the party links. However, the fact that parties are the least mentioned reason as a determiner of voting in the region as a whole, and in 12 of the 17 countries where information is available indicates that parties are not functioning effectively in organizing and channelling the competition for public office. For the majority of citizens, the differences are marked by programs and candidates to a much greater extent than by political parties. As a whole, the citizens of Latin America and the Caribbean (no data is available for Canada and the U.S.) do not perceive political parties as fulfilling their function, namely the aggregation of interests and information sourcing that their role presupposes (Mainwaing and Scully 1995, Sartori 1976).

In sum, the outlook is one of relatively weak citizen-party linkages in electoral participation, involvement with parties and participation in party and campaign activities. There are, of course, significant differences among countries. As the information in Table III-1 suggests, the links would be stronger in Honduras, Uruguay and the Dominican Republic and extremely weak in Guatemala. This individual level data is confirmed by the institutional indicators: Guatemala has one of the least institutionalized party systems in the region, whereas Honduras, Uruguay and the Dominican Republic have party systems that are much more consolidated and established (Payne et al. 2003; Payne et al. 2006).

Why Trust in Political Parties Matters

This section draws its title from the book by Marc J. Hetherington *Why Trust Matters* (2005) which looks at citizen trust in the U.S. federal government. Hetherington's results suggest that trust has an impact both at the time of choosing and voting for a presidential candidate, as well as at the moment of supporting redistributive public policies. The central argument is that trust in the government is critical when citizens feel they are paying the costs of governmental actions without receiving the benefits. In this sense, governments require great reserves of confidence in order for their redistributive programs to prosper. Although Hetherington's themes are not directly linked to the problems considered in this chapter, the underlying concern is shared; in order to function correctly, the author says, representative

---

[4] All respondents who asserted they voted in the last presidential elections were asked: (VB8) "When you voted, what was the most important reason you voted for: the candidate's personal qualities, the candidate's political party, the candidate's government plan? This question was asked in Colombia, Peru, Chile, Costa Rica, El Salvador, Panama, Guatemala, Mexico, Haiti, Nicaragua, Paraguay, Guyana, Dominican Republic, Uruguay, Venezuela, Honduras and Jamaica.

democracies require that people trust their representatives as individuals and trust in the roles that they occupy. When people do not trust their institutions, they have no incentives to adhere to the rules established by such institutions (Hetherington 2005:12)

Previous studies have found that citizens with low levels of trust in political parties are less likely to vote or to participate in campaign activities; those who do not trust parties have fewer incentives to participate in precisely the activities that involve political parties. Consequently, these citizens have a greater propensity for seeking access to politics by non-partisan means, such as direct contact with politicians, or direct action (marches and protests), or they may also do so by voting for anti-party and even anti-system options (Blackelock 2006; Dalton 2006). In extreme cases, those who least trust political parties are more likely to support non-conventional means of political participation, including illegal forms of participation. Indeed, mistrust of parties increases electoral volatility (Dalton and Weldon 2005), which in some cases can lead to political instability and lack of ability to govern.

According to the World Values Survey (WVS), political parties are the least trusted institution in the world. On a scale of zero to four, where zero represents *no confidence* and four represents *a lot of confidence*, the average value of trust in political parties is 2.08. For the rest of the institutions the mean values are: unions 2.25, parliaments 2.32, press 2.39, government 2.4, television 2.5, the justice system 2.51, the police 2.56 and the church 2.91 (Figure III-1). The data correspond to the pooled dataset of the four waves (World Values Survey 2005).

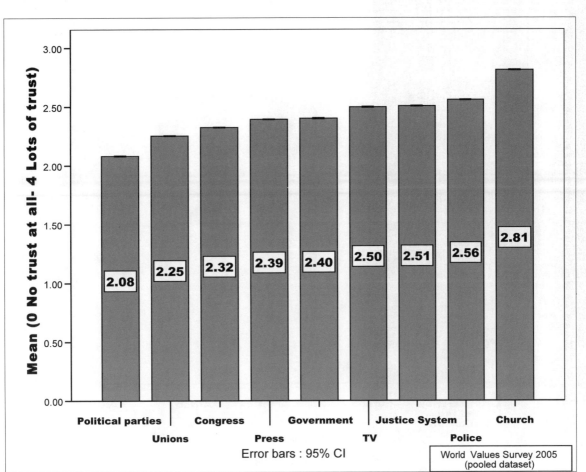

Figure III-1. Trust in political institutions worldwide

Cultural modernization theory explains the weakening of the ties among citizens and parties in the industrialized world as a consequence of general changes in citizens' preferences. It assumes that high levels of economic development need to be achieved for the attitudes that are least favorable towards parties to occur (Dalton 2006, Dalton and Wattenberg 2000, Dalton and Weldon 2005, Inglehart and Welzel 2005). The Latin American reality, however, undermines this theory at its most basic level: in Latin America and the Caribbean, where high levels of economic development are yet to be experienced, the weakest links between citizens and parties regard the issue of trust (Figure III-2). It becomes evident, therefore, that the approach developed for the industrialized democracies is not a global explanation for the weakness of the links between citizens and parties. What, then, explains such low levels of trust in political parties? What other expressions can be used to evaluate the strength of the links between citizens and parties?

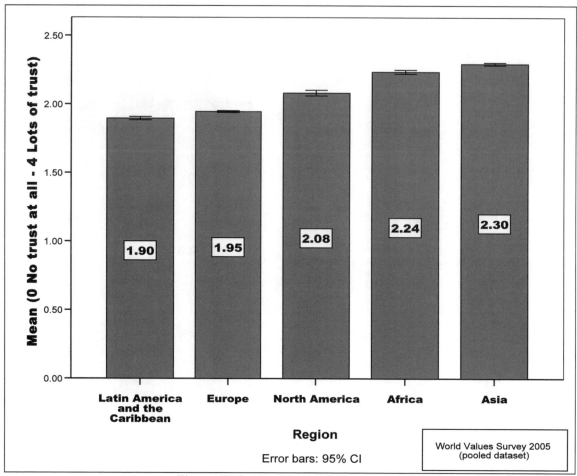

Figure III- 2. Trust in political parties worldwide

Levels of trust in political institutions are generally low throughout the region, particularly when compared to trust in non-political institutions such as the Church, the media and the military (Figure III-3). In each of the countries studied, the respondents were asked to what extent they trusted each of these and other institutions. They were asked to indicate the number that best described their position on a one to seven scale in which one meant no trust at all and seven meant a lot of trust. In order to facilitate the analysis, the responses to these questions were recoded into a zero-100 scale in which the lowest value was zero, meaning no trust at all, and the highest, 100, meant a great deal of trust. Values over 50 indicate relative trust in the institution, as they manifest, on average, confidence levels over the halfway point on the scale.

Figure III-3 presents the average values of trust in each of the eight institutions in all of the countries in the region. None of the political institutions has an average confidence level of over the mid-point on the scale (indicated by the horizontal line at the 50 confidence level) and political parties rated the worst. Not only are political parties the least trusted institution among Latin America and the Caribbean citizens as a whole but also they are the institution that inspires the least degree of confidence in each one of the countries (except in Mexico and Venezuela where parties are the second least trusted institution following the police).

The second institution that inspires the least degree of confidence, the Congress, is intimately associated with political parties, as it is their field of action. In fact, the correlation between the levels of trust and the two institutions is relatively high (Pearson's correlation coefficient of .508, for the entire sample), which suggests that the levels of trust in one and the other are related.

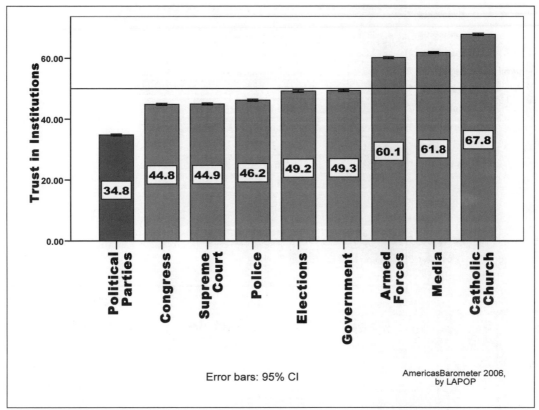

Figure III-3. Trust in institutions in Latin America and the Caribbean
To what extent do you trust…? (0 Not at all, 100 A lot) Mean, by institution[5]

---

[5] The values for Figure III-3 represent the average trust in each institution in the region (cases are weighed by country, so that all countries weigh the same in the sample and therefore they weight the same in any percentage analysis). It is noteworthy that not all questions regarding trust in the institutions were formulated in all countries; therefore some of the values presented herein are not representative of the totality of countries included in the 2006 round of the AmericasBarometer. Specifically, trust in elections excludes Mexico, Bolivia, Chile, Dominican Republic and Haiti; trust in the Armed Forces excludes countries where there are no standing armies, that is Costa Rica, Panama and Haiti; finally trust in the government excludes Bolivia.

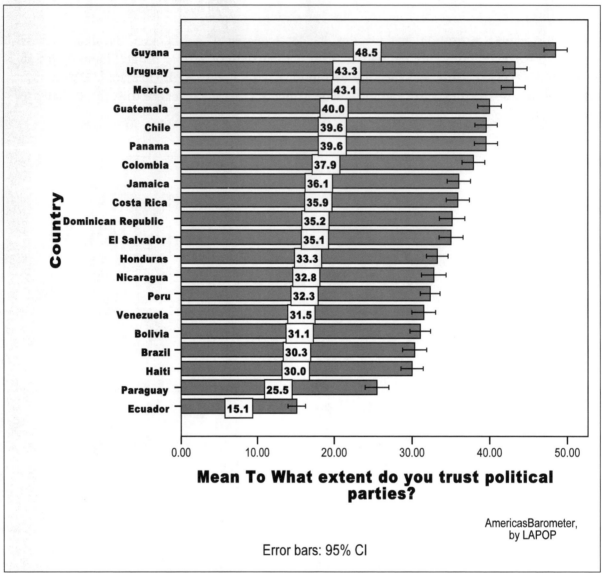

Figure III-4. Trust in political parties by country

What explains the low levels of trust in political parties in the region? There are at least two clear lines of interpretation. The first one points directly to poor party performance. This explanation emerges even in inner party circles (Achard and González 2004) and it is also supported by academic analyses: parties do not function well internally nor in relation to the rest of the relevant actors in society (Córdova Macías 2004). On the other hand, there are unmet citizen expectations. Citizens channel their frustrations arising from unmet expectations to political parties, the visible face of democratic government. In a concept called "the Central American paradox", which can certainly be extended to the region as a whole, Achard and González (2004:127) point out that although there is currently more democracy than before, citizens are less satisfied with its results, the institutions in general, and political parties in particular. According to this thesis, citizens' expectations have increased—in certain cases fed by the unrealistic promises of political parties—beyond the actual possibilities the systems might have of satisfying them. This has lead to increasing disillusionment in the system in general and political parties in particular. In the same vein, Paramio (1999:12) holds that frustration of voter expectations appears as a decisive factor when explaining citizens' low opinion of party politics.

What are the most important factors affecting trust in political parties? Is it possible to find patterns in the region in spite of the differences among countries? In the classic literature on trust in government, the perception of institutional efficacy plays an important role: citizens perceive that the better their leaders perform the more they can trust them, and perceptions of economic progress produce the same reaction (Hetherington 1998; Hetherington 2005). Consequently, it becomes imperative to analyze the impact of citizen opinions in both dimensions –government efficacy and evaluation of the economy when estimating the factors that determine trust in parties.

Prior studies that included questions about government efficacy investigated citizens' opinions regarding the efficacy of the government in areas that interviewees themselves had previously defined as prioritary (Hetherington 1998; Muller et al. 1991). The 2006-2007 round of the AmericasBarometer formulated a series of questions regarding *perceptions of government efficacy*, directly asking interviewees (independent from their prior answers regarding the problems they considered most important) to what extent they believed the current government fights poverty, promotes and protects democratic principles, battles corruption within the government, safeguards human rights, improves citizen safety, and combats unemployment. For each of these activities the respondents were asked to indicate their opinion on a scale from one to seven, in which one meant nothing and seven meant a lot. Following the standard LAPOP practice of unifying scales, the answers were re-scaled to a continuum from zero to 100 to facilitate the analysis.

In order to measure the effect of the evaluation of governments' economic performance on the level of trust in parties, two alternative measures were utilized: evaluation of the country's economic situation, and the evaluation of the economic situation of the familiy (Kinder and Kiewiet 1981). It is to be expected that in both cases the more favorable perceptions regarding the economy will lead to greater levels of trust. [6]

Citizens' connections to political parties should also have a positive impact on the level of trust in them. It is particularly expected that identification with a political party should positively affect the level trust in all parties, given that if there is one "affective orientation" towards one of the parties with a psychological identification with it (Campbell et al. 1960:121) there should be a subjacent link of trust. Consequently, it is to be expected that identification with any political party (operationalized in the affirmative answer to the question "At this time, do you currently identify with a political party?") should be associated with greater levels of trust.

---

[6] Interviewees were asked whether they would assess—both the economic situation in the country and their own household economic situations—as very good, good, neither good or bad, bad or very bad. In order to facilitate the data analysis, answers have been coded so that the higher values correspond to more favourable perceptions. Thus, values for both variables range from one to five (one reflects a "very bad" score, and five a "very good" one).

Findings from previous research suggest that trust in political institutions is related to interpersonal trust (Inglehart 1990, Inglehart and Welzel 2005; Putnam 1993); the links developed due to the level of interpersonal trust in the community would influence in a positive manner the level of trust in the system as a whole. Consequently, it is relevant to incorporate the effects of interpersonal trust on the level of trust in political parties. The 2006-2007 edition of the AmericasBarometer asked interviewees: "Speaking of people from here, would you say that people in this community are trustworthy, somewhat trustworthy, a little trustworthy, or not trustworthy at all?" The answers were ordered on a scale from one (not at all trustworthy) to four (very trustworthy).

In the same way, favorable attitudes towards the political system in general should be associated to favorable attitudes towards institutions as well (Easton 1965; Mueller et al. 1982; Seligson 2002a), which means there should also be a positive relationship between levels of support for the political system and trust in parties. The variable that collects information on support for the political system "To what extent do you believe that the country's political system should be supported?" is coded on a scale from zero (not at all) to 100 (a lot).

According to some scholars, anti-party sentiment can be at least partially explained by the rejection of corrupt practices associated with political parties (Achard and González 2004; Córdova Macías 2004; Dinerstein 2003). In this sense, it can be expected that there will be lower levels of trust in parties among those who perceive them as being corrupt. Unfortunately data on perception of corruption associated with political parties in particular is unavailable. However, there is a direct measure of individual experience with corruption. Seligson (2002b) found that direct personal experience with corruption has a negative impact on support for the political system, and the same type of negative relation is to be expected regarding trust in political parties. In the 2006-2007 round of the AmericasBarometer, citizens were asked about their experiences of being victims of attempts of bribery by the police, a public clerk, at the city hall, at work, at the courts, in the public health clinic, and at school. In order to compile the responses to these questions a "corruption victimization index" was created. This index ranges from zero to five (the initial distribution from zero to seven is re-scaled to facilitate the analysis).

The previously discussed "throw them all out" protests calling for the withdrawal of Argentinean politicians was later echoed in Bolivia and Ecuador and became a non-conventional way to claim to remove public officials from their positions. As a result, it is worth asking whether participation in public protests is related to the levels of trust in political parties. In light of the "throw them all out" experience, less trust in political parties should be expected among those who have a greater propensity to participate in protests. The 2006-2007 round of the AmericasBarometer consulted interviewees about their experience in participation in public protests; the responses were ordered on a scale of one (never participated in a protest) to three (participated sometimes).

Finally, it is necessary to control the impact that the individuals' demographic and socioeconomic characteristics (such as sex, age, education and wealth) can have on attitudes towards political parties. It is also pertinent to control the impact of the level of political knowledge and the ideological self-identification (on a scale from left to right). Finally, the

available evidence from the North-American context suggests that exposure to mass media, particularly TV news, negatively affects levels of trust (Hetherington 1998). Consequently, variables on the reception of news on radio, television, papers and on the Internet are included in order to control for this factor. With the aim of evaluating whether there are significant differences among countries, dummy variables are included for each country except for Mexico, which is taken as the reference category.

When dealing with the region as a whole, several factors are found to affect trust in parties (Table III-2). According to the results from the linear regression on trust, government efficacy in combating poverty, the fight against corruption, unemployment reduction, the promotion of democracy, and safety, identifying oneself with a political party, interpersonal trust, support for the political system, and experience of victimization by corruption are all statistically significant variables. Of the control variables, only ideology, wealth, and exposure to news on the radio have a statistically significant impact on trust in parties. The differences among countries in relation to Mexico, the reference category, are both statistically and substantively significant in most cases.

As expected, general support for the system and interpersonal trust are positively related to trust in political parties. With a 0.210 coefficient, a radical change in system support (zero to 100 points) will produce an increase of 21 points on the scale for confidence in parties. This is the greatest possible effect that could be found. Certainly, at this point it is valid to ask about the causal direction of the relation; is support for parties motivated by support for the system, or in reality is support for the system a product of trust in political parties? It is difficult to unravel this matter, and in any case there are theoretical justifications for expecting causal relations in both directions (which likely reinforce each other). In any case, the unquestionable result is that in the region trust in political parties and support for the country's political system are parallel and move in the same direction. As Mainwaring and Scully (1995:24) point out, in order for citizens to confer legitimacy to their government they must believe that said government—through the parties— at least tries to represent society.

Also in line with expectations, identification with a political party is associated with greater levels of trust in parties as institutions. Nevertheless, the impact is not dramatic: trust levels among party identifiers are, on the average, 5.8 points greater than among those who are not.

With respect to those variables that have a negative effect on trust, the individuals' experiences with corruption have the most significant impact: (-1.903), which implies that, as expected, the greater the exposure to corruption, the lower the level of trust in parties. The impact of experience with corruption can be a reduction of up to ten points on the level of trust in parties.

Table III-2. Linear Regression on confidence in political parties in Latin America and the Caribbean (*)

	B	Standard error
Evaluation of economic situation of the country	.425	.268
Evaluation economic situation of the family	.046	.293
Efficacy of government combating poverty	.052***	.011
Efficacy of government in promoting democracy	.036**	.012
Efficacy of government combating corruption	.080***	.011
Efficacy of government protecting human rights	-.003	.011
Efficacy of government improving security	.093***	.011
Efficacy of government combating unemployment	.073***	.011
Identifies with a political party	5.846***	.453
Interpersonal trust	1.582***	.235
System support	.210***	.008
Corruption victimization	-1.903***	.284
Participation in public protests	.328	.313
Political Knowledge	-4.5E-005	.002
Ideological self-placement	.247**	.084
Sex (female)	.577	.428
Age	.014	.015
Education	-.055	.062
Wealth (possession of capital goods)	-.436***	.131
News on the radio	.551**	.195
News on the TV	-.62	.250
News in the papers	.148	.227
News on Internet	-.15	.326
Guatemala	4.017***	1.241
El Salvador	-5.325***	1.131
Honduras	-5.542***	1.166
Nicaragua	-2.846*	1.179
Costa Rica	-7.604***	1.144
Panama	3.160**	1.198
Peru	-3.391**	1.121
Chile	-3.187**	1.112
Dominican Republic	-13.336***	1.126
Haiti	-2.684	1.396
Jamaica	-1.735	1.304
Guyana	9.997***	1.271
Uruguay	-10.422***	1.188
Venezuela	-7.039***	1.141
Constant	6.537***	1.781
Adjustment	.230	
ANOVA (sig)	.000	

Significance p < .05 (*), p < .01 (**), p < .001 (***)

(*) Cases corresponding to Colombia, Ecuador, Bolivia , Brasil and Paraguay have been excluded due to lack of information (some of the questions that involve independent variables were not formulated in these countries).

Contrary to expectations, the evaluation of the government regarding the performance of the economy (both at the country level and the family level) had no significant impact on trust in parties, and the perception of the efficacy of the government although statistically significant, did not substantially alter the levels of trust in parties. Also contrary to what was expected, participation in public protest had no effect on trust in political parties, which would suggest that the "throw them all out" outcry embodies a special kind of attitude towards parties: not all those who participate in protests in the region hold the same vision of parties, or at least, participation in these events does not imply significantly lower levels of trust in political parties. Neither did exposure to the media (except for the news on the radio, although with a substantially lower impact), nor political knowledge have any relation, according to this model, with trust in parties. Finally, none of the sociodemographic characteristics of the respondents (excepting wealth measured in number of capital goods, although with a substantially marginal impact) significantly affect trust in political parties.

Differences among countries (in relation to Mexico, the reference category) are statistically and substantially significant: the level of confidence in political parties varies according to the country of origin (again, in relation to Mexico) when the attitudinal factors and sociodemographic controls are kept constant.

The relatively low predictive capacity of the model presented here (Adjusted R square of 0.230) and the variations per country suggest that perhaps there are deep --even idiosyncratic--factors that contribute to explaining the trust in parties in greater detail. The difference in the levels of trust in political parties among countries did not merit a multi-level analysis, much less when it was not clear whether a single country-level variable might explain the observed variation. However, for future research it seems pertinent to consider the need to explore the influence of institutional frameworks (formal ones such as electoral rules, and informal ones such as the dynamics of inter-party competition) in determining citizen attitudes, and particularly trust in parties.

Political Parties and Democratic Consolidation in the Region

What are the implications of the preceding discussion for the democracies of the region? According to citizens' views, the political parties of the region are not performing adequately. As discussed in section two, even when the weakening of citizen-party linkages is a world-wide trend, it is particularly severe in Latin American, where democracies are still under the process of consolidation.

Political parties are not accomplishing their role of providing "information shortcuts" for voting choices; only one fifth of the inhabitants of the region chose a presidential candidate for partisan reasons. In fact, the proportion of citizens that allege partisan reasons as determiner of the vote can be as low as 4 percent, as in Venezuela. Political parties are failing to provide meaningful alternatives for leading the government; as a consequence, they do not fulfill their representational task. For representation to take place appropriately, the institutionalization of the party systems is a necessary condition. Without this

institutionalization, as Paramio (1999: 14) points out, there is no incentive structure -for the parties nor for the citizens- for democratic representation.

An institutionalized party system implies stability in inter-party competition, existence of parties with roots in society, acceptance of parties and elections as the legitimate institutions through which to gain political power, and the existence of partisan organizations with at least some degree of formal structure (Mainwaring and Scully 1995:1). When the party systems are little institutionalized there is more room for the emergence of populist and personalistic alternatives. Given that politicians depend on the masses to be re-elected, once in power they may be tempted to implement the most popular short-term policies, as opposed to mid-term policies, potentially more favorable for the country (Mainwaring and Scully 1995:22).

Trust in political parties is a key aspect when considering the prospectus for institutionalization of the party systems. If parties are not depositaries of citizens' trust, it is difficult for them to develop stable links or to become accepted as legitimate institutions in the competition for public office. If, as Dalton and Weldon (2005) observed, mistrust in parties leads to electoral volatility, the party systems of the region will not become more stable unless citizens trust them. Therefore, trust in political parties is not just a dimension of institutionalization; it is a *condition* to achieve it.

What then, are the prospects for the party systems of the region given the low level of trust in them? Notwithstanding the discouraging outlook, in most of the countries in the region there is still a reservoir of support for parties. The 2006-2007 round of the AmericasBarometer asked citizens about their opinions regarding the centrality of parties in democracies. Interviewees were asked to indicate to what extent they agreed with the statement "There can be democracy without political parties". The answers to this question (originally expressed in a 1-7 scale in which one meant "completely disagree" and seven meant "completely agree" with the statement) were inverted, so higher values show more favorable attitudes towards parties. Following the LAPOP standard procedure, the original variable –now inverted- was re-scaled to a range from zero to 100. This new variable represents the belief in the need of parties for democracy; the lower values (closer to zero) suggest attitudes less favorable to parties (higher levels of agreement with the statement that democracy can exist without them), while higher values (closer to 100) reflect more positive attitudes towards parties (rejection to the possibility of a democracy without political parties).[7]

---

[7] This modification from the original measurement of the variable does not alter, at all, the substantive distribution of preferences. Its only purpose is to ease the analysis and the comparability with other variables that use the same metric.

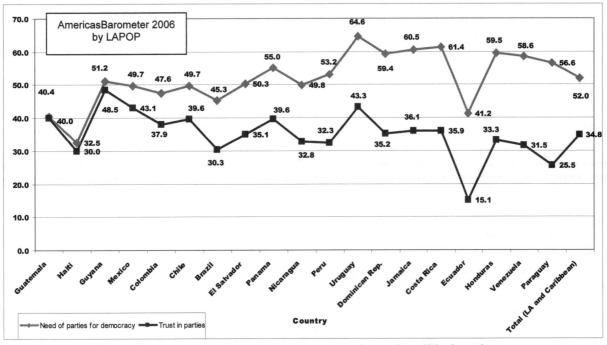

Figure III-5. Need of parties for democracy and trust in political parties

The gray line in Figure III-5 shows the values of this variable for each country side by side with averages of trust in parties (black line). Both trust in parties as well as need for parties in democracies, are presented in Figure III-5 on a scale from zero to 100, and for both variables the highest values reflect the most positive attitudes towards parties (in one case it is trust, in the other rejection of the possibility of the existence of democracy without parties). The values reported are country averages (for all the countries where the two questions were formulated) and for the region as a whole. The use of the same scale for both variables allows for direct comparison and facilitates the presentation of the differences between them, represented by the breach between the values in both lines.

In the region as a whole, and in the majority of the countries, the belief that parties are necessary for democracy is significantly greater than the levels of trust in parties. On average, there are more citizens who support with greater conviction the necessity of parties for democracy than those who claim to trust them. The difference between trust in parties and the belief that parties are central to democracy suggests that the disdain for parties is circumstantial. It is *parties as they currently function* rather than a rejection of them as an institution that keeps citizens away from parties.

This gap between trust in parties and the relatively higher rejection of democracy without parties seems to reflect an imbalance in the supply and demand of the democratic institutions (Bratton 2005: 28). Bratton points out that in order for democracy to be insured, it is necessary that popular demands be met by the supply of democratic institutions, principally by the elite; democratic consolidation would be reached when the equilibrium is produced at a high level of supply and demand. In the case of political parties, the most favorable situation

would be an increase in trust that should reach the level of expectations of party indispensability for democracy.

Rejection of democracy with no political parties, on the other hand, is not overwhelming. The average in the region is 52 points, the middle of the scale. When considering individual countries, it varies from 33 points in Haiti to 65 points in Uruguay. However, in the majority of cases rejection of democracy without parties surpasses the levels of trust, which would indicate that parties have the opportunity to recover lost ground if they improve their image and performance. Ideally, actions that aim at elevating public confidence in parties would lead to a more favorable vision of parties as necessary actors in democracy, in a dynamic process in which specific party support could feed diffuse institutional support in a representative democracy (Easton 1965), thereby strengthening the process of democratic consolidation in the region.

Democracies in the region need parties (as do all contemporary democracies) to function adequately, as they were designed to operate under representative principles, by way of channels that are institutionalized for this end. In the majority of Latin American and Caribbean countries, the agents of this representation, namely political parties, are not performing in accordance with citizen expectations. Nevertheless, the evidence suggests that should parties improve their performance (fundamentally gaining citizens' trust) there would be subsequent possibilities for party representation to become strengthened thus contributing to the strengthening of the democracies in the region.

References

Achard, Diego; Luis E. González. "Bringing All Voices Together: The State and Prospects for Political Parties Central America, Panama and the Dominican Republic." In *A Challenge for Democracy. Political Parties in Central America, Panama and the Dominican Republic*, edited by Diego Achard; Luis E. González. Washington, D.C.: Inter-American Development Bank, International IDEA, Organization of American States, United Nations Development Program, 2004.

Blakelock, Paul. "Changing Trust: Individual-Level Assessments of Political Legitimacy." Ph.D., University of Houston, 2006.

Bonnet, Alberto R. *Que Se Vayan Todos. Crisis, Insurrección Y Caída De La Convertibilidad* [cited Enero 2007]. Available from http://www.geocities.com/economistas_de_izquierda/albertobonnet_quesevayantodos.PDF.

Bratton, Michael; Robert Mattes; E. Gyimah-Boadi. *Public Opinion, Democracy and Market Reform in Africa*: Cambridge University Press, 2005.

Campbell, Angus; Philip E. Converse; Warren Miller; Donald Stokes. *The American Voter*. Chicago: The University of Chicago Press, 1960.

Córdova Macías, Ricardo. "The Crisis of Political Parties in Latin America." In *A Challenge for Democracy. Political Parties in Central America, Panama and the Dominican Republic*, edited by Diego Achard; Luis E. González. Washington, D.C.: Inter-American Development Bank, International IDEA, Organization of American States, United Nations Development Program, 2004.

Dalton, Russell J. *Citizens Politics. Public Opinion and Political Parties in Advanced Industrial Democracies*. Fourth ed. Washington, D.C: CQ Press, 2006.

Dalton, Russell J.; Martin P. Wattenberg . "Unthinkable Democracy. Political Change in Advanced Industrial Democracies." In *Parties without Partisans. Political Change in Advanced Industrial Democracies* edited by Russell J Dalton; Martin P. Wattenberg. Oxford and New York: Oxford University Press, 2000.

Dalton, Russell J.; Steven A. Weldon. "Public Images of Political Parties: A Necessary Evil?" *West European Politics* 28, no. 5 (2005): 931-51.

Dinerstein, Ana C. "¡Que Se Vayan Todos! Popular Insurrection and the Asambleas Barriales in Argentina." *Bulletin of Latin American Research* 22, no. 2 (2003): 187-200.

Easton, David. *A Framework for Political Analysis*. New Jersey: Prentice-Hall, 1965.

Giarraca, Norma. "Argentina 1991-2002: Una Década De Protesta Que Finaliza En Un Comienzo. La Mirada Desde El Interior Del País." *Argumentos* 1, no. 1 (2002): 1-8.

González, Luis E. "Las Crisis Políticas De América Latina En Los Primeros Años Del Siglo." In *Política Y Desarrollo En Honduras, 2006-2009*, edited by Diego Achard; Luis E. González. Tegucigalpa: UNDP – ASDI – AECI – DFID, 2006.

Hetherington, Marc J. "The Political Relevance of Political Trust." *American Political Science Review* 92, no. 4 (1998): 791-808.

———. *Why Trust Matters. Declining Political Trust and the Demise of American Liberalism*. Princeton and Oxford: Princeton University Press, 2005.

Inglehart, Ronald. *Culture Shift in Advanced Industrial Societies.* . New Haven: Princeton University Press, 1990.

Inglehart, Ronald; Christian Welzel. *Modernization, Cultural Change and Democracy*: Cambridge University Press, 2005.

Kinder, Donald R.; Roderick Kiewiet. "Sociotropic Politics: The American Case." *British Journal of Political Science* 11, no. 2 (1981): 129-61.

Mainwaring, Scott; Timothy R. Scully. "Introduction. Party Systems in Latin America." In *Building Democratic Institutions. Party Systems in Latin America*, edited by Mainwaring Scott and Timothy R. Scully, 1-34. Stanford: Stanford University Press, 1995.

Muller, Edward N.; Henry A. Dietz; Steven E. Finkel. "Discontent and Expected Utility of Rebellion: The Case of Peru." *The American Political Science Review* 85, no. 4 (1991): 1261-82.

Muller, Edward N.; Thomas O. Jukam; Mitchell Seligson. "Diffuse Political Support and Antisystem Political Behavior: A Comparative Analysis." *American Journal of Political Science* 26, no. 2 (1982): 240-64.

Paramio, Ludolfo. *La Democracia Tras Las Reformas Económicas En América Latina* Instituto de Estudios Sociales Avanzados (CSIC), 1999 [cited 2007]. Available from http://www.iesam.csic.es/doctrab1/dt-9903.htm.

Payne, J. Mark et al. *Democracies in Development. Politics and Reform in Latin America.* Washington, D.C.: Inter-American Development Bank, Institute for Democracy and Electoral Assistance, 2003.

Payne, Mark J.; Daniel Zovatto; Mercedes Mateo Díaz. *La Política Importa. Democracia Y Desarrollo En América Latina*. Segunda Edición ed. Washington, DC: IADB - IDEA, 2006.

Putnam, Robert D. *Making Democracy Work: Civic Traditions in Modern Italy*. Princeton: Princeton University Press, 1993.

Sartori, Giovanni. *Parties and Party Systems. A Framework for Analysis*. London New York Melbourne: Cambridge University Press, 1976.

Schattschneider, E.E. *Party Government*. Edited by Phillips Bradley, *American Government in Action*. New York: Farrar and Rinehart, 1942.

Seligson, Mitchell A. "The Impact of Corruption on Regime Legitimacy: A Comparative Study of Four Latin American Countries." *The Journal of Politics* 64, no. 2 (2002a): 408-33.

———. "Trouble in Paradise? The Erosion of System Support in Costa Rica, 1978-1999." *Latin American Research Review* 37, no. 1 (2002b): 160-85.

Survey, World Values. *World Values Survey, Four-Waves Pooled Dataset* 2005 [cited August 2006]. Available from www.worldvaluessurvey.org.

IV. Economic Performance and Support for the System: Economic Challenges for Latin American Democracies

Vivian Schwarz-Blum*

Abstract

The goal of this paper is to determine the effect that individual and system-lvell evaluations of government economic performance in Latin American and Caribbean countries have on system support.. The study makes use of a linear regression analysis in order to assess the effects of individual evaluations, and a mixed multi-level analysis to estimate the effect of national-level variables on support for the system. Results show that, in contrast to evidence gathered from highly industrialized nations, in the Latin America region individual evaluations the government's economic performance and system level factors are both important predictors of support for the system.

The study of stability of democracies has generated a substantial amount of theory and empirical evidence whose center of attention is the importance of support for the political system for the stability and even the survival of democratic regimes. The dynamics of support for the system depend, in part, on the relations between the State and the citizens of a country. The fundamental assumption in this relationship is that citizens have expectations regarding the State's performance and that said performance is judged by citizens individually. Positive or negative evaluations result in feelings of satisfaction or dissatisfaction with the State's performance, which in turn ought to lead to the willingness—or lack thereof—in the individual to support and have confidence in the State, and to consequently act in a cooperative manner with the institutions and regulations generated by the State. On the other hand, unsatisfactory evaluations ought to produce a low level of cooperation, and questioning of regulations and decisions emanating from the State, which would weaken and even destabilize the State if the sentiment of dissatisfaction is generalized among citizens.

Based on this reasoning, scholars have found that support for the political system is an important element in a democracy not only owing to its relevance for the stability of the democratic system but also because it is a vital element for the political process, given that "a democratic political system cannot survive for long without the support of a majority of its citizens" (Miller 1974).

Low levels of support for the system have been considered a threatening factor for the

* Vivian Schwarz-Blum is a PhD student in the Political Science Department at Vanderbilt University and is also part of the LAPOP crew.
** A special thanks for professors Mitchell A. Seligson and Jonathan Hiskey for their valuable advice for this study. I also thank my co-workers at LAPOP and classmates in the Political Science Department for their suggestions and comments.

stability of democracies because the consequences of long-term dissatisfaction with the government can generate, as Miller suggests, the feeling of a power vacuum and of the absence of regulations. "Feelings of powerlessness and normlessness are very likely to be accompanied by hostility toward political and social leaders, the institutions of government and the regime as a whole" (Miller 1974).

The effect of government performance on citizens can have more serious consequences than what is often believed. Bastian and Luckham (2003) propose that it is necessary to carry out an in depth study of the effects of democracies on the lives of citizens because, contrary to conventional notions, democracy is 'Janus-faced,' namely, it can generate both negative and positive consequences, depending on the power and the performance of the political players, the interest groups and the economic conditions. On the basis of the aforementioned factors, democracies can emphasize social inequalities, marginalize minorities, or intensify conflicts among social groups in the same way that they can increase the participation and inclusion of marginalized groups in the political processes, create policies of social inclusion and improve the redistribution of resources among the population.

Dissatisfaction with government performance can be changed into action at the individual level through system support. Political confidence plays a key role in the perception of legitimacy of the norms issued by a government and therefore in the degree to which an individual is willing to support the government and the regime.

Levi and Stoker (2000) emphasize the importance of the relation between political trust and that which is trustworthy, and the political consequences of the presence or absence of those elements in political regimes. Their study concentrates on phenomena which reflect confidence in the regime, such as public opinion and participation in politics and their relation to trust, social trust, and citizen cooperation with and obedience to the incumbent government with regard to the levels of trust it inspires.

This study concludes that trust is important for strengthening of the legitimacy of political regimes. The fact that citizens consider the government or politicians trustworthy has an influence on, among other things, the levels of individual participation in politics and the probability that individuals will become politically active, as well as their electoral preferences, the levels of social cooperation and individual support for government policies and for the political regime.

Aside from the Levi and Stoker study, there are several studies (Easton 1975; Easton 1976; Weatherford 1992; Hetherington 1998; Schwarz-Blum 2006) that have provided ample evidence that political trust is a fundamental part of support for the system. The LAPOP instrument for measuring the level of support for the system of a specific country is based on an index of five items that have been studied and established as valid by scholars and researchers of democracy and is intended to show the level of confidence with which interviewees consider the central elements of their political system.

These items are measured on a seven-point scale. In order to facilitate the comprehension of the analysis, the scale has been transformed into a scale from zero to 100, in

which an average closer to zero is an indicator of low levels of support for the system and an average closer to 100 is an indicator of a high level of support for the system.

The items that make up this index are measured through the following questions:

Index of Support for the System
B1. To what degree do you believe the courts in (country) guarantee a fair trial?
B2. To what degree do you respect the political institutions in (country)?
B3. To what degree do you believe that the citizen's basic rights are safeguarded by the political system in (country)?
B4. To what degree do you feel proud of living in the political system in (country)?
B6. To what degree do you think the political system in (country) should be supported?

What is the relationship between these theories and the present circumstances in the democracies of Latin America? Many Latin American democracies belong to the group of the so called "third wave of democratization" (Huntington 1991), which means that they are young democracies that are still undergoing processes of transformation and consolidation. Many of these young democracies were thought to have been consolidated to the point that they would not revert to authoritarian regimes. However, the resurgence and spread of populism that favors extremely personalized leadership in South America and Central America, indicates a growing acceptance of socialist ideologies that reject "liberal democracy" as an ideal form of government, as evidenced in the election of popular leaders such as Ortega in Nicaragua, Morales in Bolivia and Correa in Ecuador as well as the growing popularity of the governing style of Hugo Chavez. All of these factors concern citizens and scholars who are committed to "pure" democratic principles and are once again questioning the destiny of the younger democracies in Latin America.

Over the years, LAPOP studies have consistently demonstrated that the levels of support for the system vary considerably from one country to the next but tend to remain relatively stable within the countries. That is, countries with higher levels of system support tend to maintain these levels over time, and low levels of support for the system tend to remain low. A relatively rare exception to this pattern can take place when there are sudden or extreme changes in the political context of a country, such as an economic crisis, a civil war, or intense ethnic conflicts. Given that support for the system is measured individually, it is a measure that is susceptible to the influence of important or powerful events in the political circumstance. Therefore, under some circumstances, major shifts in the level of system support for the system will occur.

The following figure illustrates the distribution of support for the system in 19 Latin American and Caribbean countries measured by the AmericasBarometer in 2006-07. In the figure it can be observed that countries such as Ecuador, Paraguay, Haiti, Brazil, Jamaica and Peru have low levels of support for the system whereas Costa Rica, Mexico and Colombia show higher levels of support.

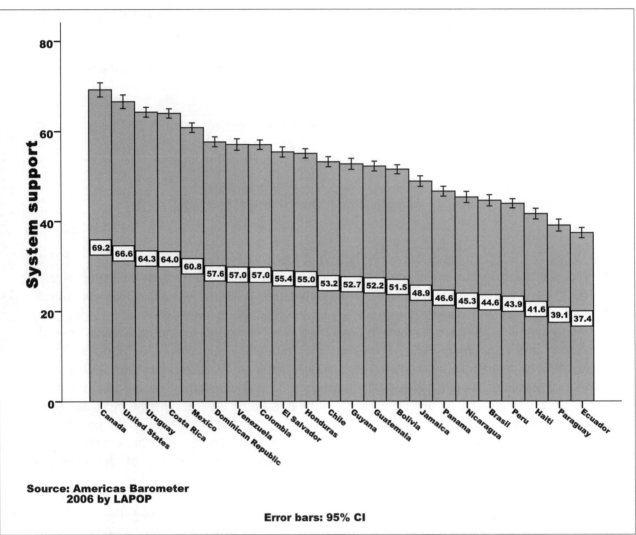

Figure IV-1. System Support: Per Country Averages. Comparative Sample, 2006-2007.

Beyond what the data says about each country specifically, on the whole they seem to indicate that the most prominent changes in the way the State is managed are occurring in countries where citizens have consistently declared themselves to be dissatisfied with the performance of democratic governments. Thus, in this chapter we are concerned with understanding the factors that reduce or increase the levels of support to the system and the conditions under which these changes occur.

In 2004, Russel Dalton published a study on the erosion of system support in advanced industrialized democracies in which he analyzed the factors that generated change in support to the system. Several other studies (Easton 1976; Weatherford 1992; Anderson and Guillory 1997) have determined that the individual assessment of government performance is one of the most important factors that influences the level of system support.

Dalton finds that, contrary to other studies, in highly industrialized countries the individual assessment of the government's economic performance does not directly cause a

decrease in support for the system since citizens tend to have long-term vision regarding economic policies. Following Dalton's line of reasoning, the rest of this chapter will analyze the degree to which individual evaluations of the economic performance of the governments in Latin American countries determine the levels of support for the system. The principal assumption in these examinations is that support for the system is strongly influenced by the satisfaction or dissatisfaction with the domestic economic situation, resulting from government performance in matters of economic policies.

The study will test two hypotheses which represent two distinct ways in which economic factors can affect support for the system: the first is the perception of the national and personal economic situations. The second test will analyze the way in which growth or reduction in the level of development of a country can affect support for the system of a specific country. In these tests, the level of development is measured by the Human Development Index which the United Nations Development Program (UNDP) generates every two years. The model will also control the influence of a country's level of wealth, measured by the Gross National Product (GNP), on the levels of support to the system. The basic assumption of this second test holds that the most wealthy and most developed countries will show greater levels of support for the system than poorer and less developed countries.

The combination of individual and aggregate factors enriches the understanding of the phenomena studied, allowing for the combination of complementary elements which affect political processes in different but simultaneous ways: the subject and the context.

The initial analysis of the determining factors for support for the system was carried out through a linear regression which takes into consideration individual perceptions of the national and personal economic situation and the perception of how generalized corruption is among public officials, controlled by the sociodemographic characteristics of the citizens interviewed. The analysis includes 19 countries from the AmericasBarometer 2006-07 in Latin America and the Caribbean: Uruguay, Costa Rica, Mexico, Dominican Republic, Venezuela, Colombia, El Salvador, Honduras, Chile, Guyana, Guatemala, Bolivia, Jamaica, Panama, Nicaragua, Brazil, Peru, Haiti and Ecuador. Costa Rica is used as a reference category for the analysis of the differences among the countries.

The results of this analysis, as seen in Table IV-1, demonstrate that contrary to what happens in industrialized countries, in Latin America individual assessment of the national economic situation and the personal economic situation do influence the decision to support the political system or not. The results of the analysis of the regression also indicate that these individual assessments and the perception of the level of generalized corruption are more robust predictors of the level of support for the system for the countries analyzed, even more important than the socioeconomic differences among individuals. In addition, the analysis suggests that government performance in matters of economic policy is important to citizens in Latin American and the Caribbean countries when determining their level of support for the system.

Furthermore, the results of the linear regression suggest that there exists a difference in support for the system which is determined by the country of residence of the people

interviewed. For example, Mexicans express greater levels of system support than Chileans, Colombians or Bolivians. In other words, although there are differences among Mexicans regarding their levels of support for the system, the support in Mexico is, on average, higher than support in Chile, Colombia or Bolivia.

Table IV-1. Analysis of the Lineal Regression of Support for the System. Comparative Sample 2006-2007.
Source: Americas Barometer by LAPOP

Model	Non-standardized coefficients		Standardized coefficients	t	Sig.
	B	St. error	Beta		
(Constant)	55.098	1.192		46.235	.000
Sex	1.187	.264	.026	4.499	.000
Age	.844	.094	.055	8.941	.000
Education	-.472	.201	-.016	-2.348	.019
Urban	1.985	.319	.040	6.225	.000
Wealth (individual possession of material goods)	-.284	.083	-.025	-3.429	.001
National economic situation	.169	.007	.168	25.629	.000
Individual economic situation	.097	.007	.087	13.266	.000
Frequency of corruption acts	-.003	.000	-.106	-17.854	.000
Mexico	-3.468	.807	-.033	-4.296	.000
Guatemala	-11.695	.846	-.107	-13.826	.000
Salvador	-7.786	.814	-.077	-9.567	.000
Honduras	-10.115	.817	-.099	-12.381	.000
Nicaragua	-17.164	.838	-.167	-20.470	.000
Panama	-18.018	.837	-.175	-21.518	.000
Colombia	-7.972	.819	-.077	-9.739	.000
Ecuador	-24.162	.806	-.240	-29.993	.000
Bolivia	-14.737	.839	-.142	-17.565	.000
Peru	-19.581	.832	-.194	-23.530	.000
Chile	-14.235	.811	-.140	-17.561	.000
RDominicana	-5.723	.815	-.056	-7.019	.000
Haiti	-20.255	.875	-.194	-23.139	.000
Jamaica	-13.796	.837	-.128	-16.483	.000
Guyana	-13.871	.838	-.129	-16.552	.000
Uruguay	-2.872	.815	-.028	-3.527	.000
Brazil	-20.448	.806	-.200	-25.376	.000
Venezuela	-7.697	.815	-.075	-9.441	.000

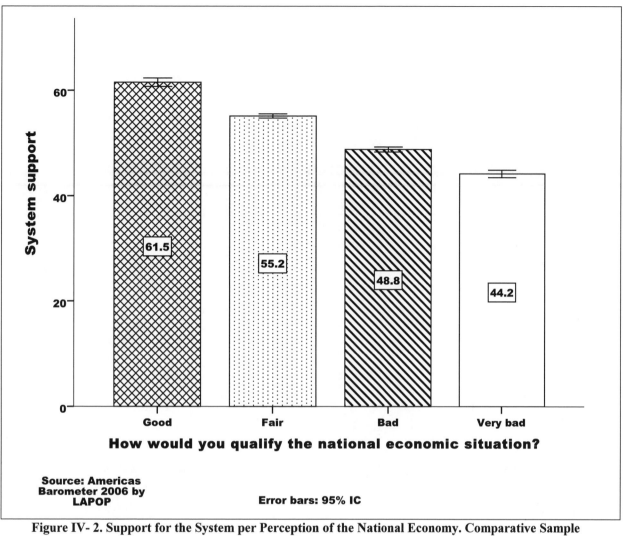

Source: Americas
Barometer 2006 by
LAPOP

Error bars: 95% IC

Figure IV- 2. Support for the System per Perception of the National Economy. Comparative Sample 2006-2007.

It can be seen in Figure IV-2 that a favorable perception of the national economic situation has a positive influence on the level of support that citizens give to the political system. In general, people who perceive that their country's economy is strong show higher levels of support for the system than do persons who have a more unfavorable perception of the national economic situation. The differences among those who think that the national economic situation is good and those who think that it is neither good nor bad, that it is bad or that it is very bad are statistically significant, as indicated by non-overlapping confidence intervals.

The perception of one's personal economic situation shows the same relationship as the tendency to support the system; people who are more satisfied with their personal economic situation show greater levels of support for the system than those who consider that their economic situation is bad or very bad. These results, both the national and personal evaluations of economic situation, are valid and statistically significant for the 19 countries included in the analysis.

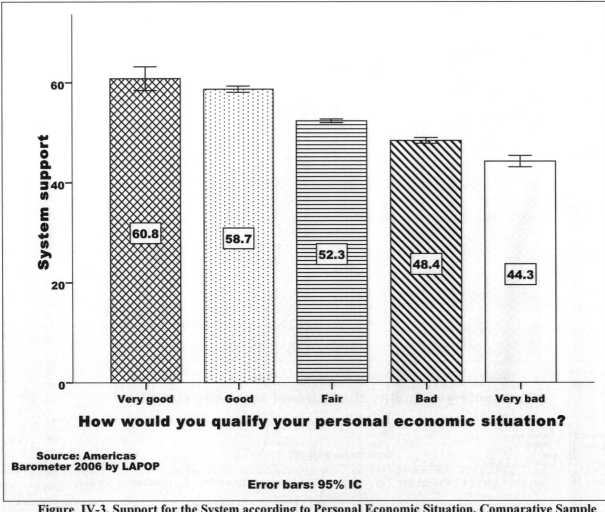

Figure IV-3. Support for the System according to Personal Economic Situation. Comparative Sample 2006-2007.

On the other hand, the perception of corruption has a negative relationship to support for the system. As can be observed in the following figure, people who perceive generalized corruption among public officials present lower levels of support for the system than those who consider that corruption is less widespread. In the final section of this volume, additional detail is provided on the impact of corruption on support.

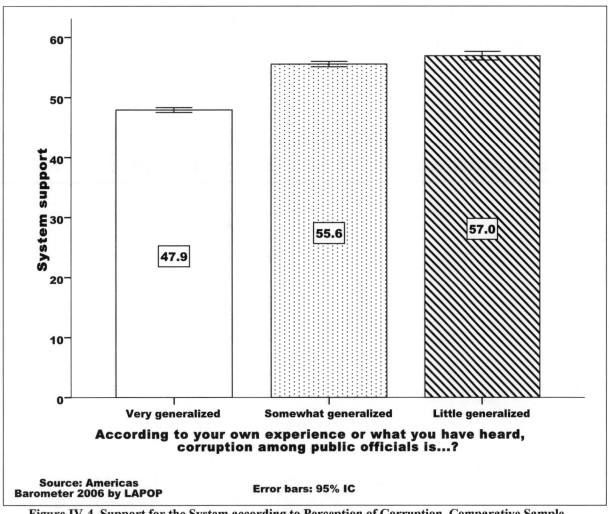

Figure IV-4. Support for the System according to Perception of Corruption. Comparative Sample 2006-2007.

Regarding the socioeconomic characteristics of respondents, the sex, age, education, and level of personal wealth, all mark differences in the level of support that citizens show. The results indicate that people who live in rural areas tend to support the system more than those who live in urban areas, and older people support the system more than the young.

The following figure illustrates the way in which the level of personal wealth[8], measured according to capital goods owned, influences system support.

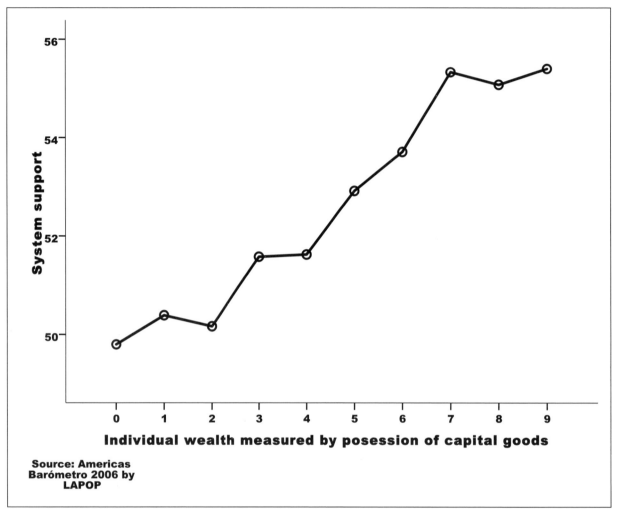

Figure IV-5. Support for the system according to level of personal wealth. Comparative Sample 2006-2007.

It can be seen in the figure that as the level of personal wealth increases, so does the level of support for the system expressed by interviewees. Nevertheless, the increase in support is not the same for all groups; rather it seems to be more moderate among people with the lowest level of wealth (on the scale from points 0 to 2) and is more pronounced among people with a medium-low to medium-high level of wealth (on the scale from points 2 to 7). It is also interesting to observe that this relationship does not happen among those with most personal wealth, where the level of support for the system remains practically constant even when the level of personal wealth increases. However, the level of support for the system in

---

[8] The personal level of wealth is measured through an additive index that results from sum of capital goods possessed by the interviewee according to her own statement. These goods vary from having access to basic services such as indoor plumbing and a sewer system to owning a car, a cell phone and other such goods.

this latter group of respondents is generally greater than the level of support among those with less personal wealth.

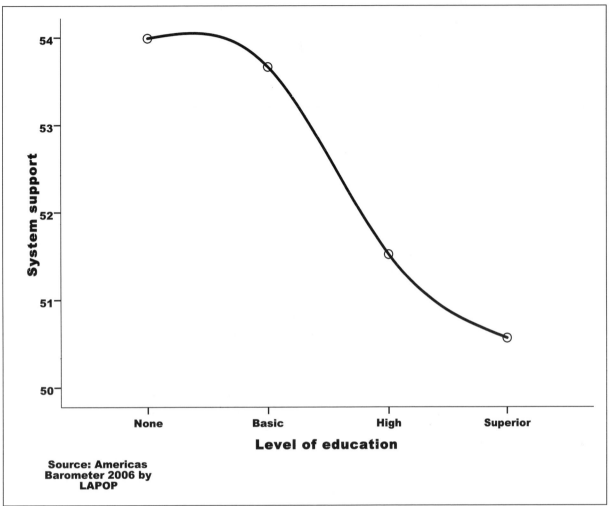

Source: Americas
Barometer 2006 by
LAPOP

Figure IV-6. Support for the System According to Educational Level. Comparative Sample 2006-2007.

As for the level of education of the respondents, Figure IV-6 illustrates a negative relationship between the educational level and support for the system. In other words, as the level of education increases, support for the system declines. People with no formal education are the ones that express higher levels of support for the system, whereas those with higher education are those that least support the system.

The following figure presents the differences in support for the system between men and women. Figure IV-7 shows that in general, women express a slightly higher level of support than do men. This difference is statistically significant—the confidence intervals do not overlap—although the differences are very small in substantive terms, since it is only one point on a scale of 100.

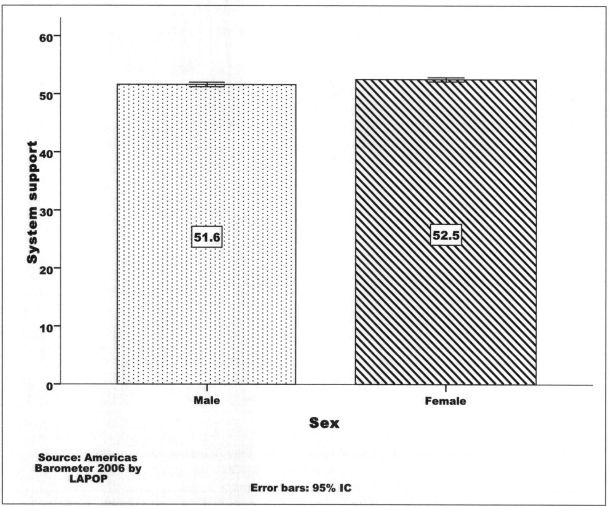

Figure IV-7. Support for the System According to Gender. Comparative Sample 2006-2007.

Development, Economic Growth and Support for the System

In the previous section, it was seen that there are significant differences in support for the system across countries. These differences cannot be attributed to any specific phenomenon in each country in an analysis with data at the individual level, as we have done until now, since there may be factors at the country level that cannot be detected at the individual level, for example the influence of the political culture, the economic situation or the political context, among many others.

However, the fact that the aspects that generate these differences cannot be detected with data on the individual level does not mean that these differences are not real. In order to determine which factor could generate these differences among countries, we will use an analysis that combines information at the individual level with aggregate national level data.

Given that the development and economic growth of a country are, to a large extent, the direct result, of the economic policies of the national government, the effect these have on support for the system is, in effect, an evaluation of government performance in the economic arena. In this section of the chapter, therefore, we concentrate on estimating the influence of economic factors on support for the system. The following analysis will estimate in two separate models the way in which the level of development in a country, measured in terms of human development[9], and the level of economic growth measured in terms of Gross Domestic Product[10], influence the different levels of support for the system among countries registered in the previous section.

Following are the results of the analysis of mixed effects of economic growth on support for the system.

Table IV-2. Analysis of Mixed Effects of Economic Growth on Support for the
System. Comparative Sample 2006-2007.

Variables	Coefficients	Error standard	z	P>z
National Economic Situation	-.0032463	.0003465	-9.37	0.000
Personal Economic Situation	-.001304	.0001476	-8.84	0.000
GDP2004	-.0000229	9.84e-06	-2.33	0.020
Constant	1.799696	.0638379	28.19	0.000
Mixed-effects REML regression		# of obs = 31626		
Group variable: country		# of groups = 20		
Prob > chi2 = 0.0000				

The results presented in Table IV-2 indicate that, as expected, the differences in national growth—measured by GDP—are statistically significant in the model and that the individual perception of the national and personal economic situation continues to be significant.

This means that the reasons, for example, for which Mexicans report higher levels of system support than do Colombians, Bolivians, or Chileans is related to individual level factors – such as satisfaction with the national and personal economic situations- as mush as with contextual economic factors at the national level. That is to say that the level of economic growth in Mexico contributes to Mexicans showing higher levels of support because they think the economy is healthy and because they feel that they live in a more developed country than some of he others, which makes them report higher levels of system support than citizens of

---

[9] The values for the Human Development Index for each country in the sample come from the 2004 estimation, the most recent available. Source: Global Report on Human Development 2006, UNDP.
[10] GDP values for each country are available only until 2004 and were taken from the Global Report on Human Development 2006, UNDP.

countries.

Table IV-3. Analysis of Mixed Effects of level of Human Development on Support for the System. Comparative Sample 2006-2007.

Variables	Coefficients	Error standard	z	P>z
Situación económica nacional	-.0032506	.0003471	-9.37	0.000
Situación económica personal	-.0013032	.0001476	-8.83	0.000
IDH2004	-.3828372	.3372549	-1.14	0.256
Cons	1.950214	.2541186	7.67	0.000
Mixed-effects REML regression		# of obs = 31626		
Group variable: country		# of groups = 20		
Prob > chi2 = 0.0000				

On the other hand, differences among countries in the level of human development are not statistically significant in the model, meaning that the national level of human development in any given country does not influence the reported level of system support in different countries.

These results provide persuasive evidence that individual political attitudes towards the political system are not only influenced by individual characteristics but that they are also influenced by structural elements that are part of the context in which the relations between individual and political system take place.

Conclusions

In this chapter the evidence has shown that the study of support for the system can be an important instrument for the evaluation of the stability of democracies. Evidence gathered from the AmericasBarometer in 19 countries in Latin America and the Caribbean for this analysis found that system support does not depend solely on political considerations; rather, it is influenced in an important way by individual evaluations of government economic performance, both in the perception of the national economic situation and in the perception of citizens' personal economic situation, contrary to what Dalton had found in highly industrialized nations.

The study also found that the perception of generalized of corruption can diminish support that citizens give to the system, reducing the levels of support proportionately to the extent of such corruption.

These elements suggest that the countries where citizens perceive that governmental economic performance generates economic problems for the country or poor conditions for the individual economy of citizens will have lower levels of support for the system than those countries in which the governments are able to maintain a healthy economy or at least a stable one.

The evidence also suggests that there are differences between the levels of support for

the system among countries that are determined at least in part by the specific characteristics of each country and that cannot be detected in the data at the individual level alone. The results of the mixed-model analysis allows us to see that these differences are also the product of differences in structural elements specific of the political system of each country, especially the levels of economic growth which influence the individual levels of system support.

References

Anderson, C. J. and C. A. Guillory. "Political Institutions and Satisfaction with Democracy: A Cross-National Analysis of Consensus and Majoritarian Systems." *The American Political Science Review* 91 (1) (1997): 66-81.

Bastian, S. and R. Luckham. Introduction. Can Democracy Be Designed? *Can Democracy Be Designed?* S. Bastian and R. Luckham. New York, Zed Books, 2003.

Dalton, R. J. *Democratic Challenges, Democratic Choices: The Erosion of Political Support in Advanced Industrial Democracies.* Oxford, Oxford University Press, 2004.

Easton, D. . "A Re-Assessment of the Concept of Political Support." *British Journal of Political Science* 5 (1975): 435-57.

Easton, D. "Theoretical Approaches to Political Support." *Canadian Journal of Political Science / Revue canadienne de science politique* 9 (3) (1976): 431 - 448.

Hetherington, M. J. "The Political Relevance of Political Trust." *American Political Science Review* 92 (4) (1998): 791-808.

Huntington, S. *The Third Wave: Democratization in the Late Twentieth Century.* Norman, University of Oklahoma Press, 1991.

Levi, M. and L. Stoker. "Political Trust and Trustworthiness." *Annual Review of Political Science* 3 (2000).

Miller, A H. "Political Issues and Trust in Government." *American Political Science Review* 68 (1974): 951-72.

Schwarz-Blum, V. Confianza en las instituciones: por que es necesaria? . D. Moreno. Cochabamba, USAID Bolivia, 2006.

Seligson, M. A. "The Impact of Corruption on Regime Legitimacy: A Comparative Study of Four Latin American Countries." *Journal of Politics* 64(2) (2002).

Weatherford, M. S. "Measuring Political Legitimacy." *American Political Science Review* 86(1) (1992): 149-166.

V. Decentralize or Centralize? Challenges for Reform of the State and Democracy in Latin America and the Caribbean[1]

Daniel Montalvo

Abstract

Since the beginning of the third wave of democratization, various debates have centered on determining how to face the challenges that persist in the democracies of Latin America and the Caribbean. A prevalent alternative in the region is decentralization, applied as a mechanism to foster the vertical balance of powers of the state. However, upon exploring citizen public opinion regarding political trust in local governments and the potential for lending support to a process of decentralization, this chapter shows that there is considerable variation in trust in municipalities and, contrary to expectations, up to 52 percent of people surveyed would like to see the national government take over municipal obligations and services. In order to determine the variables that explain these phenomena, in this research (1) a comparison is made of the individual's political trust at different levels of the government; (2) political trust is studied as a cause for support of a process of state reform; and (3) citizen support for institutional decentralization or centralization is determined. This comparative analysis of citizen perception is conducted in 19 countries, and individual case studies are carried out on extreme cases.

Numerous social scientists have debated the challenges that face democracy and democratization worldwide. For instance, Dahl (1971) considers that it is practically beyond discussion that the greater the socioeconomic level of a country, the greater the possibility for that country to consolidate its democracy. Likewise, Sorensen (1998) attributes low levels of education, urbanization and development to weak support for democracy. Other factors such as corruption, adverse political culture, and social inequality are risks for a consolidated democracy (Epstein *et al.*, 2006). Over the last two decades, several countries have attempted to decentralize their governments as a means to cope with the aforementioned challenges and, in this manner, to increase the levels of democratic governance, to mitigate poverty, and to reduce corruption.

Tulia Faletti (2005) states that in fiscal terms, "in 1980, local governments around the world collected on average 15 percent of revenue and spent about 20 percent of [national] expenditures, while at the end of the nineties these numbers expanded to 19 and 25 percent respectively, and even doubled in some regions." Therefore Latin American and Caribbean governments, with the support of several multinational organizations such as the World Bank, the United Nations Development Program (UNDP), the German GTZ, and the United States Agency

---

[1] This study has been possible thanks to USAID support of the AmericasBarometer. Additionally, our gratitude goes to the USAID Mission in Ecuador, the Department of Political Science and its staff, the Center for the Americas, the Provost's Office at the University of Vanderbilt. Special recognition goes to Professor Mitchell A. Seligson for his valuable contributions to this study, and the team at the Latin American Public Opinion Project. Also thanks to Professor Jonathan Hiskey for his extensive academic contributions.

for International Development (USAID), have extended their decentralization programs with special emphasis on the region.[2] In spite of the efforts that national governments and multilateral organizations have made to solve different problems by way of decentralization, there is scarce empirical evidence to determine whether these programs, from the point of view of the alleged "beneficiaries," have achieved their goals. To better understand the opinions of Latin American and the Caribbean citizens regarding decentralization and centralization, the AmericasBarometer in 2006-2007 included a block of questions that explore the attitudes of the region's inhabitants regarding these processes of state reform.

This chapter analyzes fiscal and administrative centralization and decentralization from the perspective of the inhabitants of 19 countries in Latin America and the Caribbean.[3] It begins with a conceptual description of centralization and decentralization, in conjunction with an historical overview of the power transfer processes, examining the centrist tradition of the Latin American and Caribbean states as an outcome of the colonial period. Next, theoretical arguments are presented for the factors that might favor the processes of state reform, starting with political trust in governmental institutions. Subsequently, countries are differentiated and described according to those whose inhabitants have greater trust in their national governments and those where municipalities are more trusted. Once political trust is determined, those who believe that municipalities should have more obligations and receive more funding and those who, on the contrary, support the national government assuming more obligations and municipal services, are described. Lastly, countries whose population would be willing to pay higher taxes to the municipality for better services are examined.

Decentralization, Centralization and Intergovernmental Transfers

Historical compilations of the processes of vertical balance of power in Latin America and the Caribbean show the centralizing heritage received from the Spanish and Portuguese colonizers in the Americas as an efficient means for extracting resources. During the 20th century the central state in almost all Latin American countries successfully increased their levels of power, authority and resource control. However, starting in the 1980s, concomitant with the transitions to democracy, systematic processes of transfer of power from the national to the local level were put in place (Seele 2004).

---

[2] The UNDP area of *Democratic Governance* for example, contributes to the formation of national capacities; it also fosters an adequate environment for effective decentralization, local governance and urban/rural development. The technical area of *Democracy and Governance* at USAID directs its efforts at fighting corruption, promoting democratic decentralization, legislative strengthening, civilian-military relations and effective implementation of public policy. Lastly, the *Decentralization and Subnational Thematic Group* at the World Bank seeks to share and deepen understanding regarding intergovernmental relationships, regional development and reduction of poverty, as well as central and local governance to reinforce the effectiveness of the different levels of government.

[3] The countries analyzed in this study, according to data availability, are: Mexico, Guatemala, Honduras, El Salvador, Nicaragua, Costa Rica, Panama, Venezuela, Colombia, Ecuador, Brazil, Peru, Paraguay, Uruguay, Chile, the Dominican Republic, Haiti, Jamaica and Guyana. The data was obtained from the 2006 Round of surveys conducted by the AmericasBarometer and the Latin American Public Opinion Project (LAPOP).

What is the theory behind decentralization and centralization in the modern nation-states of Latin America and the Caribbean? In political science terms, Tulia Falleti (2005) calls *decentralization* the process of state reform through public policies, focused on the transfer of power, responsibilities and/or resources from higher levels to lower levels of government. On the other hand, *centralization* is the process of state reform through public policies that are aimed at the restitution at higher levels of government of those faculties attributed to lower levels in a determined political context. When analyzing the components of these definitions it can be seen that primary emphasis is given to the dynamic character of these processes, rather than to the static characteristics of a system. For this reason, the character of state reform is studied and not an institutional description of a specific moment in time. The character of state reform excludes the possibility of privatization of public functions, which means that the transfer of faculties is strictly within the public sector. According to the political constitution of the states analyzed in this study, several levels of government are contemplated: (1) the national level of government, which corresponds to the national government or central government[4], (2) the intermediate level of government, that corresponds to the government of federated states, departments or provinces, (3) the local level of government, that corresponds to municipalities or city councils, and (4) other subnational levels or jurisdictions.[5]

The transfers that take place between different levels of government occur in three areas: (1) The *Political* area refers to granting space for territorial representation on the basis of electoral reforms regarding the determination of executive and legislative branches of government. Additionally, it refers to the transfer of authority to designate and remove personnel in the public sector at different governmental levels. (2) The *Fiscal* area refers to the ability to collect and distribute revenue in the form of taxes, carry out income and transfers between the different levels of government, distribute expenditures as expenses and investment, and the authority to manage public debt; and (3) The *Administrative* area, which refers to the transference of authority to grant public services (Manor 1999; Tulchin 2004; O'Neill 2005; Falleti 2005). Falleti (2005) identifies the sequence in which political, fiscal and administrative transference takes place. When authority is transferred, the preferred order is first, the transfer of administrative control and the relinquishing of responsibilities for public services; then fiscal transfer retaining political control and power. Conversely, the level of government to which authority is transferred should receive an initial transference of political control and power in order to avoid being designated or removed at the discretion of the other level of government. Once its legitimacy is insured by vote, it requires fiscal control to consolidate its institutional operation and finally exert administrative control of public services.

To better explain the processes of decentralization that have taken place during the third wave of democratization in Latin America, a number of social scientists have restated the definition in more precise terms. Kathleen O'Neil (2005) defines decentralization in terms of (1) *devolution*, the process of transfer of funds and responsibilities to officials at the intermediate and local levels, designated by the national government; (2) *delegation*, the process of conferring responsibilities to non-official organizations[6] and (3) *de-concentration*, the process of conferring

---

[4] For standardization purposes, in this study the term national government is used in reference to the central government.
[5] For example, counties, villages, parochial boards, and so on.
[6] The delegation is done by means of privatization or concession of public works.

decision-making power to a series of ministers in the executive branch. A distinction also must be made between *federalism*, which corresponds to a system of government in which sovereignty is constitutionally divided between the authority of the national government and subnational political units, and in which power is shared between the national government and intermediate governments[7], and *autonomy, in which* subnational levels of government have ample executive and legislative powers. Sovereignty as an attribute, however, belongs exclusively to the nation.

The State of Decentralization in Latin America and the Caribbean

Several researchers agree that the consolidation of state reforms such as political, fiscal and administrative transfers entered into effect with the return of democracy to Latin American and the Caribbean at the end of the 1970s.[8] Daughters and Harper (2007) argue that early state-decentralization reforms took place in the political arena, specifically with the creation of local-level representative democracies. Mayoral elections began with high expectations, given the natural advantage the local and intermediate levels have over the national level to link the needs of the population with the goods and services offered by local governments. Furthermore, another advantage lies in the facility of interpreting preferences through an increase in political participation in the community. In the mid 1990s, one of the first conditions for political decentralization was widely accomplished among the nations of Latin America and the Caribbean—democratic mayoral elections were instituted in the entire region, except in Surinam.[9] The first country to put elections for local government into effect was Mexico in 1917. This coincided with the year of its return to democracy. The last countries in the region to carry out local elections were Guyana and Panama, both in 1995, and the years of their transition to democracy were 1966 and 1989 respectively. In Table V-I the first years of mayor elections in the countries are compared, along with the years of democratic transition.

Regarding state fiscal policy reform, subnational governments have made use of three general forms of financing: (1) excise taxes,[10] (2) intergovernmental transfers,[11] and (3) the generation of income by looking for sources of financing themselves.[12] Falleti (2005) says that in the 1980s, subnational governments collected, on average, 15% of total income, and spent on average 20% of total expenditures. This data according to Daughters and Harper (2007) hides a significant difference among countries, particularly in terms of expenses and investment. In the period from 1996 to 2004, Inter-American Development Bank data reveals that, in descending order, three countries—Argentina, Brazil and Colombia—had high rates of decentralization of expenses with percentages close to 50%, placing them among the group of the most decentralized countries in the world.[13] A second group of countries—Mexico Venezuela, Bolivia, Peru and

---

[7] Generally states or provinces.

[8] See Robert Daughters and Leslie Harper (2007), Tulia Falleti (2005), Kathleen O'Neill (2005) Daniel Treisman (2002).

[9] Cuba is not taken into account in this analysis.

[10] The most common are taxes on property, vehicles, and industry and commerce.

[11] They can be made permanent and egalitarian through legislation or at the discretion of higher levels of government.

[12] This is in the case of municipal water and power companies, etc.

[13] The list of these countries includes Canada, the United State, and North-European countries (Daughters y Harper, 2007).

Ecuador—present a moderate yet equally significant level of expenditure decentralization, between 17.5% and 31.8% in 2004. It is worth mentioning that, out of the first five countries, four are federal systems of government[14], except for Colombia which has had an historically regionalist tradition that has allowed for higher levels of decentralization.

A third group of countries—Uruguay, Chile, Honduras, Guatemala, El Salvador, Paraguay, Nicaragua, Costa Rica and Panama—are characterized by low levels of expenditure decentralization, from 13% in the cases of Uruguay and Chile, to 1% and 3% in the cases of Panama and Costa Rica.

In the same vein, since the mid 1990s, a growing number of restrictions on subnational indebtedness have been put in place in order to avoid the problems of excessive debt that arose from the policies that had been adopted by Brazil and Colombia in the first instance, followed by Bolivia, Ecuador and Peru. A summary of the characteristics of subnational public indebtedness is presented in Figure V.1.

---

[14] Argentina, Brazil, Mexico and Venezuela (Central Intelligence Agency, 2007).

Table V.1. First year municipal elections, democratic transition and subnational indebtedness

Country	Municipal Mayor Elections	Year of Transition to Democracy*	Prohibition of Subnational Indebtedness**	Authorization from National Government for Indebtedness**	Restriction in the Use of Public Debt Funding**
Argentina	1983	1983		✓	✓
Belize	1981	1981	n.a.	n.a.	n.a.
Bolivia	1985	1982		✓	✓
Brazil	n.a.[a]	1985		✓	✓
Chile	1992	1990	✓		
Colombia	1988	1958		✓	✓
Costa Rica	1949	1949		✓	✓
Dominican Republic	1966	1966	n.a.	n.a.	n.a.
Ecuador	1983	1979		✓	✓
El Salvador	1985	1984		✓	✓
Guatemala	1985	1985		✓	✓
Guyana	1995	1966		✓	✓
Honduras	1982	1982		✓	✓
Jamaica	1962	1962		✓	
Mexico	1917	1917		✓	✓
Nicaragua	1992	1990	n.a.	n.a.	n.a.
Panama	1995	1989		✓	✓
Paraguay	1991	1989		✓	✓
Peru	1980	1980		✓	✓
Surinam	n.e.[b]	1987	✓		
Trinidad y Tobago	1962	1962		✓	✓
Uruguay	1984	1985	n.a.	n.a.	n.a.
Venezuela	1989	1958	n.a.	n.a.	n.a.

Sources: * Inter American Development Bank (1997).
** *Ibid* (2004)   Created by Robert Daughters and Leslie Harper (2007) and restructured by the author.
[a] n.a. Data not available [b] Local government is non-existent.

Public Opinion: Political Trust among Institutions and Support for Decentralization

What do the people of Latin America and the Caribbean think about the processes of decentralization? Do they trust national governments more, or does their trust rest more in the local levels of government? Would they be willing to back municipalities receiving more

responsibilities and resources from the national government, or do they think that the national government needs to assume more municipal responsibilities and resources? There have been many attempts at defining the ideal institutional balance between centralization and decentralization of the state, but very few studies have looked into public opinion regarding these state-reform processes. First of all, this study analyzes the level of *political trust* that people in the region have in their public institutions, focusing principally on the national government and the municipality. According to Hetherington (2005) political trust is the degree of perception that people have of whether or not the government is producing results that are consistent with their expectations. The key characteristic of this concept is the people's *perception* of government performance and not government performance in and of itself. Obviously perceptions must connect with reality, but often the link is ambiguous and indirect. This leads to several problems, not the least of which is the difficulty for citizens to determine what their government's performance really is. Much of this information is transmitted by the media, and perceptions can be distorted for political purposes. Moreover, access to the media information varies according to socioeconomic status and the citizens' level of interest in politics.

Trust in the institutions is related to support for democracy and other democratic principles. Adrian and Smith (2006) point out that in both democratic systems and in nations in the process of democratization, individuals who assess present and past regimes unfavorably also express very little trust in institutions. *Support* is defined as a foundation, confirmation or proof of an opinion or doctrine. Given the premise that political trust is, ultimately, related to support for democracy and democratic processes, it can be inferred that the greater the level of trust, for example, in the municipality, the greater the support for decentralization. This study does not analyze the inverse relationship, which is that support for decentralization causes individuals to have greater trust in the institutions because decentralization is seen from a dynamic perspective. People decide whether they will favor a greater decentralization based on personal experience with municipal government vis-à-vis their experience with the national government.

In this chapter I analyze data obtained in the 2006-07 round of surveys carried out by the Latin American Public Opinion Project (LAPOP) as part of the AmericasBarometer series. Specifically the main items used are:

> **LGL2**. In your opinion, should more obligations and more funding be given to the municipality, or should the national government be allowed to assume more municipal obligations and services?

> **B32**. To what extent do you trust your municipality?

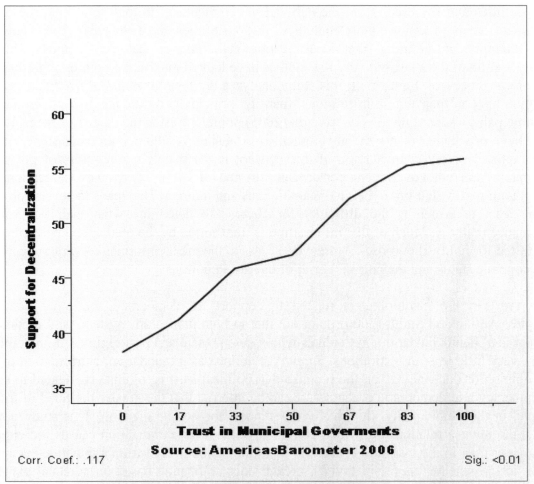

Figure V.1. Trust in the municipality per support for decentralization

The strong result of the connection between citizen support for decentralization and trust in the municipality is shown in Figure V.1. In the nineteen countries analyzed,[15] the greater the political trust in the municipality, the greater the support for decentralization. This finding verifies the hypothesis that, as for individuals, an increase in trust in the municipality means there is greater support for a process of decentralization. The latter indicates that in terms of public policy, it is of fundamental importance to take into account that citizens will support a process of transference to municipalities when they perceive that their mayors, city council members and municipal employees are performing well. That is to say, municipal officials have a fundamental role to play in building the necessary citizen support in the establishment of a process of state-decentralization because to the degree that municipalities fulfill individual expectations, the result is directly translated into citizens favoring the increase of political and economic power for local governments.[16]

---

[15] According to the available information, the following countries were included in this study: Chile, Colombia, Costa Rica, Ecuador, El Salvador, Guatemala, Guyana, Haiti, Honduras, Jamaica, Mexico, Nicaragua, Panama, Paraguay, Peru and the Dominican Republic.

[16] The relation between political Trust in the national government and support for centralization is not significant.

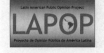

Comparative Level of Municipal Political Trust versus Other Democratic Institutions

How much political trust do the people of Latin America and the Caribbean have in municipalities? How does trust in municipalities differ from political trust in other state institutions? By assessing the ten principal institutions that are present in a democratic regime, the levels of political trust in the countries of Latin America and the Caribbean can be analyzed. Figure V.2 summarizes the results of these questions in all nineteen countries. On a scale of 100 points, where 100 means the person has a high level of trust in the institution and zero means the person has absolutely no Trust, Latin Americans and people in the Caribbean who responded to this survey gave the municipality a score of about fifty points, whereas the national government got 49 points. The average trust for all institutions is at 48 points, that is, trust in the municipality is two points above the average for the rest of the institutions, whereas trust in the national government is one point above the institutional average. It can be seen that the armed forces is the institution in which the population places the highest level of Trust, as it is 13 points over the institutional average. At the same time, political parties are the least trusted institutions, at 13 points below the average. On the graph, in black, there are the municipality and the national government. It should be noted that the difference between the level of trust in municipalities and national governments in the 19 countries is minimal (less than one point).

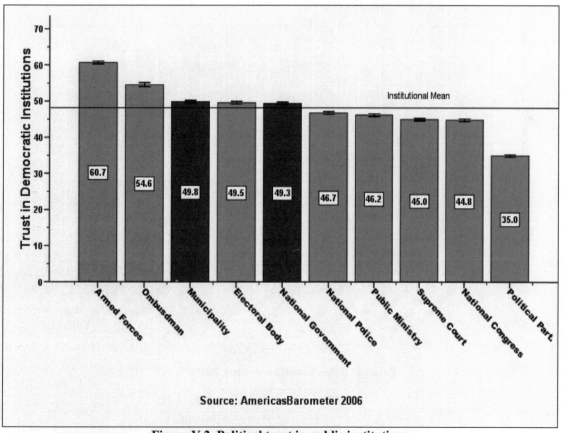

Source: AmericasBarometer 2006

Figure V.2. Political trust in public institutions.

Political Trust in Municipal Government per Country

Are these levels of trust in municipalities the same in all countries? In this section a comparative analysis is made of the level of political trust citizens have in their municipalities by country of residence. In Figure V.3 it can be seen that on a scale of zero to 100 points, where 100 means a lot of trust and zero means none at all, at 60 points, Dominican citizens are the ones who have the highest level of political trust in the municipalities, awarding them a score of 60 points. This is to say that, in the Dominican Republic, trust in the municipality in is ten points above the average political trust level for the municipalities of Latin America and the Caribbean, which is 50 points. Haiti is in last place with 30 points for trust in municipalities, 20 points below the average for the municipalities in the region. Furthermore, there exists a group of countries— Nicaragua, Guyana, Colombia and Brazil —that show a level of trust that is very close to the regional average of political trust in municipalities.

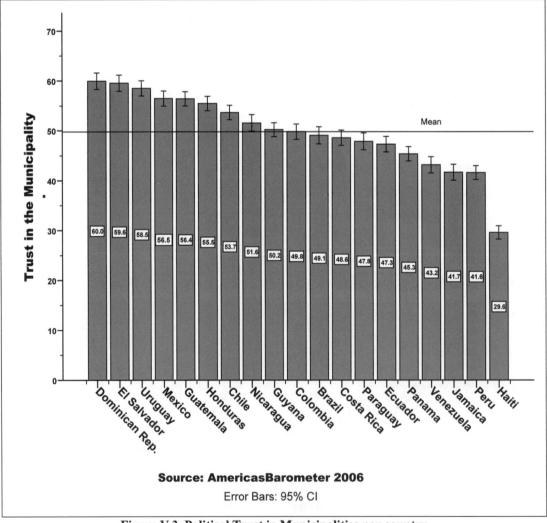

Source: AmericasBarometer 2006

Error Bars: 95% CI

Figure V.3. Political Trust in Municipalities per country

Political Trust in the Municipal Government Compared with Trust in the National Government, per Country

Despite many shared characteristics among the various Latin American and Caribbean countries studied, there are key differences in trust in municipalities and national governments. The data reveal three groupings: (1) Countries where political trust in the municipality is greater than that in the national government; (2) countries in which political trust for the national government is greater than the trust in the municipality; and (3) countries where the difference in the political trust in the national government and the municipality is not significant. Figure V.4 illustrates the three groups where there is a difference between political trust in municipalities and national government. The bars with positive scores show countries where there is more trust in the municipality, whereas bars with negative scores show greater trust in the national government.

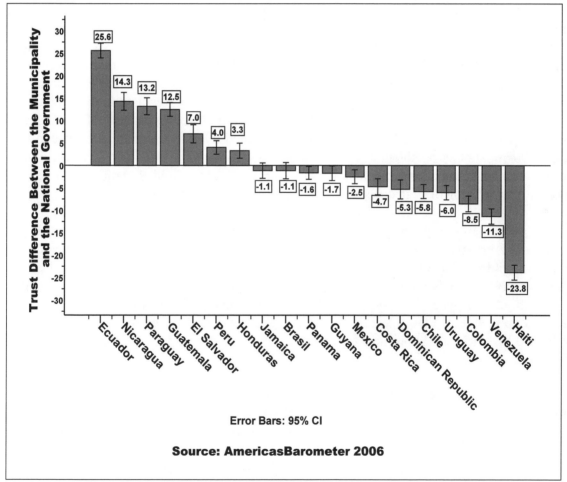

Error Bars: 95% CI

Source: AmericasBarometer 2006

Figure V.4. Political trust in the national government versus municipality

It is interesting to note that the country with the highest dispersion range between political trust in the municipality and the national government is Ecuador with almost 26 points. Thus, Ecuadorians show a higher degree of political trust in the municipality in comparison to the other Latin American and Caribbean studied. An analysis of this case indicates that the results are systematically related to the high level of political instability in Ecuador's national government in the last twelve years. According to Seligson *et al.* (2006), between 1995 and 2007, Ecuador has had eight presidents, each one holding office for an average of 1.5 years. The crisis at the national level government of Ecuador began in 1995 with the exit from the country of then vice-president Alberto Dahik, during the administration of Sixto Durán-Ballen, due to a political trial against Dahik for misuse of reserve funds. In 1997, president-elect Abadala Bucarám, after becoming involved in several corruption scandals, was removed from office through a National Congress resolution based on a constitutional provision allowing for "mental unfitness" as grounds for dismissal. Following an interim period presided over by former president of the National Congress Fabian Alarcon, presidential elections were held in 1998, and former Quito Mayor Jamil Mahuad took office. Due to a financial crisis that resulted in bank accounts being frozen, Mahuad was forced to resign in 2001 for putting the country in the worst economic crisis since the establishment of the republic. The vice-president, Gustavo Noboa succeeded him until former military man Lucio Gutierrez, who had participated in the coup d'etat against Mahuad, came to power after being elected president of the republic in 2002 (Seligson *et al.* 2004). In 2005, Gutierrez and the National Congress ordered the removal from office of all the minister judges of the Supreme Court of Justice, adducing high politicization and partiality in the Ecuadorian justice system. These events in turn provoked an abrupt reaction from a movement in the capital, and the National Congress was forced to remove Gutierrez from office by means of a constitutional definition of "abandonment of office." He was succeeded by his vice-president Alfredo Palacio, and in 2006 yet another presidential election took place (Seligson *et al.*, 2006). At the time of this writing, current Ecuadorian president Rafael Correa recently held a national referendum to authorize the rewriting of Ecuador's constitution for the twentieth time.

Political instability has not affected all levels of the government equally. For instance, the prefect of the province of Guayas, Nicolas Lapenti, has been democratically re-elected for the fourth time, and will have held office for 16 years. The municipal mayors of Quito and Guayaquil both have mayors who have been re-elected and will have been in office eight years. For all these reasons Ecuador presents itself as an extreme case in which political trust is much greater at the local government level than that of the national government. The rest of the countries studied, which have higher levels of political trust in municipalities than in the national government, show a much more moderate difference. [17]

In the second group of countries citizens express a higher level of institutional trust in the national government compared with municipalities. Figure V.4 shows the eight countries that share this characteristic in this study. In this figure, the citizens of countries below the horizontal line trust the national government more than the local government. Haiti appears at the far end with a much higher level of trust in the national government than in municipalities, with a twenty-four point difference. An analysis of this case in the report "Political Culture in Haiti: 2006" (Zephyr and Pierre, 2007) indicates that since Haitian independence in 1804, the country

---

[17] Nicaragua 14,3; Paraguay 13,2; Guatemala12,5; El Salvador 7,0; Peru 4,0; y Honduras 3,3.

has been marked by a tradition of administrative and fiscal centralization. When Haiti held its first elections for its Municipal Communal Councils in 1844, then president Riviere Herard established a law creating a series of districts and prefectures under the control of the president in order to counteract the municipal councils' political power. Subsequent governments in Haiti have employed municipal governments as extensions of central power, a process that was due to constant electoral fraud. In response to this domination by the central government, the inhabitants themselves created their own local governmental institutions which have been informally legitimized.

Local community development associations were put in place during the Duvalier regime; however, their functioning has been far from democratic (Zephyr and Pierre 2007). Called *Community Action Councils* (CAC) these associations were increasingly pressured defer to central power. Since the CAC's were tied to Duvalier's power, these institutions ceased to exist in 1986. With the advent of the new constitution in 1987, the formation of local institutions has not been permitted. For example, Departmental Assemblies in which the members of the Inter-departmental Council should be chosen were never held. It was thus impossible to establish municipalities. Starting in 1990, Haitians supported candidates from different political parties for the establishment of local governments. In 1995, local inhabitants motivated members of local groups to run for local offices. This gave rise to an important stage in the development of local governance; they did not limit themselves to supporting external political forces, rather they undertook campaigns to participate in local elections. Unfortunately, Haitian Municipalities do not have the logistical, technical or financial means to respond to the needs of their jurisdictions. In most cases, mayors depend on foreign contributions to finance small development projects. Generally such projects are financed and managed by NGOs or other international organizations in collaboration with local associations and/or neighborhood committees, thus leaving out of the equation the locally elected officials. Local level governmental projects are initiated sporadically, although the law of April 4th, 1996 calls for persons elected to occupy local offices to fully participate in local development projects. In the absence of effective municipal institutions, Haitians trust the national government rather than local governments.

Regarding the rest of the countries in this category, in spite of the fact that citizens show more trust in the national government than in municipalities, the gap is not as great as in the case of Haiti.[18] In Figure V.4 a third group of countries shows that the difference between political trust in the national and municipal government is not significant. This is to say, that these countries exhibit no statistical difference in their trust in government at the local or national levels.[19] In sum, it has been determined that on a scale from zero to 100 the inhabitants of the countries in this study give an average trust score of 45 points to ten of the most representative institutions of a democratic regime. When the countries are organized in descending order according to the sum of political trust in the national government plus trust in the municipality, the Dominican Republic is the country with the greatest level of trust in the two institutions,

---

[18] Venezuela 11.3; Colombia 8,5; Uruguay 6.0; Chile 5,8; the Dominican Republic 5,3; Costa Rica 4,7 and Mexico 2,5.

[19] Guyana, Panama, Brazil and Jamaica with a trust level of 95%. In Figure IV.4, it can be seen that the error bars coincide with the horizontal line that indicates that there is no statistical difference in the level of Trust in both levels of government.

followed by Mexico, Chile, El Salvador, Colombia, Honduras, Guyana, Costa Rica, Guatemala, Panama, Nicaragua, Haiti, Jamaica, Paraguay, Peru and finally Ecuador.

Variables that Determine Political Trust in Municipalities in Latin America and the Caribbean

This section reports on the factors that cause inhabitants to have greater trust at the local level than at the national level of government. To this end, after having determined the group of countries whose inhabitants have more trust in the municipality—Paraguay, Peru, Ecuador, Nicaragua, Honduras, El Salvador and Guatemala—a linear regression is done to determine some of the variables that explain trust in municipalities. Kenneth Newton and Pippa Norris (1999) identified at least three schools of thought regarding political trust in the institutions of the state, with the following explanatory factors: (1) Those that focus on the individuals' socio-psychological characteristics; (2) those that focus on the cultural environment of individuals, groups and communities; and (3) those that concentrate on the performance of government institutions. [20]

According to the *socio-psychological* school, Newton and Norris (1999) determined that the inner quality of trust between people, alone or joined with optimism, make-up the "basic trust" group that is formed in the first stages of psychological development as a result of the mother-child feeding experience. In that study, the authors cite Easton (1965) who concluded that the presence of trust means that the needs and interests of the members in a society are being taken care of by the authorities even if there is little supervision or scrutiny. If this school of thought is correct, it can be expected that there is an association between trust at the individual level and trust in political institutions. In order to establish which factors determine the levels of political trust in municipalities, the questions appearing in Appendix 1 were utilized. Another school of thought considers that participation in community activities and socialization increase general trust between a group of people and institutions, which means that the greater the social capital, the greater the person's general level of Trust. Finally, Newton and Norris (1999) consider that governmental institutions with good performance records generate greater trust in people; conversely, inefficient institutions generate rejection.

A model was created in order to verify these theories, which, aside from including explanatory variables from the three schools of thought mentioned above, was controlled by the standard socioeconomic variables such as: (1) urban/rural dwelling, (2) gender, (3) age, (4) educational level, (5) wealth measured by possession of capital goods and (6) dummy variables to control the country-effects. The results of this regression can be seen in Appendix 2.

The results show that the levels of political trust in the municipality do not depend on the control variables: gender or wealth measured by the possession of capital goods. What actually

---

[20] As the format of the Paraguay questionnaire is different from the one used in the rest of the countries, due to the fact that this study was not carried out by the LAPOP consortium, the results of some of the explanatory variables form "outliers" in the sample, therefore, Paraguay was removed from the rest of this analysis.

determines the level of political trust in the municipality is the level of education. As the level of education increases, political trust in municipalities *decreases*, probably because persons with higher levels of education tend to be more aware of institutional failures. This is troubling in that it is precisely the highly educated segment of the population that could accelerate the process of state reform, although they are also the most critical of the system. In addition, these results suggest that a populist candidate could obtain a great deal of benefit by pressuring the system to implement a process of decentralization. In Table V.2, as follows, there is a summary of some of the explanatory statistically significant variables and their relation—positive or negative—to political trust in municipalities.

Table V.2. Predictors of political trust in municipalities	
Variables	**Effect on political trust in the municipality**
Age	+
Education	-
Urban sector	+
Interpersonal trust	+
Satisfaction with life	+
Victim of corruption	-
Perception of municipal services	+
Attendance at town meetings	+
Victim of a criminal act	-

Table V.2 shows that as age increases and the individual resides in more urbanized areas, trust in the municipality increases. Additionally, it is shown that the greater the degree of interpersonal Trust, the greater the intensity of political trust in municipalities. This positive relation is also expressed in satisfaction with life. In the area of institutional performance according to individual requirements, people who have been victims of corruption at the level of public institutions in the last year, trust the municipality less.[21] Once again this confirms the importance of the effect of the perception of corruption on individual trust in municipalities. While it is not surprising that people distrust institutions when they have been victims of corruption in their interactions with them, an important finding of this study is that individuals can also generalize their distrust to include other state institutions. In other words, if an individual is a victim of corruption in national institutions, the same individual might decide that all state institutions are untrustworthy, including those at the local level. The same is true with victims of crime, as these people also show distrust in the municipality.

Citizens who perceive the municipality as a purveyor of services and fair treatment, show a greater level of political trust in municipalities. This is a fundamental finding in terms of a decentralization process. It is clear that in order to generate political trust and the subsequent

---

[21] In the regression, a variable was included to measure the degree of municipal-level corruption but it turned out to be non significant.

support for decentralization, mayors, city council members and other municipal officials must optimize municipal services and pay sustained and timely attention to citizen demands. This process of trust building is vital prior to a decentralization process as will be shown in later sections.

Centralize or decentralize?

Having described the reasons why people feel political trust or distrust in the municipality, it is now to be determined whether Latin American and Caribbean people in the nineteen countries included in this study want municipalities to undertake more responsibilities and receive more money from the national government, or if, on the contrary, they think the national government should assume the municipalities' responsibilities and administer their services. In order to determine the level of support for fiscal and administrative decentralization or centralization the following question was asked: [22]

> **LGL2**. In your opinion, should more obligations and more money be assigned to the municipality, or should the national government be allowed to assume more municipal obligations and services?

The results from this question are depicted in Figure V.5.

---

[22] In this study there is no analysis of public opinion regarding political decentralization and centralization

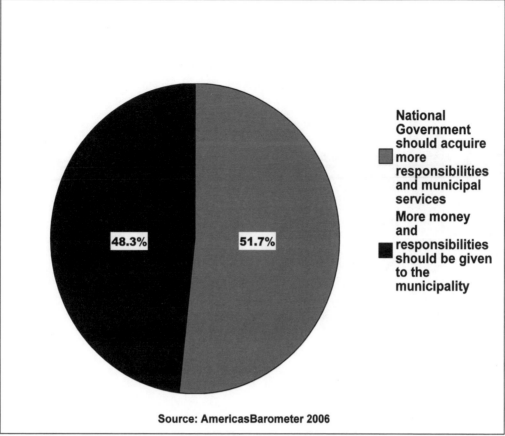

National Government should acquire more responsibilities and municipal services

More money and responsibilities should be given to the municipality

48.3%   51.7%

Source: AmericasBarometer 2006

Figure V.5. Percentage of support for state decentralization or centralization

The graph shows that the opinions of the inhabitants of the Latin American and Caribbean countries that participated in this study are closely divided between centralization and decentralization of the state. This result requires careful analysis of the countries in which people think there should be a greater process of decentralization, as well as those countries where people think that the national government should assume the municipal functions. In figure V.6 Jamaica appears first among the countries whose citizens prefer a greater fiscal and administrative transference; more than twice as many people in the population prefer a process of decentralization to one of centralization.

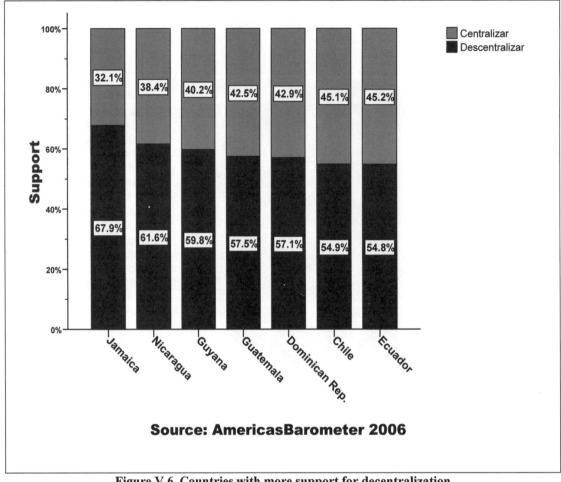

Figure V.6. Countries with more support for decentralization

This may be due in part to the fact that in early 2005 several local Jamaican authorities had prepared "Local Sustainable Development Plans." In the case of Kingston and Saint Andrew Corporation, the most populous areas of Jamaica, these plans have benefited from World Bank collaboration through financial management training and the training of Parochial Board Members in public administration.[23] The local government system in Jamaica was set up by the British in the second half of the eighteenth century. In 1944, the system of "parochial boards" was established in order to increase political representation at the local level. This system of local representation is still in place today in Jamaica. Currently, Jamaicans perceive the most serious problems the country faces to be the following: deterioration in the roadway system, water shortage and poor sewer system service. These problems correspond to the need to assign more responsibilities and resources to local governments so they can repair infrastructure and improve basic services.

In the rest of the countries—Nicaragua, Guyana, Guatemala, the Dominican Republic, Chile and Ecuador—over 50% of persons surveyed were in favor of transferring more

---

[23] Parochial Board Members are elected by popular vote at the local level.

responsibilities and resources to the municipalities. However, there is a second group of countries in which interviewees considered that the national government should be the one to assume more obligations and municipal services. The results regarding administrative and fiscal centralization are summarized in Figure V.7.

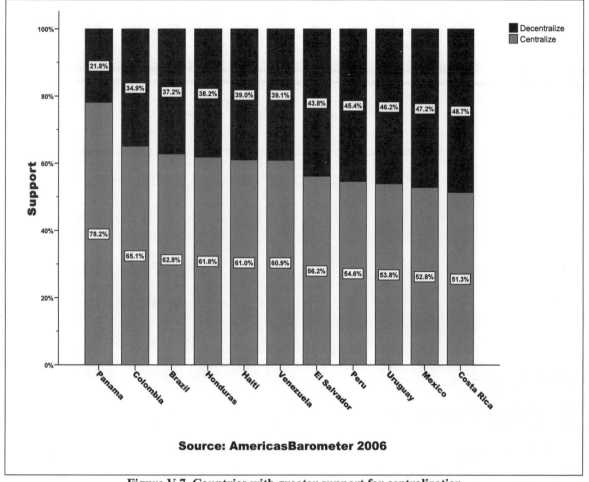

Source: AmericasBarometer 2006

Figure V.7. Countries with greater support for centralization

It can be seen that Panamanians who consider that the national government ought to assume more municipal obligations and services are 3.5 times more numerous than those who favor decentralization.. These results are similar to those of Daughters and Harper (2007) who found Panama to be the least decentralized country in the region.[24] In the study for the BID *Municipal Development and Decentralization Support Program*, Nessim *et al.* (2003) stated that tax revenue for Panamanian municipalities constitutes taxes on economic activity, vehicle circulation tax, and construction permits. Property tax is not a municipal tax. This means that at the national level, two out of every three municipalities do not have enough resources to cover operating costs. For this reason, the quality of municipal services is poor and in general produces an unfavorable opinion of municipal governments. The difference is less in the rest of the

---

[24] In fiscal and administrative terms; in terms of political decentralization, along with Guyana, Panama has been one of the last countries to implement local elections for municipal mayors.

countries—Colombia, Honduras, Haiti, El Salvador, Peru, México and Costa Rica—in spite of the fact that they belong to the group of countries with greater support for centralization than decentralization of the state.

The battery of questions used to explain some of the explanatory variables for support for centralization or decentralization of the state appears in Appendix 3. Also, the following socio-demographic control variables were included: (1) urban/rural dwelling; (2) gender; (3) age; (4) educational level; (5) wealth measured by possession of capital goods; and (6) dummy variables to control the country-effects. The results of the binomial logistic regression can be seen in Appendix 4. Table V.3, sums up some of the statistically significant explanatory variables and their relation to the centralization or decentralization of the state.

Table V.3. Predictors for Decentralization and Centralization	
Variables	Effect on decentralization or centralization of the state
Sex (Male)	Decentralization
Age	Decentralization
Urban sector	Decentralization
Level of education	Decentralization
Incumbent government's efficiency	Centralization
Political knowledge	Decentralization
Perception of Municipal Services	Decentralization
Trust in the municipality	Decentralization
Interest in politics	Centralization

Table V.3 shows that in socio-demographic terms, sex, age, educational level and the geographic area where Latin Americans and Caribbean people live, determine their support for decentralization. Therefore, men, persons who are older or possess a higher educational level and residents of urban areas, are more in favor of fiscal and administrative decentralization. Likewise, people with more political knowledge, who have requested municipal personnel assistance or who perceive that municipalities treat citizens fairly and fulfill their needs, also tend to exhibit greater support for descentralization. Nevertheless, people who have in interest in

politics and consider that the incumbent national government is efficient, show greater support for centralization. This could be because people who are interested in politics seek public office in the national level of the government, and for this reason they do not choose decentralization as it could take power from the national government.

Finally, interviewees were asked, "Would you be willing to pay higher taxes to the municipality in order for it to be able to give better municipal services or do you believe it is not worthwhile to pay more taxes to the municipality?" Except in Haiti, where eighty percent of those interviewed said they would be willing to pay higher taxes, more than sixty percent of people in the nineteen countries analyzed in this study answered that it was not worthwhile to pay more taxes, The refusal to pay more taxes is understandable, since people do not, as a rule, volunteer to pay taxes.

Conclusion

This chapter has analyzed public opinion regarding financial and administrative centralization and decentralization state reforms in Latin America and the Caribbean. In spite of enormous efforts made for decentralization in the region, there are few empirical studies of the population's opinion regarding these processes of reform. This analysis is an attempt to address this deficit by means of a nineteen country survey in the region that makes possible the analysis of levels of trust in the central government and municipalities and the support that the people of Latin America and the Caribbean give the processes of decentralization and centralization.

Contrary to what might be expected regarding massive support for decentralization, the population of Latin America and the Caribbean is divided in its opinion regarding this process. Nearly half of the people think that more obligations and resources should be given to municipalities, while the other half believe that it is the central government that should assume municipal obligations and administer resources. This coincides with the minimal difference between trust in the national and local governments. Therefore, it is necessary to determine the support governments and international organizations and other cooperation organizations receive from the population when planning to aid reform processes in the transference of resources and responsibilities at an intergovernmental level.

A case by case analysis of the relation between trust in the municipality and the national government, and the ensuing support for centralization or decentralization, has found that in Ecuador, Guatemala and Nicaragua inhabitants trust their municipalities more, and would be willing to support a decentralization process. In the case of Guyana and Jamaica, although the level of trust is practically the same for national government and municipality, people in these countries would be willing to support the process of decentralization. Finally, Chile and the Dominican Republic show lower levels of trust in their municipalities, but would give decentralization a chance. In Peru, Honduras and El Salvador, in spite of the fact that people trust their municipalities more than the national government, they show more support for the process of centralizing the state. In the case of Panama, Brazil and Mexico, there is practically no

distinction between municipal and national government trust, but people prefer that the national government assume more municipal obligations and services. To conclude, the people of Chile, Colombia, Haiti, Uruguay and Venezuela trust their national governments more and support state centralization.

A factor to be considered in subsequent studies is the decentralization of the judicial branch of government. All the literature reviewed for this study mentions three factors in decentralization—administrative, political and fiscal—but in all of them decentralization of judiciary institutions has not been addressed. In the end, a complementary analysis of this investigation would consist of determining the levels of balance of power in different levels of government by way of formal modeling and game theory.

References

Agresti, Alan and Barabara Finlay. *Statistical Methods for the Social Sciences*. International Edition ed. New Jersey: Prentice-Hall, Inc., 1997.

Barczak, Monica. "Representation by Consultation? The Rise of Direct Democracy in Latin America." *Latin American Politics and Society* 43, no. 3 (2001): 24.

Bardhan, Pranab. "Decentralization of Governance and Development." *Journal of Economic Perspectives* 16, no. 4 (2002): 20.

Barr, Robert. "Parties, Legitimacy and the Motivations for Reform: Devolution and Concentration in Latin America." (2001): 27. Publication data?

Bunce, Valerie. "Comparative Democratization: Big and Bounded Generalizations." *Comparative Political Studies* 33, no. 6/7 (2000): 32.

Cameron, John. "Municipal Democratization in Rural Latin America: Methodological Insights from Ecuador." *Bulletin of Latin American Research* 24, no. 3 (2001): 24.

Campbell, Tim. *The Quiet Revolution: Decentralization and the Rise of Political Participation in Latin American Cities*. Pittsburgh: University of Pittsburgh Press, 2003.

Chang, Eric. "Electoral Incentives for Political Corruption under Open-List Proportional Representation." *The Journal of Politics* 67, no. 3 (2005): 15.

Charles, Andrian and James Smith. *Political Democracy, Trust and Social Justice*. Boston: University Press of New England, 2006.

Christopher Garman, Stephan Haggard, and and Eliza Willis. "Fiscal Decentralization: A Political Theory with Latin American Cases." *World Politics* 53 (2001): 32.

CIA, Central Intelligence Agency. "The World Factbook." Washington, 2007.

Dahl, Robert. *Polyarchy; Participation and Opposition*. New Heaven: Yale University Press, 1971.

Daughters, Robert, Leslie Harper. "Fiscal and Political Decentralization Reforms." In *The State of State Reform in Latin America*, edited by Eduardo Lora, 87 - 121. Washington: Stanford University Press, 2007.

Epstein, David. "Democratic Transitions." *American Journal of Political Science* 50, no. 3 (2006): 19.

Escobar-Lemmon, Maria. "Political Support for Decentralization: An Analysis of the Colombian and Venezuelan Legislatures." *American Journal of Political Science* 47, no. 4 (2003): 15.

Falleti, Tulia. "A Sequential Theory of Decentralization: Latin American Cases in Comparative Perspective." *American Political Science Review* 99, no. 3 (2005): 20.

Freire, James Keese and Marco. "Decentralisation and Ngo–Municipal Government Collaboration in Ecuador." *Development in Practice* 16, no. 2 (2006): 14.

Garman, Christopher, Stephan Haggard, and and Eliza Willis. "Fiscal Decentralization: A Political Theory with Latin American Cases." *World Politics* 53 (2001): 32.

Grote, Joachim vonBraun and Ulrike. "Does Decentralization Serve the Poor?" *IMF* (2000): 32.

Hetherington, Marc. *Why Trust Matters?* New Jersey: Princeton University Press, 2005.

Hiskey, Jonathan, and Mitchell Seligson. "Pitfalls of Power to the People: Decentralization, Local Government Performance, and System Support in Bolivia." *Studies in Comparative International Development* 37, no. 4 (2003): 25.

Joseph Tulchin, Andrew Selee. *Decentralization and Democratic Governance in Latin America*. Washington: Woodrow Wilson International Center for Scholars, 2004.

Kenneth Newton, Pippa Norris. "Trust in Public Institutions: Faith, Culture or Performance?" (2000). This looks like an incomplete entry

Lagos, Martha. "How People View Democracy: Between Stability and Crisis in Latin America." *Journal of Democracy* 12, no. 1 (2001): 9.

Licha, Isabel. "Citizen Participation and Local Government in Latin America: Advances, Challenges and Best Practices." *IADB* (2002): 8.

Lucero, Jose. "High Anxiety in the Andes: Crisis and Contention in Ecuador." *Journal of Democracy* 12, no. 2 (2001): 15.

Manor, James. *The Political Economy of Democratic Decentralization*. Washington, 1999.

Nessim, Heli, Ana María Linares, Iveta Ganev, Diego Buchara, Julio Norori, Javier Aguilar, Silvia Echeverría, Huáscar Eguino. "Programa Multifase De Desarrollo Municipal Y Apoyo a La Descentralización ", 15: BID, 2003.

Newton Kenneth and Pippa Norris. "Trust in Public Institutions: Faith, Culture or Performance?" *Harvard University* (2000): 26.

O'Neill, Kathleen. "Decentralization as an Electoral Strategy." *Comparative Political Studies* 36, no. 9 (2003): 24.

O'Neill, Kathleen. *Decentralizing the State: Elections, Parties, and Local Power in the Andes*. New York: Cambridge University Press, 2005.

Perez, Maria Garcia-Guadilla and Carlos. "Democracy, Decentralization and Clientelism: New Relationship and Old Pratices " *Latin American Perspectives* 29, no. 5 (2002): 21.

Pérez-Liñán, David Altman and Aníbal. "Assessing the Quality of Democracy: Freedom, Competitiveness and Participation in Eighteen Latin American Countries" *Democratization* 9, no. 2 (2002): 15. format??

Peruzzotti, Catalina Smulovitz and Enrique. "Societal Accountability in Latin America." *Journal of Democracy* 11, no. 4 (2000): 12.

Radcliffe, Sarah, Nina Laurie and Robert Andolina "Reterritorialised Space and Ethnic Political Participation: Indigenous Municipalities in Ecuador." *Space & Polity* 6, no. 3 (2002): 17.

Roberts, Kenneth. "Social Inequalities without Class Cleavages in Latin America's Neoliberal Era." *Studies in Comparative International Development* 36, no. 4 (2002): 31.

Sadoulet, Alain de Janvry and Elisabeth. "Rural Poverty in Latin America: Determinants and Exit Paths." *Food Policy* 25 (2000): 21.

Selee, Andrew. "Exploring the Link between Decentralization and Democratic Governance." In *Decentralization and Democratic Governance in Latin America*, edited by Andrew Selee Joseph Tulchin, 35. Washington, 2004.

Seligson, Mitchell. "The Impact of Corruption on Regime Legitimacy: A Comparative Study of Four Latin American Countries." *The Journal of Politics* 64, no. 2 (2002): 26.

Seligson, Mitchell , Polibio Cordoba. *Auditoría De La Democracia Ecuador*. Quito: Cedatos, 2006.

———. *Audiutoría De La Democracia Ecuador*. Quito: Cedatos, 2004.

Sorensen, Georg. *Democracy and Democratization: Processes and Prospects in a Changing World* Westview Press, 1998.

Sukhtankar, Carol Graham and Sandip. "Does Economic Crisis Reduce Support for Markets and Democracy in Latin America? Some Evidence from Surveys of Public Opinion and Well Being." *Journal for Latin American Studies (UK)* (2004).

Treisman, Daniel. "Decentralization and Inflation: Commitment, Collective Action or Continuity." *The American Political Science Review* 94, no. 4 (2000): 22.

———. "Defining and Measuring Decentralization: A Global Perspective." (2002): 38. Publication data?

Zéphyr, Dominique, Yves-François Pierre, and Abby Córdova. *Culture politique de la démocratie en Haïti: 2006*. Edited by Latin American Public Opinion Project. Nashville, TN: Vanderbilt University, 2007.

Appendix 1

LS3. Changing the subject, in general how satisfied are you with your life? Would you say that you are ..? (1) Very satisfied (2) Somewhat satisfied (3) Somewhat **dis**satisfied (4) Very **dis**satisfied (8) DK

IT1. Now, speaking of the people from here, would you say that people in this community are generally very trustworthy, somewhat trustworthy, not very trustworthy or untrustworthy ..?

NP1. Have you attended a town meeting, city council meeting or other meeting convened by the mayor in the past 12 months?

SGL1. Would you say that the services the municipality is providing are…? **[Read options]**
(1) Very good (2) Good (3) Neither good nor poor (fair) (4) Poor (5) Very poor (8) Doesn't know

SGL2. How have they treated you or your neighbors when you have had dealings with the municipality? Have they treated you very well, well, neither well nor badly, badly or very badly? (1) Very well (2) Well (3) Neither well nor badly (4) Badly (5) Very badly (8) Doesn't know

VIC1. Have you been a victim of any type of crime in the past 12 months?
(1) Yes [continue] (2) No [go to AOJ8] (8) DK [go to AOJ8]

EXC2. Has a police official ask you for bribe during the past year?

EXC6. During the past year did any public official ask you for a bribe?

EXC11. During the past year did you have any official dealings in the municipality/local government?
If the answer is No → mark 9
If it is Yes→ ask the following:
During the past year, to process any kind of document (like a license, for example), did you have to pay any money above that required by law?

EXC13. Are you currently employed?
If the answer is No → mark 9
If it is Yes→ ask the following:
At your workplace, did anyone ask you for an inappropriate payment during the past year?

EXC14. During the past year, did you have any dealings with the courts?
If the answer is No → note down 9
If it is Yes→ ask the following:
Did you have to pay a bribe at the courts during the last year?

EXC15. Did you use the public health services during the past year? **If the answer is No → mark 9**
If it is Yes→ ask the following:
In order to receive attention in a hospital or a clinic during the past year, did you have to pay a bribe?

EXC16. Did you have a child in school during the past year?
If the answer is No → mark 9
If it is Yes→ ask the following:
Did you have to pay a bribe at school during the past year?

EXC17. Did anyone ask you for a bribe to avoid having the electricity cut off?

EXC18. Do you think that the way things are, sometimes paying a bribe is justified?

EXC19. Do you think that in our society paying bribes is justified because of poor quality public services, or do you think it is not justified?

Appendix 2

Coefficients

Model		Unstandardized Coefficients		Standardized Coefficients	t	Sig.
		B	Std. Error	Beta		
1	(Constant)	6.540	1.423		4.596	.000
	Sex (male)	.439	.377	.007	1.165	.244
	Age	.367	.134	.018	2.746	.006
	Education	-.769	.287	-.020	-2.682	.007
	Urban sector	1.162	.449	.018	2.589	.010
	Wealth	-.187	.115	-.013	-1.616	.106
	Interpersonal trust	.077	.006	.078	12.031	.000
	Life satisfaction	.021	.007	.019	2.805	.005
	Corruption victimization	-2.108	.250	-.056	-8.439	.000
	Municipal service perception	.153	.019	.114	7.975	.000
	Attend city hall meetings	.424	.022	.282	19.475	.000
	Delinquency victimization	-.019	.005	-.024	-3.742	.000
	Ecuador	2.919	1.139	.024	2.564	.010
	El Salvador	13.077	1.146	.108	11.415	.000
	Guatemala	12.328	1.174	.097	10.501	.000
	Honduras	8.723	1.170	.071	7.452	.000
	Nicaragua	8.082	1.141	.065	7.085	.000
	Peru	4.093	1.108	.034	3.693	.000
	Dominican Republic	13.018	1.166	.106	11.160	.000
	Chile	11.839	1.185	.097	9.991	.000
	Costa Rica	7.004	1.209	.058	5.794	.000
	Guyana	9.433	1.189	.069	7.932	.000
	Jamaica	7.755	1.212	.054	6.399	.000
	Panama	6.382	1.153	.050	5.537	.000
	Mexico	15.672	1.167	.128	13.431	.000
	Uruguay	11.564	1.199	.095	9.646	.000
	Venezuela	2.874	1.255	.020	2.291	.022

a. Dependent variable: Trust in the Municipality

Appendix 3

N1. To what extent would you say the current administrationfights poverty.

N3. To what extent would you say the current administration promotes and protects democratic principles.

N9. To what extent would you say the current administrationfights government corruption.

N10. To what extent would you say the current administration protects human rights.

N11. To what extent would you say the current administration improves the security of our citizens.

N12. To what extent would you say the current administration fights unemployment.

Now we want to know how much information about politics and the country is transmitted to the people...
GI1. What is the name of the current president of the United States? **[Don't read,** George Bush]
(1) Correct (2) Incorrect (8) Do not Know (9) No Answer

GI2. What is the name of the President of Congress in country? **[Don't read,** insert name]
(1) Correct (2) Incorrect (8) Do not Know (9) No Answer

GI3. How many provinces does dcountry have? **[Don't read,** insert number of provinces]
(1) Correct (2) Incorrecto (8) Do not Know (9) No Answer
NICARAGUA AND PANAMA ACCEPT WITH OR WITHOUT COMARCAS

GI4. How long is the presidential/prime minister term in country? **[Don't read,** insert number of years]
((1) Correct (2) Incorrect (8) Do not Know (9) No Answer

GI5. What is the name of the president of Brazil? **[Don't read,** Luiz Inácio Lula da Silva, also accept "Lula"]
(1) Correct (2) Incorrect (8) Do not Know (9) No Answer

SGL1. Would you say that the services the municipality is providing are…? [Read options]
(1) Very good (2) Good (3) Neither good nor poor (fair) (4) Poor (5) Very poor   (8) Doesn't know

SGL2. How have they treated you or your neighbors when you have had dealings with the municipality?
Have they treated you very well, well, neither well nor badly, badly or very badly? (1) Very well (2) Well (3) Neither well nor badly   (4) Badly (5) Very badly (8) Doesn't know

VIC1. Have you been a victim of any type of crime in the past 12 months?
(1) Yes [continue] (2) No [go to AOJ8]   (8) DK [go to AOJ8]

EXC2. Has a police official ask you for bribe during the past year?

EXC6. During the past year did any public official ask you for a bribe?

EXC11. During the past year did you have any official dealings in the municipality/local government?
If the answer is No → mark 9
If it is Yes→ ask the following:
During the past year, to process any kind of document (like a license, for example), did you have to pay any money above that required by law?

EXC13. Are you currently employed?
If the answer is No → mark 9
If it is Yes→ ask the following:
At your workplace, did anyone ask you for an inappropriate payment during the past year?

EXC14. During the past year, did you have any dealings with the courts?
If the answer is No → note down 9
If it is Yes→ ask the following:
Did you have to pay a bribe to the courts during the last year?

EXC15. Did you use the public health services during the past year? **If the answer is No → mark 9**   **If it is Yes→ ask the following:**   In order to receive attention in a hospital or a clinic during the past year, did you have to pay a bribe?
EXC16. Did you have a child in school during the past year?   **If the answer is No → mark 9**   **If it is Yes→ ask the following:**   Did you have to pay a bribe at school during the past year?
EXC17. Did anyone ask you for a bribe to avoid having the electricity cut off?
EXC18. Do you think that the way things are, sometimes paying a bribe is justified?
EXC19. Do you think that in our society paying bribes is justified because of poor quailty of public services, or do you think it is not justified?
Now, moving on to a different topic, sometimes the people and communities have problems that they cannot solve by themselves, and so in order to solve them they request help from a government official or agency.
In order to solve your problems have you ever requested help or cooperation from...?
CP2. A member of congress/parliament
CP4A. Some local public official (e.g, a mayor, municipalcouncilperson, provincial official)
B14. To what extent do you trust the national government?
B32. To what extent do you trust the Mayor's office of your municipality?

have chosen leftist political parties to be in charge of the government. Daniel Ortega, former president of Nicaragua from 1985 to 1990, and leader of the Frente Sandinista de Liberación Nacional (FSLN) was reelected as president in November 2006. In Ecuador, Rafael Correa won the presidency in the second round of the election with the support of leftists' political parties and indigenous movements.

The movement of Latin America to the left has led journalists, political analysts and political scientists to look for explanations. The most widespread of these suggests that Latin Americans' vote for political parties on the left is a backlash against the neoliberal model implemented in the region mainly during the 1990s. A deeper concern is the implications of this shift to the left for the stability of democracy under these new leftist's governments. This chapter attempts to explore both of these issues using AmericasBarometer 2006-2007 public opinion data set.

To anticipate, the research comes to three main conclusions. First, Latin Americans are not voting leftist parties because they are against neoliberal policies. The current shift to the left in Latin America is far more a result of popular discontent with the voters' economic situation than anything else. Second, the electoral prospect that leftist parties have by capitalizing on social discontent depend heavily upon the number of "untainted opposition" parties available in the political system. In countries like Brazil and Uruguay where leftist parties embody the only "untainted opposition," it was easier for them to capitalize on popular discontent than in Mexico, where a party on the right also represented an "untainted opposition." Finally, rather than a threat to the stability of democracy the findings of the research show that the rise of the left is actually good news for the future of democracy in the region because Latin Americans have been able to demonstrate to themselves, at least, that governments can now incorporate the formerly excluded opposition left-oriented parties into the political game. Democracy is at risk when, as was the case in Mexico for over 50 years, opposition parties are always on the losers' side. Throughout the region, for many years, several leftist political parties were consistent losers in the electoral game, leading some of them to dismiss electoral democracy as a valid means to achieve power. Therefore, the arrival of left-leaning parties to the government of several Latin American countries, rather than being a cause of concern, should be considered an indicator of a healthy democracy and a mechanism to strengthen democratic support among citizens. Latin Americans are proving capable of making their political leaders accountable, removing them from office when they do not accomplish what was expected of them, and changing those in charge of the government by voting for "untainted parties." The recent shift towards the left in Latin America has helped to intensify and strengthen democracy in the region by incorporating losers into the political game.

The first section of this chapter discusses the argument that the vote for leftist parties in Latin America is a backlash against the neoliberal model implemented in the region. This argument is tested for three country cases in which leftist parties have been increasing their electoral support during the last decade: Brazil, Mexico and Uruguay. The second section describes each of these country cases and states the theories and hypotheses used to evaluate the argument. In the third section, I present the models and results of the statistical tests which show that Latin-Americans´ vote for left-of-center parties is not a rejection of market-oriented policies but a reaction to the state of the economy. The second argument tested is that the vote for the left

Appendix 4

Coefficients

		B	S.E.	Wald	df	Sig.	Exp(B)
Step 1(a)	Male	.085	.031	7.634	1	.006	1.089
	Age	.057	.011	27.439	1	.000	1.058
	Urban sector	.193	.036	27.923	1	.000	1.213
	Education	.172	.025	47.993	1	.000	1.187
	Wealth	.006	.010	.377	1	.539	1.006
	Government efficacy	-.003	.001	17.936	1	.000	.997
	Political Knowledge	.004	.001	34.513	1	.000	1.004
	Municipal service perception	.012	.001	185.704	1	.000	1.012
	Trust in the Municipality	.006	.001	116.514	1	.000	1.006
	Trust in the Nacional Government	-.001	.001	1.837	1	.175	.999
	Interest in Politics	-.109	.017	40.742	1	.000	.897
	Help request in the mayor's office	.001	.000	2.378	1	.123	1.001
	Help request in a Ministry	.001	.001	3.664	1	.056	1.001
	Delinquency victimization	.000	.000	.011	1	.917	1.000
	Corruption victimization	.014	.020	.481	1	.488	1.014
	Ecuador	1.314	.099	177.803	1	.000	3.719
	El Salvador	.912	.096	89.407	1	.000	2.489
	Guatemala	1.577	.101	245.647	1	.000	4.842
	Honduras	.685	.097	49.583	1	.000	1.983
	Nicaragua	1.810	.100	327.056	1	.000	6.111
	Peru	1.048	.097	117.442	1	.000	2.853
	Dominican R.	1.543	.098	246.783	1	.000	4.680
	Chile	1.505	.098	234.202	1	.000	4.503
	CRica	1.221	.100	147.967	1	.000	3.392
	Guyana	1.550	.105	216.838	1	.000	4.713
	Jamaica	2.023	.109	345.640	1	.000	7.563
	Haiti	1.022	.103	98.012	1	.000	2.780
	Mexico	1.145	.102	126.660	1	.000	3.143
	Uruguay	.894	.101	79.082	1	.000	2.445
	Brazil	.753	.101	55.351	1	.000	2.124
	Venezuela	.961	.104	85.007	1	.000	2.615
	Constant	-2.695	.148	330.785	1	.000	.068

b. Dependent Variable: Decentralization versus Centralization.

VI. Is the Vote for the left a Risk or Opportunity for Democracy in Latin America?

Rosario Queirolo*

Abstract

What is the impact that market-oriented economic reforms have had on the vote for leftist parties in Latin America? Are Latin Americans voting for the left based on their ideological stances or because parties on the left merely benefit from voters' discontent towards traditional parties? Latin Americans can vote left because they want more state intervention in the economy, a more egalitarian economic distribution, or more investment in social policies. Alternatively, it is possible to argue that voters are not policy oriented, they only care about outcomes, and they are voting left because the neoliberal model failed to deliver sustainable economic development and to overcome the endemic problem of unemployment. My central argument is that the recent increase of leftist parties in Latin America comes about as a result of voters punishing political parties that were unable to improve the economic well-being of their electorates. In addition, this article compares the attitudes towards democracy of those Latin Americans identified as leftists with those that declared themselves as rightists to explore if the movement to the left represents a risk or opportunity for democracy. The evidence from AmericasBarometer 2006-07 indicates that leftists are not significantly less democratic than rightists.

Is the vote for the left a risk for democracy in Latin America? Since the final years of the Twentieth Century, many Latin American countries have elected governments that identified themselves with the ideological left. In 1999, Hugo Chávez, a former coup plotter, was elected President of Venezuela after campaigning against the "Washington consensus" model, and promising to upend the old social order and improve the lives of the poor. Brazil also veered toward the left with the victory of the Workers Party (Partido dos Trabalhadores, PT) in the 2002 general elections. In Argentina, a left-wing political faction of the Peronist Party headed by Néstor Kirchner won the 2003 election; while in neighboring Uruguay, the Broad Front (Frente Amplio) a left-leaning coalition party which has steadily increased its electoral participation since it was founded in 1971, finally gained the presidency in 2004. Chile has been governed by a center-left coalition since its return to democracy; the chair of the government has alternated between social democrats and socialists, and in the 2005 election a female socialist candidate became President. Also in 2005, Bolivians decided to grant Evo Morales, the presidential candidate of Movimiento al Socialismo (MAS), and an important leader of the coca producers' union, the chance to govern one of the poorest countries in Latin America. Manuel López Obrador, the presidential candidate for the Partido Revolucionario Democrático (PRD) in México, lost the presidential election held in July 2006 by less than 1% of the votes in a very controversial and disputed election. More recently, at the end of 2006, Nicaragua and Ecuador

---

* Professor of Political Science at the Universidad de Montevideo.

represents a risk for the embryonic Latin American democracies. Rather than weaken democratic prospects, the success of several leftist parties in the region makes democracy stronger by channeling social discontent through institutional mechanisms. The fourth section explains this argument and states the hypotheses used to assess its validity. The fifth section shows the statistical results of these tests performed using the Americas Barometer 2006-2007 dataset. To conclude, I discuss the implications for democracy and political accountability in the region.

First Argument: Voting Left as a Backlash Against the Washington Consensus

During 1980s and 1990s, the "neoliberal model" based on the so-called "Washington Consensus," was implemented to various degrees in Latin American countries. Market oriented economic reforms were initiated in the 1980s, or even earlier in Chile, Uruguay, Argentina, and Colombia (Morley, Machado and Pettinato 1999).[1] In this chapter the terms "Washington Consensus," "market-oriented economic reforms," "structural reforms," "neoliberal model," or "orthodox policies" are used interchangeably, and it is assumed that all of these terms refer to the same set of policies described by Williamson as the so-called "Washington Consensus." To remind the reader, the set of policy reforms grouped as "Washington Consensus" can be summarized as involving fiscal discipline, public expenditure restrictions, tax reform, interest rate liberalization, a competitive exchange rate, trade liberalization, liberalization of restrictions on foreign direct investment, privatization, deregulation, and reinforcement of property rights.

Many scholars have undertaken the task of measuring the success or failure of the Washington Consensus (Dutch 2003; Escaith and Morley 2001; Huber and Solt 2004; Kuczynski and Williamson 2003; Lora and Panizza 2002; Lora, Panizza and Quispe-Agnoli 2004; Stallings and Peres 2000), and many others have analyzed the impact of particular policy reforms (Lora and Barrera 1997). Regardless of the differences between those studies, they agree that after two decades of reforms the expected results of economic growth was far from universally achieved. While all agree that fiscal responsibility has spread throughout the region, and hyper inflation seems to be thing of the past, sustainable economic growth and, for our purposes more importantly, improvement of social indicators have been illusive. The Chilean case is an important exception to the overall uneven pattern, but it is difficult to point to other cases in which growth and social indicators have improved steadily.

Regardless of the objective outcomes of the neoliberal model, Latin Americans' disenchantment with it can be seen everywhere. Many of the strongest supporters of the model have recognized that the outcome was not the one that they were hoping for. International organizations, which strongly supported the "neoliberal model" such as the International Monetary Fund, the World Bank and the Inter-American Development Bank, have acknowledged that the reforms did not produce the expected results, and they now suggest four different types of follow-up reforms to overcome this failure: "crisis proofing, completing first-generation reforms, advancing second-generation reforms, and improving equality" (IDEA 2004). From this

---

[1] Morley et al. (1999) point out that most of the rise in the trade and financial reform indexes during the 1970s are due to the policies implemented in Chile, Uruguay, Argentina, and Colombia.

perspective, it was not the reforms that were at fault, but the failure to implement them fully and effectively that these follow-up reforms are attempting to address. Many scholars who initially supported the "Washington Consensus" as the way to achieve development later moved away from this idea, and became its critics: Jeffrey Sachs (2005), Joseph Stiglitz (2002) and Dani Rodrik (2001) are leaving examples of this shift. Some have argued that the international community has shown signs of "reform fatigue" (Edwards 1997).[2] The lack of public support for the Washington Consensus can also be seen among the general public; there is a widespread loss of confidence in the benefits of pro-market reforms among opinion leaders, and a less proactive stance toward reforms is the current mainstream among Latin America's policymakers (Lora, Panizza and Quispe-Agnoli 2004; Panizza and Yañez 2005).

In the view of many political analysts, the current increase in the vote for the left in Latin America is a consequence of "reform fatigue." Simply stated, this argument says that because voters are tired of market-oriented economic reforms and their consequences, they are voting in favor of parties that allow more state intervention in the economy. *The Economist* magazine states this argument as follows: "Rightly or wrongly, voters blamed the slowdown on the free-market reforms known as the Washington Consensus. As happens in democracies, they started to vote for the opposition- which tended to be on the left." (The Economist 2006).

However, this is not the only answer. Others have pointed out that, behind this shift to the left, there lies primarily a need for a change. Popular discontent at traditional parties unable to solve problems of poverty, corruption and inequality led Latin Americans to vote for political parties perceived as being more likely to deliver a better standard of living. To put it simply, according to this view, Latin America's shift to the left is rooted less in ideological stances than in a desire to punish incumbents for poor economic performance.

This chapter disentangles what is true in each of these arguments. What is the impact that market-oriented economic reforms have had on the vote for leftist parties in Latin America? Are Latin Americans voting for the left depending on their ideological stances or because parties on the left merely benefit from voters' discontent towards traditional parties? Latin Americans can vote left because they want more state intervention in the economy, a more egalitarian economic distribution, or more investment in social policies. After a decade of neoliberal economic reforms, they may be claiming that it's "time for a change" (Schlesinger 1986), and consequently, may behave in a policy-oriented way. Alternatively, it is possible to argue that voters are not policy oriented, they only care about outcomes, and they are voting left because the neoliberal model failed to deliver sustainable economic development and to overcome the endemic problem of unemployment. These two explanations are not incompatible, both can be true. Latin Americans may be voting left because they do not want more market-friendly economic policies, and also because they are punishing incumbent parties for poor economic performance.

My central argument is that the recent increase of leftist parties in Latin America comes about as a result of voters punishing political parties that were unable to improve the economic

---

[2] "Reform fatigue" is a concept coined by Sebastian Edwards (1997) that encompasses citizens' tiredness with the sacrifices required by economic reforms in their respective countries.

well-being of their electorates. Most Latin Americans have faced economic hardship during successive governments under a variety of political parties, and recent research demonstrates that voters have long-term economic memories (Benton 2005) and punish not only the incumbent party for the material suffering; they also rebuke parties that governed before the incumbent came to power. Left-of-center parties took advantage of this popular discontent and capitalized on social and economic dissatisfaction when they were outside the governing coalitions and remained in the opposition. As a result, by voting left-oriented parties, Latin Americans seem to be looking for credible political alternatives to the status quo rather than becoming anti-market in their policy positions.

Theories, Hypotheses and Country Cases

Latin American voting behavior is usually understood as being highly volatile and unpredictable due to the lack of strong party and ideological identifications. Latin Americans seem mainly to base their vote choice on short-term factors such as economic conditions (Cantón and Jorrat 2002; Roberts and Wibbels 1999) and candidate image (Echegaray 2005; Weyland 2003). It is within this context that the recent victories of leftist parties have become puzzling. If ideology and party identification are not relevant voting clues in Latin America (Echegaray 2005), why are voters choosing parties identified with the ideological left? Is the vote for leftist parties another example of economic voting theory according to which voters punish the incumbent party for poor economic results? Are electorates in Latin America mainly choosing leftist parties because their candidates are, on average more appealing than are the candidates from parties of the center and right? Or, alternatively, are Latin-Americans becoming more ideological and policy-oriented by voting for the left because ideology does indeed matter and voters are rejecting the neoliberal paradigm?

Taking into account the research on voting behavior done on Western Europe and the United States, and building on the results of previous studies about Latin American voting, I will test two theories to explain the rise of the left in Latin America: *economic voting theory*, and *the cleavages created by political processes* (Przeworski and Sprague 1986; Torcal and Mainwaring 2003). In particular, the individual level analysis aims to understand what the role is of economic evaluations (economic voting theory), and ideology and policy issues (cleavages created by political processes) in the recent rise of the left in Latin America. At the same time, I will be testing if Latin Americans are policy-oriented (ideology and policy issues are significant determinants of the vote), outcome-oriented (economic evaluations are the significant predictors of the vote), or both. The following sub-sections briefly describe each of the said theories, summarize the major research done in Latin America using each of them, and go over the main hypotheses and variables by which the theories are going to be tested.

Economic voting theory

The literature on voting behavior in Latin America is dominated by the economic voting explanation. Economic voting theory states that if the economy is doing fine, voters will reelect the incumbent party; while in bad times, citizens will punish the incumbent at the ballot box. The theory has taken four major forms: pocketbook vote, sociotropic vote (Kinder and Kiewiet 1981), retrospective vote, and prospective vote (MacKuen, Erikson and Stimson 1992). These distinctions lead to four possible combinations in which citizens can appraise the economic situation: evaluating how good or bad the economic situation of the country has been during the past (retrospective sociotropic), taking into account voters' expectations of how the country's economic situation is going to be in the future (prospective sociotropic), thinking on how good or bad their family's economic situation has been in the recent past (retrospective pocketbook), or considering their expectations for their family's economic future (prospective pocketbook).

Economic voting theory has noticeably proved its predictive power in the stable economic and political contexts of the United States and Western Europe (Fiorina 1981; Kinder and Kiewiet 1981; Lewis-Beck 1986; Lewis-Beck 1988; Lewis-Beck and Belluci 1982; MacKuen, Erikson and Stimson 1992; Nadeau and Lewis-Beck 2001). And there is a consensus regarding the idea that Americans and Europeans respond "to changes in general economic conditions much more than to changes in the circumstances of personal economic life" (Kinder 1998).

In Latin America, scholars have tested the relationship between economic downturns and voting for incumbent parties in single-country case studies (Cantón and Jorrat 2002; Domínguez and McCann 1995; Mora y Araujo and Smith 1984; Remmer 2003; Roberts and Arce 1998; Seligson and Gómez 1989; Weyland 1998), and through comparative studies (Echegaray 2005; Remmer 1991; Roberts and Wibbels 1999; Remmer 1993), but the evidence is far from conclusive. Economic evaluations matter for Latin-Americans depending on the election. For example, Weyland found that Venezuelans were Pocketbook voters from 1989 to 1993 (Weyland 1998), but Sociotropic voters when they elected Hugo Chávez in 1998 (Weyland 2003). Cantón and Jorrat (2002) and Echegaray (2005) also find that the impact of the economy on Latin Americans' vote choice varies across countries and elections. Despite these distinctions, scholars confirm that voters in Latin America tend to treat elections as plebiscites on the economic performance and capabilities of the government.

If economic factors are important determinants of the fortune of incumbents, are there any specific economic conditions that favor leftist parties in comparison with centrist or rightist parties? Following the economic voting explanation, I expect that voters who evaluate negatively the economic situation will punish the incumbent. In countries where the incumbent is a leftist party, citizens will reward or punish it depending on the economic performance. But in countries where leftist parties were never in charge of the government and represent a "credible" or "untainted" opposition, electorates which are economically dissatisfied with the economy will cast their vote in favor of them.

H1: *The more negatively a voter evaluates the national economic situation, the greater the probability he or she will vote for the opposition. In particular, voters who are discontented will reward leftist parties when they were not in charge of the government.*

To put it simply, if a voter has a negative economic evaluation (x1) and leftist parties represent a "credible" or "untainted" opposition (x2), he or she will vote for the left (y).

The variables to test the economic voting theory are four: retrospective sociotropic vote, retrospective pocket-book vote, prospective sociotropic vote and retrospective sociotropic vote. *Sociotropic vote* measures the evaluation of the country's economic situation; the higher the value, the worse the evaluation. *Pocketbook vote* measures the evaluation of the family's economic situation; the higher the value of the variable, the worse the family's economic assessment is. *Prospective* measures the expectations regarding the economic future, while *retrospective* measures the evaluation of the country economic situation in comparison with the past.

Cleavages Created by Political Process

In determining which theory and voting clues best explain the vote for leftist parties in Latin America, it is essential to include ideology. Ideology is regarded as one of the most influential voting clues. Electorates use the overarching continuum between left and right, or from liberal to conservative, as a shortcut to processing political information and making their electoral decisions. Since Converse (1964) there has been a great deal of debate about how readily voters rely on ideology when voting, and to what extent citizens organize their political opinions around the ideological dimension. The same doubts are cast regarding the importance of ideology to predict Latin Americans' voting behavior. Echegaray (2005) considers that ideological clues are an irrelevant source of guidance for Latin American voters, but he does not empirically test this contention. Differing from Echegaray's position, this study will test the impact of ideological clues on the vote for leftist parties. Two main reasons make the inclusion of ideology reasonable.

First of all, around seven out of ten Latin Americans were able to place themselves in the ideological dimension according to the AmericasBarometer for 2006-2007. This percentage varies depending on the country; left and right ideological labels mean more to Chileans and Uruguayans than to Argentineans. But, as a first appraisal, ideological thinking is part of most Latin Americans' political behavior. Second, there is empirical research pointing to ideology as a relevant voting clue for Latin Americans (Cameron 1994; Torcal and Mainwaring 2003). Torcal and Mainwaring (2003) point out: "class emerges as a major cleavage in party systems to the extent that parties of the left emphasize class issues," and they called this phenomenon the cleavage created by political processes (Przeworski and Sprague 1986; Torcal and Mainwaring 2003).[3] This theoretical approach to cleavage formation pays attention to how cleavages are created by political elites and political factors. The left/right ideological division can also be considered a cleavage created by political process. In other words, politicians can activate this cleavage as a way to get votes. All this suggests that it is appropriate to test for ideological clues:

H2: *Ideological self-placement is likely to determine the vote for the left irrespective of social and structural determinants.*

---

[3] Torcal and Mainwaring (2003) test the existence of these political cleavages in the Chilean case with three cultural-ideological divisions that can be used by political leaders to articulate conflict: the authoritarian/democratic cultural division, the perception of social inequality, and religious differences.

An alternative way to test the ideological cleavage is to analyze if policy positions are determinants of voting behavior. Voting for the left is usually associated with support for government involvement and regulation of the economy, income redistribution, and an increase in social spending (Fuchs and Klingermann 1990; Inglehart and Klingermann 1976; Kitschelt and Hellemans 1990). In addition, and due to the difficulty in obtaining survey data that deals with citizens' perceptions and opinions towards market-oriented economic reforms, the analysis of policy preferences is the best way to approach this issue. Consequently, I hypothesize that:

H3: *Those Latin Americans who support government involvement and regulation of the economy, income redistribution and an increase in social spending will be more likely to vote for leftist parties, while those who are against these policy issues will be more likely to vote for rightist parties.*

Ideology is measured by the ideological self-placement of the respondent in a dimension that ranges from "0" meaning Left, to "10" meaning Right. Different policy issues are also used as independent variables to test the ideological cleavage: support for privatization, support for agrarian reform, support for nationalization, opinion towards redistribution, opinion about state regulations and state interventionism.

The Cases

My argument that the recent increase of leftist parties in Latin America comes about as a result of voters' punishing political parties that were unable to improve the economic well-being of their electorates and rewarding "untainted political parties" is tested in three country cases: Brazil, Mexico and Uruguay. I argue that leftist parties can capitalize social discontent when: 1) they represent a credible or untainted opposition, and even more so when 2) they are the only untainted opposition in the political system. A "credible" or "untainted" political party is a party that was never in charge of the government and cannot be held responsible for the country's welfare.

Brazil, Mexico and Uruguay are all cases in which leftist parties have increased their share of the vote since 1980s, but the electoral trajectories followed by left-of-center parties in each country differ. In Brazil, leftist parties gained access to the government in 2002. Before that, in 1994, the Partido Social Democracia Brasileira (PSDB), a social democrat party, carried Fernando Henrique Cardoso to the presidency. However, when the PSDB was elected to Brazil's national government, it had already moved to the right of the ideological scale (Power 2001/2002). Therefore, the first time that a left-of-center party gained access to Brazil's national government after the return to democracy was in 2002 through Luis Inácio "Lula" da Silva, the long-time leader of the Partido dos Trabalhadores (PT). After the experience of the PSDB government, the most "credible" opposition was embodied by the PT.

In Uruguay, leftist parties have progressively increased their electoral participation since the return to democracy in 1984, and after twenty years of democracy, in 2004 a left-leaning coalition called the Encuentro Progresista-Frente Amplio (EP-FA) won the presidency. The

search for new alternatives has led Uruguayans to vote for the Frente Amplio, a left-leaning coalition party which represents the only "credible" or "untainted" opposition after a long succession of Partido Colorado and Partido Nacional governments.

Mexico represents a different example for the same phenomenon. Leftist parties, in particular the Partido Revolucionario Democrático (PRD), have increased their share of the vote during the 1990s, and by doing so, have helped to raise competitiveness in the Mexican electoral arena. The PRD received almost a fifth of the votes cast in the 1994 and 2000 presidential elections, and in 2006 it lost the presidency by fewer than 500,000 votes in a highly controversial vote count. However, the electorate's search for something new ended up with their favoring the two credible and untainted opposition parties: PAN, a center-right political party and the PRD, a leftist party.

All these leftist parties, PT, PRD, and EP-FA, are examples of professional parties: they care about party building, they have relatively strong party organizations, and they mobilize political support in addition to social support. In that sense, they are more similar to Concertación in Chile than to Movimiento al Socialismo (MAS) in Bolivia or Hugo Chávez's party, the Movimiento Quinta República in Venezuela. They are usually categorized as the "institutional" left in Latin America, contrary to the "populist" left represented mainly by the Movimiento Quinta República. Regardless of these commonalities, there are several differences between these countries that make the case selection relevant. I will only refer to those characteristics that are pertinent for the purpose of this research: differences in their party and political systems, and differences in the level of economic reforms.

The differences between Brazilian, Mexican and Uruguayan party and political systems are large. Brazil is usually defined as a case of party underdevelopment and weakly-established political institutions (Ames 2001; Mainwaring 1999; Mainwaring and Scully 1995). Its multiparty system has been described as "highly fragmented, electoral volatility is comparatively high, more than one-third of sitting legislators change parties during a term, and individualism, clientelism and personalism rather than programmatic appeals dominate electoral campaigns" (Samuels 2006). For a long time, Mexico was characterized as a weakly-institutionalized political system (Mainwaring and Scully 1995) with single-party dominance in the shape of the long-ruling Partido Institucional Revolucionario (PRI). The PRI was in charge of the national government from 1929 to 2000, and opposition parties were unable to win a majority in the lower chamber of congress until 1997 when the single, dominant-party system was broken in favor of a multiparty system. It was not until 2000 that the Partido de Acción Nacional (PAN), a right-leaning party, ousted the PRI from the presidency. Uruguay has had a very stable party system (Mainwaring 1995), with three major political parties, Partido Colorado (PC), Partido Nacional (PN) and Frente Amplio (FA), and one minor party, Partido Independiente (PI). It was with the emergence of the Frente Amplio in 1971 that the party system experienced a major change evolving from a two-party system to a multiparty system (Gillespie and González 1989; González 1991).

To put it simply, Brazil, Mexico and Uruguay are dissimilar in their levels of party system institutionalization and numbers of political parties. Mainwaring and Scully (1995) classify Brazil as an inchoate party system, Mexico as a hegemonic party system, and Uruguay as an

institutionalized one. Several things changed by the end of the 1990s - one is that Mexico can no longer be considered a hegemonic party system. In terms of the number of parties, Mexico and Uruguay have experienced important transformations by becoming multiparty systems and raising their level of party competition. Recent research shows that the number of parties affects the way in which voters hold governments accountable; multiparty systems strengthen voters' ability to punish several parties at a time, and therefore, popular discontent may be lower in countries with more permissive electoral rules that allow small parties to gain congressional representation (Benton 2005).

Market-oriented economic reforms were also implemented very differently in Brazil, Mexico and Uruguay. Brazil and Mexico are classified as slow reformers: they started reforms later and adopted less structural reforms; while Uruguay is considered a gradual reformer: reforms were adopted earlier, but they were milder and carried out in a gradual way (Lora 1997/2001). The differences in the reforms pursued in Brazil, Mexico and Uruguay also depend on the area being reformed. Brazil presents some of the highest privatization reform and labor reform indexes. On the other hand, Mexico ranks low on their tax reform and labor reform indexes, but high on the financial reform index. Finally Uruguay has one of the lowest levels of privatization in the region but one of the highest indexes of trade reform (Lora 1997/2001).

The Model and Results

In order to test if policy preferences or ideological identifications are more important than economic assessments when Latin Americans vote leftist parties, I use survey data collected in the three country cases at the time of their pivotal elections. The Uruguayan data comes from a pre-election survey carried out by CIFRA, González, Raga y Asociados before the 2004 election, the election in which the left got access to the government.[4] The survey is national and includes 1,500 respondents. The comparison between the percentage intending to vote for leftist parties in this survey with the proportion that actually voted for the left when the elections were held, strengthen the validity of the analysis: the election result was 54% and the survey predicted a 60%.

To test the hypotheses in the 2002 Brazilian presidential election, when PT won for the first time the presidency, I use data from Brazil's 2002 National Election Study (BNES), a national post-election voter behavior survey which includes 2,513 respondents[5]. Because this survey does not include questions about economic evaluations, I also test the model with a 1998 pre-election national survey carried out by Datafolha which includes 4,380 cases and the data collection occurred during July. As is the case for Uruguay, Brazilian survey data also fits very well the proportion intending to vote left with the proportion that actually voted left: in 2002, 68% of the respondents said that had voted left and the actual percentage was 77%[6].

---

[4] I would like to thank the directors of CIFRA, Luis E. González and Adriana Raga for giving me access to this data, and generously allowed me to include some specific questions in the 2004 survey.
[5] I want to thank Rachel Meneguello and Simone Aranha from the Center for Studies on Public Opinion (CESOP) at the University of Campinas (UNICAMP) in Brazil for giving me access to Datafolha and BNES data.
[6] This result is counterintuitive because post-election surveys usually over represent the winner.

The vote for leftist parties in the 2000 Mexican presidential election is analyzed through the Post-Electoral Cross-Section survey carried out as part of the Mexico 2000 Panel Study[7]. This survey includes 1,199 cases collected from July 6 to July 9 at respondents' homes. As for Brazil and Uruguay, the proportions intending to vote left according to the Mexican data correspond very closely with proportions actually voting left when the elections were held, ensuring the validity of the analysis. For the 2000 Mexican post-electoral survey, it is only possible to separate the vote for PRD (not for others leftist parties), and the comparison between the survey and election proportions is the following: 15% to 19% respectively. In all the surveys, data was collected by personal, door-to-door interviews in the respondents' homes[8].

The dependent variable is a dummy variable that measures the intention to vote for a left-of-center party, value 1 means that the person intended to vote for the left, while 0 represents the vote intention for the remaining political parties. The following political parties were classified as left-of-center in the presidential elections analyzed: in Uruguay, the Frente Amplio and Nuevo Espacio/Partido Independiente; in 1998 Brazil, the PT, PPS and PSTU; in 2002 Brazil, the PT, PSB, and PSTU; and in Mexico only PRD because it was not possible to separate the vote for other leftist parties that have been put together under the "other" category in the dataset.

I have used two independent variables, *sociotropic vote* and *pocketbook vote*, to test the economic voting theory. *Sociotropic vote* measures the evaluation of the country's economic situation; thus, the higher the value, the worse the evaluation. *Pocketbook vote* measures the evaluation of the family's economic situation. The *Retrospective Sociotropic, Prospective Sociotropic, Retrospective Pocketbook* and *Prospective Pocketbook* variables measure citizens' economic assessments of the country and their own situation in comparison with the past and economic expectations for the future. *The Sociotropic vote* and *Pocketbook vote* in 1998 Brazilian survey, measure respondent's evaluation of the *Plano Real* for the country and for voters' own life. Higher values correspond to negative evaluations.

Ideology is one of the independent variables I used to test the political cleavage; I measured it by situating the ideological self-placement of the respondent in a dimension that ranges from "1" meaning left to "10" meaning right. *Ideology* is measured in two ways. The other way to measure an interviewee's ideology and test the political cleavage is through a series of questions asking citizens' opinions toward a series of policy issues: state interventionism, redistribution, state regulations of private firms, agrarian reform, nationalization, and privatizations. Higher values in each of these policies correspond with liberal positions, which I expect to be negative correlated with the vote for leftist parties.

Other variables are included in the model as control variables: *age, education, family income, household level,* and *urban voter (residence). Age, education* and *family income* have a

---

[7] Participants in the 2000 Mexico Panel Study included (in alphabetical order): Miguel Basañez, Roderic Camp, Wayne Cornelius, Jorge Domínguez, Federico Estévez, Joseph Klesner, Chappell Lawson (Principal Investigator), Beatriz Magaloni, James McCann, Alejandro Moreno, Pablo Parás, and Alejandro Poiré. Funding for the study was provided by the National Science Foundation (SES-9905703) and *Reforma* newspaper.

[8] The sample size of each survey is reduced after deleting all the missing values. The final N of is reported in the tables that present the regression results.

straightforward interpretation; low values denote young people, low education, and low income. *Household level* is measured in two ways. First, as an ordinal variable that classifies the interviewees in categories based on an indicator of their household, higher values correspond to higher socioeconomic level; and second as a houseware index in which higher values also correspond with high socioeconomic level. *Urban Voter* is a dummy variable representing the region in which the respondent lives; it takes the value of 1 when the person lives in an urban area and 0 when he/she lives in a rural area or in other smaller cities and towns.

Finally, I also include partisanship as control variable using four dummy variables; each dummy represents one category of partisanship: party identification with left-of-center parties, party identification with parties at the center, party identification with right-of-center parties and those that lack partisanship. Each category is entered into the model as a dummy variable that takes the value of 1 when the person belongs to it and 0 when he/she does not. Those that have no partisanship are the base category in the regression.

Results

The first thing to notice is that economic voting explains Latin Americans' vote for leftist parties in Brazil and Uruguay, but not in Mexico. Regressions results in Table VI-1 indicate that Brazilians and Uruguayans who negatively evaluated the economic situation, tended to vote more for left-of-center parties than for center or rightist ones. Citizens who were discontented with the results that the economy had on their own lives, or in the country's well-being, voted for left-of-center parties, while those that made a positive evaluation reelected the incumbent government or voted for other non-leftist party. The positive signs on the sociotropic and pocketbook coefficients in Table 1 indicate that the worse the economic evaluation, the higher the probability to vote for the left. This evidence supports hypothesis 1, which states that "the more negatively a voter evaluates the national economic situation, the greater the probability he or she will vote for the opposition. In particular, voters who are discontented will reward leftist parties when they were not in charge of the government." In Brazil and Uruguay, leftist parties were not responsible for the government until 2002 and 2004, respectively.

However, Mexico presents a different case. In the 2000 presidential election, economic assessments neither favored nor undermined leftist parties' electoral chances. As other scholars have pointed out, PRI's defeat in 2000 has nothing to do with the economy; on the contrary, the economic achievements of Zedillo's presidency were acknowledged by most Mexicans (Lawson and McCann 2004). In other words, economic evaluations did not favor leftist parties' electoral chances.

Ideological considerations also play a role in explaining Latin Americans' voting behavior, but this does not mean that voters chose leftist parties at the ballot box because they are rejecting neoliberalism. Ideological identifications reach significance in Brazil and Uruguay, but not in Mexico; and policy stances are not relevant voting cues in none of them, with the exemptions of privatizations and the agrarian reform in Brazil. In order for political cleavages to become active, politicians need to emphasize them. Torcal and Mainwaring (2003) point out that

political cleavages are created by political elites as a way to get votes. The ideological cleavage only becomes relevant if political leaders and political parties structure political conflict in ideological terms. Ideology, measured as the individual self placement on the ideological scale, is a significant predictor of the vote for the left in Brazil and Uruguay: a one unit increase in ideology (one space to the right on the ideological scale) decreases the probability of voting for a left-of-center party rather than voting for a center or rightist party. This evidence supports Hypothesis 2 which states that "ideological self-placement is likely to determine the vote for the left irrespective of social and structural determinants."

On the other side, Mexican politics revolved around a regime cleavage (pro-PRI vs. anti-PRI) at least until 2000. During that time, the ideological dimension remained inactive, or at least, as a minor-league dimension (Domínguez and McCann 1995, Domínguez and McCann 1996, Greene 2002, Klesner 2004, Klesner 2005, Magaloni and Poiré 2004a, Moreno 1998, Moreno 1999). Regression results demonstrate that Mexicans' ideological self-placement does not determine their vote. In 2000, individuals who placed themselves on the left side of the ideological dimension did not significantly differ in their vote from those that placed themselves on the right.

An alternative way to test the ideological cleavage, and the argument that Latin Americans' shift toward the left is an anti-market response, is to analyze if policy positions are determinants of voting behavior. To do so, I include a series of variables that measure electorates' opinions towards: state interventionism, redistribution, state regulation of private firms, agrarian reform, nationalization, and privatizations. The results shown in Table VI-1 indicate that with the exception of the opinions towards privatizations and agrarian reform in Brazil, none of these variables are significant determinants to vote for a left-of-center political party. These results refute Hypothesis 3 which states that "Latin Americans who support government involvement and regulation of the economy, income redistribution and an increase in social spending will be more likely to vote for leftist parties, while those who are against these policy issues will be more likely to vote for rightist parties." Despite ideology being a relevant voting predictor, none of the policy issues traditionally associated with the ideological distinction explains why Latin Americans choose a leftist party. These results strengthen the argument that Latin Americans' voting behavior is not an ideological rejection of the Washington Consensus.

Latin Americans who had voted left in these pivotal elections do not have a clear socioeconomic profile. Contrary to the 2006 Latinobarómetro Report which hypothesizes that poor Latin Americans might be voting left, while wealthy ones will be voting right (Latinobarómetro 2006), regression results reported in Table 1 dismisses this argument. Only in Brazil, those with a low family income have a higher probability to vote leftist parties in 1998 and 2002, but this pattern does not exist in Mexico or Uruguay. Neither other socioeconomic variables like education or the household socioeconomic level reach significance in any of these countries.

Table VI-1. Vote Determinants for leftist Parties: Economic Voting vs. Ideology

Independent Variables:	Brazil 1998	Brazil 2002	Mexico 2000	Uruguay 2004
Economic Voting				
Sociotropic Vote	0.344***			0.416**
	(.068)			(.182)
Pocket-book Vote	0.686***			0.369**
	(.062)			(.191)
Sociotropic Retrospective			-0.038	0.054
			(.182)	(.216)
Pocketbook Retrospective			0.141	-0.037
			(.213)	(.222)
Sociotropic Prospective				0.403
				(.294)
Pocketbook Prospective				-0.418
				(.284)
Ideology				
Ideological selfplacement		-0.064**	-0.037	-0.798***
		(.020)	(.048)	(.098)
Opinion state interventionism		-0.006		
		(.012)		
Opinion redistribution			-0.010	
			(.055)	
Opinion state regulations		-0.019		
		(.015)		
Opinion agrarian reform		-0.431**		
		(0.141)		
Opinion nationalization		0.015		
		(.015)		
Opinion privatizations	-0.248***		-0.051	
	(.048)		(.078)	
Control variables				
Education	0.039	-0.002	0.102	-0.138
	(.029)	(.017)	(.149)	(.086)
Family income	-.001**	-0.001***		0.094
	(.000)	(.000)		(.064)
Household SES			-0.106	
			(.213)	
Household SES (houseware index)			-0.109	
			(.133)	
Age	0.001	-0.018***	0.012	-0.010
	(.000)	-0.005	(.012)	(.008)
Urban Voter		-0.167	-0.084	-0.903**
		(.157)	(.237)	(.293)
Partisanship (1)				
Left	1.967***	2.069***	2.736***	dropped
	(.133)	(.225)	(.445)	
Right	-0.449***	-0.662***	-2.651***	-2.557***
	(.128)	(.160)	(.431)	(.335)
Center	0.065	-0.970		
	(.124)	(1.289)		
Constant	-2.713***	2.496***	-0.910***	3.806**
	(0.230)	(.594)	(.431)	(1.505)
Pseudo R squared	0.22	0.18	0.58	0.49
Wald chi2	577***	181***	198***	185520***
Number of observations	2900	1215	710	571

(1) No partisanship is the reference category. *p< .10, ** p< .05, *** p< .01
Note: Entries are binary logit coefficients with robust standard errors
In 2004, STATA dropped party identification with leftist parties from the regression
because they perfectly predict voting for Leftist parties.

Partisanship is a strong predictor of voting for leftist parties in these pivotal elections in Brazil, Mexico and Uruguay; it reaches statistical significance in all of them. Latin Americans identified with a leftist political party tend to vote for a left-of-center party in presidential elections, while those identified with a party that belongs to the ideological right also vote within the same bloc.

To sum up, the evidence from these three country cases show that Latin Americans vote leftist parties as a way to punish incumbents or traditional parties which were not able to provide the expected economic well-being. Despite ideology being a relevant voting clue, electorates in the region are not voting left because they are against the market or strongly in favor of more state intervention in the economy. They vote for leftist parties because these parties were able to capitalize the social and economic discontent prevalent in the region. The possibilities of leftist parties capitalizing on Latin Americans' social discontent depend on the number of "credible" or "untainted" opposition. In countries like Brazil and Uruguay, where leftist parties embody the *only* "credible opposition," it is easy to capture votes from those unhappy with the status quo. But in countries where more than one "credible opposition" exists like in Mexico, leftist parties have to win over the vote of voters who take into account other considerations, mainly the party's capacity to govern.

Second Argument: Voting Left as a Risk for Latin American Democracy

The recent success of leftist parties in Latin America led some policy analysts to question the impact that leftist governments could have for democracies in the region. Behind this question, there is a fear that leftist parties could undermine the stability of democracy in Latin America. My argument is that the electoral success of leftist parties in Latin America, rather than being of source of concern, should be taken as an indicator of the democratic maturity of the region.

Despite the fact that almost all of Latin America emerged from its transition to democracy some years ago, it still needs to consolidate and improve the quality of its democracy (Roberts 1998). In order for democracies to work properly, they need at least a minimum of popular support (Easton 1953), and recent research has shown that support for democratic political institutions and democratic systems depends in part on which side of the winning-losing equation citizens are (Anderson, Blais, Bowler, Donovan and Listhaug 2005). Citizens that have voted for a party that lost the election (losers) tend to have lower levels of support for democracy than winners. As a result, democracies could become unstable if losers are continuously ignored in the political game, excluded from the political process, and if they are always the same people. To make democracy strong and stable, according to basic theories of democracy, it is better to have alternation in power and it is essential to incorporate minorities (Anderson, Blais, Bowler, Donovan and Listhaug 2005). Following this argument, the recent success of leftist parties in the region can be taken as good news.

In order to test if democracy is in danger due to the success of leftist parties, I test if Latin Americans who considered themselves leftist differ in their support for democracy from those that consider themselves rightist or centrist. I hypothesize that:

H4: Latin-Americans who identified themselves with the left are not less democratic than those who considered themselves centrist or rightist.

Results

To test the previous hypothesis, I use AmericasBarometer 2006-2007 public opinion survey. This survey covers 23 countries in North America, the Caribbean, Central America and South America; it is by far the most comprehensive source available to measure democratic values and behaviors in the Americas. It was carried out during 2006-2007 by LAPOP (Latin American Public Opinion Project) at Vanderbilt University,[9] and it uses a national probability sample of voting-age adults. For the purpose of this article, I will only use data from Mexico, Guatemala, El Salvador, Honduras, Nicaragua, Costa Rica, Panama, Colombia, Ecuador, Bolivia, Peru, Paraguay, Chile, Uruguay, Venezuela, Brazil and Dominican Republic because the focus is on Latin America; hence I exclude the English-speaking Caribbean and North American cases.

Table VI-2 presents a means comparison analysis of different attitudes and opinions towards democracy using ANOVA. How strongly citizens defend democracy is measured, in part, by attitudes toward political tolerance. In the AmericasBarometer we are able to use the Political Tolerance scale that combines four different indicators[10]: 1) There are people who speak negatively of the country's form of government, not just the incumbent government but the system of government. How strongly do you approve or disapprove of such people's **right to vote**? 2) How strongly do you approve or disapprove that such people be allowed **to conduct peaceful demonstrations** in order to express their views? 3) How strongly do you approve or disapprove of such people being permitted **to run for public office**? 4) How strongly do you approve or disapprove of such people appearing on television **to make speeches**? The answer categories go from 1=Strongly disapprove to 10=Strongly approve. Democratic attitudes, or more political tolerance, correspond to higher values. The index goes from 1 to 100, and it shows a Cronbach's Alpha of .870 for the pooled sample of countries indicating that all the items have enough in common to be together.

The Civil Liberties scale is another way to measure how democratic Latin Americans are. The scale merges five indicators: 1) To what degree do you approve or disapprove of a **law prohibiting public protests**? 2) To what degree do you approve or disapprove of a **law prohibiting the meetings of any group that criticizes the nationality political system**? 3) To what degree would you approve or disapprove **if the government censored television**

---

[9] I want to thank Profesor Mitchell A. Seligson, LAPOP director, for giving me access to this data.

[10] When one respondent does not answer one or two of the four questions comprised in the scale, the mean of the remaining questions is imputed to those questions in order to avoid loosing the observation. However, when more than two questions are not answered, the case is considered as missing data.

programs? 4) To what degree would you approve or disapprove **if the government censored books in public school libraries**? 5) To what degree would you approve or disapprove **if the government censored any of the media that criticized it**? The answer categories go from 1=Strongly disapprove to 10=Strongly approve. In this case, the scale was reversed to keep the comparability with the rest of the variables and scales. Therefore, higher values also correspond with stronger democratic attitudes. The index goes from 1 to 100, and it shows a Cronbach's Alpha of .788 for the pooled sample of countries[11].

TableVI-2. Attitudes towards democracy

		Mean	N	Std Deviation	F	Sign.
Political Tolerance scale						
	Left	56.7	5171	27.988		
	Center	53.2	7474	25.682	26.126	.000
	Right	54.5	6588	28.154		
Civil Liberties scale						
	Left	74.6	4653	21.948		
	Center	71.4	6523	21.337	38.404	.000
	Right	71.1	6125	22.420		
Democracy may have problems, but it is better than any other form of government (1)						
	Left	4.99	5119	1868		
	Center	5.10	7395	1653	71.725	.000
	Right	5.36	6498	1.714		

Source: AmericasBarometer 2006-2007
(1) Democracy may have problems, but it is better than any other form of government. To what extent do you agree or disagree with these statements? The answers categories goes from 1= Strongly disagree and 7=Strongly agree.

The results shown in Table VI-2 indicate that leftists in Latin America have, in general, levels of political tolerance no different from those who consider themselves close to the Right. It is only those in the political center who have lower tolerance scores. Leftists are stronger defenders of civil liberties than rightists. However, those who perceived themselves close to the right, are more in favor of the position that "democracy may have problems but it is still the best form of government" than those identified with the left. To sum up, two out of three indicators support hypothesis 4, which states that Latin Americans who feel themselves close to the left are not less democratic than those who considered rightist or centrist. In other words, the attitudes of Latin Americans do not provide strong evidence that the shift towards the left in the region could imply any danger for democratic prospects.

---

[11] The Civil Liberties scale uses the same procedure to impute missing values than the Political Tolerance scale does. When one respondent does not answer one or two of the four questions comprised in the scale, the mean of the remaining questions is imputed to those questions in order to avoid loosing the observation. However, when more than two questions are not answered, the case is considered as missing data. The N is lower because some of these questions were not asked in some of the countries.

It is possible that the analysis of the pooled sample hides strong country effects that might contradict the results, but in most countries the differences are not significant. The attitudes measured by the Civil liberties scale show a similar lack of significance. To make things even more complicated, Figure VI-1 shows evidence that rightists are more pro-democracy, and have higher levels of support for the idea that "democracy may have problems but it is better than any other form of government" in almost every country with the exception of Chile, Bolivia, Uruguay and Guatemala. In several of these cases the differences are significant.

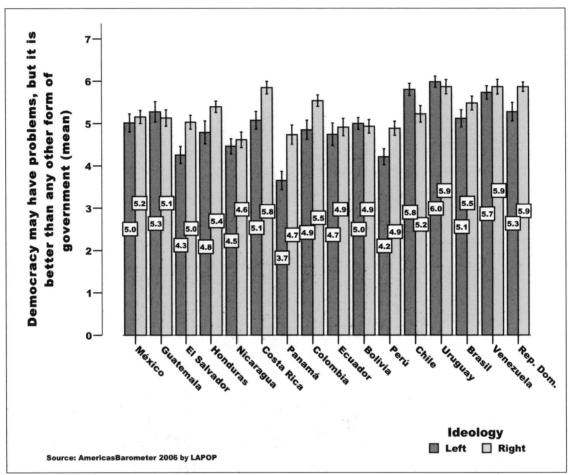

Source: AmericasBarometer 2006 by LAPOP

Figure VI-1. Democracy is the best form of government by country

Table VI-3 reinforces that last idea: rightists are more or equally democratic than their fellows on the ideological left[12]. It is important to mention that the majority of Latin Americans, in each country, think that electoral democracy is always the best. However, there are some differences between leftists and rightists. In Costa Rica, Colombia, Nicaragua, Ecuador, Peru, Venezuela and Panama, rightists are more democratic; while in Chile, Uruguay, Guatemala and Honduras, leftist are stronger supporters of electoral democracy. Finally, in Dominican Republic, Brazil, Mexico and El Salvador, the differences are irrelevant.

---

[12] The exact wording of the question is the following: "There are people who say that we need a strong leader that does not have to be elected. Others say that although things may not work, electoral democracy, or the popular vote, is always the best. What do you think?

Table VI-3. Authoritarianism vs. democracy by country

Country		Strong leader who does not have to be elected	Electoral democracy is the best	Total
Brazil				
	Left	13	87	100
	Center	11	89	100
	Right	12	88	100
Costa Rica				
	Left	8	92	100
	Center	5	95	100
	Right	2	98	100
Chile				
	Left	4	96	100
	Center	8	92	100
	Right	16	84	100
Dominican Rep.				
	Left	13	87	100
	Center	10	90	100
	Right	12	88	100
Colombia				
	Left	15	85	100
	Center	8	92	100
	Right	9	91	100
Mexico				
	Left	13	87	100
	Center	12	88	100
	Right	12	88	100
Guatemala				
	Left	18	82	100
	Center	21	79	100
	Right	29	71	100
El Salvador				
	Left	13	87	100
	Center	12	88	100
	Right	14	86	100
Honduras				
	Left	14	86	100
	Center	12	88	100
	Right	16	84	100
Nicaragua				
	Left	21	79	100
	Center	20	80	100
	Right	17	83	100
Ecuador				
	Left	21	79	100
	Center	17	83	100
	Right	13	87	100
Peru				
	Left	24	76	100
	Center	15	85	100
	Right	13	87	
Panama				
	Left	35	65	100
	Center	28	72	100
	Right	26	74	100
Uruguay				
	Left	3	97	100
	Center	5	95	100
	Right	7	95	100
Venezuela				
	Left	15	85	100
	Center	15	85	100
	Right	12	88	100
All the countries				
	Left	**15**	**85**	**100**
	Center	**14**	**86**	**100**
	Right	**13**	**87**	**100**

Source: AmericasBarometer 2006-07 by LAPOP

An alternative way to check if leftists in Latin America are significantly more or less democratic that rightists is through regression analysis. Table V.4 shows the impact that ideological self placement has on different indicators of democratic support after controlling by place of residence (urban versus rural), sex, age, wealth and education. The first thing to notice is that being leftist or rightist is a significant determinant of all the indicators of democratic support with the exception of political tolerance. Second, leftists are stronger opponents to government censorship than rightists. But on the other hand, the evidence is strong in showing that rightists are more supportive of Churchill's idea of democracy ("democracy is the best form of government"), and even more important, they are significantly less willing to overthrow democracy by force. Regression results also indicate that more educated citizens, those with a higher economic status, and older people show higher levels of democratic support than their younger, less educated and less well-off fellows. Women, as other studies show, are more intolerant and more likely to support government censorship than men.

Table V.4 Determinants of Democratic Support

Independent variables	Political Tolerance scale	Civil Liberties scale	Democracy is the best form of government	Opposition to overthrow an elected government (2)	Authoritarianism vs. Democracy (1)
Urban-Rural	-.040***	-.052***	-.008	-.026***	.021
Sex	-.057***	-.060***	-.010	.036***	.033
Age	-.005	.036***	.083***	.089***	.009***
Wealth	.100***	-.055***	.142***	.110***	.124***
Education	.077***	.136***	.043***	.031***	.028***
Ideological selfplacement	-.008	-.038***	.093***	.071***	.024**
Adjusted R squared	.031	.042	.042	.032	.024

(1) Because Authoritarianism vs. Democracy is a dichotomous variable (0 is Authoritarianism and 1 is Democracy), entries are binary logit coefficients and the last cell shows the Nagelkerke R Square.
(2) The exact wording of the question is the following: "Now we are going to use another card. The new card has a 10-point scale, which goes from 1 to 10, where 1 means that you strongly disapprove and 10 means that you strongly approve. I am going to read you a list of some actions that people can take to achieve their political goals and objectives. Please tell me how strongly you would approve or disapprove of people taking the following actions: of people participating in a group wanting to carry out a violent overthrow of an elected government". The scale was reversed to keep the comparability with the rest of indicators.
Note: Entries are Beta coefficients from OLS regression models. * p<.10, **p<.05, ***p<.01.
Urban-Rural: Urban 0, Rural 1; Sex: Male 0, Female 1; Age, Wealth and Education: higher values correspond with more age, more wealth and more years of education. Ideological selfplacement goes from 1 Extreme left to 10 Extreme right. In all the dependent variables, higher values correspond with democratic attitudes.
Source: AmericasBarometer 2006-2007 by LAPOP.

To sum up, and despite all the country differences found, the results provide evidence to answer the question if democracy is at risk due to the shift towards the left that the region has been experiencing. First, it is important to notice that the majority of Latin Americans have democratic attitudes irrespective of their ideology. This finding is good news for the stability of democracy in the region. Second, the differences between leftists and rightists on their level of democratic support depend on the country and the indicator used to measure democratic support.

Leftists have higher levels of political tolerance and are stronger supporters of civil liberties than rightist, but rightists show higher levels of support than leftists to the idea that democracy is the best form of government in almost all the countries. Even more, rightists are less willing to overthrow a democratic elected government that their fellows on the left are. To put it simply, there is evidence that leftists in the region cannot be considered substantially weaker supporters of democracy than rightists, but it is also not true that they are more democratic than their fellows on the ideological right.

Conclusion

Taking all these arguments into account, the findings of this article represent a reasonable positive picture on the prospects for democracy as a result of the rise of the left. First, they show how Latin Americans have broadened the arena of political contention by electing governments that incorporate left-oriented parties into the political game. The future of democracy can be in danger if one important group of political actors are always on the losers' side. For many years, several leftist political parties in the region played as losers in the electoral game. Therefore, the arrival of left-leaning parties to the government of several Latin American countries, rather than being a cause of concern, should be considered an indicator of a healthy democracy and a mechanism to strengthen democratic support among citizens. Second, the results of this study show that when Latin Americans have institutional and democratic ways to channel their discontent, they go for them. At least in Brazil, Mexico and Uruguay, voters prefer to vote for "untainted parties" rather than looking for non-democratic alternatives to achieve their demands.

In addition, this article supports the idea that Latin Americans are more outcome-oriented than policy-oriented, and the current shift towards the left in the region is more the result of the citizens' economic discontent than a bandwagon effect against market-oriented economic policies.

Latin Americans are capable of making their political leaders accountable, remove them from office when they do not accomplished what was expected of them, and change those in charge of the government by voting for "untainted parties." The success of "untainted parties" in Brazil, Mexico and Uruguay implies an increase in institutionalization, in political representation, and a sign of political maturity (López 2005). In a region demanding a more accountable and responsive democracy, the examples of Brazil, Mexico and Uruguay show a way this can be done. The recent shift towards the left in Latin America has helped to intensify and strengthen democracy in the region by incorporating losers into the political game.

Even though Latin America is better off because of the more pluralist nature of elections, it is still an open question how the left will behave in office. The analysis performed with the AmericasBarometer 2006-07 data show that Latin Americans that identified themselves with the left are not substantially less democratic than rightists, but not more democratic either. Therefore, in order to figure out where the region is headed as it moves to the left, we need to look at what leftist governments do: deepening democracy or return to undemocratic political practices. Chile, Brazil and Uruguay are countries in which leftist governments are acting with respect to democracy. But the picture is not so clear in countries as Venezuela, Bolivia, and even Ecuador.

It is still premature to say if leftists' governments in this last group of countries will make democracy more stable or represent a risk.

References

Ames, Barry. *The Deadlock of Democracy in Brazil.* Ann Arbor: The University of Michigan Press, 2001.

Anderson, Christopher J., André Blais, Shaun Bowler, Todd Donovan, and Ola Listhaug. *Losers' Consent. Elections and Democratic Legitimacy.* Oxford: Oxford University Press, 2005.

Benton, Allyson Lucinda. "Dissatisfied Democrats or Retrospective Voters? Economic Hardship, Political Institutions and Voting Behavior in Latin America." *Comparative Political Studies* 38 (4) (2005):417-442.

Cameron, Maxwell. *Democracy and Authoritarianism in Peru: Political Coalitions and Social Change.* New York: St. Martin's Press, 1994.

Cantón, Darío and Jorge Raúl Jorrat. "Economic Evaluations, Partisanship, and Social Bases of Presidential Voting in Argentina, 1995 and 1999." *International Journal of Public Opinion Research* 41 (4) (2202):413-427.

Converse, P. The Nature of Belief Systems in Mass Publics. In *Ideology and Discontent*, ed. D. Apter. Glencoe: The Free Press, 1964.

Domínguez, Jorge I., and James A. McCann. "Shaping Mexico's Electoral Arena: The Construction of Partisan Cleavages in the 1988 and 1991 National Elections." *American Political Science Review* 89 (1) (1995):34-48.

Domínguez, Jorge I. and James A. McCann. *Democratizing Mexico: Public Opinion and Electoral Choices.* Vol. 89, *American Political Science Review.* Baltimore, MD: Johns Hopkins University Press, 1996.

Dutch, Raymond M. State of the Latin American Political Economy: The James A. Baker III Institute for Public Policy of Rice University, 2003.

Easton, David. *The Political System*: Knopf, 1953.

Echegaray, Fabián. *Economic Crises and Electoral Responses in Latin America.* Maryland: University Press of America, 2005.

Economist, The. The battle for Latin America's soul. *The Economist*, 20 May (2006).

Edwards, Sebastian. "Latin America's Underperformance." *Foreign Affairs* 77 (2) (1997).

Escaith, H. and S. Morley. "El efecto de las reformas estructurales en el crecimiento de América Latina y el Caribe: una estimación empírica." *El Trimestre Económico* 68 (2001).

Fiorina, Morris P. *Retrospective Voting in American National Elections.* New Haven: Yale University Press, 1981.

Fuchs, Dieter and Hans-Dieter Klingermann. The Left-Right Schema. In *Continuities in Political Action*, ed. Jennings K. et al. Berlin: Walter de Gruyter (1990).

Gillespie, Charles and L.E. González. Uruguay: The Survival of Old and Autonomous Institutions. In *Democracy in Developing Countries, vol. 4: Latin America*, ed. Juan J. Linz Larry Diamond, and Seymour M. Lipset. Boulder, Colorado: Lynne Rienner Publishers, 1989.

González, Luis E. *Political Structures and Democracy in Uruguay.* Notre Dame: University of Notre Dame Press, 1991.

Greene, Kenneth. Opposition Party Strategy and Spatial Competition in Dominant Party Regime. A Theory and the Case of Mexico. *Comparative Political Studies* 35 (7) (2002):755-783.

Huber, Evelyn and Fred Solt. "Successes and Failures of Neoliberalism." *Latin American Research Review* 39 (3) (2004).

IDEA. Reform Fatigue. Washington DC: Inter-American Development Bank, 2004.

Inglehart, Ronald and Hans-Dieter Klingerman. Party Identification, Ideological Preference and the Left-Right Dimensions among the Western Mass Publics. In *Party Identification and Beyond: Representations of Voting and Party Competition*, ed. I. Budge, I Crewey D. Farlie. Chichester: Wiley, 1976.

Kinder, Donald R. Opinion and Actions in the Realm of Politics. In *Handbook of Political Psychology* (1998).

Kinder, Donald R. and D. Roderick Kiewiet. "Sociotropic Politics: The American Case." *British Journal of Political Science* 11 (2) (1981):129-161.

Kitschelt, Herbert and Staf Hellemans. "The Left-Right Semantics and The New Politics Cleavage." *Comparative Political Studies* 23 (2) (1990):210-238.

Klesner, Joseph L. The Structure of the Mexican Electorate: Social, Attitudinal, and Partisan Bases of Vicente Fox´s Victory. In *Mexico´s Pivotal Democratic Election. Candidates, Voters, and the Presidential Campaign of 2000*, edited by J. I. a. C. L. Domínguez. Stanford: Stanford University Press, 2004.

Klesner, Joseph L. Electoral Competition and the New Party System in Mexico. *Latin American Politics and Society* 47 (2) (2005):103-142.

Kuczynski, Pedro-Pablo and John Williamson, ed. *After the Washington Consensus: Restarting Growth and Reform in Latin America*. Washington DC: Institute for International Economics, 2003.

Latinobarómetro, 2004. Annual Report (2004).

Latinobarómetro, 2006. Annual Report (2006).

Lawson, Chappell and James McCann. "Television News, Mexico´s 2000 Elections and Media Effects in Emerging Democracies." *British Journal of Political Science* 35 (2004):1-30.

Lewis-Beck, Michael. "Comparative Economic Voting: Britain, France, Germany, Italy." *American Journal of Political Science* 30 (2) (1986):315-346.

Lewis-Beck, Michael. . *Economics and Elections: The Major Western Democracies*. Ann Arbor: University of Michigan Press, 1988.

Lewis-Beck, Michael, and Paolo Belluci. "Economic Influences on Legislative Elections in Multiparty Systems: France and Italy." *Political Behavior* 4 (1982): 93-107.

López, Santiago. "Partidos Desafiantes en Amerérica Latina: Representación Política y Estrategias de Competencia de las Nuevas Oposiciones." *Revista de Ciencia Política* 25 (2)(2005):37-64.

Lora, Eduardo. Structural Reforms in Latin America: What Has Been Reformed and How to Measure it. In *Working Paper Green Series #348*. Washington DC: Inter-American Development Bank, 1997/2001.

Lora, Eduardo and F. Barrera. Una década de reformas estructurales en América Latina: el crecimiento, la productividad y la inversión, ya no son como antes. Washington DC: Inter American Development Bank, Research Department, 1997.

Lora, Eduardo, and Ugo Panizza. Structural Reforms in Latin America under Scrutiny. In *Research Paper*. Washington DC: Inter American Development Bank, 2002.

Lora, Eduardo, Panizza, Ugo and Myriam Quispe-Agnoli. "Reform Fatigue:Symptoms, Reasons and Implications." *Federal Reserve Bank of Atlanta Economic Quarter* (Second Quarter), (2004).

MacKuen, Michael, Robert Erikson and James Stimson. "Sociotropic Politics: The American Case." *British Journal of Political Science* 11 (2) (1992):129-161.

Mainwaring, Scott. *Rethinking Party Systems in the Third Wave of Democratization. The Case of Brazil*. Stanford, CA: Stanford University Press, 1999.

Mainwaring, Scott and Timothy R. Scully, ed. *Building Democratic Institutions: Party Systems in Latin America*. Stanford, CA: Stanford University Press, 1995.

Mora y Araujo, Manuel, and Peter H. Smith. Peronism and Economic Development: The Elections of 1973. In *Juan Perón and the Reshaping of Argentina*, ed. F. C. Turner and J. E. Miguens. Pittsburgh: University of Pittsburgh Press., 1984

Moreno, Alejandro. Party Competition and the Issue of Democracy: Ideological Space in Mexican Elections. In *Governing Mexico: Political Parties and Elections*, edited by M. Serrano. London: University of London, 1998.

Moreno, Alejandro. Ideología y voto: dimensiones de competencia política en México en los noventa. *Política y Gobierno* 6 (1) (1999):45-81.

Nadeau, Richard and Michael S. Lewis-Beck. "National Economic Voting in U.S. Presidential Elections." *Journal of Politics* 63 (1) (2001):158-181.

Panizza, Ugo and Mónica Yañez. "Why are Latin Americans so unhappy about reforms?" *Journal of Applied Economics* VIII (1) (2005).

Power, Timothy. "Blairism Brazilian Style? Cardoso and the "Third Way" in Brazil." *Political Science Quarterly* 116 (4) (2201/2002).

Przeworski, Adam and John Sprague. *Paper Stones*. Chicago: University of Chicago Press, 1986.

Remmer, Karen and Francois Gélineau. "Subnational electoral choice. Economic and Referendum Voting in Argentina, 1983-1999." *Comparative Political Studies* 36 (7) (2003):801-821.

Roberts, Kenneth M. and Erik Wibbels. "Party Systems and Electoral Volatility In Latin America: A Test of Economic, Institutional, and Structural Explanations." *American Political Science Review* 93 (3) (1999):575-590.

Roberts, Kenneth M. and Moisés Arce. "Neoliberalism and Lower-Class Voting Behavior in Peru." *Comparative Political Studies* 31 (2) (1998):217-246.

Rodrik, Dani and Francisco Rodríguez. Trade Policy and Economic Growth: A Skeptic's Guide to the Cross-National Evidence. In *NBER Macroeconomics Annual 2000*, ed. B.S. and K. Rogoff Bernanke. Cambridge: Massachusetts Institute of Technology Press, 2001.

Sachs, Jeffrey; McCord, Gordon and Wing Thye Woo. Understanding African Poverty: Beyond the Washington Consensus to the Millennium Development Goals Approach. In *Africa in the World Economy,* ed. Jan Joost and Age Akkerman Teunissen. The Hague: FONDAD, 2005.

Samuels, David. "Sources of Mass Partisanship in Brazil." Latin American Politics and Society, 2006.

Schlesinger, Arthur M., Jr. The Cycles of American History. Boston: Houghton-Mifflin, 1986.

Seligson, Mitchell, and Miguel Gómez. Ordinary Elections in Extraordinary Times: The Political Economy of Voting in Costa Rica. In *Elections and Democracy in Central (1989) America*, ed. J. Booth and M. Seligson. Chapell Hill: University of North Carolina Press.

Stallings, Barbara, and Wilson Peres. Growth, Employment, and Equity: the Impact of Economic Reforms in Latin America and the Caribbean. Washington D.C.: Brookings Institution , 2000.

Stiglitz, Joseph. *Globalization and Its Discontent.* W.W.Norton & Company, 2002.

Torcal, Mariano, and Scott Mainwaring. "The Political Recrafting of Social Bases of Party Competition: Chile, 1973-95." *British Journal of Political Science* 33 (2003):55-84.

Weyland, Kurt. "Peasants and Bankers in Venezuela? Presidential Popularity and Economic Reform Approval, 1989-1993." *Political Research Quarterly* 51 (2) (1998):341-362.

Weyland, Kurt. "Economic Voting Reconsidered. Crisis and Charisma in the Election of Hugo Chávez." *Comparative Political Studies* 36 (7) (2003):822-848.

Part II. Challenges to Democracy from Civil Society

VII.   Social Trust, Economic Inequality, and Democracy in the Americas *

Abby B. Córdova Guillén**

Abstract

The main task of this research is to identify sources of social trust in Latin America by exploring why the most politically and economically developed countries in the Americas, namely Canada and the United States, have higher levels of social trust than their neighbor countries. The major thesis of this chapter is that the lower levels of social trust in Latin America are in part explained by the highly unequal distribution of economic resources in many countries in the region because social trust is unlikely to proliferate in an environment that foster polarization and social conflict between haves and have nots. The empirical evidence of this chapter suggests that the lack of a substantial improvement in the distribution of income in Latin America poses a challenge to democracy given that economic inequality triggers social mistrust. This chapter also finds that social trust rather than civic participation is the functionally most important component of social capital in Latin America, since it consistently promotes the type of political attitudes favorable to democracy, such as support for democracy and political tolerance. This conclusion reinforces the findings of previous works and suggests that efforts to strengthen civil society in the region are not likely to advance democracy unless higher civic participation is accompanied by a considerable increase in the levels of social trust, which in turn seems to require a more equitable distribution of income.

> "You can't build trust when some groups feel left out of the society and believe that others control the resources."[1]

Is economic inequality eroding Latin America's social capital? Paradoxically, even though the emergence of democracy in Latin America has opened important participation channels for its citizenry, civic and political participation during the democratization period has taken place in an environment characterized by low social trust, challenging the notion that civic participation and interpersonal trust, the two main components of social capital, always go hand in hand (Putnam 1993). Taking into account that a high level of social trust has been found in the literature to be more effective in deepening democracy than the level of participation in voluntary organizations alone (Inglehart and Welzel 2005), the importance of identifying sources of social trust in order to strengthen social capital in Latin America speaks for itself. The main hypothesis of this chapter is that the relatively low levels of social trust in Latin America are in part explained by the highly

* The author is grateful to the comments and suggestions provided by Professor Mitchell A. Seligson on previous versions of this chapter and to the Department of Political Science at Vanderbilt for its financial support. In addition, the author would like to thank the members of Latin American Public Opinion Project (LAPOP) team. Any omissions and errors are entirely the author's responsibility.

**The author is currently a member of the LAPOP team and a PhD student in political science at Vanderbilt University.

[1] Eric M. Uslaner, "Producing and Consuming Trust," *Political Science Quarterly* 115, no. 4 (2000). p.580.

unequal distribution of economic resources in the region, which is the region with the highest income inequality in the world. In other words, this chapter claims that economic inequality breeds social distrust, resulting in an overall negative effect on democracy.

Many definitions of "social trust" can be found in the literature; for example, Newton (2001) defines social trust as "the actor's belief that, at worst, others will not knowingly or willingly do him [her] harm, and at best, that they will act in his [her] interests" (202). Generally, social trust is conceived as the ingredient that makes possible interaction between individuals who might not know each other well and who do not necessarily share the same interests and values, but who are willing to undertake collective actions. Therefore, social trust is found to be key for democracy because it facilitates participation and cooperation among individuals with different backgrounds (Fukuyama 1995, Inglehart 1999, Putnam 1993, Uslaner 2002), fostering political tolerance. However, some societies seem more prone to creating social trust than others, and economic conditions, in particular, appear to play an important role in the formation of social trust.

As the quotation by Uslaner (2000) at the beginning of this chapter suggests, interpersonal trust is unlikely to flourish in societies where the fruits of economic growth are distributed highly unevenly since conflicts between the haves and have-nots are likely to be more profound, undermining solidarity and cooperation and, in turn, weakening the creation of the type of social capital conducive to better democracies. Although economic growth per se has been found to be an important determinant of democratic political stability, research has shown that the probability of democratic breakdown is greater in nations with high levels of economic inequality (Przeworski 2000). Indeed, much research has pointed to the importance of economic equality in democratization as well as in conflict prevention (Boix 2003, Karl 2000, Lipset 1961, Muller and Seligson 1987).

Lipset (1961), for example, stresses the importance of transforming the class structure of democratic societies from a "elongated pyramid" to a "diamond" shape, pointing out that "a large middle class tempers conflict by rewarding moderate and democratic parties and penalizing extremist groups" (51). Indeed, social conflict and personal violence seem to be more common in societies with a highly unequal income distribution (Fajnzylber, et al. 2002, Fajnzylber, et al. 1998). The argument this chapter offers is that economic inequality hinders the process of democratic consolidation in Latin America by inhibiting the formation of social trust. Mistrustful societies are unlikely to create an environment favorable to democracy since low social trust is associated with greater opportunities for conflict.

In addition, civic participation in an environment characterized by low social trust is likely to be less meaningful for democracy because membership in civic organizations in this case might be associated with "particularized" rather than "generalized" trust (Uslaner 2002, 2000), which suggests that trust materializes within but not across civic groups. For this reason, this study argues that the kind of civic participation that is most important for Latin American democracies is the one that is accompanied by high levels of interpersonal trust. Thus, this chapter attempts to determine how Latin American countries could boost their levels of social trust so that the participation opportunities that have been brought about by the emergence of democracy can be translated into a widespread democratic culture and therefore stronger democracies. In other words, how can social capital be made to work in Latin America in a way consistent with the

predictions of the bulk of the social capital literature, namely, that interpersonal trust and civic participation go together and reinforce each other (Putnam 1993). The focus of this chapter has important policy implications as well as theoretical relevance. Although the strengthening of civil society has been at the core of democratization programs for the region (Campbell 2003, Seligson 2006), and has been a very important part of USAID's democracy efforts (Finkel, et al. 2007), this chapter claims that civic participation by itself is unlikely to foster democracy unless it forms part of a broader agenda that includes policies that facilitate the conditions for the construction of generalized social trust, such as economic policies designed to promote equality.

Since both economic equality and socioeconomic development have been identified as notable sources of social trust, this study also analyzes whether the effect of economic equality on social trust remains significant once the impact of socioeconomic development is considered. Indeed, it has been said that feelings of economic security are also likely to produce more trust in others because economic well-being reduces competition for scarce resources, ameliorating social conflict (Inglehart and Welzel 2005). Besides structural factors, namely the degree of development and economic equality, the individual level determinants of interpersonal trust are also explored. In particular, this work explores the role of personal experience with crime as well as the standard socio-economic and demographic individual characteristics in the formation of interpersonal trust. In attempting to identify the determinants of social trust in order to find mechanisms to strengthen social capital in Latin America, this study departs from previous works that have considered social trust to be an enduring characteristic, above all a cultural trait, rather than a social phenomenon that can be shaped through public policy.

Methodologically, a multilevel analysis of the determinants of social trust is carried out, taking into account individual and country-level characteristics and exploring why it is that, on average, individuals who live in the more politically and economically developed countries in the Americas (i.e., Canada and the United States) have much higher levels of social trust than individuals living in neighbor countries. Indeed, at the country-level, there is overwhelming evidence, mainly from the World Values Survey data, that there is a strong positive correlation between social trust and political and economic development (Inglehart and Welzel 2005, Norris 2002). As it will be shown, the empirical evidence presented in this work confirms those results.

The data used in this study come from face-to-face interviews in nineteen Latin American nations, including Caribbean countries, drawn from the AmericasBarometer in 2006-2007 carried out by LAPOP, and phone survey data gathered also by AmericasBarometer during the same year in Canada and the United States. In total, the database includes over 32,000 individual interviews. The 2006-07 round of surveys facilitated comparisons between two clusters of nations with dissimilar levels of social trust and political and economic development. Specifically, these data make it possible to examine why Latin American and Caribbean countries have a lower level of social trust than Canada and the United States. In order to answer this question, the LAPOP data are combined with aggregate data about the degree of socioeconomic development and economic inequality at the country level. The objectives of this chapter are the following:

- Briefly review the social capital literature, placing special emphasis on the role of social trust and its determinants.

- Measure the level of social capital in the Americas, and determine the strength of the relationship between social trust and civic participation.
- Examine whether the social trust gap between Latin America and Canada and the United States is determined by differences in personal experience with crime and socioeconomic and demographic characteristics.
- Explore the effect of structural factors, specifically economic inequality and socioeconomic development, on social trust vis-à-vis individual-level characteristics.
- Demonstrate the importance of interpersonal trust for democracy in Latin America, vis-à-vis participation in civic organizations by examining whether trusting individuals are more likely to embrace a democratic culture.

A Brief Review of the Literature

The notion that a "civic culture" is important for the consolidation of democracy has a long tradition in political science. Social trust has been identified as one of the main characteristics of a civic culture. For example, Banfield (1958) concluded that "Montegrano," a town located in the south of Italy, was characterized by the almost complete lack of trust among individuals, which made their cooperative participation in collective enterprises extremely difficult. As a result, the local government suffered from almost complete political incapacity, which in turn made improving the economic circumstances of the village impossible. Similarly, Almond and Verba (1963) found that among the five countries they analyzed, the ones with less stable democracies, Mexico being one of them, also had lower levels of interpersonal trust.

More recently, the importance of social trust was dramatically reemphasized with the publication of *Making Democracy Work,* in which Putnam (1993) made the term "social capital" popular. At the heart of the social capital theory rests the idea that democratic governments in trusting societies are more accountable and responsive to the demands of their citizens because civic and political participation in those societies is likely to be higher, and therefore governments are, at the same time, more likely to represent the interests of the bulk of the population. Putnam suggests that the main components of social capital are interpersonal trust and civic participation. In fact, for Putnam there is a reciprocal relationship between interpersonal trust and civic participation, suggesting that where civic participation is high, social trust should also be high, and vice versa. However, as it will be shown in this chapter, although civic participation is relatively high in many Latin American countries, the level of social trust is low, empirical evidence that contradicts Putnam's theory.

The common characteristic among the aforementioned works is that they understand political outcomes to be products of a "civic culture" that is rooted in the historical legacy of nations and therefore in the cultural values transmitted from generation to generation. From this perspective, social trust is predominantly a cultural phenomenon, making changes in the levels of social trust

difficult since by their very nature, cultural traits are enduring.[2] This also implies that some cultures are more favorable to democracy than others.

Following Max Weber's ideas, Western Protestant values are seen more compatible with democracy than other value systems. Indeed, many of the politically and economically successful countries in the world are at the same time those whose cultures have been rooted in Protestant traditions Even though the so-called "Confucian ethic" civilizations have made impressive gains in recent years. For example, Harrison (1985) evaluates the causes of underdevelopment in Latin America, and concludes that what impedes prosperity in Latin American countries are Catholic values and traditions imbedded in the Hispanic culture. These views are shared by Inglehart (Inglehart 1990, 1988, 1999, Inglehart and Welzel 2005), who understands civic attitudes, including social trust, as cultural products, although he acknowledges that structural factors, socioeconomic development in particular, can shape the levels of social trust specially in already politically and economically advanced societies.

These "culturalist" approaches have been challenged by the empirical evidence, since, for example, social trust and civic participation appear to have experienced important declines in the United States in recent decades (Putnam 2000, 1995), suggesting that some other factor besides deep-seated cultural traits might be affecting the levels of social capital in the U.S., given that dramatic cultural changes are unlikely to take place within a relatively short period of time. Putnam argues that the decline in civic activism in the United States is explained, in part, by the increased number of hours people spend watching television, which deter individuals from interacting with others. In addition, he claims that television viewing has also made people less trusting because television programs tend to overstate negative aspects and portray the world as a "mean" place (Putnam 1996).

The Putnam thesis has not gone unchallenged. While many agree that there has been a decline in social trust in the U.S., the explanation is not to be found in television viewing. Uslaner (1998, 2005), for example, rejects Putnam's explanations for the decline in social capital in the United States. Instead, he argues that the recent rise in economic inequality in the United States better explains the waning of interpersonal trust (Uslaner and Brown 2005), and adds that the decline in civic participation is the effect of the decline in social trust.

Indeed, other authors have also suggested that the elements that make up a "civic culture," among them social trust, are not entirely cultural, but the byproduct of structural factors (Armony 2004, Jackman and Miller 1998, Muller and Seligson 1994). Therefore, civic attitudes are more malleable than what some proponents of the culturalist view suggest. Structural factors are important, and consequently social trust can be shaped by the products of public policies. This is the theoretical framework that has inspired this study. Regardless of the role that culture might play, this study argues that the quality of social capital in Latin America can be improved if and only if the appropriate set of public policies is implemented. Economic equality has been found to be an important structural factor that affects the level of social trust in democratic nations

---

[2] Cultures can change over time, as Inglehart has demonstrated in his studies of Europe. Ronald Inglehart, *Culture Shift in Advanced Industrial Society* (Princeton, N.J.: Princeton University Press, 1990).

(Armony 2004, Uslaner and Brown 2005), and its role in shaping Latin America's social capital vis-à-vis other structural and individual factors is investigated here.

Social Capital in Latin America in Comparative Perspective

Following Norris (2002)'s approach, this study measures social capital using two indicators: social trust and civic activism.[3] The following item in the AmericasBarometer survey measures the level of interpersonal trust:

> **IT1**. Now, speaking of the people from around here, would you say that people in this community are generally very trustworthy, somewhat trustworthy, not very trustworthy or untrustworthy?

Social trust, in this study, then, refers to how confident individuals feel about people outside their immediate family circle. As mentioned before, the type of trust that is likely to enhance democracy is the one that makes individuals sympathetic to people who may have different beliefs, ideologies, or backgrounds than one's own, and consequently this type of trust ought to contribute to the establishment of more harmonious and, ultimately democratic societies (Putnam 2000, Uslaner 2002). Figure VII.1 shows the average level of social trust in each country, based on AmericasBarometer's measure of interpersonal trust.[4] As expected, the average level of social trust is much lower in Latin American and Caribbean countries than in Canada and the United States, confirming the trend found in the World Values Survey data. The two richest and more democratic countries in the sample show a much higher level of social trust. Out of the twenty one countries examined, Canada has the highest level of social trust, with an average of 82.8 points, and Haiti has the lowest level, with an average of only 42.1 points. The United States has the second highest level of social trust, a level that is not statistically significantly different to that of Canada.[5]

---

[3] Factor analysis of the AmericasBarometer 2006 dataset revealed that the measures of social trust and civic activism here used belong to different dimensions, which suggest that each of them is a distinct component of social capital, confirming Norris' (2002) findings. Norris states that social trust is the "cultural" dimension of social capital, and civic activism the "structural" dimension. In contrast to Norris, however, a single index of social capital was not constructed because a Cronbach Alpha test revealed that there is a low reliability of an index constructed using both of these components, which suggest that, at least in the Americas, social trust and civic participation do not always go together.

[4] The original interpersonal trust variable in the survey was recoded into a 0-100 scale in order to retain comparability with the other chapters in this volume, and therefore facilitating cross-chapter comparisons.

[5] Although the AmericasBarometer 2006 included data for Brazil, this country was excluded from the analysis in this chapter because the wording of interpersonal trust variable is different.

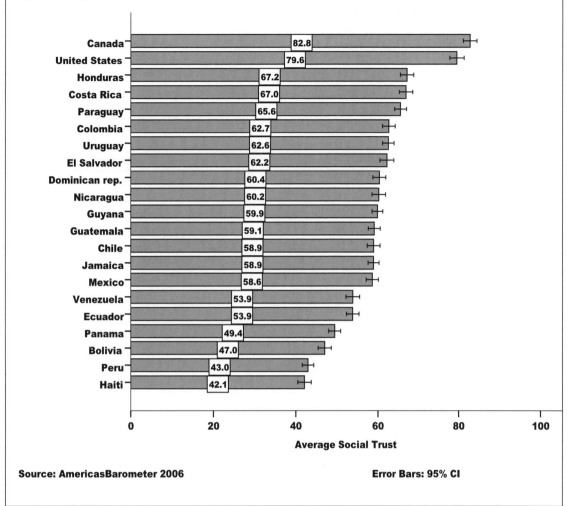

Figure VII-1. Average Social Trust by Country

In order to measure the level of civic activism, an index of "civic participation" was constructed, which indicates whether a respondent stated having participated in meetings of *at least one* of the following secular voluntary organizations: a parents' association at school (the equivalent of the U.S. PTA), a committee or council for community improvement, an association of professionals, an association of merchants or farmers, and meetings of a political party or movement.[6] Figure VII.2 shows the percentage of the population in each country that participates in at least one of these four types of civic organizations. The three countries with the highest level of civic participation, based on the index here developed, are Bolivia, Peru, and Canada, with

---

[6] Although the survey included an item about participation in meetings of religious organizations, it was not included in the index because factor analysis shows that participation in this type of organizations belongs to a different dimension or component of civic participation. It is likely that respondents to this item include their participation in religious services as part of their "count" of participation, and the analysis shows this kind of activity to be distinct from other forms of civil society activism. In addition, although the survey asked how frequently respondents participated in the meetings of all these organizations, a dichotomous index, instead of a scale, was preferred, because the reliability of the four items included in the index of civic participation was low. Low reliability means that the organizations do not naturally group together, which is understanable; members of farmer associations are not likely to be members of professional associations.

78.2, 73.8, and 72.4 percent of the population, respectively, participating in the civil society. In sharp contrast, the countries with the lowest percentage of the population participating in meetings of civic organizations are Panama (45.4), Costa Rica (46.5), and Uruguay (47.2). On the face of it, at least, these results do not conform to expectations.

While it was expected that Canada would show a high level of civic participation, it was also expected that the U.S. would also be at the top, but it was not. Nonetheless, in absolute terms, participation in the civil society in the U.S. is respectably high (67.5%). The real surprises are at the top and bottom for Latin America. Panama, Uruguay, and Costa Rica are well established democracies, with the latter widely considered to be the oldest and most consolidated democracy in the region. Yet, these three nations score at the very bottom. Similarly, Chile, in many ways a leading example of a successfully re-democratized country, is also low. On the other hand, Bolivia scores at the very top, a country with a fragile democracy and a turbulent democratic history in which elected regimes have frequently been forced from office.

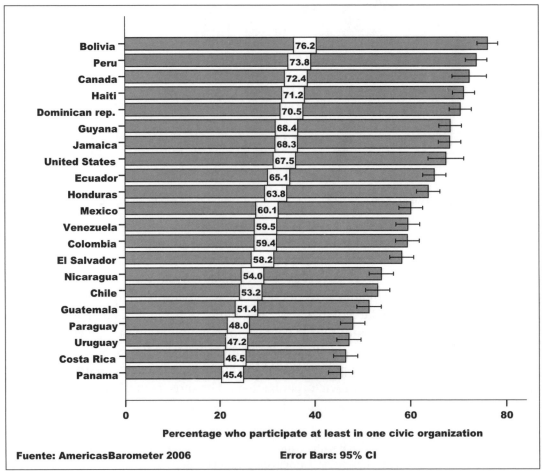

Figure VII-2. Civic Participation in the Americas

Figure VII.3 clusters the countries analyzed into regions of high and low social capital, namely Latin American and Caribbean countries and Canada and the United States.[7] At the regional level, social capital, measured by social trust and civic participation, is higher in Canada and the United States than in Latin America, although social capital differentials between these two regions are more substantial for social trust. While the civic participation differential between the means of the two regions is only 9.8 points, the difference in social trust is 23.7 points. As observed in the previous figures, in some Latin American countries civic activism is higher than in Canada and the United States, but social trust is significantly lower in Latin America. Overall, the less politically and economically developed regions in the Americas show lower levels of social trust.

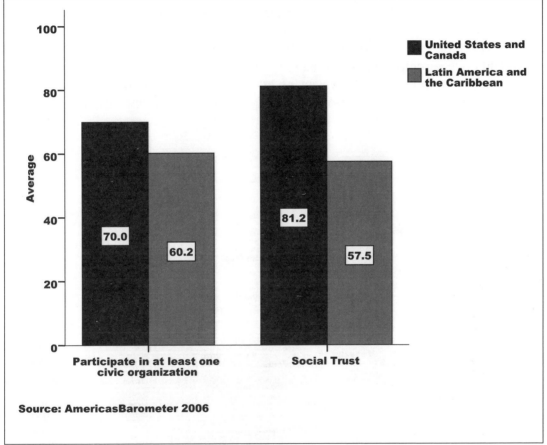

Figure VII-3. Social Capital by Region

A Weak Link: Social Trust and Civic Participation

In this section, we assess the proposition that social trust and civic activism form a "virtuous circle" given that these two elements of social capital have been thought to reinforce each other, and therefore it is assumed that high social trust leads to participation in civil society, and vice

---

[7] Herein, the term "Latin America" in this chapter is used to refer to all countries in the survey, except Canada and the United States.

versa (Putnam 1993). As noted in the introduction of this chapter there are reasons to question this putative link, especially as Armony (Armony 2004) has shown that participation very frequently does *not* lead to trust (or democratic outcomes). He notes the extremely high levels of participation in some areas in Weimer,Germany, precisely the areas in which the Nazis first gained control. The AmericasBarometer data reinforce this doubt.

Figure VII.4 shows the relationship between interpersonal trust and civic participation at the country level. It can be observed that the relationship between interpersonal trust and civic participation is not well defined. For example, while Costa Rica has a relatively high level of interpersonal trust in comparison to other Latin American countries, it also has one of the lowest levels of civic participation. On the other hand, the Latin American countries with the highest civic participation (Bolivia, Peru, and Haiti) show the lowest levels of interpersonal trust. Only Canada and the United States show a relatively high average level of social trust *and* civic participation. This suggests that at the country level there is no clear-cut association between social trust and civic participation, as Putnam (1993)'s social capital theory suggests that there is. This finding is not entirely novel, however, as other survey-based studies have also found that social trust and civic participation do not go always together (Newton 2001, Norris 2002, Seligson 2002).

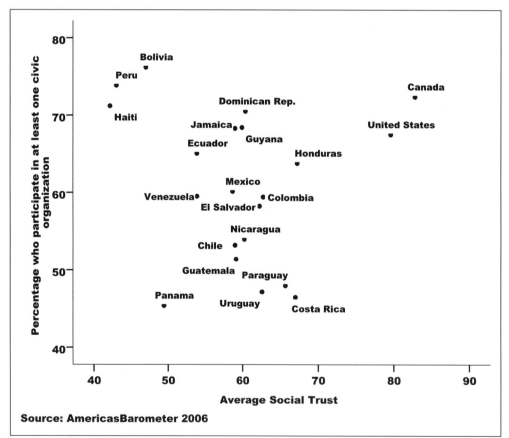

Figure VII-4. A Weak Link: Social Trust and Civic Participation

In light of these finding, it must be asked, at the individual level, if a higher level of interpersonal trust leads to, or is at least associated with, higher levels of civic activism. Figure VII.5 again shows that this seems to be the case only in Canada and the United States where individuals who have a higher level of interpersonal trust also show a higher average level of civic participation. In Figure VII.5, the line that represents the Northern countries has a steep slope, indicating that social trust is very closely linked to civic participation. In contrast, in the Latin American region, higher levels of social trust do not seem to be associated with higher levels of participation in the civil society, as reflected by the almost flat line in the figure. While in Latin America about 60 percent of the individuals who have the highest level of social trust participate in at least one type of civic organization, in Canada and the United States over 70 percent do. This supports Norris' (2002) observation that the contextual (i.e., national) level of social trust matters for civic participation. Even if the individual level of interpersonal trust is high, this only results in civic activism if other members of society also show high levels of trust.

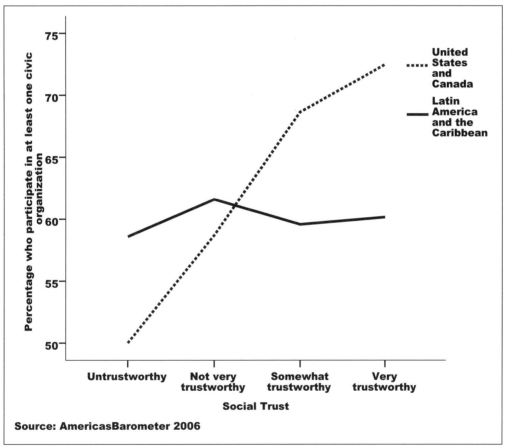

Figure VII-5. The Link between Social Trust and Civic Participation: and individual level analysis

However, Figure VII.5 also indicates that in Latin America even individuals who have no confidence in others at all do indeed participate in meetings of secular civic organizations. A larger percentage of respondents in Latin America with the lowest level of social trust are members of civic organizations than in Canada and the United States. This suggests that in Latin

America civic organizations may not bring together people of different beliefs, ideologies, or backgrounds, since social trust facilitates interaction between dissimilar individuals. Indeed, it could be argued that the benefits of civic participation for democracy are more likely to be maximized in heterogeneous rather than homogenous organizations since plural civic organizations have been found to foment political tolerance (Theiss-Morse and Hibbing 2005). In general, the results suggest that other factors seem to be more important in Latin America for bringing about civic participation than social trust.

In fact, at the individual level, in Latin America the level of education proved to be a more important predictor of civic participation than social trust. Indeed, the effect of social trust on civic participation in Latin America, although positive and statistically significant, is negligible.[8] Figure VII.6 shows that there is a relatively strong relationship between the individual level of education and civic participation. This confirms the uneven character of social capital. Those who have more human capital are more likely to join voluntary organizations, since they have the means (i.e., "resources," in Verba's terminology) to participate more effectively (Putnam 2000, Verba, et al. 1995). However, Figure VII.6 also shows that a substantial percentage of persons without formal education in Latin America, over 50 percent, do participate in meetings of secular civic organizations.

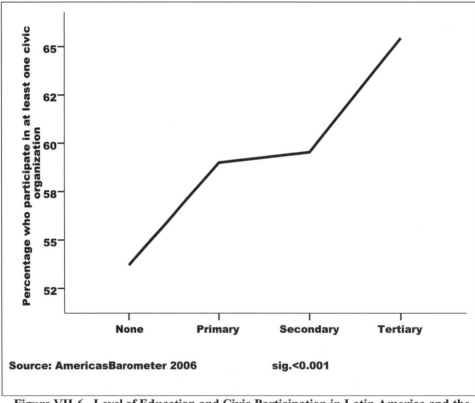

Figure VII-6. Level of Education and Civic Participation in Latin America and the Caribbean

---

[8] The results of the regression analysis can be found in appendix VII.1. The "design effect" of the sample was taken into account for the estimation of the standard errors of the coefficients in all the regressions in this chapter.

Explaining the Social Trust gap in the Americas: Do Individual Characteristics Matter?

This section explores whether the lower level of social trust in Latin America relative to Canada and the United States is explained by individual level factors, such as the varying socio-economic and demographic characteristics and personal experiences. Levels of social trust in Latin America and Canada and the United States are compared taking into account the individual characteristics of respondents. If individuals with similar characteristics, but living in very dissimilar social contexts, show different levels of social trust, it would suggest that structural factors might be more important in explaining social trust differentials in the Americas than individual characteristics.

Socio-economic Characteristics

Do education differentials explain the lower level of social trust in Latin America and the Caribbean? It is well documented in the literature that more educated individuals show higher levels of social trust (Newton 2001, Putnam 1995). As a result, one hypothesis that emerges is that the lower level of social trust in Latin America is explained by lower levels of schooling in this region. If this were the case, it might be observed that individuals with very low levels of education in Latin America also have lower levels of social trust while well educated individuals would show levels of social trust similar to that of Canada and the United States. Figure VII.7 clearly rejects this hypothesis.

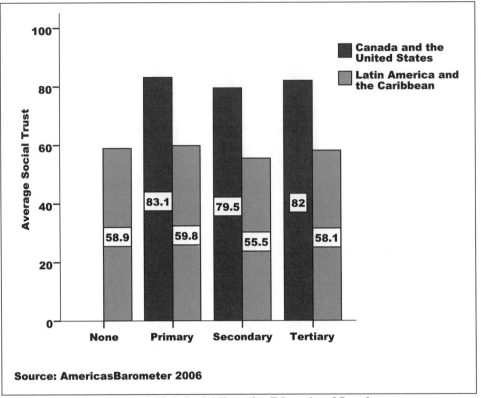

Figure VII-7. Social Trust by Educational Level

Schooling does not seem to explain the lower level of social trust in Latin America. There are no significant differences in the average level of trust across educational levels in the two regions. And, the gap in social trust between Latin America and Canada and the United States remains large at each level of education. In fact, the social trust differential is still about 23 points at each educational level, similar to the overall regional gap observed in Figure VII.3.

Demographic Characteristics

Are demographic characteristics responsible for the lower level of social trust in Latin America? Specifically, the first issue is whether men and women have similar levels of social trust in Latin America and Canada and the United States or if there is a gender bias in social capital that explains social trust differentials across regions. Second, it must be determined whether there are differentials in the age composition of the population in these two regions that would explain the social trust gap. Indeed, previous works have found that that in general social trust seems to vary by sex and age. There is evidence that men and middle age persons tend to be more trusting (Newton 2001), and therefore gender differences, along with differentials in the age composition of the population are also plausible factors explaining why the two sets of countries here analyzed show different levels of social trust. The following two figures help to answer these questions.

Figure VII.8 shows that, on average, there are no substantial differences in the level of social trust between men and women either in Latin America or in Canada and the United States. Therefore, the gap in social trust between regions is still evident even when the sample is split across genders.

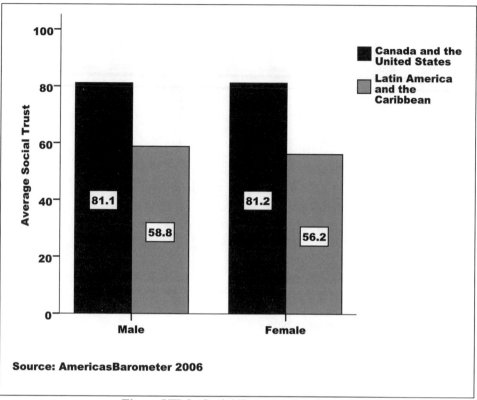

Figure VII-8. Social Trust by Gender

Figure VII.9 shows that the age composition of the population in the two regions is not the factor explaining the social trust gap either. In both regions, the trend is similar: older people are, in general, more trusting. The differentials in social trust across regions remain constant at about 20 points in each age cohort.

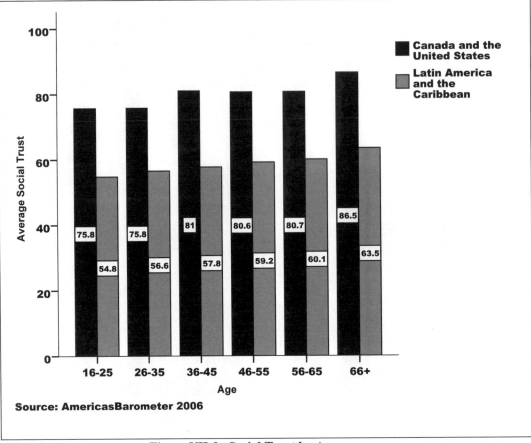

Figure VII-9. Social Trust by Age

Personal Experience with Crime

Finally, this section evaluates whether the higher rate of crime victimization in Latin America relative to Canada and the United States explains the social trust gap between these two groups of countries. The 2006-07 AmericasBaromenter data on individual crime victimization show that, as expected, on average, crime rates are higher in Latin American countries than in Canada and the United States. While in Latin America, according to the AmericasBarometer survey, the percentage of the population victimized by crime is 17.5, in Canada and the United States that figure is 11.7 percentage points. Since individuals who are victims of crime might be less likely to trust others in their communities, the higher crime victimization rate in Latin America is a plausible candidate to explain the social trust gap in these two regions. In fact, there is evidence that social trust and crime victimization are negatively correlated (Lederman, et al. 2002). Figure VII.10 shows, however, that differentials in crime victimization rates do not seem to explain the social trust gap.

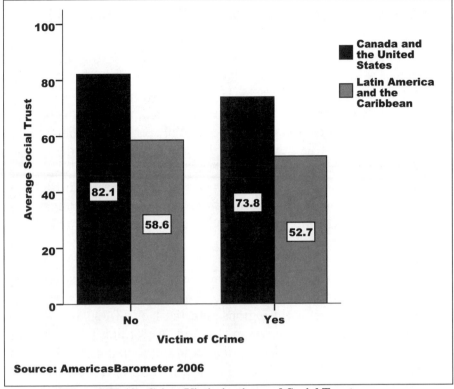

Figure VII-10. Crime Victimization and Social Trust

Although, as expected, on average those who reported having been victims of crime show a lower level of interpersonal trust, this does not explain the differential in social trust between the two regions analyzed here. If crime victimization were an important factor explaining social trust differentials, similar levels of social trust could be found in both regions among those who did not have a personal experience with crime; however, clearly this does not seem to be the case. The average level of social trust is lower in Latin America, regardless of whether a person has been a victim of crime or not, even though in both regions trust is lower among those who have been victimized by crime. Since we know that criminals do not seek out their victims based upon the latter's level of trust, we know that low trust is a product of being a victim rather than the other way around.

In conclusion, this section did not find empirical support for the hypothesis that socio-economic and demographic individual characteristics or personal experience with crime explain why in Latin American countries individuals are less trusting of people outside their family group than in Canada and the United States. Without further analysis, the evidence presented so far seems to lend support to the thesis that deep-seated "cultural" traits might be important determinants of the type of a civic culture that one finds in different regions of the world. Although this study does not test the "culturalist" thesis directly, the following section provides evidence that structural economic factors explain, at least in part, why in the Americas some societies are more trusting than others.

Economic Inequality and Social Trust: A Multi-level Analysis

Until now, the analysis performed in this study has shown that the Latin American region unambiguously has a lower average level of social trust than the much more economically developed and democratic Canada and the United States; moreover, we have observed that the social trust gap in these two regions does not seem to be explained by gender biases, differentials in schooling, the age composition of the population, or differentials in the level of crime victimization across regions. The next step in the analysis is to determine whether the "context" matters, and if so, what structural factors in these countries seem to explain such social capital differences. In this section, we test the hypothesis that countries with higher income inequality show lower levels of social trust, or in other words, that individuals living in countries characterized by a particularly unequal distribution of income are more likely to distrust people in their communities.

The study of the consequences of economic inequality for social trust, and therefore democracy, is especially important for Latin America, which has the most unequal income distribution compared to other world regions, and the lack of equality is particularly notorious when it is compared to that of the developed world. According to recent data from the World Bank, "whereas the richest tenth of the population in the region earn 48 percent of total income, the poorest tenth earn only 1.6 percent. By contrast, in developed countries the top tenth receive 29 percent of total income, compared to 2.5 percent for the bottom tenth."[9] In fact, although income inequality has been rising in the United States in recent years, it still has a lower level of inequality than any of the Latin American and Caribbean countries examined in this chapter. This study argues that the great economic inequality in Latin America is hindering social capital by lowering the overall level of social trust.

In order to test this hypothesis, we estimated a Hierarchical Linear Model (HLM) which takes into account the fact that individuals are nested within countries. The properties of these statistical models make it possible to assess how individual characteristics affect the dependent variable, in this case the individual level of interpersonal trust and at the same time whether structural characteristics shape individuals' attitudes.[10] In other words, this statistical tool allows us to explore why, once individual characteristics are controlled for, an individual living in a Latin American country shows a lower level of social trust than an individual with similar characteristics living in the United States or Canada; that is how the context affects the average level of social trust in a country. As mentioned before, the main claim of this chapter is that income inequality is an important structural variable that explains, at least in part, the lower level of social trust in Latin American countries.

At the individual level, four variables were included in the model: years of schooling, gender, age, and crime victimization. These are the same variables analyzed in the previous section using data from the AmericasBaromenter surveys. At the country level, two competing structural

---

[9] David M. De Ferranti, *Inequality in Latin America : Breaking with History?*, World Bank Latin American and Caribbean Studies. *Viewpoints* (Washington, DC: The World Bank, 2004). p.1-1.
[10] For an overview of HLM, see Douglas A. Luke, *Multilevel Modeling* (Thousand Oaks, Calif.: Sage Publications, 2004).

variables were tested: income inequality and socioeconomic development. The economic inequality data comes from the World Bank Development Indicators, and correspond to the most recent estimate of the Gini coefficient available for each country in the sample.[11] The socioeconomic development variable corresponds to the UNDP Human Development Index for 2004, the most recent available.[12]

Table VII.1 summarizes the results of the multilevel model.[13] All the variables included in the model are statistically significant and show the expected effect on interpersonal trust. On average, males, more educated, and older individuals show a higher level of interpersonal trust, while victims of crime are more likely to distrust people in their communities. In addition, the results show that social trust is higher in more developed countries and in those where income inequality is lower.

Table VII-1. Structural and individual predictors of social trust: Hierarchical Linear Model

Variables	Coef.	Standard Err.
Structural (country-level)		
Income inequality (Gini)	-0.101**	0.052
Socio-economic development (HDI)	0.116**	0.051
Individual-level		
Years of Schooling	0.040***	0.006
Male	0.092***	0.011
Age	0.080***	0.006
Victim of crime	-0.195***	0.014
Constant	0.003	0.052
Note: *Standardized coefficients for continuous variables		
**p-value<0.05		
***p-value<0.001		
Number of observations: 31.859		
Number of groups (countries): 21		
R-squared (total): 5.5%		
R-squared (structural variables): 5.3%		
R-squared (individual variables): 0.2%		

Structural factors, economic inequality and socioeconomic development, on the other hand, are much more important predictors of social trust than individual level factors. This conclusion was drawn because although the results revealed that 5.5 percent of the total variance is explained by structural and individual factors, about 5.3 percent of the total variance is explained by

---

[11] The Gini coefficient can have a value between zero and one; it measures the extent of income inequality in a country. A larger Gini indicates a greater degree of income inequality.

[12] The Human Development Indicator (HDI) is a composite measure of the level of socioeconomic development in a country. It encompasses three measures of socioeconomic well-being: economic resources (GDP per capita at purchasing power parity), an index of education, and a health indicator, as measured by life expectancy at birth. The HDI ranges between zero and one, with a higher value denoting a higher level of development.

[13] Appendix VII.2 shows the decomposition of the variance of our social trust variable. The results show that about 10% of the total variation in social trust is due to cross-country differences. This relatively small variation across countries is explained by the fact that although there is a substantial difference in the average social trust between Latin American and Northern countries (Canada and the United States), this difference is being offset by the smaller differences in social trust across Latin American countries.

structural factors alone. [14] Moreover, the statistical analysis shows that socioeconomic development and economic inequality have almost the same effect on social trust (although in contrary directions) as shown by the absolute value of the coefficient for each of these variables. This finding reinforces the results shown in the previous section; individual characteristics are less important in explaining interpersonal trust differentials. This means that the most important sources of social trust are neither personal characteristics nor experience with crime, but rather the economic context of the place of residence. Figures VII.11 and VII.12 show the relationship between social trust and income inequality, and socioeconomic development at the country-level, accordingly.

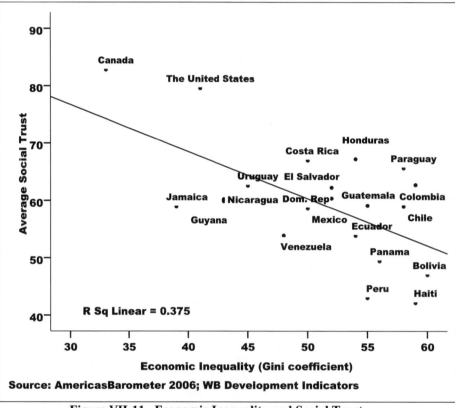

Figure VII-11. Economic Inequality and Social Trust

As can be observed in Figures VII.11 and VII.12, inequality and development are two forces working in opposite directions that affect social trust. This suggests that although improving the socioeconomic development of Latin American countries is important, improvements in the standard of living of the population alone are not likely to result in a significant increased in social trust, and therefore in stronger democracies, unless an improvement in the distribution of income also takes place.

---

[14] Although the explanatory power of the model seems to be small, since it only explains 5.5 percent of the total variance, it is important to keep in mind that regression analysis based on survey data usually yields low R-squared values.

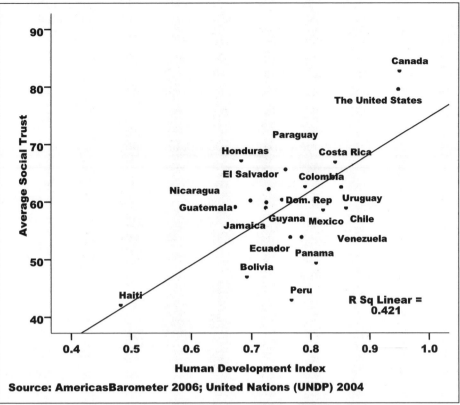

Figure VII-12. Socioeconomic Development and Social Trust

Furthermore, the findings of this section suggest that efforts to strengthen the rule of law and to mitigate social violence in Latin America are more likely to have a positive impact on democracy if at the same time the sources of conflict are mitigated. The great economic inequality faced by most Latin American countries constitutes a source of social conflict. Indeed, as mentioned before, prior research has found that social violence is more common in countries with higher economic inequality (Fajnzylber, et al. 2002, Fajnzylber, et al. 1998), and the results of this study suggest that a possible intervening factor explaining that outcome is the lower levels of social trust found in highly unequal societies. Therefore, in order to reduce social violence, an increase in social trust seems necessary, which in part can be achieved through a better distribution of wealth.

The Importance of Social Trust for Latin American Democracies

In the previous section, we identified sources of social trust in the Americas. In this section, we demonstrate that increasing the levels of social trust is imperative for fomenting a widespread democratic culture in Latin America. In general, we expect that individuals with a higher level of interpersonal trust will show a higher support for democracy, and we also expect them to be more willing to respect the civil liberties and political rights of minorities or of those whom they are more likely to disagree with. A democratic culture has been argued to be a

prerequisite for the consolidation of democracy (Diamond 1999), and support for democracy and political tolerance are indispensable values of highly democratic individuals. Interpersonal trust encourages those values. Trusting individuals are expected to oppose authoritarian rule since they are more likely to feel confident in cooperating with others and peacefully accept political outcomes even when such outcomes do not directly favor them. Indeed, the empirical evidence suggests that trusting individuals have a higher probability to tolerate and support policies that benefit minorities and the poor (Uslaner 2004). Therefore, trusting individuals are also likely to have a higher political tolerance because they are more willing to interact with people unlike themselves, and consequently, more likely to respect the rights and worldviews of others.

Figure VII.13 demonstrates that, in general, the higher the individual level of interpersonal trust, the higher the average support for democracy in Latin America. The significant positive relationship between interpersonal trust and support for democracy holds even after taking into account the individuals' evaluation of the economic situation of the country, their satisfaction with the way democracy works, their approval of current government, participation in civic organizations, and individual demographic and socioeconomic characteristics.[15]

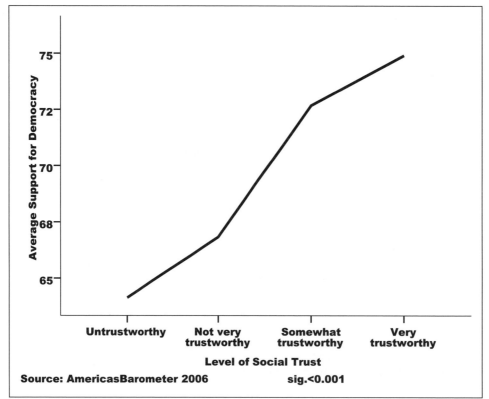

Source: AmericasBarometer 2006   sig.<0.001

Figure VII-13. Support for Democracy and Social Trust in Latin America and the Caribbean

---

[15] The regression results for support to democracy are show in Appendix VII.3. The "support for democracy" variable corresponds to the ING4 variable in the AmericasBarometer survey which asks individuals to state the extent to which they agree with the following proposition in a scale from 1 to 7: "Democracy may have problems, but it is better than any other form of government." To what extent do you agree or disagree with this statement?"

In order to test the proposition that higher interpersonal trust is associated with higher political tolerance at the individual level, the "political tolerance" index developed by Mitchell Seligson of LAPOP was included as dependent variable in the multivariate statistical analysis.[16] Figure VII.14 shows that there is a positive relationship between interpersonal trust and political tolerance. This association remains significant even after controlling for the effect of civic participation, approval of current government, and other individual characteristics.

Besides showing that higher interpersonal trust translates into higher support for democracy and political tolerance, the statistical analysis revealed that interpersonal trust is consistently the most important component of social capital in Latin America, a finding that supports the recent world-wide study of Inglehart and Welzel. When the effect of civic participation on support for democracy and political tolerance are examined, the only mode of civic participation that has a positive effect on support for democracy is participation in meetings of religious organizations; however, participation in such meetings is at the same time associated with lower political tolerance. On the other hand, although participation in meetings of a political party or movement is the only mode of civic participation likely to significantly increase political tolerance, paradoxically, activism in political organizations has a negative effect on support for democracy.

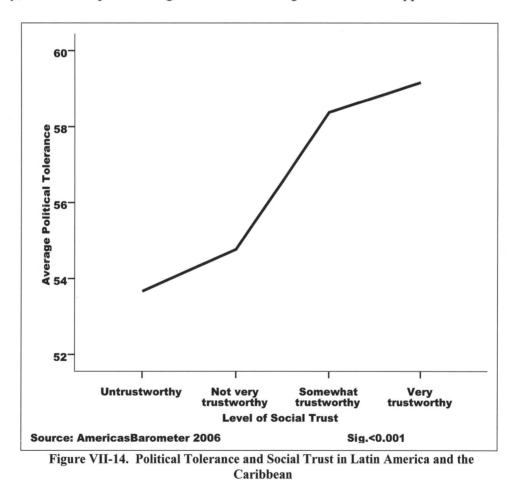

Figure VII-14. Political Tolerance and Social Trust in Latin America and the Caribbean

---

[16] The regression results for political tolerance are shown in Appendix VI.4. The political tolerance index is based on items D1, D2, D3, and D4 in the survey.

Conclusion

This chapter has demonstrated that social trust is the most important component of social capital in the Americas; when civic participation does not take place in an environment characterized by generalized social trust, as it seems to be the case in Latin America, civic activism is unlikely to contribute to the configuration of a democratic culture. In addition, this study, based on the AmericasBarometer data, confirmed the trend found in previous studies; the most politically and economically developed countries in the sample, namely Canada and the United States, show the highest levels of social trust, which reinforces the importance of social trust for development. For this reason, the main task of this chapter was to identify "sources" of social trust, and therefore explain why Latin American countries have a lower level of social trust. This chapter showed that, in general, individual characteristics and personal experience with crime have a significant impact on the individual level of interpersonal trust, and that these individual factors are not responsible for the social trust differentials between Latin America and Canada and United States. The statistical analysis showed that the most important predictors of social trust are structural rather than individual factors, namely economic inequality and socioeconomic development.

Indeed, the results show that even if the effect of economic development is taken into account, economic equality remains a significant source of trust. Specifically, the findings suggest that economic development is likely to enhance democracy by increasing the levels of social trust as long as there is a substantial improvement in the distribution of economic resources. A conclusion that gives support to the thesis that although economic development fosters democracy, individuals are likely to embrace the kind of values necessary to support democracy only if socioeconomic development is also accompanied by economic equality (Lipset 1961, 1959).

Taken together, these results suggest that although Latin American countries, in general, have progressed in some areas, reflected for example in the increased years of schooling in the region (IADB 2006), the impact of these advances on democracy is perhaps offset by the lack of a substantial improvement in the distribution of income in the region. Therefore, fiscal reform that seeks redistribution is imperative for democracy in Latin America. This chapter concludes that unless significant advances in both socioeconomic development and the distribution of economic resources occur, the likelihood of democratic consolidation in Latin America and the Caribbean will be inhibited.

References

Almond, Gabriel A., and Sidney Verba. *The Civic Culture: Political Attitudes and Democracy in Five Nations*. Princeton: Princeton University Press, 1963.

Armony, Ariel. *The Dubious Link : Civic Engagement and Democratization*. Palo Alto: Stanford University Press, 2004.

Banfield, Edward. *The Moral Basis of a Backward Society*. Chicago: The Free Press, 1958.

Boix, Carles. *Democracy and Redistribution, Cambridge Studies in Comparative Politics*. Cambridge, UK ; New York: Cambridge University Press, 2003.

Campbell, Tim. *The Quiet Revolution : Decentralization and the Rise of Political Participation in Latin American Cities, Pitt Latin American Series*. Pittsburgh, Pa.: University of Pittsburgh Press, 2003.

De Ferranti, David M. *Inequality in Latin America : Breaking with History?, World Bank Latin American and Caribbean Studies. Viewpoints*. Washington, DC: The World Bank, 2004.

Diamond, Larry. *Developing Democracy: Toward Consolidation*. Baltimore: Johns Hopkins University Press, 1999.

Fajnzylber, Pablo, Lederman Daniel, and Loayza Norman. "Inequality and Violent Crime." *Journal of Law and Economics* 45, no. 1 (2002): 1.

Fajnzylber, Pablo, Daniel Lederman, and Norman Loayza. *Determinants of Crime Rates in Latin America and the World : An Empirical Assessment, World Bank Latin American and Caribbean Studies. Viewpoints*. Washington, D.C.: World Bank, 1998.

Finkel, Steven E, Aníbal Pérez-Liñán, and Mitchell A. Seligson. "The Effects of U.S. Foreign Assistance on Democracy Building, 1990-2003." *World Politics* 59 (2007): 404-39.

Fukuyama, Francis. *Trust: The Social Virtues and the Creation of Prosperity*. New York: The Free Press, 1995.

Harrison, Lawrence E. *Underdevelopment Is a State of Mind: The Latin American Case*. Boston, MA: Center for International Affairs, Harvard University and University Press of America, 1985.

IADB. "Education, Science and Technology in Latin America and the Caribbean, a Statistical Compendium of Indicators."

Inter-American Development Bank, 2006.

Inglehart, Ronald. *Culture Shift in Advanced Industrial Society*. Princeton: Princeton University Press, 1990.

———. "The Renaissance of Political Culture." *American Political Science Review* 82, no. 4 (1988): 1203-30.

———. "Trust, Well-Being and Democracy." In *Democracy and Trust*, edited by Mark E. Warren, 88-120. Cambridge: Cambridge University Press, 1999.

Inglehart, Ronald, and Christian Welzel. *Modernization, Cultural Change, and Democracy : The Human Development Sequence*. Cambridge, UK ; New York: Cambridge University Press, 2005.

Jackman, Robert W., and Ross A. Miller. "Social Capital and Politics." *Annual Review of Political Science* 1, no. 1 (1998): 47-73.

Karl, Terry Lynn. "Economic Inequality and Democratic Instability." *Journal of Democracy* 11, no. 1 (2000): 149.

Lederman, Daniel, Loayza Norman, and Menendez Ana Maria. "Violent Crime: Does Social Capital Matter?" *Economic Development and Cultural Change* 50, no. 3 (2002): 509.

Lipset, Seymour Martin. *Political Man: The Social Basis of Politics*. 1981 (expanded edition) ed. Baltimore, MD.: Johns Hopkins University Press, 1961.

———. "Some Social Requisites of Democracy: Economic Development and Political Legitimacy." *American Political Science Review* 53 (1959): 65-105.

Luke, Douglas A. *Multilevel Modeling*. Thousand Oaks, Calif.: Sage Publications, 2004.

Muller, Edward N., and Mitchell A. Seligson. "Civic Culture and Democracy: The Question of the Causal Relationships." *American Political Science Review* 88 (1994): 635-54.

———. "Insurgency and Inequality." *American Political Science Review* 81 (1987): 425-51.

Newton, Kenneth. "Trust, Social Capital, Civil Society, and Democracy." *International Political Science Review* 22, no. 2 (2001): 201.

Norris, Pippa. *The Democratic Phoenix: Reinventing Political Activism*. Cambridge: Cambridge University Press, 2002.

Przeworski, Adam. *Democracy and Development : Political Institutions and Well-Being in the World, 1950-1990*. Cambridge: Cambridge University Press, 2000.

Putnam, Robert. "The Strange Death of Civic America." *The Independent* 1996, 13.

Putnam, Robert D. *Bowling Alone: The Collapse and Revival of American Community*. New York: Simon & Schuster, 2000.

———. *Making Democracy Work: Civic Traditions in Modern Italy*. Princeton, NJ: Princeton University Press, 1993.

———. "Tuning in, Tuning Out: The Strange Disappearance of Social Capital in America." *PS, Political Science & Politics* 28, no. 4 (1995): 664.

Seligson, Mitchell A. "Can Social Capital Be Constructed? Decentralization and Social Capital Formation in Latin America." In *Developing Cultures : Essays on Cultural Change*
edited by Lawrence E. Harrison and Jerome Kagan, xvi, 399 p. New York: Routledge, 2006.

———. "The Renaissance of Political Culture or the Renaissance of Ecological Fallacy." *Comparative Politics* 34 (2002): 273-92.

Theiss-Morse, Elizabeth, and John R. Hibbing. "Citizenship and Civic Engagement." *Annual Review of Political Science* 8, no. 1 (2005): 227-49.

Uslaner, Eric M. *The Moral Foundations of Trust*. New York: Cambridge University Press, 2002.

———. "Producing and Consuming Trust." *Political Science Quarterly* 115, no. 4 (2000): 569-90.

———. "Social Capital, Television, and The "Mean World": Trust, Optimism, and Civic Participation." *Political Psychology* 19, no. 3 (1998): 441-67.

Uslaner, Eric, M. . "Trust and Social Bonds: Faith in Others and Policy Outcomes Reconsidered*." *Political Research Quarterly* 57, no. 3 (2004): 501.

Uslaner, Eric M. , and Mitchell Brown. "Inequality, Trust, and Civic Engagement." *American Politics Research* 33, no. 6 (2005): 868.

Verba, Sidney, Kay Lehman Schlozman, and Henry E. Brady. *Voice and Equality : Civic Voluntarism in American Politics*. Cambridge, Mass.: Harvard University Press, 1995.

Statistical Analysis

Appendix VII.1

Dependent Variable : Civic participation in at least in one civic organization* (Nineteen Latin American countries)						
	Odds Ratio	Linearized Std. Err.	t	P>t	[95% Conf.Interval]	
Social Trust	1.001	0.000	2.850	0.004	1.000	1.002
Education	1.139	0.023	6.440	0.000	1.095	1.185
Approval current government	1.202	0.077	2.890	0.004	1.061	1.362
Age	1.006	0.001	5.930	0.000	1.004	1.008
Male	0.967	0.009	-3.820	0.000	0.950	0.984
Wealth	0.769	0.020	-10.230	0.000	0.732	0.809
Guatemala	0.715	0.080	-2.980	0.003	0.573	0.891
El Salvador	0.900	0.088	-1.080	0.282	0.742	1.091
Honduras	1.162	0.122	1.430	0.153	0.946	1.426
Nicargua	0.780	0.082	-2.360	0.018	0.635	0.959
Costa Rica	0.587	0.060	-5.250	0.000	0.481	0.716
Panama	0.512	0.062	-5.500	0.000	0.403	0.650
Colombia	0.904	0.100	-0.900	0.366	0.727	1.125
Ecuador	1.174	0.113	1.670	0.094	0.973	1.418
Bolivia	2.014	0.222	6.340	0.000	1.622	2.501
Peru	1.752	0.194	5.070	0.000	1.410	2.177
Paraguay	0.607	0.066	-4.600	0.000	0.491	0.751
Chile	0.698	0.080	-3.150	0.002	0.558	0.873
Uruguay	0.546	0.056	-5.890	0.000	0.447	0.668
Venezuela	0.959	0.118	-0.340	0.736	0.753	1.222
Dom. Rep.	1.527	0.157	4.120	0.000	1.248	1.868
Haiti	1.520	0.189	3.370	0.001	1.191	1.940
Jamaica	1.437	0.156	3.340	0.001	1.162	1.778
Guyana	1.394	0.150	3.090	0.002	1.129	1.720
*Logistic Regression Model; standard errors take into account design effect Reference country: Mexico Number of observations: 29.605						

Appendix VII.2

Variance Decomposition Dependent Variable: Interpersonal Trust	
Random-effects Parameters	
Between groups	.103
Within groups	.927
Total	1.020
Percentage of variance explained by between groups differences:	10%
Statistical significance : 0.000; Number of observations: 32.274; Number of groups: 21	

173

Appendix VII.3

Dependent Variable : Support for Democracy (ING4)* (Eighteen Latin American countries)						
	Coef.	Linearized Std. Err.	t	P>t	[95% Conf. Interval]	
Social Trust	0.049	0.007	7.110	0.000	0.035	0.062
Religious org.	1.406	0.494	2.850	0.004	0.438	2.375
Parents' association	-3.315	0.772	-4.290	0.000	-4.830	-1.801
Community org.	-0.439	0.806	-0.540	0.586	-2.019	1.142
Professionals, etc. org.	-2.373	1.096	-2.170	0.031	-4.523	-0.223
Political party or movement	-2.401	1.204	-1.990	0.046	-4.763	-0.039
Education	2.871	0.298	9.620	0.000	2.286	3.456
Approval current government	10.920	1.069	10.210	0.000	8.823	13.018
Satisfaction with democracy	0.135	0.010	13.600	0.000	0.115	0.154
Economic situation	-0.643	0.242	-2.650	0.008	-1.118	-0.167
Wealth	0.428	0.128	3.350	0.001	0.177	0.678
Age	0.140	0.013	10.910	0.000	0.115	0.166
Male	0.626	0.352	1.780	0.075	-0.064	1.316
Guatemala	0.410	1.525	0.270	0.788	-2.582	3.402
El Salvador	5.378	1.865	2.880	0.004	1.719	9.036
Honduras	-5.943	1.487	-4.000	0.000	-8.859	-3.027
Nicaragua	0.410	1.525	0.270	0.788	-2.582	3.402
Costa Rica	-4.407	1.575	-2.800	0.005	-7.497	-1.317
Panama	7.635	1.443	5.290	0.000	4.805	10.466
Colombia	-13.249	1.968	-6.730	0.000	-17.109	-9.389
Ecuador	1.335	1.503	0.890	0.375	-1.612	4.282
Bolivia	-0.286	1.623	-0.180	0.860	-3.470	2.898
Peru	-2.343	1.425	-1.640	0.100	-5.139	0.453
Chile	-6.713	1.696	-3.960	0.000	-10.041	-3.386
Uruguay	3.615	1.730	2.090	0.037	0.221	7.009
Venezuela	8.650	1.550	5.580	0.000	5.610	11.690
Dom. Rep.	8.462	2.245	3.770	0.000	4.058	12.865
Haiti	8.672	1.503	5.770	0.000	5.724	11.621
Jamaica	8.961	2.192	4.090	0.000	4.662	13.260
Guyana	7.828	1.577	4.960	0.000	4.735	10.920
Constant	2.914	1.606	1.810	0.070	-0.237	6.064

*Linear Regression Model (OLS); standard errors take into account design effect
Reference country: Mexico
Number of observations: : 25.468; R-squared: 0.11

Appendix VII.4

Dependent Variable : Political Tolerance* (Nineteen Latin American countries)						
	Coef.	Linearized Std. Err.	t	P>t	[95% Conf. Interval]	
Social Trust	0.038	0.007	5.460	0.000	0.024	0.051
Religious org.	-0.876	0.475	-1.840	0.065	-1.807	0.056
Parents' association	-2.335	0.711	-3.290	0.001	-3.729	-0.941
Community org.	-1.004	0.793	-1.270	0.205	-2.559	0.551
Professionals, etc. org.	1.656	1.058	1.570	0.118	-0.419	3.731
Political party or movement	4.175	1.082	3.860	0.000	2.053	6.296
Approval current government	-8.280	0.892	-9.290	0.000	-10.029	-6.532
Education	3.899	0.301	12.970	0.000	3.309	4.488
Wealth	0.330	0.123	2.680	0.007	0.089	0.571
Edad	0.006	0.013	0.460	0.648	-0.019	0.031
Male	2.431	0.329	7.380	0.000	1.785	3.077
Guatemala	-2.566	1.354	-1.890	0.058	-5.222	0.091
El Salvador	0.350	1.274	0.270	0.784	-2.149	2.848
Honduras	-8.805	1.592	-5.530	0.000	-11.926	-5.683
Nicaragua	-3.015	1.679	-1.800	0.073	-6.308	0.278
Costa Rica	4.016	1.484	2.710	0.007	1.104	6.927
Panama	-7.471	1.800	-4.150	0.000	-11.001	-3.941
Colombia	-3.708	1.491	-2.490	0.013	-6.632	-0.783
Ecuador	-11.038	1.392	-7.930	0.000	-13.769	-8.307
Bolivia	-11.977	1.375	-8.710	0.000	-14.673	-9.281
Peru	-4.242	1.466	-2.890	0.004	-7.117	-1.367
Paraguay	0.704	1.635	0.430	0.667	-2.502	3.910
Chile	-1.003	2.065	-0.490	0.627	-5.053	3.046
Dom. Rep.	5.469	1.914	2.860	0.004	1.716	9.223
Haiti	8.920	1.856	4.810	0.000	5.280	12.560
Jamaica	3.798	1.668	2.280	0.023	0.526	7.069
Guyana	7.690	1.998	3.850	0.000	3.772	11.608
Constant	15.711	1.569	10.010	0.000	12.633	18.788

*Linear Regression Model (OLS); standard errors take into account design effect
Reference country: Mexico
Number of observations: 28.231
R-squared: 0.09

VIII.   National Identity and Ethnic Minorities in the Americas[*]

Daniel Moreno[**]

Abstract

This chapter focuses on the strength of the bond between citizens and the national political community in the sample of countries included in the AmericasBarometer 2006-7 by LAPOP. Two research questions are explored: First, how does the ethnic minority status affect the sense of national belonging among citizens? And second, what is the effect that the level of development has on the sense of national belonging? A multi-level analysis is employed to determine the effect that ethnic identity, as an individual level variable, and the level of development as a country level variable have on the sense of national belonging. Evidence suggests that, excepting three countries, ethnic minority status does not have a relevant effect on the strength by which citizens relate to the national political community; this finding seems to be independent from the level of development of a country. At the national level, human development appears to be an important predictor of the average strength of the bond between citizens and the nation.

This chapter focuses on the connection citizens have to their national political community. In particular, it explores the relationship between ethnic identity and the sense of national belonging, taking into consideration the fact that it is possible for there to be important differences in this relation according to each country's level of development.

This topic has become more relevant in the last two decades, during which ethnic identities have become more important as part of a trend that could very well be called global (Brysk 2000; Connor, 1994). In the 1990s, the breakdown of Yugoslavia and the civil war in Rwanda were the most visible signs, albeit not the only ones, of the potentially negative consequences of the exacerbation of identity on political stability in those countries. In present times, there are citizens in different Latin American countries who question the legitimacy of the national state itself; this makes observers point at the bonds between citizens and the State as a possible explanation for differences in the quality of democracy in the region.

In this chapter responses are sought for the following questions: Following a world-wide trend of politicization of ethnic identities, has this trend become a threat to democracy in the

[*] This chapter has been prepared thanks to financial support from USAID/Bolivia and the Center For the Americas at Vanderbilt University. Suggestions and commentary by Mitchell A. Seligson and the LAPOP team members were particularly useful for this paper. Any errors and omissions are only the author's own.

[**] Ph.D. candidate at Vanderbilt University; Fellow of the Center for the Americas 2006-2008.

Americas? What role does the level of national development play in the relation between identities and the feeling of national belonging? What other variables may explain the relative strength of the link between the citizen and the national political community? In order to perform this analysis, the entire sampling of the AmericasBarometer for the year 2006-07 is used.

The National Political Community

The sense of national belonging is one of the most important conditions for democracy. In order to feel motivated to participate in democracy as well as to abide by the law, citizens need to recognize the State they live in as legitimate. From this insight, and following the line drawn by Mill (1993), Rustow suggests that the strength of the bond between citizen and State is an indispensable condition for democracy (1970).

Being part of a nation in some way implies that one's own destiny is joined to that of the rest of its citizens. It also implies that all citizens accept and recognize the legitimate power of the State. The national political community, the nation of citizens, can therefore be understood as an imaginary community, as it has been defined in Anderson's (1993) seminal work; that is, as a community of persons who, without knowing each other, imagine they share the same bond of fraternity and equality.

In spite of the importance of this area of study, comparative politics has paid very little attention to this matter, and empirical studies based on quantitative information have been scarce or nonexistent (Juviler and Stroschein 1999). A notable exception has been the Smith and Jarkko study (2001).

Most studies that deal with national identity do so only tangentially, often stemming from the greater concept of system support, as part of what has been called "diffuse support" (Dalton 1999; Dalton 2004; Easton 1965; Easton 1975; Muller, Jukam and Seligson 1982; Norris 1999). In this chapter, an explicit distinction is made between the concepts of support for the system and that of belonging to a national political community. Although it seems clear that feeling oneself part of a political nation is a necessary condition for showing support for the political and institutional system, it should not be considered part of the same theoretical construct.

National Belonging: Is it Necessary for Democracy?

To what extent is this sense of belonging to a national political community important for democracy? To respond to this question, two elements of that support that are central to democracy will be analyzed: system support—which refers to the relation between citizens and State, as well as political tolerance—which speaks of a horizontal relationship between citizens within the framework of a democratic State.

The LAPOP 2006-2007 data is revealing and demonstrates that the feeling of belonging to a national political community has a positive effect on these democratic values. Figure VIII.1 shows the relationship of national pride, described and analyzed below, with support for the political system, measured as described in chapter IV of this volume.

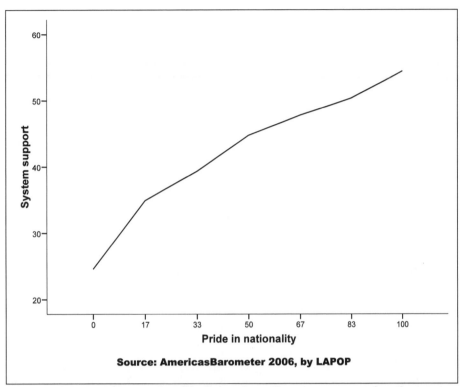

Source: AmericasBarometer 2006, by LAPOP

Figure VIII.1: Effects of pride in nationality on support for the system

This figure indicates that the correlation is clear: people who feel greater pride in their nationality tend to be more supportive of the country's political system. The relationship is strong (r=0.230) and statistically significant (p<0.001). Regarding support for the system and national pride, it is possible, however, that both variables measure concepts that are too closely connected to establish a causal relationship between the two variables.

To determine the existence of a causal relationship, another value that is central to democracy, political tolerance, is examined. Tolerance has to do with citizen respect for the right of others to think and act in a manner that is different and perhaps opposite from their own (Adorno, et al. 1950; Gibson 1992). This variable is described and analyzed in chapter IX of this volume. Figure VIII.2 shows the relationship between political tolerance and the measure of acceptance with regards to the idea of common values, the other variable considered in this chapter.

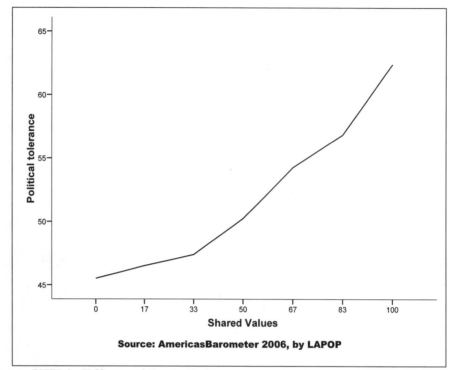

Source: AmericasBarometer 2006, by LAPOP

Figure VIII.2: Effects of the belief in common values on political tolerance

The correlation between the two variables is strong and significant (r=0.18, p<0.001). The appropriate test of robustness of this relationship is a lineal regression analysis in which statistical control factors that generally explain political tolerance (such as education, age, income and gender) are taken into account. Each additional ten points on the common values scale increase the average political tolerance by 2 units on its 0 to 100 scale. Hence, shared values matter for this vital element of democratic political culture.

This relationship suggests furthermore the possibility of assuming a causal relationship by means of which a greater sense of attachment to the national political community, measured by the scale of common values, results in a greater level of political tolerance. This hypothesis also has its own logical consistency; the more a person feels part of a national community, the greater the person's predisposition to showing respect for different members of this community will be. In this sense, to feel part of the national political community could lead to the recognition of the 'other' as a citizen, or as the 'legitimate other' as Mouffe (2000) puts it.

The Strength of the National Political Community in the Countries Studied

This chapter empirically analyzes two variables that refer to the strength of the bonds that link citizens to the national political community. The first stems from the following question used in the LAPOP survey: *How proud are you of being (Mexican, Guatemalan, etc.)?*

The second variable comes from the question that reads *In spite of our differences, as (Mexicans, Guatemalans, etc.) we have values that unite us as a country. To what extent do you agree with this statement?* Both questions were initially measured on a 1 to 7 scale, in which 1 means "Not at all" and 7 "Very much"; values were recoded into a zero to 100 scale to present the results more easily. These questions are normally used in studies regarding this topic, and are supported in the literature (Norris 1999).

The two variables measure two different dimensions of the bond between individuals and the national political community. The first directly addresses the level of pride that a person feels for his or her nationality and is based on the idea that the feeling of belonging to a national community is reflected in the pride of being a part of it. The second focuses on the idea that the nation exists beyond the territory of the State, in the values shared by its citizens (or at least in the belief that these values exist). These two variables have a correlation of .247 (p<0.001), which means that they are related but not very high, which suggests that the variables do indeed measure different dimensions of the concept.

Figure VIII.3 presents national averages for the two variables focused on in this chapter.

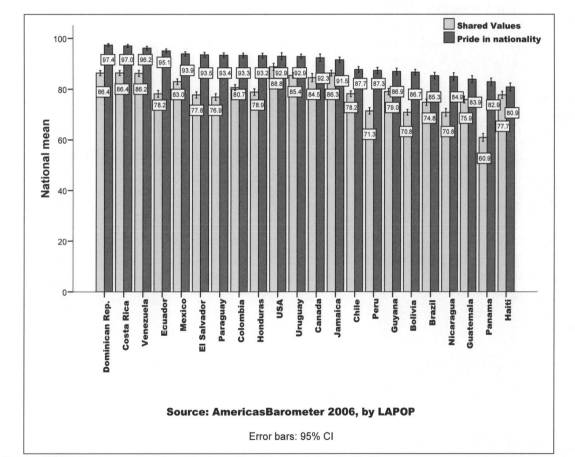

Figure VIII.3: Averages for National pride and the belief in common values, per country

It can be seen that national pride levels are relatively high in all countries in the study, although the "I's" corresponding to the error bars suggest that countries can be classified into

four groups[1]. The highest averages belong to the Dominican Republic, Costa Rica, and Venezuela. The next group of countries consists of Ecuador, Mexico, El Salvador, Paraguay, Colombia, Honduras, the United States, Uruguay, Canada and Jamaica. The third group is made up of Chile, Peru, Guyana, Bolivia, Brazil, Nicaragua, Guatemala and Panama. The lowest registered value belongs to Haiti.

The variation is much higher for the item that measures the level of agreement with the idea of common values. The United States is the country with the highest national average for this variable, and seems to stand out among the rest. Following the U.S. is the group including the Dominican Republic, Costa Rica, Jamaica, Canada, Venezuela, Uruguay, and Mexico. Next is the group is made up of Colombia, Guyana, Honduras, Ecuador, Chile, El Salvador, Paraguay, Brazil and Guatemala. Much lower values belong to Bolivia and Nicaragua, whereas Panama has an even lower average which sets it apart from any other country in the series.

Previous analysis suggests that national pride tends to be higher in stable and institutionalized democracies than in countries with more fragile democracies (Smith and Jarkko 2001). Although the data shows that countries with more stable democracies have higher levels of national pride, the relationship does not appear to be linear: the most consolidated democracies in the region, Canada and the United States, show lower averages than those of less consolidated democracies such as Ecuador or the Dominican Republic. This explanation, therefore, does not seem to clearly explain the opinions expressed in countries in the region.

An alternative explanation for these differences is the level of development in each country. Following, I present the national averages of each country according to the level of human development as measured by the United Nations Development Program[2] (UNDP 2006) Figures VIII.4 and VIII.5 show the relation between the national averages of the two focus variables and the Human Development Index calculated for each country.

---

[1] The "I" that each bar includes represents the confidence interval of the average presented. As a rule of thumb, if the "I" s of two bars overlap, it cannot be assumed that the averages are statistically different.

[2] The Human Development Index is an indicator composed of economic (GNP per-capita calculated according to Purchasing Power Parity), educational (the country's educational index), and health (the population's life expectancy) aspects. The UNDP calculates the value of the index for every country in the world bi-annually. For further information see http://hdi.undp.org.

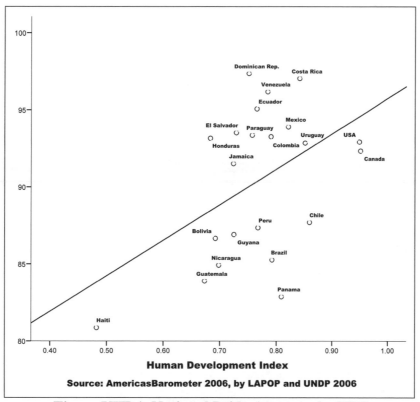

Source: AmericasBarometer 2006, by LAPOP and UNDP 2006

Figure VIII.4: National Pride Averages by HDI

It is clear that the relation between the level of human development and national pride is positive. Excluding Panama from the sample, the correlation is strong and significant (r=0.535, p<0.05). In spite of this strength, the relationship is not unequivocal nor is it monotonic. The further a country is from the line of regression, the lower the predictability of its average level of pride according to its level of human development. For example, Costa Rica, Brazil, Dominican Republic and Ecuador are above the expected average value, whereas Brazil, Chile and Guatemala are below the expected levels. Panama was excluded from the sample because it is clearly an outlier, as will be evident below. There are many factors that might explain the pride citizens have in their nationality, ranging from the performance of the national team in world soccer matches, which could be the case in Ecuador (Seligson, et al. 2006b) to the internal perception of the country's image abroad.

As Graph VIII.5 below shows, the relationship between human development and "common values" does not seem to be very strong at first look; this can be explained again by the presence of Panama. This is an atypical case, an outlier, which "pulls" the regression line; once this case is removed from the sample, the relation becomes strong and significant (r=0.497, p<0.05).

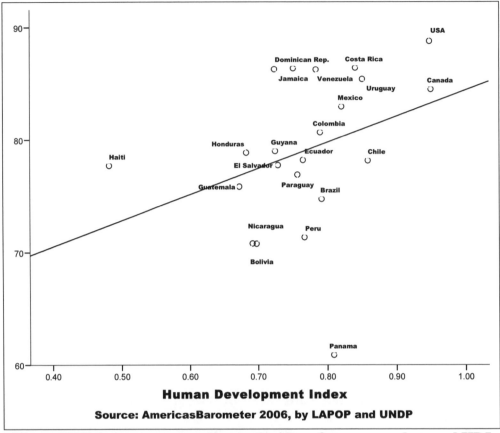

Figure VIII.5: Average according to the idea of common values and HDI

Considering national averages at the country level, the Human Development Index appears to be a factor that weighs heavily when predicting both national pride and agreement with the idea of common values. Using national averages in this type of analysis is helpful when comparing countries or registering the effects of contextual variables on matters germane to this study. However, national averages do not tell the whole story; the great differences among citizens within each country are best explained by individual characteristics, and not those of the country. This problem in the analysis is known as the "ecological fallacy" and is a common failing in the analysis of cross-national survey data (Seligson 2002).

National Belonging and Ethnic Identity. Questioning Assumptions

One of the central defining characteristics of individuals, which in theory, at least, can become a focus point for strengthening the bond between the citizen and the state or nation, is ethnic identity. There are authors for whom ethnic diversity represents an obstacle to liberal democracy (Chua 2003; Horowitz 1985; Rabushka and Shepsle 1972; Snyder 2000); the main argument for this point of view is that ethnic identities, understood as the "primordial" belonging to a group (Geertz 1963; Stack 1986; Van Evera 2001), create stronger alliances among members than those that can be created by national states that are made up of different ethnic groups. Tragic examples such as Yugoslavia and Rwanda in the 1990s are commonly

184

used as evidence for this supposed contradiction between democracy and strengthened ethnic identity.

However, this position has increasingly been debated, principally using a less "essentialist" conception of ethnic identity, in which identities are understood as complex, fluid, and malleable social constructs. This means that for some authors, ethnic diversity is not necessarily a problem for the democratic stability of a country (Abizadeh 2002; Chandra 2006; Gutmann 2003) and that ethnic differences are relevant only when they go hand in hand with social and economic differences that systematically transform ethnic patterns into mechanisms for social stratification.

One implication of the "primordialist" position in this debate is that ethnic identities would tend to be stronger than national identity. This means that ethnic minorities in the countries studied may exhibit a weaker feeling of belonging to the national community than individuals who belong to the majority ethnic group. In order to test this theory, a dichotomous variable was created assigning a value of 1 to persons who identified themselves as part of a minority group in the country and 0 to those who identified themselves as part of the majority ethnic group.

The variable was generated by the question: *How do you describe yourself?* This question was included as an item in the LAPOP questionnaire with slight variations in question wording and adjustments to the possible categories listed for each country. In most Latin American countries the majority was considered to be a group constituted by a combination of respondents who identified themselves as "white" and "*mestizo*" (mixed Native American and European), whereas "indigenous" (Native American) and "afro descendants" are part of the minority category;[3] in the United States those who identified themselves as racially "white" were classified the majority, whereas in Canada the individuals classified as part of the majority did not identify themselves with any other category except Canadian (principally French-Canadian). In Brazil, individuals who identified as '*branco*' and '*pardo*' where coded as non-minorities. In Haiti, those identified as "white" were classified as the minority. Three of the twenty-two countries surveyed by LAPOP in 2006-2007 were not included in the analysis: Paraguay, where there were no questions regarding ethnic identification on the questionnaire, as well as Jamaica and Guyana, where classifying individuals according to the options on the questionnaire is particularly complicated.[4]

Figure VIII.6 illustrates the percentage of people in each country who were coded as belonging to an ethnic minority. It can be seen that the relative number of people who were

---

[3] Although it is true that in some Latin American countries such as Guatemala and Bolivia the majority population could be "indigenous" (Gurr 1993; Van Cott 2005; Yashar 2005), the national governments have historically been made up of citizens who can be classified as "mestizos" or "white". Of course, the recent election of Evo Morales in Bolivia represents a substantial change in these power relations, and this has had important effects on citizen opinions and attitudes *vis-à-vis* the State, as confirmed by LAPOP studies (Seligson, *et al.* 2006). Despite their relative majority, and following the rule of thumb applicable for other Latin American countries, indigenous groups in Bolivia and Guatemala can be classified as *minorities* in terms of their access to power.

[4] Details of those questionnaires applied in the surveys in each of the countries are available on the LAPOP internet web page (www.lapopsurveys.org).

classified as part of the minority varies greatly from country to country, from over 40% in Guatemala to less than 5% in Nicaragua.

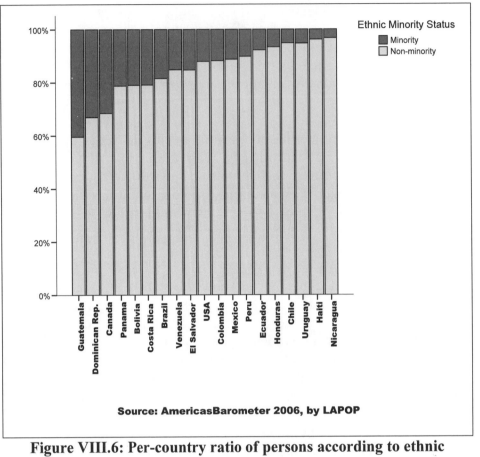

Figure VIII.6: Per-country ratio of persons according to ethnic minority status.

What effect does being part of an ethnic majority or minority have on the individual's sense of belonging to the political community? After running a linear regression analysis for each of the two dependent variables that include a person's age, sex, educational level and income as statistical controls, the differences between the ethnic majority and minority are evident in only a handful of countries. Figure VIII.7 shows the effect of the differences between majority and minority groups in the countries studied, where the difference is robust after introducing the social demographic controls. The dependent variable is pride in one's own nationality.

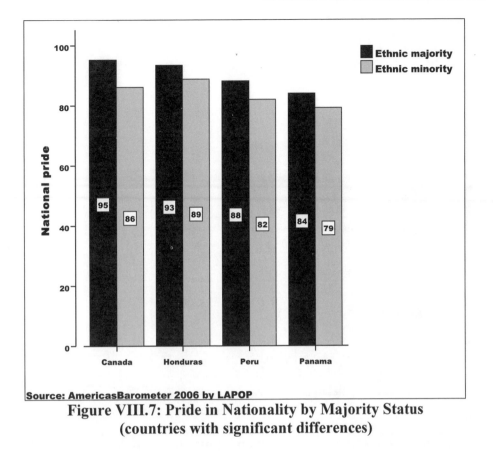

**Figure VIII.7: Pride in Nationality by Majority Status
(countries with significant differences)**

Only in Canada, Honduras, Peru and Panama do minorities feel less proud of their nationality than the ethnic majority. In Canada this factor reflects the greatest differences, as the figure shows. It is notable that in the few cases where there are differences between the majority and the ethnic minority, the minority group's averages are lower than the majority's. Therefore, only in these countries is the result what could be expected from a "primordialist" vision of ethnic identities.

When comparing the variable that measures the level of agreement with the idea of common values it can be seen that the results are very similar. Figure VII.8 shows this, as follows:

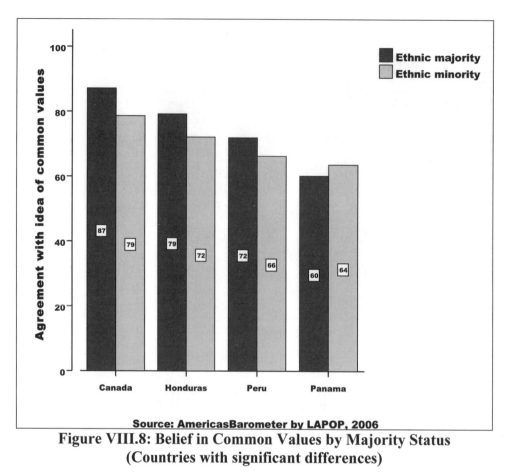

Source: AmericasBarometer by LAPOP, 2006

**Figure VIII.8: Belief in Common Values by Majority Status
(Countries with significant differences)**

The countries in which ethnic identity has some effect on the sense of national belonging are the same one appearing in the previous case. Again, the greatest differences are in Canada. The main difference in evidence upon comparing these results with those viewed previously, is that people who identify themselves as part of ethnic minority groups in Panama remain more convinced that there are common values that bond Panamanians together than the members of the white/*mestizo* majority. The minority variable in Panama shows a paradoxical behaviour: one of the variables is affected positively, the other is affected negatively.

Aside from the paradoxical case of Panama, it can be seen that the countries in which the differences between majority and minority groups are most important are Canada, Honduras and Peru. Those who identify themselves as indigenous, black or mulatto in Honduras and Peru, and as French-Canadian or members of another racial group in Canada, systematically exhibit a lesser attachment to the national political community of their respective countries than those who feel they are part of the ethnic group coded as the majority. This suggests a weaker inclusion of these populations in the national project represented by these three states.

The key question that arises from these observations, then, is: What factors cause ethnic identity to have a significant effect on the sense of belonging to the national political community in one country and not in others? Why are ethnic differences on these survey questions relevant in Peru but not in Ecuador, relevant in Honduras but not in Nicaragua? In other words, what do Canada, Honduras and Peru have in common that differentiates them from the rest of the countries in the group?

Combining Individual Factors and Contextual Factors

There are statistical tools that allow us to determine the influence that national factors, such as the Human Development Index or the Gross National Product, exert simultaneously with the effect that individual factors have, such as the person's gender and age, or personal status as a member of an ethnic majority or minority. One of these tools is multi-level statistical analysis, or hierarchical linear modelling, which allows for the combining of information regarding national and individual factors (Luke 2004; Raudenbush and Bryk 2002). A multi-level analysis model is basically a generalized linear regression model (GLM) in which the independent variable effects are allowed to vary randomly, that is to say, that they are not constant.[5]

Using the combined base of countries studied by LAPOP in 2006-2007[6], a series of statistical analyses were carried out; various equations were used to test the relations between both dependent variables and independent variables at the individual level (gender, age, ethnic minority status), as well as the Human Development Index for the year 2006 as a variable corresponding to the country.

In the same way, an interaction term between an individual level variable (ethnic status) and a national level (HDI) was included[7]. If this term proved to be statistically significant, we would then be able to assume that the effect of being part of an ethnic minority varies according to the level of human development in these countries. Table VIII.1 which we present next, presents the most important results for each variable[8].

---

[5] The model used is known as *Random Effects Maximum Likelihood* (REML).

[6] The combined base excludes Guyana, Jamaica and Paraguay for lack of information in the 'minority' variable. Panama is excluded as well due to its paradoxical behaviour regarding both variables. Therefore, 15 countries with a total of 24,426 interviews are considered here.

[7] Given that the number of countries is relatively small, the inclusion of more than one variable at this level would be a problem.

[8] The results presented for all variables come from models with random intercepts and slopes estimated for the variable "minority" in which the interaction term was not included in order to avoid collinearity. The interaction term was incorporated into subsequent models based on those now described. Results in the shaded cells of table VIII.1 correspond to the models including the interaction term.

Table VIII.1: Results of multi-level analysis on the two dependent variables

Dependent Var. Independent Var.	National Pride[+]	Common Values[+]
Minority status	*-0.64 (-0.85)*	***-1.60 (-2.37)****
Age	**0.36 (4.18)****	**0.50 (4.95)*****
Educational Level	-0.06 (-0.37)	**1.80 (8.87)*****
Gender (Women)	-0.11 (-0.46)	**0.57 (1.99)****
HDI	***24.9 (2.69)****	***24.87 (2.20)****
HDI X Minority	*-11.81 (-1.54)*	*-10.78 (-1.51)*
Constant	70.7 (9.83)***	54.49 (6.19)***
SD Minority/ Constant / Residual[++]	2.6 / 4.1 / 20.3	1.88 / 4.99 / 23.6
N individuals / country	27,179 / 18	26,684 / 18
+ Values are coefficients (z value) ++ Random Effects * p<.05; ** p<.01; *** p<.001		

In the combined eighteen-country database that is considered here, being part of an ethnic minority significantly diminishes the average belief in common values, but has no effect on the variable that measures national pride. This is the average result for the entire region (it has been observed that averages can be different in each particular country), and this is independent from the level of development in the country, the person's age, educational level and gender.

Age has a highly significant positive effect on the sense of belonging to a national political community. Once age is controlled by other factors, the older people tend to feel more pride in their nationality and to be surer of the existence of common values than do younger citizens. Therefore, young people feel less attached to the nation that they live in, perhaps strongly marked by the idea of "universal citizenship" that comes out of the information technology revolution.

The other two variables at the individual level which are included in the model are educational level and gender. Both affect significantly only the idea of common values. The higher a persons' level of education, the higher tends to be her conviction that there are values which unite the citizens in her country. Women are found to agree more with the existence of common values in their countries than men; this might indicate that men see internal differences in each country as something more unsolvable than women do.

The Human Development Index, a country level variable included in this analysis, has a positive and significant effect on national pride as well as on the variable of common values, as mentioned before. The higher the level of human development in a country, the greater the citizens' pride in their nationality and the more they tend to believe in the existence of values that unite the country. This result is independent of people's educational level and the other factors considered in the model.

In the analysis, the variable that has no statistical significance is the interaction term between human development and minority status. This means that, among countries under consideration, the level of development does not mediate the effect of minority status on the levels of feeling of belonging to the national political community. However, as previously stated, the number of countries available for analysis is small and represents a truncated distribution of the universe of countries in the world. It is possible, with a world-wide sample, that the effect of belonging to an ethnic minority on the individual's connection with the national political community might vary according to the country's level of development although probably not linearly.

In short, it can be said that in the sample made up of the Americas, ethnic minority or majority status has a small or nonexistent effect on the strength of the bond between individuals and the national political community. People who are classified here as members of an ethnic minority are less persuaded of the existence of common values among citizens in their countries than those who belong to the group characterized as majority, yet their level of national pride is indistinct from that of the majority. These findings suggest that some research in this field may have exaggerated the impact of ethnic differences for variables related to the bond with the national political community.

Conclusions

Three main conclusions can be drawn from the analysis presented in this chapter. First, ethnic minority status in and of itself has no effect on the variables that assess the strength of the bond between the citizen and the national political community. The heightened focus on ethnic identities in recent years seems to pose no risk to consolidated nations or their democracies. National pride is, generally, the same for ethnic minorities and majorities, whereas the idea of the existence of common values is slightly lower among minorities than among national ethnic majorities. There are, however, three countries in which minorities appear to be less integrated into the national political community: Canada, Honduras and Peru. These three cases merit further consideration in order to uncover factors that are common to the three nations or specific to each country, which might explain the potentially problematic insertion of minorities into the national political community.

Second, a country's human development has an effect on national pride. It has been observed that the higher the level of human development, the more citizens feel proud of their nationality and the greater their belief that they are brought together by shared values. However, contrary to expectations, the level of development does not seem to affect the relationship between ethnic minority status and national belonging. It has been found that ethnic differences matter in countries that are in very different places in the UNDP's international human development ranking: Canada is number 6, Peru number 92 and Honduras number 117 among the 177 countries for which the UNDP has information (UNDP 2006). It is probable that if the level of development mediates the effect between ethnic minority status and the sense of belonging to a national political community, it does so in a non-linear manner. In any case,

Limitations of this study derived from the use of a sample restricted only to the region make the arrival to further reaching conclusions on this issue somehow problematic. [9]

The third conclusion is that the variables that measure the bond between citizens and the national political community can aid in understanding the possibilities of the state of democracy in different countries. It has been shown that national pride is strongly related to support for the system and that the idea of common values are strongly associated with political tolerance. In the future, those interested in promoting democracy would do well to pay more attention to the conditions in which citizens form part of the national political community as an important factor in explaining the growth in the political culture of democracy.

Finally, it is necessary to point out the relevance that the study of the relationship between ethnic identities and political participation has beyond the issue of inclusion in the national political community considered in this chapter. While it has been shown here that ethnic minority status matters for the strength of the political community in some countries, it is still unclear how and under what conditions identities are relevant for more specifically political behaviours and attitudes, such as voting preferences and ideological positioning. These are questions that remain to be answered, and that the construction of datasets such as the AmericasBarometer can help to clarify.

---

[9] It is certainly possible that there are other factors that may explain the differences between these countries and others in the region, which were neither taken into account theoretically nor empirically in this chapter. Finally, it is not possible to discard the hypothesis which says that these differences are significant in each country for contextual reasons that are specific to each country and not due to the existence of a common explanatory factor. In any case, the only way to determine this is by means of a multi-level statistical analysis, using more cases at the country level, which could incorporate more country-specific variables and in this way test the effect of other factors on the variables we have focused on in this chapter.

References

Abizadeh, Arash. "Does Liberal Democracy Presuppose a Cultural Nation? Four Arguments." *American Political Science Review* 96, no. 3 (2002): 495-509.

Adorno, TW, Frenkel-Brunswik Else, Daniel Levinson, and Nevitt Sanford. *The authoritarian personality*. New York: Harper & Row publishers, 1950.

Anderson, Benedict. *Comunidades Imaginadas*. México: Fondo de Cultura Económica, 1993.

Brysk, Alison. *From Tribal Village to Global Village: Indian Rights and International Relations in Latin America*. Stanford: Stanford University Press, 2000.

Chandra, Kanchan. "What is Ethnic Identity and Does It Matter?" *Annual Review of Political Science* 9 (2006): 397-424.

Chua, Amy. *World on fire*. New York: Doubleday, 2003.

Connor, Walker. *Ethnonationalism: The Quest for Understanding*. Princeton: Princeton University Press, 1994.

Dalton, Russell. "Political Support in Advanced Industrial Democracies." In *Critical Citizens*, edited by Pippa Norris. Oxford: Oxford University Press, 1999.

———. *Democratic Challenges, Democratic Choices: The Erosion of Political Support in Advanced Industrial Democracies*. Oxford: Oxford University Press, 2004.

Easton, David. *A Systems Analysis of Political Life*. New York: Willey, 1965.

———. "A Reassessment of the Concept of Political Support." *British Journal of Political Science* 5 (1975): 435-57.

Geertz, Clifford. "The Integrative Revolution: Primordial Sentiments and Civil Politics in New States." In *Old Societies and New States: The Quest for Modernity in Asia and Africa*, edited by Clifford Geertz. New York: Free Press of Glencoe, 1963.

Gibson, James. "The Political Consequences of Intolerance: Cultural Conformity and Political Freedom." *American Political Science Review* 86, no. 2 (1992): 338-56.

Gurr, Ted Robert. *Mnorities at Risk. A Global View of Ethnopolitical Conflict*. Washington DC: United States Institute for Peace Press, 1993.

Gutmann, Amy. *Identity in democracy*. Princeton - Oxford: Princeton University Press, 2003.

Horowitz, Donald. *Ethnic Groups in Conflict*. Berkeley: University of California Press, 1985.

Juviler, Peter, and Sherrill Stroschein. "Missing boundaries of comparison: The political community." *Political Science Quarterly* 114, no. 3 (1999): 435-53.

Luke, Douglas. *Multilevel Modeling: Quantitative Applications in the Social Sciences*. Newbury Park, CA: Sage, 2004.

Mill, John Stuart. *Utilitarianism, On Liberty, Considerations on Representative Government, Remarks on Bentham's philosophy*. London- Vermont: Everyman, 1993.

Mouffe, Chantal. *The democratic paradox*. London: Verso, 2000.

Muller, Edward, Thomas Jukam, and Mitchell Seligson. "Diffuse Political Support and Antisystemic Political Behavior." *American Journal of Political Science* 26, no. 2 (1982).

Norris, Pippa, ed. *Critical Citizens: Global Support for Democratic Governance*. Oxford: Oxford University Press, 1999.

Rabushka, Alvin, and Kenneth Shepsle. *Politics in Plural Societies: A Theory in Democratic Instability*. Columbia: C. Merrill, 1972.

Raudenbush, S. W., and A.S. Bryk. *Hierarchical Linear Models: Applications and Data Analysis Methods*. 2nd ed. Newbury Park: Sage, 2002.

Rustow, Dankwart. "Transitions to Democracy: Toward a Dynamic Model." *Comparative Politics* 2, no. 3 (1970): 337-63.

Seligson, Mitchell A. "The renaissance of political culture or the renaissance of the ecological fallacy?" *Comparative Politics* 34, no. 3 (2002): 237-92.

Seligson, Mitchell, *et al. Auditoría de la democracia. Informe Bolivia 2006*. Cochabamba: USAID - LAPOP - CIUDADANIA, 2006a.

———. *Auditoria de la democracia. Ecuador 2006*. Quito: CEDATOS - LAPOP, 2006b.

Smith, Tom, and Lars Jarkko. *National Pride in Cross-National Perspective* National Opinion Research Center, 2001 [cited. Available from http://www.issp.org/Documents/natpride.doc.

Snyder, Jack. *From Voting to Violence: Democratization and Nationalist Conflict*. New York: Norton, 2000.

Stack, John, ed. *The Primordial Challenge: Ethnicity in the Contemporary World*. New York: Greenwood Press, 1986.

UNDP. *Human Development Report 2006* 2006 [cited. Available from http://hdr.undp.org.

Van Cott, Donna Lee. *From movements to parties in Latin America: The evolution of ethnic politics*. New York: Cambridge University Press, 2005.

Van Evera, Stephen. "Primordialism Lives!" *APSA - CP: Newsletter of the organized section in comparative politics of the American Political Science Association* 12 (2001): 20-22.

Yashar, Deborah. *Contesting Citizenship in Latin America: The Rise of Indigenous Movements and the Postliberal Challenge*. Cambridge ; New York: Cambridge University Press, 2005.

IX. Challenges of Tolerance in the Americas[1]

Diana Orcés

Abstract

This chapter analyzes the importance of political and social tolerance for democracy. Citizens who have higher levels of tolerance are more willing to accept and respect the political rights and civil liberties of the minorities and those whom they may disagree. If the rights of minorities to express themselves freely are not guaranteed, how can democracy be sustained over the long term? For this reason tolerance is of great importance for the persistence of democracy as a form of government. In this chapter, a comparison of political and social tolerance is made across countries in which differences between political and social tolerance are partly attributed to cultural factors such as British, French, and Spanish colonial traditions. Nonetheless, the primary task of this research is to explain which individual-level factors determine differences in levels of tolerance. The most important finding in this chapter is the critical role that education plays in raising levels of tolerance: higher levels of education lead to higher levels of tolerance.

Is tolerance necessary for democracy? While most citizens support democratic norms worldwide, this same group of citizens is unlikely to extend democratic rights to "disliked groups" (Peffley and Rohrschneider 2003). Consequently, if "disliked groups" or minorities generally are denied the right to express themselves freely and their rights are not guaranteed, how can one guarantee the continuation of democracy over the long term (Seligson and Córdova 1993)?[2] For this reason, tolerance is necessary for the persistence of democracy as a system of government. Moreover, tolerance is necessary for democracy not only because it provides an environment of political freedom and diversity as well as the opportunity for political opposition's representation, but also because it may help promote the norms that make for a peaceful coexistence among divergent groups living together under a single political system.

In this chapter, the main objective is to examine the importance of political tolerance for democracy. First, the differences in levels of political tolerance across countries will be explored, focusing on Latin American and Caribbean contexts.[3] In order to accomplish that objective, an index of political tolerance will be developed to measure the acceptance by citizens of the rights

---

[1] This research project benefited from the financial support provided to the AmericasBarometer and a graduate fellowship for the author's education by USAID. The author is also grateful for the computer-equipped office space provided by the Center of the Americas and the Provost at Vanderbilt University. The author is highly indebted to her Latin American Public Opinion Project (LAPOP) colleagues for constantly given advice and guidance throughout the process of working on this research, and especially to Professor Seligson for his unconditional support and for making this research possible in the first place.

[2] The point of departure for the theoretical basis for a stable democracy is Seligson and Córdova's (Seligson and Córdova 1993; Seligson 2000) study. Nations can become authoritarian if tolerance is low even if system support is high, according to that research.

[3] North American countries are included in the first part of the analysis to contrast differences in levels of political tolerance between established democracies and emergent democracies.

of citizens who are persistent critics of their system of government. Next, the factors that influence political tolerance will be analyzed, focusing on the critical role that education plays for raising levels of political tolerance. The last section of this chapter will be devoted to another dimension of tolerance, what is termed here as "social tolerance," measured by the expressed level of acceptance of the political rights of homosexuals. The chapter concludes with the implications of the findings.

Political Tolerance

The literature on political tolerance points to the difficulty posed by its measurement. For instance, Stouffer (1955) focused on measures related to the willingness of citizens to extend civil rights to those who have different political views, such as socialists, atheists, and communists. He predicted that levels of tolerance would increase noticeably in future years. Sullivan et al. (1982) criticized Stouffer's approach by finding that increases in tolerance were merely an illusion because in reality the dislike toward those specific groups (especially communists) decreased, while the level of generalized intolerance remained unchanged. Prothro and Grigg (1960) studied the tolerance of the majority toward minorities and concluded that majorities strongly support the principles of tolerance but fail to do so with respect to specific minority groups (e.g., communists, blacks, gays). Thus, finding the most appropriate way to measure political tolerance has remained a challenge for social scientists (Dahl 1971; Gibson and Bingham 1982; McClosky 1983; Gibson 1992a). [4]

The AmericasBarometer 2006-2007 round of surveys carried out by the Latin American Public Opinion Project (LAPOP) has its own measures of political tolerance, which have been found to be reliable in prior studies, and have the advantage as well of providing comparisons across time and countries. The 2006-2007 survey covers four aspects of democratic rights, and rather than focusing on a specific minority group (e.g., communists), it looks at the rights of people who persistently "only say bad things about" their country's form of government. The following questions were asked in all countries; response categories ranged from 1 "firmly disapprove" to 10 "firmly approve":

D1. There are people who speak negatively of the country's form of government, not just the incumbent government but the system of government. How strongly do you approve or disapprove of such people's **right to vote**?
D2. How strongly do you approve or disapprove that such people be allowed **to conduct peaceful demonstrations** in order to express their views?
D3. How strongly do you approve or disapprove of such people being permitted **to run for public office**?
D4. How strongly do you approve or disapprove of such people appearing on television **to make speeches**?

---

[4] For key studies on political tolerance, see (Gibson 2006) (Gibson 2005a) (Gibson 2005b) (Gibson 2002) (Gibson 1987) (Gibson 1989) (Gibson 1992b)(Gibson and Duch 1991) (Gibson and Duch 1993).

The advantage of this methodology is that it does not exclude those who do not select a "least-liked" group; neither does it link the answer to a specific group.[5] Its shortcoming is that it focuses only on those who always speak negatively about the form of government. A consequence of this measure is that the people who disagree with the form of government tend to be more tolerant toward those who think the same way they do. Yet, that defect is easily resolved by controlling for the political preferences of the respondents (Seligson, *et al.* 2006).

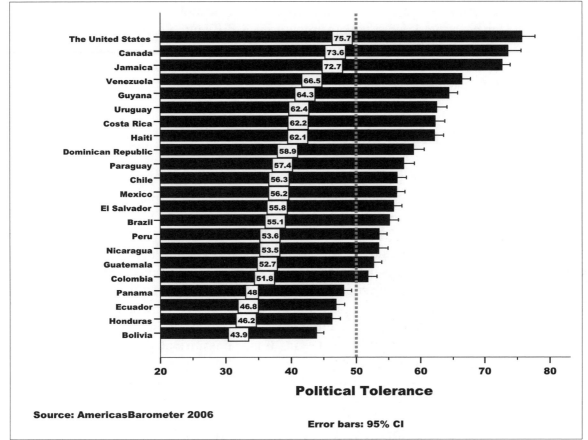

Figure IX-1. Political Tolerance by country

Figure IX-1 shows that on a scale from 0 to 100 the average level of political tolerance is far higher in the United States, Canada, and Jamaica than it is in any of the Spanish-speaking or French-speaking countries in the study. In contrast, Panama, Ecuador, Honduras, and Bolivia demonstrate the lowest levels of political tolerance—below 50 points on scale from 0 to 100. These results may suggest that countries that are stable democracies enjoy higher levels of political tolerance, possibly because "when civil liberties have been in place for longer periods, citizens have more opportunities to apply democratic norms to disliked opponents" (Peffley and Rohrschneider 2003: 245). For instance, the United States and Canada have a long history of democratic governance (i.e., from 1787 and 1867 respectively[6]). However, these results also suggest that even though established democracies enjoy higher levels of political tolerance, they

---

[5] The current conventional format of tolerance items is to ask respondents to select their "least liked group." In a LAPOP study of Nicaragua, nearly half of the respondents refused to select a group.

[6] http://www.infoplease.com/countries.html

are far from achieving universal agreement on tolerance. Thus, even among the countries at the top of the group, a culture of political intolerance is present among an important segment of the population (Gibson 1992b).

Other cases in the sample that enjoy high levels of political tolerance are Costa Rica and Venezuela[7] which, like the United States and Canada, have the longest democratic tradition of any of the Latin American and Caribbean cases in the sample (i.e. from 1949 and 1959 respectively). However, the order of the other countries is difficult to explain. Haiti has relatively high levels of political tolerance, but does not have a British colonial background and no history of democracy. At the other end, Bolivia is very low, perhaps as a consequence of being the most deeply ethnically divided of any country in the sample.

Why Does Political Tolerance Differ Across Countries?

It is noteworthy that Jamaica (73) and Guyana (64) compared to other non-North American countries in the study enjoy high levels of tolerance despite their short history of democratic performance (i.e., from 1962 and 1992 respectively) and lower levels of economic and political development similar to countries in Latin America. Why, then, are their levels of political tolerance relatively high? Latin America and Caribbean countries have been characterized by a long history of political and economic instability. At the same time, widespread inequality has been present in the region (Patrice 2003). Many scholars contend that one explanation for the differences in political and economic situations between developed and developing countries in the Americas is cultural legacies of colonization. The success of northern hemisphere countries, namely the United States and Canada, is attributed to its English-Protestant tradition that generated stronger political and economic institutions (Engerman and Sokoloff 2002). In contrast, the underdeveloped nature of Latin American countries is attributed to the unequal institutional framework by the Spanish conquest (Yeager 1995).[8]

Do these cultural and institutional factors relate to the differences observed in political tolerance? One common characteristic that the U.S., Canada, Jamaica, and Guyana share is their British colonial heritage. Therefore, it seems that one factor to be related to tolerance may be colonial heritage (Seligson 1987).

Various authors concur that culture plays an important role in contributing to both economic development and democracy (Harrison and Huntington 2000). Similarly, Lawrence Harrison (1985) argues that Latin America is underdeveloped and unstable because its culture was mainly influenced by the antidemocratic values of traditional Spanish. Harrison also indicates that these values are transmitted from generation to generation through a socialization process. Furthermore, Huber et al. (1993) points out that some of the differences between Central

---

[7] Ibid. Because of many political and economic changes that Venezuela has experienced in the past few years, a more in depth explanation of Venezuela's high political tolerance will be presented at the end of this section.

[8] The "encomienda" system established by the Spaniards in Latin America is believed to have contributed to the "institutionalization" of inequality, meaning that all the political and economic power belonged to the elites while the masses derived little benefit.

America and Caribbean countries were caused by their development in the 1930s. According to these authors:

"British colonialism was important because it was an alternative to the Central American pattern of landlord or military control of the state, and thus an alternative to the use of labor unions and allied political parties. Consequently, the 30's marked the beginning of organized political life, and opened the way for the subsequent consolidation of civil society in the West Indies, whereas in Central America they solidified the pattern of the primacy of the coercive apparatus of the state and of state control over the repression of civil society, exercised either by landowner-military collations or the military alone" (79).

Therefore, higher levels of political tolerance in Jamaica and Guyana may be attributed to the processes of their colonization. Even though these accounts do not provide a complete explanation, they do offer some insight into the important role that colonialism played in these countries. Nevertheless, more empirical evidence needs to be obtained to explain the differences in political tolerance in these countries.

Which Individual-level Factors Influence Differences in Political Tolerance?

The primary research question in this chapter is to determine and explain the factors that account for the differences in levels of political tolerance. As suggested at the beginning of this chapter, tolerance matters because it legitimizes the democratic system by guaranteeing the rights of the minorities. As Gibson (1992b) points out, "tolerance matters because it is connected to a set of beliefs about the legitimacy and appropriateness of self-expression" (343). Thus, it is central to this study to evaluate the factors that contribute to levels of political tolerance.

In order to determine which factors influence political tolerance, the sample of countries included in this study is divided into three regions: 1) North America and the Caribbean; 2) Central America; and 3) South America.[9] Differences between men and women and their levels of education will be examined, beginning with the role of education in raising levels of political tolerance and in greater acceptance of "disliked groups." Education is believed to be a critical element because it enhances political tolerance even among those who have negative feelings toward a specific group (Lawrence 1976; Bobo and Licari 1989; Golebiowska 1995). Therefore, it is expected that while higher levels of education should lead toward higher levels of political tolerance, it is the quality of the education that may well have a greater impact on political tolerance. Similarly, while various studies show that women tend to have lower levels of political tolerance than men, there is reason to believe that education will have an impact on women's tolerance and that differences between both men and women will be mitigated by higher levels of education. Thus, it is expected that women will show lower levels of political tolerance than men, yet the higher the levels of education women achieve, the lower their deviation from men.

---

[9] North American countries are included in the first part of the analysis to contrast the differences in levels of political tolerance between established and emergent democracies.

North America and the Caribbean

Figures IX-2 and IX-3 show some variation from the standard pattern of relationship between education and political tolerance across various North American and Caribbean countries. The results for Canada and the United States[10] show that men are more tolerant than women at all levels of education. The remaining cases conform to the general pattern, except that in Haiti, education seems to play no role for women, and secondary education has the strongest positive effect for men. Guyana is the one case in which gender does not distinguish respondents by their levels of tolerance. It is worth noting that there are no statistically significant differences between men and women in Mexico, Haiti, and Guyana whereas the United States and Canada[11] show significant differences at the highest level of education.

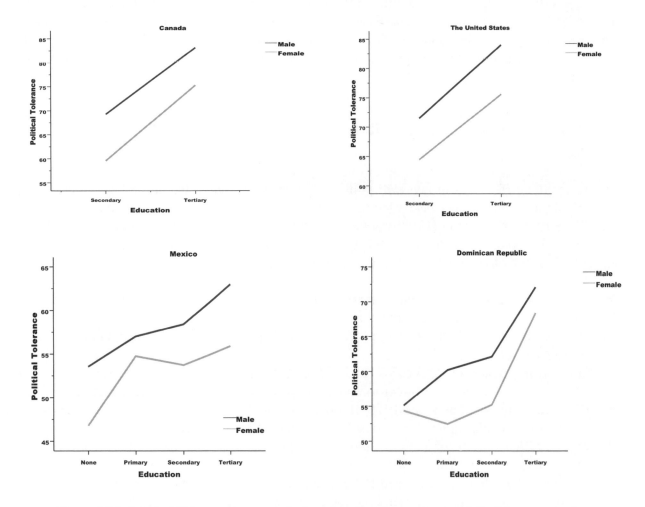

Figure IX-2. Political Tolerance by sex and education: North American and Caribbean countries

---

[10] The "primary education" category was excluded in the U.S. and Canadian graphs since there were only 2 and 6 cases, respectively. The "no education" category was excluded in the case of Guyana with only 7 cases. The reason for this decision is that means are unreliable when sample sizes are very small.

[11] The Dominican Republic shows statistically significant differences throughout all levels of education except at the highest level.

200

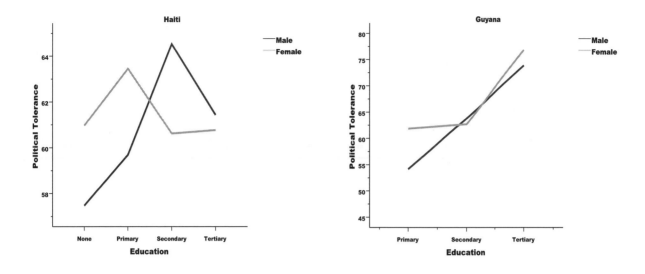

Figure IX-3. Political Tolerance by sex and education: Haiti and Guyana

These results do not support the idea that differences between men and women are mitigated by higher levels of education. Even when women achieve higher levels of education, they still exhibit lower levels of tolerance compared to men. Some research suggests that women tend to be more conservative than men. Ewa Golebiowska (1999) points out that "women are less tolerant because of their weaker commitment to abstract norms of democracy, partially due to their lower levels of political expertise. Women are also less willing to put up with groups outside the political mainstream because they perceive more threat from such groups, partially deriving from their greater commitment to moral traditionalism and intolerance of uncertainty" (58).

Central America

Figure IX-4 show a clearer pattern of the relationship between education and political tolerance in the Central American region in comparison to the region previously examined. Costa Rica, El Salvador, Nicaragua, and Panama illustrate that political tolerance increases with higher levels of education. However, this pattern disappears among women in Honduras.

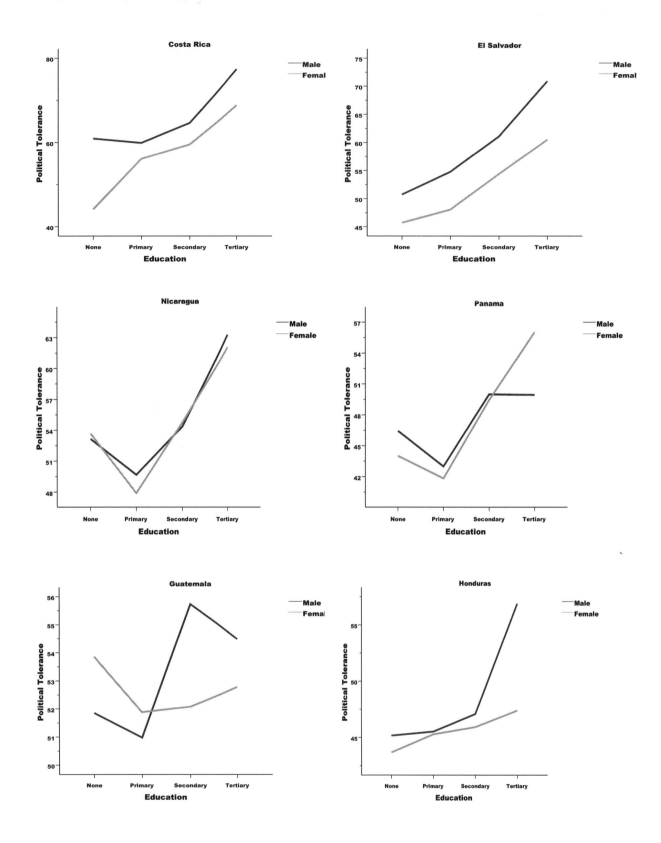

Figure IX-4. Political Tolerance by sex and education: Central American countries

Similarly, Panama shows a relationship between education and political tolerance with the exception of the highest levels of education, at which women have more tolerance than men. However, the difference is not statistically significant. The only Central American country that demonstrates marked differences in tolerance between men and women is El Salvador. One could speculate that while acquiring higher levels of education influences political tolerance, it is the quality of the education that has a greater impact on political tolerance (Moreno and Seligson 2006). Guatemala is the single country in the region without a clear pattern for women, but in the case of men it conforms to the general pattern.

South America

Figure IX-6 indicates that political tolerance increases with higher levels of education in Colombia, Bolivia, Chile, and Paraguay. This relationship appears to hold among men whereas among women, the relationship disappears with the exception of Chile. In Venezuela, Ecuador, and Peru (IX-5) education plays no role for men or women. Colombia is the only country in the region that shows statistically significant differences by sex.

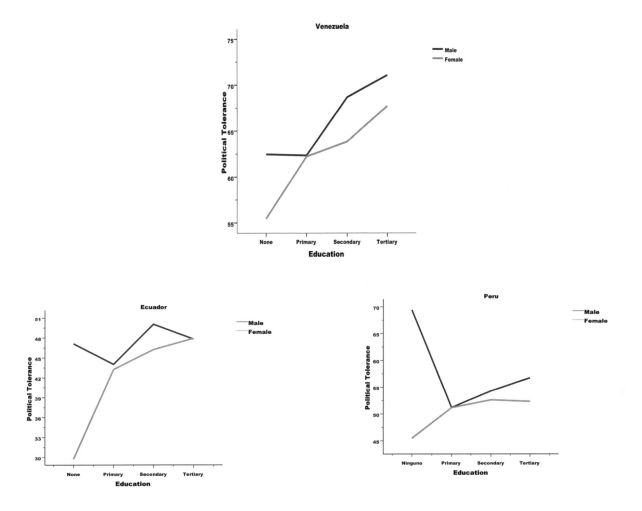

Figure IX-5. Political Tolerance by sex and education: Venezuela, Ecuador, and Peru

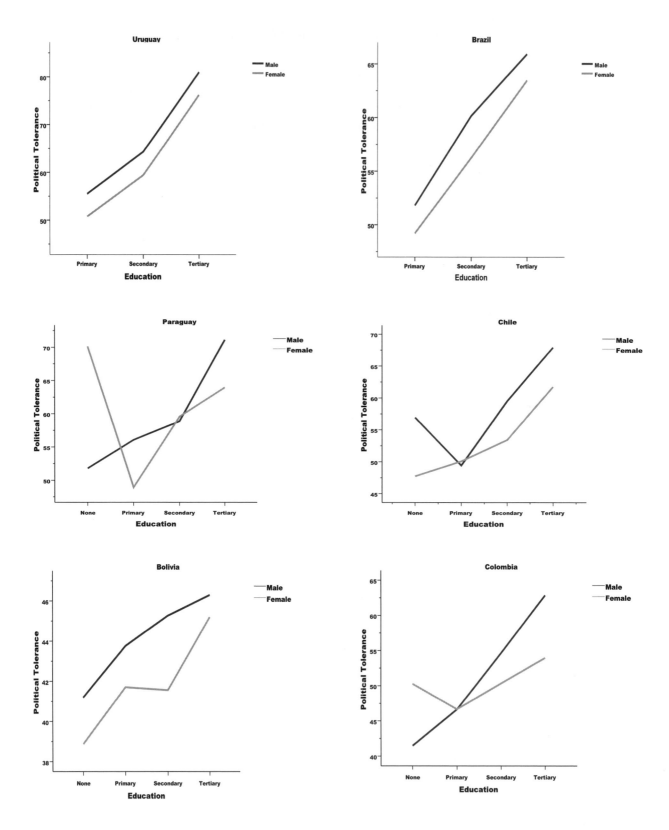

Figure IX-6. Political Tolerance by sex and education: South American countries

To sum up, the influence of education on political tolerance is evident among countries that are considered established democracies. For instance, the United States, Canada, and Costa Rica show a sharp impact of education and tolerance; the higher the level of education, the higher the effect on increasing levels of political tolerance. However, there are developing democracies that also present marked statistical differences between levels of education (i.e., El Salvador, Nicaragua, Guyana, and the Dominican Republic. We also find this pattern in South America, except for Paraguay and Peru. These results may suggest that while higher levels of education should lead to higher levels of political tolerance; it is the quality of education that has a greater impact on political tolerance (Moreno and Seligson). Furthermore, even with higher levels of education for females, the differences in political tolerance between men and women are not eliminated,[12] perhaps because, as some research suggests, women are more traditional than men.

Methods and Results

An ordinary least-squares (OLS) linear regression model is used to estimate the effects of the predictor variables. The model includes a set of theoretically relevant socio-demographic variables as well as a measure of support for the system.[13] The dependent variable, political tolerance, consists of an index of four questions presented at the beginning of this chapter. Similarly, a measure of attendance to religious organizations[14] is incorporated in the model. It is expected that regular attendance at meetings of such organizations will have a negative effect on political tolerance since it relates to support for more traditional values. A measure of interpersonal trust is also included in the model where those with low levels of interpersonal trust are expected to have less political tolerance.[15] In addition, a measure of the President's job approval is incorporated to control for the opposition to the current government.[16] The socio-demographic variables include measures of age, wealth, and area of residence; a dummy variable representing females and dummy variables representing "primary education," "secondary education," and "higher education." This division of levels of education will help predict the influence that the level of education has on political tolerance. Finally, dummies of all the countries under examination are also incorporated to render a clear assessment of how political tolerance differs across countries and across regions.[17]

The results in Table IX-1 show that education is a significantly positive factor predicting political tolerance, especially among respondents with secondary and higher education. Similarly, women tend to have lower levels of tolerance than men. Residing in urban areas as opposed to rural areas increases levels of political tolerance. For theoretical reasons, system support was

---

[12] In countries that show statistical significant differences between levels of education.

[13] The creation of the "System Support" index is presented elsewhere in this volume.

[14] **CP6.** Meetings of any religious organization, do you attend their meetings at least once a week, once or twice a month, once or twice a year, or never? The variable was recoded reversing the scale by assigning higher values to those who attend religious organizations regularly.

[15] **IT1.** Now, speaking of the people from here, would you say that people in this community are generally (1) very trustworthy, (2) somewhat trustworthy, (3) not very trustworthy or (4) untrustworthy?

[16] **M1.** Speaking in general of the incumbent administration, would you say that the job being done by the President is: (5) Very good (4) Good (3) Neither good nor bad (fair) (2) Bad (1) Very bad

[17] In this section of the chapter, the United States and Canada are excluded from the analysis since the study focuses on the Latin American and Caribbean contexts.

included in the model which shows that system support influences positively political tolerance. On the other hand, regular attendance to religious organizations, lower levels of interpersonal trust, and approval of the President's job has a negative effect on political tolerance. As mentioned previously, political tolerance refers to the rights of those who persistently "only say bad things" about the country's form of government. Therefore, the finding that indicates that those who approve the President's job are less tolerant conforms to the general expectation since they will be less likely to sympathize with the opposition.

Table IX-1. Factors that explain political tolerance: results of the linear regression

	Unstandardized Coefficients		Standardized Coefficients		
	B	Std. Error	Beta	t	Sig.
System Support	.097	.008	.080	11.867	.000
Primary Education	.158	.916	.003	.173	.863
Secondary Education	4.040	.934	.072	4.326	.000
Higher Education	9.077	1.009	.128	8.994	.000
Female	-2.787	.339	-.050	-8.233	.000
Age	-.080	.123	-.004	-.648	.517
Wealth	.236	.104	.017	2.268	.023
Urban Areas	1.592	.404	.027	3.938	.000
Attendance to a religious organization	-.011	.004	-.016	-2.552	.011
Interpersonal Trust	-1.062	.189	-.035	-5.621	.000
President's job approval	-2.756	.198	-.093	-13.916	.000
Mexico	-4.243	1.010	-.035	-4.200	.000
Guatemala	-6.011	1.073	-.046	-5.602	.000
Salvador	-3.379	1.032	-.028	-3.275	.001
Honduras	-12.019	1.035	-.098	-11.608	.000
Nicaragua	-6.118	1.080	-.048	-5.667	.000
Panama	-10.376	1.069	-.084	-9.702	.000
Colombia	-7.230	1.047	-.059	-6.908	.000
Ecuador	-13.684	1.045	-.111	-13.097	.000
Bolivia	-15.500	1.093	-.120	-14.178	.000
Peru	-7.407	1.071	-.060	-6.918	.000
Paraguay	-1.513	1.062	-.012	-1.424	.154
Chile	-4.352	1.023	-.036	-4.254	.000
Uruguay	1.760	1.039	.014	1.695	.090
Venezuela	4.901	1.034	.040	4.741	.000
Dominican Republic	.895	1.040	.007	.860	.390
Haiti	5.365	1.174	.039	4.571	.000
Jamaica	12.998	1.089	.096	11.935	.000
Guyana	4.504	1.070	.035	4.208	.000
(Constant)	45.330	1.683		26.930	.000

a Dependent Variable: political tolerance
b Country of reference: Costa Rica
c Reference level of education: none

R Square .096
Adj R Square .094
Estimated std. error 26.697

Ecuador and Bolivia have the lowest levels of political tolerance. Perhaps these findings could be attributed to the political instability in these countries in recent years. For instance,

Ecuador has had seven different presidents in a ten year period. The latest, President Lucio Gutiérrez, was overthrown in April 2005 after the Ecuadorian congress decided to shut down the Supreme Court.[18] In addition, various events marked by corruption (e.g. the Cabrera and Zambrano cases) had become the trademark of the Ecuadorian political arena. Therefore, it is no surprise that political tolerance of citizens is low. Nonetheless, a finding that remains puzzling is the relative high levels of political tolerance that Venezuela reveals despite its drastic political and economic changes in the past few years.

The case of Venezuela

Venezuela is a federal republic with a multiparty system and one of the most stable democracies in Latin America since 1959. President Hugo Chávez Frias was elected in December 1998 and assumed power in early 1999. In July 1999, a constituent assembly was formed to rewrite the constitution and it was followed by the creation of a constitutional assembly. Chávez won reelection in December 2006 with 63% of the vote. By 2007, Chávez had taken important steps to further consolidate his power and create his model of a socialist state. In January, the National Assembly voted to allow Chávez to rule by decree for a year and half. A few months later, he shut down one of the main opposition television station, RCTV. In August, the National Assembly voted to abolish presidential term limits. Chávez has proposed many reforms to the 1999 Constitution that would further consolidate his power.[19]

Table IX-2. Factors that explain political tolerance in Venezuela: results of the linear regression

	Unstandardized Coefficients		Standardized Coefficients		
	B	Std. Error	Beta	t	Sig.
System Support	.063	.037	.059	1.690	.091
Primary Education	4.418	4.685	.062	.943	.346
Secondary Education	9.750	4.562	.180	2.137	**.033**
Higher Education	11.381	4.635	.201	2.455	**.014**
Female	-4.759	1.447	-.088	-3.288	**.001**
Age	.789	.558	.041	1.413	.158
Wealth	-.010	.475	-.001	-.020	.984
Urban Areas	-1.787	3.652	-.013	-.489	.625
Attendance to a religious organization	.037	.018	.054	2.014	**.044**
Interpersonal Trust	-1.219	.757	-.044	-1.610	.108
President's job approval	-3.848	.939	-.160	-4.098	**.000**
"Antichavista" sentiment	7.838	2.052	.141	3.819	**.000**
(Constant)	44.112	7.315		6.030	**.000**

a Dependent Variable: political tolerance	R Square .078
	Adj R Square .070
c Reference level of education: none	Estimated std. error 26.035

---

[18] Congress decided to close the Supreme Court in December 2004; it was not reinstituted until almost a year later.
[19] Tarver and Frederick. 2005. <u>The History of Venezuela</u>. Greenwood Press: Westport, CT.
http://www.venezuelanalysis.com/files/images/2007/10/Constitutional-Reform-Fact-Sheet-2007.pdf
http://www.infoplease.com/ipa/A0108140.html

An ordinary least-squares (OLS) linear regression model is used to have a better assessment of the factors that explain the high levels of political tolerance in this country. The model includes the same variables as in the previous model, in addition to an index of "antichavista" sentiment.[20]

The results in Table IX-2 show that education is a significantly positive factor predicting political tolerance, especially among respondents with secondary and higher education. Similarly, as reported above, women tend to have lower levels of tolerance than men. The strong and positive significant effect that remains among those with "antichavista" sentiment even after controlling for the approval of the President's job, indicates that the wording of the tolerance items is having an impact. That is, the tolerance questions talk about those who "only say bad things about our system of government." Hence, critics of the Chávez style of rule are much more tolerant of those views than those who are not critical of it.[21]

Social Tolerance

This section examines another type of tolerance, social tolerance, which is related to the acceptance of persons and groups perceived as different. In other words, social tolerance involves "full recognition and acceptance of the identity and uniqueness of differences that are seen as not reducible to invisibility by their bearers" (Persell, Green and Gurevich 2001: 208). In this section of the chapter, social tolerance is referred to as the acceptance of minority groups perceived as different. Social tolerance will be measured through the level of acceptance of the rights of homosexuals. Respondents were asked the following question:

> **D5.** And now, changing the topic and thinking of homosexuals, how strongly do you approve or disapprove of such people being permitted to run for public office?

The contrast between higher levels of political tolerance[22] and lower levels of social tolerance is worthy of note. Figure IX-7 shows that while certain countries demonstrate relatively high levels of social tolerance (e.g., Panama, Colombia, and Bolivia), they are far from achieving the same levels as political tolerance, and even then, both types of tolerance remain distant from being in the positive end of the continuum. Similarly, the figure shows a striking contrast between North America and Latin America and the Caribbean. Canada and the United States have, on average, the highest social tolerance levels, with 76 and 70 points respectively on the 0 to 100 scale, while Haiti is the country with the lowest levels of social tolerance.

---

[20] Do you (1) strongly agree, (2) somewhat agree, (3) somewhat disagree, (4) strongly disagree:

C1ch. Do you feel proud of being associated with Hugo Chavez

C3ch. Hugo Chavez's actions make you respect him even more

C4ch. Hugo Chavez weighs the ethical and moral consequences of what he does

C5ch. Hugo Chavez expresses a convincing vision of the future

The index was recodified as a dummy variable: 0. Favor Hugo Chavez 1. Oppose Hugo Chavez

[21] For further details on Chávez see: Damarys Canache, "From Bullets to Ballots: The Emergence of Popular Support for Hugo Chávez," *Latin American Politics and Society*, Vol. 44, No. 1. (Spring, 2002), pp. 69-90.

[22] To make comparisons with the Figure illustrating political tolerance across countries, see page 3.

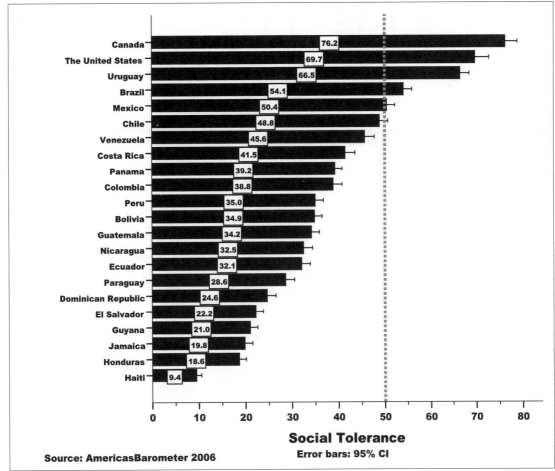

Figure IX-7. Social Tolerance by country

At the same time, Uruguay and Brazil (i.e., 67, 54 respectively) show high levels of social tolerance compared to other countries in the region. The majority of countries have levels lower than 50 points on a scale from 0 to 100, in contrast to only four countries that had levels of political tolerance below 50 points. The most surprising result is that Caribbean countries that have the highest levels of political tolerance are those with the lowest levels of social tolerance, at least when social tolerance is measured in terms of homosexuals. The gap between political and social tolerance in Caribbean countries may be the result of their historical cultural orientations or even a reaction to the AIDS epidemic, but at present this is merely speculation.

In this section, the same analysis in the first part of this chapter is done including one more variable: ethnic identity. This variable is included in the model to determine if ethnic identity is a significant factor that explains social tolerance. It is expected that Latin American countries will have lower levels of social tolerance because of the traditional Catholic disapproval of homosexuality.

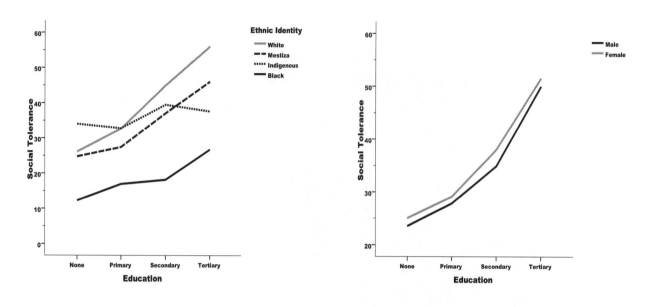

Figure IX-8. Social Tolerance by education and ethnic identity

Figure IX-9. Social Tolerance by sex and education

Figure IX-8 illustrates that education increases levels of social tolerance.[23] Notwithstanding, there are clear differences in levels of social tolerance by ethnic identity. Whites and *mestizos* show higher levels of social tolerance, whereas blacks have the lowest levels. Yet, as will be shown in the regression results, this is largely a result of their average (low) levels of education and income.

Figure IX-9 shows differences in levels of social tolerance between men and women by level of education. Here, the results are fascinating since they show that tolerance toward homosexuals is higher among women than among men whereas in political tolerance, the opposite is true. One can speculate that women have higher levels of social tolerance probably because when they were asked if they agree or disagree with homosexuals running for public office, women might have thought about men in particular. In some ways their answers may suggest that women are less sensitive about the issue. Still, education has a significant impact on increasing levels of social tolerance among both men and women. The factors that have an impact on social tolerance will be analyzed through an ordinary-least squares regression model.

---

[23] These results are based on the pooled sample.

Methods and Results

The regression model is the same as the one presented in the previous section of this chapter, except that it differs by the inclusion of ethnic identity. Four dummies representing blacks, whites,[24] *mestizos* and indigenous groups are incorporated in the model. The rest of variables remain the same.[25]

Table IX-3. Factors that explain social tolerance: results of the linear regression

	Unstandardized Coefficients		Standardized Coefficients		
	B	Std. Error	Beta	t	Sig.
System Support	.088	.011	.055	8.408	.000
Primary Education	-.859	1.183	-.011	-.726	.468
Secondary Education	4.705	1.208	.063	3.896	.000
Higher Education	*13.099*	1.304	.140	10.049	.000
Female	2.949	.436	.040	6.769	.000
Mestizo	1.320	.571	.017	2.314	.021
Indigenous group	4.576	1.158	.026	3.952	.000
Black	-.033	1.064	.000	-.031	.975
Age	-.980	.158	-.039	-6.191	.000
Wealth	.931	.134	.051	6.942	.000
Urban Areas	2.445	.521	.031	4.689	.000
Attendance to a religious organization	-.051	.005	-.059	-9.638	.000
Interpersonal Trust	-1.384	.243	-.034	-5.701	.000
President's job approval	-.781	.255	-.020	-3.066	.002
Guatemala	-13.608	1.405	-.078	-9.683	.000
Salvador	-26.672	1.311	-.165	-20.350	.000
Honduras	-27.180	1.321	-.168	-20.583	.000
Nicaragua	-14.152	1.369	-.084	-10.340	.000
Costa Rica	-9.764	1.318	-.061	-7.410	.000
Panama	-7.154	1.348	-.044	-5.307	.000
Colombia	-10.378	1.320	-.063	-7.865	.000
Ecuador	-17.503	1.341	-.106	-13.054	.000
Bolivia	-13.483	1.433	-.078	-9.412	.000
Peru	-16.365	1.354	-.101	-12.089	.000
Paraguay	-17.320	1.408	-.104	-12.298	.000
Chile	-2.946	1.320	-.018	-2.233	.026
Uruguay	14.893	1.362	.091	10.938	.000
Venezuela	-7.839	1.323	-.048	-5.925	.000
Dominican Republic	-22.853	1.327	-.139	-17.217	.000
Haiti	-33.696	1.765	-.184	-19.096	.000
Jamaica	-27.355	1.686	-.151	-16.220	.000
Guyana	-26.940	1.448	-.155	-18.599	.000
(Constant)	38.411	2.134		18.001	.000

a Dependent Variable: social tolerance	R Square .161
b Country of reference: Mexico	Adj. R Square .160
c Reference of level of education: none	Estimated std. error 34.14

[24] Whites are the reference group.

[25] In this section of this chapter, the United States and Canada are also excluded from the analysis since the study focuses on the Latin American and Caribbean contexts.

211

Contrary to original expectations, the results in Table IX-3 show that even though the effect on social tolerance of being black is negative, the effect is insignificant when other factors, especially wealth and education, are included. Therefore, the notion that blacks tend to particularly dislike homosexuals is not supported by the data. The lower social tolerance found among blacks was instead a function of their lower levels of education and wealth rather than their ethnicity. Another unanticipated result is that whites were found to have the highest levels of social tolerance when the bivariate relationship was presented. Yet, when included in the regression and controlled by socio-demographic variables and other theoretically related variables, other ethnic identities express greater social tolerance than whites, especially those who identify themselves as indigenous. Indigenous groups have less access to education; therefore, one would have expected that this group would have lower levels of social tolerance. However, the results show that when controlled for education and overall SES, social intolerance is lower among the indigenous than among, whites. One could argue that their levels of social tolerance may reflect greater acceptance of others as a result of having been themselves victims of intolerance. Nevertheless, further research is necessary to provide more empirical evidence to explain the reasons indigenous groups have the highest levels of social tolerance.

Other results presented in Table IX-3 indicate that respondents residing in urban areas as opposed to rural areas are more socially tolerant. Similarly, when education, wealth, and other variables are controlled for, women tend to show higher levels of social tolerance than men. System support also influences positively social tolerance. On the other hand, regular attendance at meetings of religious organizations, lower levels of interpersonal trust and approval of the President's job performance has a negative effect on social tolerance. As mentioned earlier, those who attend religious organizations regularly tend to be more conservative. Once again, higher levels of education play an important role. The difference of the effects on social tolerance between secondary and higher education are sharp. Even though secondary education has a positive significant effect on tolerance, the effect of higher education is greater by far. These results reinforce the notion that education is a critical factor in raising levels of social and political tolerance.

Conclusion

In this chapter, a comparison of political and social tolerance across countries showed that Jamaica, Guyana, and Haiti compared to other Latin American and Caribbean countries, enjoy high levels of political tolerance despite their relatively short history of democratic rule and, in the case of Guyana and Haiti lower levels of economic and political development compared to many other countries in the study. These results point to the conclusion that perhaps British and French colonialism contributed to the establishment of certain norms and values that enhance political tolerance among these countries. On the other hand, these same countries showed the lowest levels of social tolerance. The study also found that "antichavistas" in Venezuela are those with high levels of political tolerance reflecting their greater acceptance of critics of the system. The most important finding in this chapter, however, is the critical role that education plays in raising levels of political and social tolerance: higher levels of education lead to higher levels of tolerance. Therefore, if tolerance is an important goal of democratization, governments ought to endorse policies that increase the quantity and quality of their educational systems so that

tolerance will increase, which in turn will help to ensure the rights of minorities will remain secure.

References

Bobo, Lawrence, and Frederick C. Licari. "Education and Political Tolerance: Testing the Effects of Cognitive Sophistication and Target Group Affect." *The Public Opinion Quarterly* 53, no. 3 (1989): 285-308.

Dahl, Robert A. *Polyarchy: Participation and Opposition*. New Haven: Yale University Press, 1971.

Engerman, Stanley L., and Kenneth L. Sokoloff. "Factor Endowments, Inequality, and Paths of Development Among New World Economies." *Economia* 3, no. 1 (2002): 41-109.

Gibson, James L. "On the Nature of Tolerance: Dichotomous or Continuous?" *Political Behavior* 27 (2005a): 313-23.

Gibson, James L. "Homosexuals and the Ku Klux Klan: A Contextual Analysis of Political Tolerance." *Western Political Quarterly* 40 (1987): 427-48.

———. "The Structure of Attitudinal Tolerance in the United States." *British Journal of Political Science* 19 (1989): 562-70.

———. "Alternative Measures of Political Tolerance: Must Tolerance Be "Least-Liked?"" *American Journal of Political Science* (1992a): 562-71.

———. "The Political Consequences of Intolerance: Cultural Conformity and Political Freedom." *American Political Science Review* 86, no. 2 (1992b): 338-56.

———. "Becoming Tolerant? Short-Term Changes in Russian Political Culture." *British Journal of Political Science* 32 (2002): 309-34.

———. "Parsimony in the Study of Tolerance and Intolerance." *Political Behavior* 27 (2005b): 339-45.

———. "Enigmas of Intolerance: Fifty Years after Stouffer's Communism, Conformity, and Civil Liberties." *Perspectives on Politics* 4 (2006): 21-34.

Gibson, James L., and Richard D. Bingham. "On the Conceptualization and Measurement of Political Tolerance." *The American Political Science Review* 76, no. 3 (1982): 603-20.

Gibson, James L., and Raymond M. Duch. "Elitist Theory and Political Tolerance in Western Europe." *Political Behavior* 13 (1991): 191-212.

———. "Political Intolerance in the USSR: The Distribution and Etiology of Mass Opinion." *Comparative Political Studies* 26 (1993): 286-329.

Golebiowska, Ewa. "Individual Value Priorities, Education, and Political Tolerance." *Political Behavior* 17, no. 1 (1995): 23-48.

———. "Gender Gap in Political Tolerance." *Political Behavior* 21, no. 1 (1999): 43-66.

Harrison, Lawrence E. *Underdevelopment Is a State of Mind: The Latin American Case*. Boston: University Press of America, 1985.

Harrison, Lawrence E., and Samuel P. Huntington, eds. *Culture Matters: how values shape human progress*. New York: Basic Books, 2000.

Huber, Evelyne, Dietrich Rueschemeyer, and John D. Stephens. "The Impact of Economic Development on Democracy." *Journal of Economic Perspectives* 7, no. 3 (1993): 71-85.

Lawrence, David G. "Procedural Norms and Tolerance: A Reassessment." *The American Political Science Review* 70, no. 1 (1976): 80-100.

McClosky, Herbert and Alida Brill. *Dimensions of Tolerance: What Americans Believe about Civil Liberties* New York: Russell Sage Foundation, 1983.

Moreno, Daniel, and Mitchell Seligson. "Educación y tolerancia política en Bolivia." In *La cultura política de los bolivianos. Aproximaciones cuantitativas. Educación y tolerancia política en Bolivia*, edited by Mitchell Seligson and Daniel Moreno. Cochabamba: Cidadanía-LAPOP-USAID, 2006.

Patrice, Franko. *The Puzzle of Latin American Economic Development*. Edited by 2nd. New York: Rowman & Littlefield Publishers, Inc, 2003.

Peffley, Mark, and Robert Rohrschneider. "Democratization and Political Tolerance in Seventeen Countries: A Multi-Level Model of Democratic Learning." *Political Research Quarterly* 56, no. 3 (2003): 243-57.

Persell, Caroline H., Adam Green, and Liena Gurevich. "Civil Society, Economic Distress, and Social Tolerance." *Sociological Forum* 16, no. 2 (2001): 203-30.

Prothro, J.W., and C.W. Grigg. "Fundamental Principles of Democracy: Bases of Agreement and Disagreement." *The Journal of Politics* 22 (1960): 276-94.

Seligson, Mitchell A. "Costa Rica and Jamaica." In *Competitive Elections in Developing Countries*, edited by Myron Weiner and Ergun Ozbudun. Durham, North Carolina: Duke University Press 1987.

———. "Toward A Model of Democratic Stability: Political Culture in Central America." *Estudios interdisciplinarios de América Latina y el Caribe* 11, no. 2 (2000).

Seligson, Mitchell A., and Ricardo Córdova. *Perspectivas para una democracia estable en El Salvador*. San Salvador: IDELA, 1993.

Seligson, Mitchell A., Daniel Moreno, Diana Orcés, and Vivian Schwarz-Blum. *Auditoría de la democracia: Informe Ecuador 2006*. Quito: Cedatos-Gallup International-LAPOP-USAID, 2006.

Stouffer, Samuel. *Communism, Conformity, and Civil Liberties*. New York: Doubleday, 1955.

Sullivan, John L., James Piereson, and George E. Marcus. *Political Tolerance and American Democracy*. Chicago: University of Chicago Press, 1982.

Yeager, Timothy J. "Encomienda or Slavery? The Spanish Crown's Choice of Labor Organization in Sixteenth-Century Spanish America." *The Journal of Economic History* 55, no. 4 (1995): 842-59.

Part III. Challenges to the Rule of Law

X. The Impact of Violent Crime on the Political Culture of Latin America: The Special Case of Central America

José Miguel Cruz

Abstract

The objective of this chapter is to analyze the impact of criminal violence, measured both in terms of victimization as well as in terms of insecurity, on support for democracy in Latin America, particularly in Central America, taking into account the degree of consolidation and stability of democracy in those countries. In other words, the general hypothesis of this work is that crime erodes democratic political culture in Latin American countries, taking into account, above all, that many of these countries have a relatively recent history of democratization, as is the case of most Central American countries: Guatemala, El Salvador, Honduras, Nicaragua and Panama. The results show that although perceptions of victimization and insecurity play an important role in eroding democratic political culture in some cases, it is also necessary to consider citizens' perception on government performance regarding public security. This condition, how the government is perceived, seems to have a more important leverage in some democratizing countries.

In the early twenty-first century, violence has become a great social problem worldwide. According to the World Health Organization's *World Report on Violence and Health* (Krug et. al. 2002), approximately 1.6 million people lose their lives each year due to violence: violence is one of the most frequent causes of mortality among people aged 15 to 44. With the exception of Sub-Saharan Africa, Latin America and the Caribbean stand out as some of the most violent regions in the world. However, much of the violence in Africa is due to civil wars and ethnic conflicts, the principle sources of violence in Latin America are social violence and crime.

According to statistics published by the World Health Organization (WHO) on the rate of homicide in Latin American countries in the 1990s, there were 27 deaths per 100,000 inhabitants, more than twice the world average of 13 deaths per 100,000 inhabitants (Krug et. al. 2002). In this context, Central America has emerged as the most violent sub-region in Latin America of late. With homicide rates oscillating between 45 to 55 deaths per 100,000 inhabitants, countries like El Salvador, Guatemala and Honduras are considered countries with the most severe rates of criminal violence in the world (Gaviria and Páges, 1999).

Very little research has been done on the political impact of common or criminal violence. From the perspective of political science, violence has not always been examined under the mode of political violence, that is, as an instrument to access—or vie for—political power, or as a catalyst for the forces that go on to become the State (Bates 2001; Tilly 2003). Apart from a few recent studies and compilations (see Garland et al. 2003; Karstedt 2006), the impact of non-political violence on politics has not been explored, particularly in Latin America. This may be so because historically, when the survival of Latin American

democracies has been considered, the economic and social performance of its regimes has been taken into account more than the capacity to insure public safety.

The surge of criminal violence in societies worldwide has drawn attention to the possible effects it may have on political processes, and particularly on democracy (Bodemer 2003). Although there are some recent studies on the impact of criminal violence on democracy and political culture (Pérez 2003; Seligson and Azpuru; Cruz 2003; Cruz 2000), most academic papers focus on the impact of democracy on the functioning of the criminal justice system or on criminal violence itself (Karstedt and Lafree 2006). Therefore, very little is known about the impact that criminal and common violence have had on democracy and, above all, on the processes of democratization that many Latin American countries have been undergoing for several years.

This becomes more relevant if one considers the fact that violence is an increasingly pressing problem for many new, stable democracies (LaFree and Tseloni 2006). The objective of this chapter is to analyze the impact of criminal violence, measured both in terms of victimization as well as in terms of insecurity, on support for democracy in Latin America, particularly in Central America, taking into account the degree of consolidation and stability of democracy in those countries. In other words, the general hypothesis of this work is that crime erodes democratic political culture in Latin American countries, taking into account, above all, that many of these countries have a relatively recent history of democratization, as is the case of most Central American countries: Guatemala, El Salvador, Honduras, Nicaragua and Panama.

In order to perform this analysis, information is drawn from records from the AmericasBarometer database at Vanderbilt University. This database collects a wide spectrum of citizen opinions and attitudes from twenty Latin American and Caribbean countries regarding democracy, politics, corruption, institutional performance, tolerance, criminal violence, citizen confidence and other issues[1].

In addition to theoretical considerations and a review of the conditions of violence in Latin America, this work presents the results of the study in two major parts. The first focuses on analyzing the relation between criminal violence and attitudes that support democracy in Latin American countries as a whole. This is done by means of multivariate analyses of the results from all countries in the general database of the AmericasBarometer 2006-2007. The second part specifically focuses on the countries of Central America. The fundamental objective of this study is to elucidate the impact of criminal violence where crime is particularly high, and this is the case for the northern Central American region.

Conditions for Democracy, Political Culture, Legitimacy and Violence

"Conditions for democracy" are those circumstances that make a regime operational and which prevent it from being overthrown by an authoritarian regime (Rustow 1999; Linz 1989).

---

[1] Countries included in this analysis are: Bolivia, Brazil, Chile, Colombia, Costa Rica, Dominican Republic, Ecuador, El Salvador, Haiti, Honduras, Guatemala, Guyana, Jamaica, Mexico, Nicaragua, Panama, Paraguay, Peru, Uruguay, and Venezuela.

This study does not analyze the factors that lead to the establishment of democracy, or the beginning of a democratic transition; rather, it examines the factors that will aid in the sustainability and the development of democratic regimes once the transition has taken place. This is the case of Central American regimes with the exception of Costa Rica. Two general categories explain the circumstances that make a democracy function: first, the focus on macroeconomic and social situations, which are linked to the economic and political performance of those regimes; the second, the existence of a group of values, norms and attitudes held by citizens who support the regime's performance. The latter has to do with political culture.[2]

It is not the objective of this study to focus on the impact of a regime's economic performance on democracy. Studies of economic performance (Lipset 1960/1996; Przeworski 1996; Muller and Seligson 1986) state that when a society produces, for example, economic growth, reduction of inequality and economic wellbeing, it is less likely that the regime will rupture, and therefore more likely that its democracy will "prosper." Economic performance is, from this perspective, an important condition for the survival of a regime, particularly if it is democratic.

This study focuses the role of subjective and socio-cultural factors on the sustainability and preservation of democracy, in other words, political culture. The concept of political culture was originally developed by Almond and Verba (1963), who defined it as the set of psychological orientations towards politics of the members of a society. This was later taken up by Lipset (1994: 3) who said that "democracy requires a culture of support, that a part of the citizenry and the political elite accept the principle that is the basis for freedom of speech, communication, association, religion and the rights of association of parties, the rule of law, human rights, among others."

In its empirical relation to democracy and democratization, however, the notion of political culture is not equally viewed among researchers given that it implies different values and attitudes. In this regard, it is possible to identify three principle perspectives on the relation between political culture and democratization. The first focuses on cultural values and argues that a stable democracy depends on a satisfactory life, on interpersonal trust, and the population's resistance to revolutionary change. According to Inglehart (1988), these values can emerge as the result of economic growth stimulated by capitalism, or as the result of historical factors related to religion and ideology. The second approach stems from Putnam's (1993) social capital theory, which lists the system of norms of social reciprocity, social trust, and social participation networks as important factors for the functioning of democracy. This means that democracy will function and endure in societies in which people trust each other, participate in organizations and hold values of social reciprocity. The third perspective points to the link between political culture and democracy, focusing on legitimacy and political support for the system. This is developed in Lipset's work (1996) on efficiency and legitimacy, and has been developed empirically by several authors (Diamond 1993; Seligson 2000; Norris 1999).

---

[2] There exists another type of explanation related to political and social structures (see, for example, Lijphart, quoted in Rustow, 1999), and to historical conditions, as Karl (1990) pointed out. Nevertheless, that type of explanation is better adapted to transitions than to the processes of democratization. For some excellent studies of Central American regimes from an historical perspective, see Paige (1996) and Mahoney (2001).

According to this perspective, which is the fundamental framework for this study, a democratic system can only subsist when the population—masses and elites—are certain that the existing political institutions are the most adequate for society (Lipset 1960); that is to say, when most of the population see this regime as *"the only game in town"* (Linz and Stepan 1996). This certainty is not created from one day to the next. In democratic regimes, which do not depend on force, legitimacy is the product of system performance, it emanates from the perceptions of satisfaction of basic necessities of the majority of the population, and it is related to the real behaviour of authorities and power groups (Lipset 1960). As Diamond (1993: 13) points out: legitimacy "stems in part from the performance of a democratic regime over time, but it is also influenced (especially in the early stages of the regime) by the manner in which specific democratic institutions are articulated with the traditional and legitimate forms of authority and then by the socialization, the expansion of education, and other types of social and cultural change."

Diamond's views contain considerations which are relevant in the study of Latin America, and particularly so in the case of Central America. First, system performance is a serious challenge to governments that are learning how to function as democratic regimes for the first time. Given that there are no personal or institutional memories about how democracy operates, or if there were any, they have vanished for the new generations, the pressure for results is exceptional, particularly when a link between democracy and satisfaction of needs is perceived, as in the case of Latin America (Moreno 2001). Second, in societies with a long authoritarian tradition, such as those in Central America, traditional sources of authority—the police and the armed forces—are related to the arbitrary use of force, as are the institutions that they administer, (Holden 1996). Thus, the assessment of system performance, which is the basis for legitimacy, is not based solely on economic growth and distribution of wealth as Lipset originally proposed. It is also constituted by evaluating social reforms by upright and transparent governments which respect and preserve the rules of the democratic game; and, within the scope of this study, by their capacity to maintain the law and order (Diamond 1993).

The rampant violence in Latin American, particularly in Central America, can harm the political culture that is necessary for these democracies to survive. It can affect them in different ways. First, it can erode the attitudes that lend legitimacy to the system (Perez 2003; Seligson and Azpuru 2004; Cruz 2003). Violence also erodes social capital, that is, interpersonal trust, trust in the institutions, and attitudes that favor citizen participation that is necessary for the construction and maintenance of democracy (Karstedt and LaFee 2006; Sullivan and Transue 1999). Moreover, violence promotes support for authoritarian responses which weaken democracy (Kurtenbach 2003). Insecurity and fear of violence which dominates societies with high levels of crime or in which there is a perception of high crime rates, produces anxious citizens who, in turn, become "bad democrats" (Loader 2006, p. 216). Violence stimulates citizen support for repressive measures which often violate the rule of law, which is essential for the functioning of a stable democracy.

The limited amount of literature about common violence and democracy[3] has focused on the impact of crime on institutional performance and on the establishment of the rule of law (see Mendez et al. 1999; Aguero and Stark 1998). Beyond measuring the impact on public legitimacy most studies have analyzed the impact of violence and insecurity on social capital and tolerance, assuming that they are fundamental values for democratic functioning (Moser and Holland 1998; Moser and McIlwaine 2001).

It is for these reasons, and because of the lack of empirical studies that portray the link connecting violence, citizen insecurity and support for the system, that this study intends to test the theoretical and empirical relation between political culture, support for democracy and common violence in the countries of Latin America, and particularly in Central American countries, taking up the analytical framework proposed by Cruz (2000). The premise is that violence and insecurity erodes support for the system because they reduce credibility in the system's institutions and they foment attitudes which support alternative authoritarian regimes.

Of course violence and insecurity are not the only factors that generate the lack of legitimacy and support for the democratic regime. Neither would it be right to say that violence is necessarily the most important factor in eroding the conditions that support or lead to democracy. Notwithstanding, it would not be wrong to say that violence and insecurity can play a fundamental role in destabilizing the democratic processes by debilitating legitimacy, social capital and the rule of law.

Specifically this study is based on the theoretical framework proposed by Seligson (2000), according to which high levels of support for the system and a long-term attitude of political tolerance in the population are fundamental conditions for the maintenance and survival of a stable democracy. Therefore, the following pages seek to establish the impact of criminal violence on the combination of these attitudes which sustain a stable democracy.[4]

Criminal Violence in Latin America

Although the crime rate in Latin America is the highest in the world, violence in Latin America differs substantially among and within the countries of the region. For years Colombia has been considered the most violent country in the region with homicide rates of over 80 deaths per 100,000 inhabitants, whereas Chile and Uruguay have rates that are lower than 5 deaths per 100,000 people (De Mesquita Neto 2002). At the end of authoritarian regimes and

---

[3] Most of the literature that links the concepts of violence and democracy focuses on political violence and not on crime and common violence.

[4] This methodology has been chosen instead of simply assessing the impact on support for the political system because in the latter case, it could be that people support the predominant political system, but at the same time do not necessarily support a democratic regime. The use of Seligson's model, which combines support for the system and political tolerance, allows for a better approximation to an unequivocally democratic political culture. On the other hand, this method also offers an advantage over measuring support for democracy using only one item on the AmericasBarometer survey (for example ING4: "Democracy may have problems but it is better than any other form of government"). The use of this model implies the use of a more complex and standardized measure, and is less likely to produce the type of slant that appears frequently when using single items.

civil wars, Latin American countries have not only "discovered" new forms of violence, but their institutions have also begun to develop record systems that have revealed the real magnitude of the problem of violence.

According to a World Bank study (Moser, Winton and Moser 2004), the homicide rates in the Latin American region have increased by 50% since the 1980s, and most of the victims of violence are young people between the ages of 15 and 25. The study points out that the growing levels of violence have exacerbated social and political problems, and at the same time they have generated high economic costs in some Latin American countries.

In recent years, some countries have risen to the top of regional violence and crime statistics. El Salvador, Guatemala and Honduras published information that placed them at the same level as Colombia and some cities in Brazil. A study funded by the Inter American Development Bank (IDB) in the mid 1990s showed that El Salvador had homicide rates of over 100 deaths per 100,000 inhabitants (Cruz and Gonzalez 1997) from 1994 to 1997. Another IDB publication showed that in the years following the Peace Agreements, Guatemala had levels of almost 150 violent homicides per 100,000 inhabitants (Buvinic et al. 1999). Although some of these numbers may be overestimated due to the methods of recording (CIEN, 2002; Aguilar 2001), the truth is that in these Central American countries violence is much higher than in the rest of the region (Arriagada 2001; Wielandt 2005). Table X.1 shows the most recent data on the homicide rates in Latin America.

Table X.1. Homicide Rates in Latin America and the Caribbean (the most up-to-date data available)

Country	Homicide Rate (per 100,000 inhabitants)
Argentina	4.7*
Bolivia	18.5
Brazil	20.0
Chile	3.0
Colombia	40.0
Costa Rica	6.0
Cuba	6.2*
Ecuador	14.8**
El Salvador	55.5
Guatemala	35.5
Guyana	6.6*
Honduras	41.0
Jamaica	35.0*
Mexico	18.0
Nicaragua	10.0
Panama	11.0
Paraguay	12.6*
Peru	10.3**
Dominican Republic	12.0
Uruguay	4.0
Venezuela	33.0

Sources: Mockus and Acero, (no date);
  * Krug et al. (2004);
  **Carrión (2004).

In Table X.1 it can be seen that the great majority of countries in Latin America have homicide rates that are equal to or above the global worldwide rate (12/100,000 inhabitants). Only countries such as Argentina, Chile and Uruguay in the Southern Cone, Costa Rica in Central America, and Cuba and Guyana in the Caribbean are clearly below this average. As has already been pointed out, the countries in the northern triangle of Central America are, by far, the most affected by violence, with homicide rates greater 35 deaths per 100,000 inhabitants; they are followed by countries that are part of the Caribbean region, such as Mexico, Colombia and Venezuela, whose rates are also high.

It is worthwhile to point out that the countries in the Andean region also have relatively high homicide rates given that they have experienced a noticeable increase in recent years. According to Carrión (2004), the homicide rates in countries such as Ecuador and Peru have almost quadrupled over a five year span.

The violence that affects many Latin American countries is expressed not only by homicides but also by the incidence of crime and other expressions of violence. The increase in juvenile gangs or "*maras*" in Central America, which control entire urban areas where the authorities cannot counter them; the increase of organized crime in countries such as Mexico, Brazil, Haiti, to levels that openly defy the states; corruption among government officials in charge of security; and the increase of street crime in some countries that have until now been considered less violent, such as Argentina or Costa Rica (see for example, Dammert 2000) generate a feeling of insecurity that affects all citizens.

A survey done by the United Nations Interregional Crime and Justice Research Institute in the mid 1990s showed that in the six Latin American countries surveyed, over 85% qualified crimes such as theft, injury and sexual assault as serious or very serious (Gabaldón 2001). In other words, criminal violence that takes many forms in Latin American countries translates to citizen insecurity, which in turn affects governability as well as the relations among citizens and those between citizens and institutions.

Methodological Aspects

This study is based on data generated by the 2006-2007 edition of the Latin American Public Opinion Project's (LAPOP) AmericasBarometer. It uses the results of a survey of over 30,000 Latin American citizens in twenty countries of Latin America and the Caribbean. The study uses the results of a survey that is unique in its scope, nature and commitment to the scientific method[5], and begins with the fundamental assumption that people's beliefs, attitudes and life-experience are important categories for the analysis of political facts, and that surveys are a means in which to approach them.

---

[5] Full information regarding LAPOP and the AmericasBarometer can be found at: http://sitemason.vanderbilt.edu/lapop/about_us.

Data

This study uses data from LAPOP's 2006-2007 surveys. The surveys were applied in all the countries during various periods throughout the year. In each country, national probability samples were designed in order to precisely represent the population, and a total of 1,500 adult citizens over the age of 18 were interviewed.[6]

Items and Variables

Violence, Victimization and Insecurity

In order to assess the impact of violence on the democratic political culture of Central American citizens, two independent variables will be used. The first variable measures the level of violence by personal victimization per crime and collects what could be called "objective" levels of violence. The second variable measures the level of perceived insecurity as a product of the violence that prevails in the environment and gathers what might be referred to as the "subjective" side of violence.

In the first case, only one item regarding mediation of victimization (VIC1) is used to determine the levels of crime and violence in the analysis and the models. People were asked whether they had or not been victims of some violent incident during the twelve months prior to the interview. In the second case, insecurity was also measured with only one item, AOJ11.

Democratic Political Culture

Generally, the dependent variable is the political culture that supports democracy. However, given that this culture has many dimensions in which violence can have an impact, a series of indicators which refer to the factors of a political culture that supports democracy are used in the general analysis of the data. These dimensions are: a) support for a stable democracy, following Seligson's model (2000); b) interpersonal trust, measured by way of item IT1; c) support for electoral democracy as opposed to rejection of authoritarian leaders, through number AUT1; and d) support for the rule of law, measured by item AOJ8.

There are important theoretical reasons to consider these dimensions part of a political culture that supports democracy. First, Seligson has presented vast empirical evidence of the relevance of combining support for the system and interpersonal tolerance as one of the fundamental actions for democracy. Second, interpersonal trust is reminiscent of relevant social capital theories (Putnam 1993; Fukuyama 1995), particularly regarding regimes that attempt to build a social fabric that may promote political participation. On the other hand, rejection of authoritarian leadership in order to support electoral democracy becomes more important especially in light of longstanding authoritarian traditions. This dimension is included to analyze the issue of citizens who support a democratic system in general, trust in others, but are

---

[6] Except for Nicaragua where surveys were carried out starting at age 16.

willing to continue supporting authoritarian leadership through elections (Bermeo 2003). Finally, abiding by the rule of law means that in a democracy all citizens respect the law and require that institutions do the same (Mendez 2003).

The following table summarizes all the variables used in this study.

Table X.2. Variables in the first part of the analysis

Condition	Name of variable	Indicator	Item on the questionaire
Violence	Victimization by crime	Percentage of people victimized over the last year	VIC1: ¿Have you been the victim of a criminal act in the last twelve months?
	Insecurity due to crime	Insecurity scale average (0-100)	AOJ11: Talking about the place or neighborhood you live in, and thinking about the possibility of being the victim of a hold-up or robbery, do you feel very safe, somewhat safe, a little unsafe or very unsafe?
Government Performance	Perception that the government is fighting crime	Government performance perception average (1-7)	N11: To what extent would you say the current administration improves the security of our citizens?
Political Culture	Support for stable democracy	Combination of high tolerance and high support for the system (0-1)	Basic series B1-B6 Basic series D1-D4
	Interpersonal trust	Interpersonal trust-scale average (0-100)	IT1: Now, speaking of people around here, would you say people in your community are: very trustworthy, somewhat trustworthy, a little trustworthy or not at all trustworthy?
	Rejection of authoritarian leaders	Authoritarian leader rejection average (0-100)	AUT1: There are people who say we need a strong leader who does not have to be elected by vote. Others say that although things are not working electoral democracy, that is popular elections, is always better. What do you think?
	Consent to the rule of law	Average on the scale in which the police ignore the law (0-100)	AOJ8: In order to capture criminals, do you believe the authorities always have to respect the law or can they act outside the law on occasion?

Empirical Hypothesis

The empirical hypothesis of this chapter holds that victims of crime or violence and those who show high levels of insecurity as a result of victimization tend to exhibit less support

for the political system and less tolerance; in other words, they tend to have a political culture that does not favor stable democracy. In addition, they more frequently favor the presence of a strong leader who overlooks electoral democracy and justifies the authorities acting outside the law as long as they fight crime. These hypotheses will be evaluated using statistical tests of significance to establish a probable relation between victimization and insecurity and the aforementioned cultural values.

Victimization, Insecurity and Democratic Political Culture in the Region

The first step is to establish whether criminal violence, measured by the AmericasBarometer survey as criminal victimization and perceptions of insecurity, affects the percentage of citizens that have a political culture favorable toward a stable democracy. In order to do that, a series of regressions were run to establish the impact of insecurity and violence; control variables such as gender, age, education, family income, and city size (as a proxy of urbanization) were also added. In addition, a variable tapping government performance in public security was also included in the models. Given that the impact of violence and insecurity can be mediated by the functioning of the regime in the public security sphere, the citizens' perception of the performance of the regime was also incorporated into the models. The assumption behind this is that support for democracy can also be influenced by citizens' perceptions regarding the government's work in the security arena, and cannot only be influenced by the objective and subjective conditions of security alone.

Hence, attitudes of support for stable democracy, interpersonal trust, support for electoral democracy (as opposed to approval for authoritarian leadership), and support for rule of law were regressed on the independent variables depicted above. The results are shown in Table X.3.

As it can be seen in Table X.3, the variable of crime victimization does not play any important role on the attitudes leading to supporting a stable democracy (second column). Crime victimization is not statistically significant and, along with the city size condition, it does not make a difference in the attitudes of support for stable democracy. We are not surprised by this finding since crime victims make up only a small part of the population. Conversely, perceptions of insecurity do have a negative effect upon the attitudes of stable democracy. This means that in general, people who feel more unsafe because of crime tend to have lower attitudes of support for stable democracy than the rest of the population. Thus, the problem of criminal violence seems to have a negative effect on stable democracy only through the perceptions of insecurity produced by violence, but not through direct victimization—at least not in the way that it has been measured in the AmericasBarometer survey. However, the variable that turned out to have a substantive effect and a statistical significant impact on the support for stable democracy was the assessment of government performance in the public security area. The latter means that insofar as Latin Americans perceive that their governments are tackling crime, there is a greater more probability that they will have stronger supporting attitudes for a stable democracy.

Table X.3. Predictors of support for a stable democracy, interpersonal trust, support for electoral democracy and support for the rule of law in Latin America and the Caribbean, 2006-2007.

	Support for a stable democracy	Interpersonal trust	Support for electoral democracy	Support for the Rule of Law [a]
City size	.018 (.010)	1.873** (.130)	.030* (.013)	.003 (.009)
Gender (Female)	-.074* (.030)	-1.335 ** (.386)	.048 (.039)	.054* (.027)
Age	.006** (.001)	.145* (.013)	.011** (.001)	.008** (.001)
Family income	.047** (.007)	1.356** (.085)	.057** (.009)	-.027** (.006)
Education	.022** (.004)	-.116** (.050)	.042** (.005)	.014** (.004)
Crime victimization	.000 (.000)	-.017* (.005)	.000 (.001)	-.003** (.000)
Perception of insecurity	-.102** (.016)	-8.837** (.209)	-.030 (.021)	-.133** (.015)
Assessment on government performance in security [b]	.288** (.008)	1.013** (.106)	.096** (.010)	.034** (.007)
Constant	-2.209** (.108)	61.804** (1.370)	.304* (.137)	.048** (.096)
R^2	.090 (Nagelkerke)	.116	.023 (Nagelkerke)	.018 (Nagelkerke)
X^2 o F	1471.25	372.40	287.26	313.91
N	23,923	22,751	22,159	24,167

* p < .05
** p < .001
[a] Brazil not included
[b] Bolivia not included.

In fact, perceptions of government performance in each of the areas assessed by the AmericasBarometer survey (tackling poverty-N1, decreasing corruption-N9, democratic principles promotion-N3, human rights promotion-N10, and tackling unemployment-N12) have a statistically significant relationship with the support for stable democracy, but in none the effect is larger —with the exception of human rights promotion—than when assessing the improvement of public security.

This is particularly important. It means that having positive perceptions about the performance of the government in the public security area is more relevant than being a victim of crime and violence, or than the perceptions of insecurity. When examining the figures by country, one can find that this relationship is statistically significant in every Latin American and the Caribbean country included in the sample[7]. Figure X.1 clearly shows this relationship.

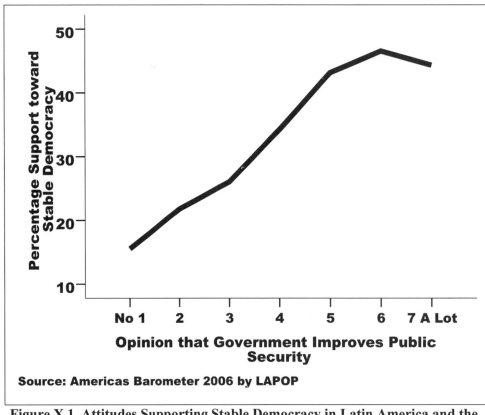

Figure X.1. Attitudes Supporting Stable Democracy in Latin America and the Caribbean according to assessment of government performance in public security, 2006-2007.

All these results, however, should not downplay the importance of perceptions on insecurity. As it can be seen in the next figure, the percentage of people holding attitudes supportive of a stable democracy increases insofar as people feel safer from violence. Hence, people supporting stable democracy goes from 22 percent among those who feel themselves very unsafe up to 32 percent among those who feel very safe. This relationship is found in the overall sample, and it is significant in most countries, with the exception of Guatemala, El Salvador, Ecuador, Bolivia, and Chile.

---

[7] In Bolivia, the question N11 was not included in the questionnaire; hence this country is not included in the analyses tapping government performance.

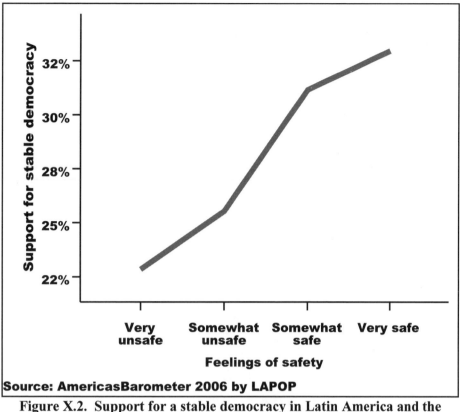

Source: AmericasBarometer 2006 by LAPOP

**Figure X.2. Support for a stable democracy in Latin America and the
Caribbean according to citizen perception of safety, 2006-2007**

On a related topic, when interpersonal trust is regressed on the violence and insecurity variables, the results show that all the conditions have a significant effect on interpersonal trust, even the crime victimization condition. As can be seen in Table X.3, being a victim of crime and having perceptions of insecurity erode the overall levels of interpersonal trust in the Latin American region. By the same token, perceptions of government performance in the public security area also have a positive effect on interpersonal trust. Nevertheless, perception of insecurity seems to play a more important role in the levels of people's trust than assessment of regime's performance in public security.

When examining the effects of these variables using bivariate analyses at the country level, it can be seen that perceptions of insecurity tend to have a significant effect more frequently than crime victimization or than perceptions of government performance (see Table X.4). In all the countries included in the sample, perceptions of insecurity are related to interpersonal trust with negative signs. Conversely, when exploring the effects of crime victimization, it turns out that this variable does not have any effect in Bolivia, Chile, Costa Rica, Jamaica, or Panama; whereas the effect of perceptions of government performance turns out to be insignificant in Costa Rica, the Dominican Republic, Ecuador, Nicaragua, and Panama. In short, perceptions of insecurity are the most important eroding condition for interpersonal trust.

Table X.4. Relationships of statistical significance between crime victimization, perceptions of insecurity and perceptions of government performance in security, and interpersonal trust according to country, Latin America and the Caribbean 2006-2007 (bivariate analyses)

Country	Independent Variables		
	Victimization	Insecurity	Government performance
Bolivia		**	---
Brazil	**	**	*
Chile		**	*
Colombia	*	**	*
Costa Rica		**	
Dominican Republic	*	**	
Ecuador	*	**	
El Salvador	**	**	**
Guatemala	**	**	*
Guyana	*	**	**
Haiti	*	**	*
Honduras	**	**	**
Jamaica		**	*
Mexico	**	**	**
Nicaragua	*	**	
Panama		**	
Paraguay	*	**	*
Peru	*	**	**
Uruguay	**	**	**
Venezuela	**	**	**

Dependent Variable: Interpersonal Trust.
* p < .05
** p < .001

When regressing support for electoral democracy (or rejection of authoritarian leadership) on violence and insecurity variables, the coefficients of the logistic regression shown in Table X.3 point out that only the perception of regime's performance plays an important role in supporting electoral democracy and rejecting authoritarian leadership. Victimization events and the levels of insecurity do not seem to affect support for electoral democracy, at least in statistical terms.

Although the effect of perception of government performance is significant in the entire region, in some countries the relationship is non-existent. The way in which citizens perceive their government's work in the security arena is important in order to reject authoritarian leaders in Guatemala, Nicaragua, Panama, Colombia, Haiti, the Dominican Republic, Venezuela, Chile, Paraguay, and Uruguay; but it does not seem to have the same importance in Mexico, El Salvador, Honduras, Costa Rica, Ecuador, Peru, Brazil, Jamaica, or Guyana. Therefore, it is sounder to think that the perceptions about the government's functioning are relevant to rejecting authoritarian leadership only in some regions of Latin America.

Concerning the support for the rule of law, the results of the regression shows that the variables of violence and insecurity have an effect upon the backing of the rule of law. Support for the rule of law was measured using question AOJ8, which explores whether people approve

or not the police overlooking the law when prosecuting criminals. This variable proved to be significantly related to crime victimization, to perceptions of insecurity, and to perceptions of government performance. Results from the logistic regression (Table X.3, column 5) point out that being a victim of crime in Latin America erodes citizens' commitment with the law when the police fight crime; perceptions of insecurity produce the same effect: to the extent that the interviewees feel more unsafe, they are more willing to support the police when acting outside of the law in order to catch criminals. This erodes the rule of law (see Figures X.3 and X.4).

Equally important is the result that reveals that citizens who approve the government's functioning are more willing to demand that the police follow the laws and rules. In other words, people who assess negatively the performance of the government are more ready to consent to police acting outside of the law. Such results have important implications for the discussion of support for democracy and the rule of law. This means that it is crucial that governments be perceived as able to deal with security issues so that citizens can commit themselves to the rule of law.

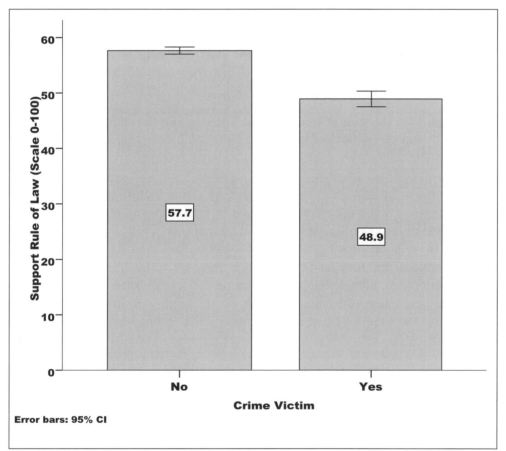

Figure X.3. Support for the Rule of Law in Latin America and the Caribbean and crime victimization, 2006-2007.

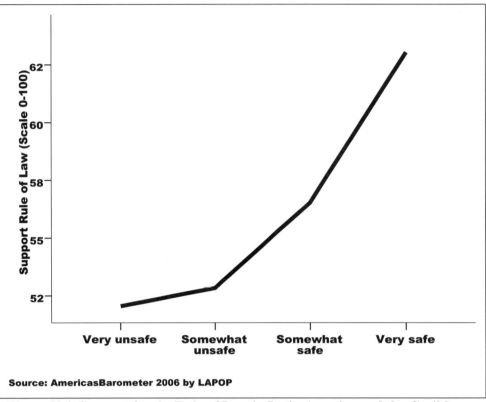

Figure X.4. Support for the Rule of Law in Latin America and the Caribbean, and perceptions of insecurity, 2006-2007.

Although support for the rule of law is influenced by crime victimization, perceptions of insecurity, and perceptions of government performance in the entire region[8], it is necessary to explore whether these variables have the same effect at the national level. Table X.5 presents an overview of the bivariate relationships by country. As shown, in Costa Rica, Panama, and the Dominican Republic, none of the independent variables turn out to be statistically significant. However, in the other countries, at least one variable came out significant to predict the support for the rule of law. The perception of insecurity again, seems to play an important role in most of the countries: citizens tend to reject institutional behavior that is outside of the law insofar as they feel safe from violence.

---

[8] With the exception of Brazil because the item AOJ8 was not included in their questionnaire.

Table X-5. Statistically significant relationships between crime victimization, perceptions of insecurity and perceptions of government performance in security, and the support for the rule of law according to country, Latin America and the Caribbean 2006-2007 (bivariate analyses)

Country	Independent variables		
	Victimization	Insecurity	Government Performance
Bolivia	*	*	---
Chile	**	*	*
Colombia		*	
Costa Rica			
Dominican Republic			
Ecuador	*	**	
El Salvador		**	
Guatemala	**	**	*
Guyana	**	**	**
Haiti		**	**
Honduras	**	*	*
Jamaica	*		**
Mexico	**	*	
Nicaragua		**	
Panama			
Paraguay	*	**	
Peru	*		
Uruguay		*	
Venezuela	**	*	*

Dependent variable: Support for the Rule of Law.
* p < .05
** p < .001

In sum, crime victimization and perceptions of insecurity affect attitudes of support for democracy, namely those which maintain a stable democracy, bolster interpersonal trust, reject authoritarian leadership (and support electoral democracy), and encourage the rule of law. This is especially true in the case of perception of insecurity concerning crime and violence. Insecurity affects, in substantive and significant terms, the attitudes that are essential for maintaining a stable democracy; it also affects interpersonal trust, the beliefs that authorities must not disobey the law, and the support for the procedures of electoral democracy.

Crime victimization, although important in some cases, does not seem to have the relevance found in the perceptions of insecurity in predicting democratic political culture attitudes. Victimization has only a crucial effect when related to the rule of law, and up to some point when related to interpersonal trust. Nevertheless, victimization does not have significant effects in rejecting authoritarian leaders, nor in the overall attitudes that are useful for a stable democracy. Two possible explanations can be drawn from this. First, victimization affects only a small portion of the population. Even in the most problematic societies victimization does not reach everyone, so the effect of these kinds of events are limited to a tiny fraction of the population. Second, victimization has been measured with some limitations because surveys do not capture all kinds of violence occurring in a society (think, for instance, in homicides).

All in all, these findings suggest that there are ways to explore the impact of violence on the political culture of democracy. These results seem to imply that perceptions of the performance of the regime are important when considering support for democracy. This will be more deeply studied in the next section of the present chapter devoted to study the relationship between violence and attitudes of support for stable democracy in Central America.

Violence and Attitudes of Support for Democracy in Central America

In this section the impact of violence on the Central American sub-region will be analyzed. There are two reasons to do so. First, because as has been mentioned before, the northern Central American region, comprised of Guatemala, El Salvador and Honduras is, for many reasons, the most violent region in the world regarding criminal violence. At the same time, Nicaragua, Costa Rica and Panama, with homicide rates of less than 15 per 100,000 inhabitants, suggests that it is also one of the least violent regions in Latin America (see Figure IX.1). This presents a unique opportunity to compare countries with similar cultures in the same geographical area but strikingly different in their incidence of violence. Second, Central America countries have very different histories in terms of their democratic consolidation. In this region comparisons can be drawn between Costa Rica, the most stable country in Latin America in terms of democracy (Booth 1998), and Guatemala, El Salvador and Nicaragua, which have undergone transitions to democracy for the first time in their respective histories (Torres-Rivas 2001) following years of armed conflicts. Interesting comparisons can also be made regarding Honduras and Panama which have recently transitioned from military governments to democracies but which have had certain levels of democracy in the past (Remmer 1985)[9].

Therefore, this has to do with the possibility of comparing countries that show two conditions that are important in understanding the impact violence has on attitudes that are behind the consolidation of democracy. The position of these countries regarding these conditions is presented in Table X.6.

---

[9] To state that countries such as Honduras and Panama have had a certain level of democracy in the past is not a statement free of controversy. For many authors, these countries have not had democratic regimes in the past, but rather electoral regimes that have constantly been subjected to supervision by the military or oligarchic groups (Remmer 1985; Mahoney 2001). These groups have allowed certain liberties and processes of political alternating to take place but have not achieved the level of consolidation and institutionalization reached in Costa Rica. In any case, during some periods of the twentieth century, these regimes have differentiated themselves from the more inflexible authoritarian character of their neighbors Guatemala, El Salvador and Nicaragua.

Table X.6. Central American countries according to levels of criminal violence and stage of democracy

	Stable Democracy	Recent Transition from an authoritarian government: "Recovered" Democracies.	Transition together with end of military conflict: Foundational Democracies
Non violent (rate < 15/100,000 hab.)	Costa Rica	Panama	Nicaragua
Violent (rate > 40/100,000)		Honduras	Guatemala El Salvador

Thus, criminal violence can have an impact on these countries in differentiated manners, both in terms of the degree of violence that they face, as well as the function of the democratic/authoritarian traditions prevalent in these regimes. Countries such as Guatemala, El Salvador and Nicaragua are considered foundational democracies: they have no institutional memory of the way a democracy functions and their populations have had to learn to live in the new political culture that requires the abandonment of authoritarianism.[10] It is logical then, to think that the problems posed by high levels of violence would have a greater impact on the popular support for a stable democracy. On the other hand, in countries such as Honduras and Panama which have a previous history of quasi-democratic regimes, the challenge lies in re-establishing the institutions and values to support democracy. This task can be made less difficult when a certain type of memory exists, even if it is tenuous. The case model for this is Costa Rica. Compared to its neighbors, Costa Rica has a longstanding democratic tradition, with institutions and values that have been firmly established for decades. Therefore, the challenges posed by violence or economic crises should have less of an impact on the political culture that supports a stable democracy.

To test the impact of the variables of violence on the support for a stable democracy a statistical analysis was run on data by means of binary logical regressions, taking as the dependent variable the support for a stable democracy. Unlike the graphs and analysis of the previous section, this exercise includes demographic variables such as gender, age, education and the size of the population where the respondent lives. In addition, two variables related to the topic of violence were introduced into the models, variables which might play an important role on the impact on political attitudes. One of these variables is the presence of juvenile gangs in the respondent's neighborhood; the other is the evaluation of government performance in the area of citizen security. The summary of these results is presented in Table X.7.[11]

The figure shows the variables that have enough statistical weight to state that they influence democratic political culture in each per-country regression that are significant in predicting support for a stable democracy. Consequently, for example, the results show that in Guatemala, the size of the city where the respondent lives, the perception of gang presence in the community and the evaluation of the Guatemalan government's performance in the area of public security are all conditions that are statistically associated to a political culture that supports democracy.

---

[10] It is important to recall that these transitions implied the cessation of armed conflicts and the retreat of the military from politics (Córdova 1996).

[11] See appendixes for more on the specific results of the regressions.

More concretely, the Guatemala results indicate that people living in small cities or rural areas, those who perceive gang presence in their communities, and those who evaluate the Guatemalan government's security policies positively tend to show greater demonstrations of a political culture that supports a stable democracy. In El Salvador, results clearly show that the respondent's gender—that is, being a woman—and the perception of the performance of the government in office in the area of security are the factors influencing support for a stable democracy. In Honduras, people who are not as afraid of becoming victims of violence and those who do not perceive the presence of gangs in their communities show greater support for a stable democracy as well as the positive evaluation of governmental performance in the area of public security. In Nicaragua, results again point to the importance of government performance but they also show that variables such as city size, family income and the perception of security play an important role as well, although a less significant one.[12] In Costa Rica, aside from positive evaluation of government security policies, personal characteristics appear to play a greater role: older people with a higher educational level and higher income are more committed to supporting democratic political culture than the rest of the population. Finally, in Panama only the perception of security and the positive evaluation of governmental work contribute to political culture that supports democracy.

Table X.7. Predictors of support for stable democracy in each Central American country

Variables	Guatemala	El Salvador	Honduras	Nicaragua	Costa Rica	Panama
City size	**			*		
Respondent gender		***				
Respondent age					**	
Respondent educational level					**	
Respondent income level				*	**	
Degree of victimization						
Perception of security			**	*		**
Gang presence	*		**			---
Evaluation of government performance in the area of public security	***	***	***	***	***	***

* p< .100
** p < .050
*** p< .001

Note: In the case of Panama, the gang presence variable was not included in the regression because it was not asked about in the local survey.

These results point to the fact that despite the results of previous section when a multivariate analysis is run on the conditions that contribute to support for a stable democracy, personal victimization loses its power of prediction in countries where it had previously

---

[12] We opted for showing the variables that have a significance level of p< .1. Although this is particularly high for statistical significance in the social sciences, it can be useful for registering those variables that have a more diffuse effect on democratic political culture and that could be overlooked in the regression. All in all, variables with this type of significance should be considered with much more care and the best is to give due relevance to variables that show a level of statistical relevance of p< .05.

appeared to be of importance, that is to say in Honduras and in Nicaragua. Additionally when determining the most important factors in the presence of a political culture that supports democracy from the perspective of the incidence of violence, the most important condition is not insecurity or victimization; rather, it is the perception of what governments do to combat these problems. In other words, support for a stable democracy is more the result of perception of institutional performance than the absence of these problems.

Actually, results indicate that when the variable of perception of security is introduced into the models the effect of personal victimization on the attitudes of support for a stable democracy vanishes in Honduras and Nicaragua where there was a simple relation. This would suggest that in these countries, from the point of view of support for democracy the perception of security is more important than the fact of having been a direct victim of violence. People who have been direct victims of crime tend to feel more insecure and this insecurity shared by many others affects the attitudes of support towards a stable democracy. Although these results may seem to contradict the idea that direct violence affects democratic attitudes it must be remembered that the degree of victimization that is accounted for in this study is partial in that it refers only to victimization due to economic factors and excludes many of the more serious types of victimization that take place in Latin America. In truth, the results suggest that the most important variable regarding citizen attitudes is not violence but the insecurity that it produces. This is not a new consideration as it has already been pointed out in other studies (Gabaldón 2004) but it demonstrates that when working on the topic of democratic political culture, perceptions related to violence cannot be overlooked.

In this context, the findings regarding the importance of perception of government performance in the area of public security turns out to be revealing. In the previous section it was seen that in the majority of per-country bivariate analyses perception of security played an important role in determining attitudes of support for democracy. In other words, in all Central American countries except Guatemala and El Salvador, insecurity due to crime significantly reduces support for stable democracy. Nevertheless, the results presented in this section show that for Nicaragua and Costa Rica the perception of governmental efforts becomes more important than insecurity, such that when introducing this last variable in the regressions the effect of the sense of security disappears. As seen in Table X.7 (and appearing in the Appendixes), the variable of governmental performance evaluation is the most important condition for predicting support for a stable democracy. This suggests that at the time of examining the impact of criminal violence on political culture it is important to consider not only the insecurity engendered by crime, but also and above all, to consider the manner in which citizens perceive governmental actions in the fight against crime. From the citizen standpoint what government does to combat violence is more important in supporting a democratic regime than the existence of violence or insecurity in and of themselves. In other words, the erosion of a political culture that supports democracy fundamentally comes from the loss of legitimacy, the result of governmental actions, and not so much from the fact of there being violence and insecurity or not.

There is no doubt that both aspects are related. In many countries criminal violence increases or decreases as a result of the actions of government. Nonetheless, this is not always perceived by people when evaluating the state of their societies. When government

performance in terms of security is assessed citizens say that their commitment to democracy depends more on the system's performance in facing problems than the problems themselves. This was originally proposed by Lipset and restated by Klingemann (1999) when they stated that the legitimacy of a democratic system is greatly influenced by its own performance.

The preceding is important because at the time of considering the possibilities of survival of democracy as a product of citizen support it indicates the need to pay attention to political institutions and not to the problems. Democracy is maintained, strengthened or weakened not because of the existence of more or less serious problems in society but because of the actions the institution undertakes in facing these problems and the manner in which these actions are perceived by the public. From the perspective of political culture the problem of violence is a problem for democracy because it affects the perception of system performance, but in so doing, it also affects the conviction that the rule of law has to be respected, and weakens the opposition to authoritarian leadership. Therefore, violence is a problem for maintaining democratic stability.

This can be seen much more clearly in the results of a series of questions included in the AmericasBarometer with the objective of identifying the conditions in which citizens would be willing to support a *coup d'etat*. Figure X.5 shows these results for the countries of Central America grouped by the function of level of violence.

Among the conditions listed— unemployment, social protest, criminal violence, high inflation and corruption— crime stands out as the condition by which most citizens would support a *coup d'etat*. This is as true for Central American countries that have serious violence problems as it is for the other countries included in the AmericasBarometer. However, it is in Guatemala, El Salvador and Honduras where the level of citizen justification for a *coup d'etat* is the highest. Over half of Guatemalans, Salvadorans and Hondurans said they would approve of a *coup d'etat* as a response to the levels of violence that exists in those countries. No other condition reaches this level of approval and nothing else stands out as notably among the violent countries and the non-violent ones. In other words, support for the break with democracy due to criminal violence is the highest in precisely those countries where violence is a serious problem. In no other circumstance or country is there so much support for a break with democracy as in those countries where violence prevails.

Under no circumstances should this data be taken as a predictor of a *coup d'etat*. Instead, this data needs to be taken as an indicator of the level of erosion of legitimacy that regimes face when they co-exist with high levels of criminality. The results shown in the graph only exemplify what has already been said before: violence affects the perception of the system's performance and it is this very perception that weakens the prospects of a political culture that would support democracy. The fact that people might "justify" a *coup d'etat* due to the high levels of violence fundamentally constitutes a response to modify a regime perceived incapable of providing security.

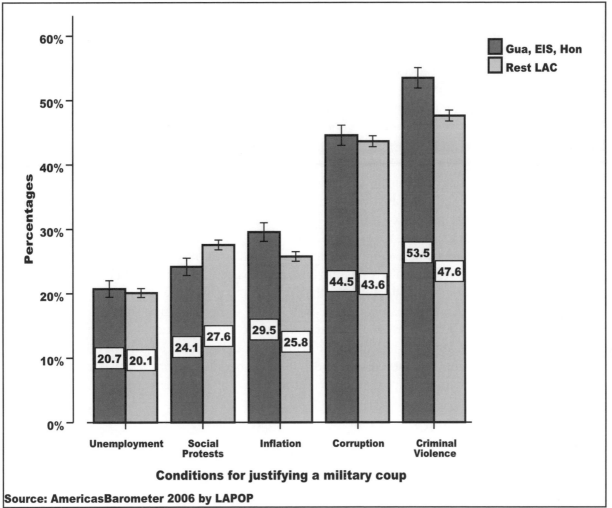

Source: AmericasBarometer 2006 by LAPOP

Figure IX.5. Conditions that might justify a *coup d'etat* in Central American countries with problems of violence compared to the rest of countries, 2006-2007.

Conclusions

Criminal violence affects the prospects of a stable democracy. This is particularly true in most of the countries in Central America. Violence creates insecurity and contributes to convincing citizens that the institutions in office do not provide adequate security nor do they do enough to combat crime. This should not be a problem of legitimacy because in a democracy institutions can be modified, reformed or strengthened, and their representatives can be called to account, relieved or backed following a series of democratic procedures. What is certain is that data indicate that when citizens live in an environment of insecurity, and when they do not have a positive evaluation of the performance of the institutions that are in charge of security, an erosion in the attitudes that support a stable democracy becomes apparent to the degree that in countries where violence is one of the most serious social problems, over half of the people justify a *coup d'etat* as a manner of dealing with the problem of criminal violence.

The impact of violence on democratic political culture, therefore, is not related only to the prevalence of crime and insecurity but above all to the conditions that erode the legitimacy of the institutions that are in charge of providing security and as a result, cause people to detach themselves from democratic values, ignore the rule of law and support authoritarian alternatives. This is not to say that the most violent countries are irredeemably on the way to the collapse of their proto-democratic regimes. It does mean that criminal violence, particularly of the most severe kind that translates into generalized insecurity, constitutes a clear threat to the processes of democratic consolidation.

This is particularly true in the countries that are most affected by violence in Central America. Having examined the transitional character of most of these countries, there remains little doubt regarding the impact of violence and insecurity on citizen support for democratic regimes in those countries. Violence is pernicious to the frail path to democratization in the Central American countries where democratization is recent, not only because it directly erodes the rule of law, or because it threatens the citizens' most basic human rights but also because it can destroy the infrastructure of legitimacy that is necessary for new regimes. As stated by Seligson (2002), Latin America has a long history of instability and authoritarian regressions. Central America is no exception to this negative tendency; countries in this region were unstable long before having known democratic regimes. Judging from history in other latitudes there is no reason to think that the current and hybrid democratic regimes are free from these setbacks, particularly when violence continues to affect Central American citizens.

References

Agüero, Felipe and Stark, Jeffrey. (eds). *Fault Lines in Post-Transition Latin America.* Miami: North-South Center Press, 1998.

Aguilar, Jeannette. *Metodologías para la cuantificación del delito.* San Salvador: Fundación de Estudios para la Aplicación del Derecho (FESPAD), Centro de Estudios Penales de El Salvador (CEPES) (2002).

Almond, Gabriel and Verba, Sydney. *The Civic Culture: Political Attitudes and Democracy in Five Nations.* Princeton: Princeton University Press, 1963.

Bates, Robert. *Prosperity and Violence. The political economy of development.* New York: Norton, 2001.

Bermeo, Nancy. *Ordinary People in Extraordinary Times. The Citizenry and the Breakdown of Democracy.* Princeton: Princeton University Press, 2003.

Bodemer, Klaus. *El nuevo escenario de (in)seguridad en América Latina ¿Amenaza para la democracia?* Caracas: Nueva Sociedad, 2003.

Booth, J. Costa Rica: Quest for Democracy. Boulder: Westview Press, 1998.

Buvinic, Mayra; Morrison, Andrew; and Shifter, Michael. "La violencia en América Latina y el Caribe". In: Fernando Carrión (ed.). *Seguridad ciudadana, ¿espejismo o realidad?* Quito: FLACSO Ecuador- OPS/OMS, 2002.

Carrión, Fernando. "Seguridad ciudadana en la comunidad andina". *Iconos* 18 (2004): 119-129.

Centro de Investigacion Económicas Nacionales. (CIEN). *Estudio sobre la magnitud y el costo de la violencia en Guatemala.* Guatemala: CIEN, 2002.

Córdova Macías, Ricardo. "Executive-Legislative Relations and the Institutionalisation of Democracy". In: Rachel Sieder (ed.). *Central America: Fragile Transition.* London: Macmillan Press, 1996.

Cruz, José Miguel. Violencia y democratización en Centroamérica: el impacto del crimen en la legitimidad de los regímenes de posguerra. *América Latina Hoy 35 (2003):* 19-59.

———. "Violencia, democracia y cultura política." *Nueva Sociedad 167 (2000):* 132-146.

Cruz, José Miguel y González, Luis Armando "Magnitud de la violencia en El Salvador". *Estudios Centroamericanos 588 (1997):* 953-966.

Dammert, Lucía. "Violencia criminal y seguridad pública en América Latina: la situación en Argentina". Serie políticas sociales No. 43. Santiago de Chile: CEPAL, 2000.

De Mesquita Neto, Paulo. "Crime, Violence, and Democracy in Latin America". Paper presented in the Conference Integration in the Americas. Albuquerque, New Mexico: April 5, 2002.

Diamond, Larry. "Introduction: Political Culture and Democracy". In: Larry Diamond (ed.). *Political culture and democracy in Developing Countries.* London: Lynne Rienner Publishers, 1993.

Fajnzylber, Pablo; Lederman, Daniel and Loayza, Norman. *Crimen y violencia en América Latina.* Bogotá: Alfa y Omega, 2001.

Fukuyama, Francis. *Trust. the social virtues and the creation of prosperity.* New York: Free Press, 1995.

Gabaldón, Luis Gerardo. "Seguridad ciudadana y control del delito en América Latina". Análisis y propuestas. El observatorio de Nueva Sociedad. [Puede encontrarse en: http://www.seguridadregional-fes.org/upload/1772-001_g.pdf] (Última fecha de acceso: 4 de marzo de 2007).

Gabaldón, Luis Gerardo. "Desarrollo de la criminalidad violenta en América Latina: un panorama". En: Bodemer, Klaus et al. *Violencia y regulación de conflictos en América Latina.* Caracas: Nueva Sociedad, 2001.

Garland, Allison; Holding, Heather A.; Ruthenburg, Meg; and Tulchin, Joseph. (eds.). "Crime and the threat to democratic governance". Washington, D.C.: Woodrow Wilson Center for International Scholars, 2003.

Gaviria, Alejandro & Pagés, Carmen. "Patterns of Crime Victimization in Latin America". Working Paper No. 408. Washington, D.C: Interamerican Development Bank, 1999.

Holden, Robert. "Constructing the Limits of State Violence in Central America: Towards a New Research Agenda". *Journal of Latin American Studies 28,* 2 (1996): 435-459.

Inglehart, Ronald. "The Renaissance of Political Culture". *American Political Science Review 8 (1988):* 1203- 1230.

Karstedt, Susanne. "Democracy, values, and violence: paradoxes, tensions, and comparative advantages of liberal inclusion". *The Annals of the American Academy of Political and Social Science* 605 (6) (2006): 50-81.

Karstedt, Susanne y Lafree, Gary. "Democracy, Crime and Justice". *The Annals of the American Academy of Political and Social Science* 605 (6) (2006): 6-23.

Klingemann, Hans-Dieter. "Mapping political support in the 1990's: A global Analysis.". En: Pippa Norris (ed.). *Critical citizens. Global support for democratic governance.* Oxford: Oxford University Press, 1999.

Krug, Etienne H.; Dahlberg, Linda L.; Mercy, James A.; Zwi, Anthony B.; and Lozano Rafael. (eds). *World Report on Violence and Health.* Geneva: World Health Organization Publications, 2002.

Kurtenbach, Sabine. El nuevo escenario de (in)seguridad en América Latina: ¿amenaza para la democracia?. En: Klaus Bodemer. *El nuevo escenario de (in)seguridad en América Latina ¿Amenaza para la democracia?* Caracas: Nueva Sociedad, 2003.

LaFree, Gary y Tseloni, Andromachi. "Democracy and crime: a multilevel analysis of homicide trends in forty-four countries, 1950-2000". *The Annals of the American Academy of Political and Social Science* 605 (6) (2006): 26-49.

Linz, Juan and Stepan, Alfred. "Hacia la consolidación democrática". *La Política 2 (1996):* 29 – 49.

Linz, Juan. *La quiebra de las democracias.* Madrid: Alianza Editorial, 1989.

Lipset, Seymour M. "The Social Requisites of Democracy Revisited". *American Sociological Review 59,* 1 (1994): 1-22.

————. *Political man.* London: Mercury Books, 1960.

Loader, Ian. "Policing, Recognition, and Belonging". *The Annals of the American Academy of Political and Social Science* 605 (6) (2006): 210-223.

Londoño, Juan L., Gaviria, Alejandro & Guerrero, Rodrigo (eds.). *Violencia en América Latina. Asalto al desarrollo.* Washington, D.C.: Banco Interamericano de Desarrollo, 2000.

Mahoney, James. "Radical, reformist, and aborted liberalism: Origins of national regimes in Central America." *Journal of Latin American Studies* 33, 2 (2001): 221-256.

Méndez, Juan. "Problems of Lawless Violence: Introduction." In: Juan Méndez, Guillermo O'Donnell and Paulo Sergio Pinheiro (ed.). *The (Un)Rule of Law & the Underprivileged in Latin America.* Notre Dame: University of Notre Dame Press, 1999.

Mockus, Antanas y Acero, Hugo. "Criminalidad y violencia en América Latina. La experiencia exitosa de Bogotá." *Seguridad Sostenible* 22 (sin fecha).

Moreno, Alejandro. "Democracy and Mass Beliefs Systems in Latin America". In: Roderic Ai Camp (ed.). *Citizens views of Democracy in Latin America.* Pittsburgh: University of Pittsburgh Press, 2001.

Moser, Caroline y Holland, Jeremy. *La pobreza urbana y la violencia en Jamaica.* Washington D.C.: El Banco Mundial, 1997.

Moser, Caroline y McIlwaine, Cathy. *Violence in a Post-Conflict Context: Urban Poor Perceptions from Guatemala.* Washington, D.C.: World Bank Publications, 2001.

Moser, Caroline; Winton, Ailsa y Moser, Annalise. "Violence, Fear, and Insecurity among the Urban Poor in Latin America". En: Marianne Fay (ed.). *The urban poor in Latin America.* Washington, D.C.: The World Bank, 2005.

Muller, Edward y Seligson, Mitchell A. "Inequality and Insurgency". *American Political Science Review 81,* 2 (1987): 425-452.

Norris, Pippa. "Introduction: The Growth of Critical Citizens?" In: Pippa Norris (ed.). *Critical Citizens. Global Support for Democratic Government.* Oxford: Oxford University Press, 1999.

Pérez, Orlando. Democratic Legitimacy and Public Insecurity: Crime and Democracy in El Salvador and Guatemala. *Political Science Quaterly,* 118 (4) (2003). Winter 2003-2004.

Programa de las Naciones Unidas para el Desarrollo. (PNUD). *La democracia en América Latina: Hacia una democracia de ciudadanas y ciudadanos.* Buenos Aires: Alfaguara, 2004.

Przeworski, Adam; Alvarez, Michael; Cheibub, José Antonio; and Limongi, Fernando. "What makes democracies endure?" *Journal of Democracy 7,* 1 (1996): 39-55.

Putnam, Robert A. *Making Democracy Work.* Princeton: Princeton University Press, 1993.

Remmer, Karen. "Redemocratization and the impact of authoritarian rule in Latin America". *Comparative Politics* 17, 3 (1985): 253-275.

Rustow, Dankwart. "Transitions to democracy: Toward a Dynamic Model". In: Lisa Anderson (comp.). *Transitions to Democracy.* New York: Columbia University Press, 1999.

Seligson, Mitchell A. "The Impact of Corruption on Regime Legitimacy: A Comparative Study of Four Latin American Countries". *The Journal of Politics 64,* 2 (2002): 408-433.

————. "Toward a Model of Democratic Stability: Political Culture in Central America". *Estudios Interdisplinarios de América Latina y el Caribe 11,* 2 (2000): 1 – 22.

Seligson, Mitchell y Azpuru, Dinorah. "Las dimensiones y el impacto político de la delincuencia en la población guatemalteca". En Luis Rosero Bixby (ed)., *Población del istmo 2000: Familia, migración, violencia y medio ambiente.* San José: Centro Centroamericano de Población, 2000.

Tilly, Charles. *The Politics of Violence.* Cambridge: Cambridge University Press, 2003.

Torres-Rivas, Edelberto. "Foundations: Central America". En: Manuel Antonio Garretón and Edward Newman, (eds). *Democracy in Latin America. (Re)Constructing Political Society.* New York: United Nations University Press, 2001.

Wielandt, Gustavo. "Hacia la construcción de lecciones del posconflicto en América Latina y el Caribe. Una mirada a la violencia juvenile en Centroamérica". *Serie Políticas Sociales 115*. Santiago de Chile: CEPAL, 2005.

Appendixes: Binary Logistic Regression Tables According to Country

Table X.A.1: Guatemala. Variables in the Equation(b)

		B	S.E.	Wald	df	Sig.	Exp(B)
Step 1(a)	size	.095	.046	4.303	1	.038	1.100
	q1	.009	.135	.005	1	.946	1.009
	q2	.006	.005	1.559	1	.212	1.006
	ed	.025	.019	1.781	1	.182	1.026
	q10	.002	.042	.001	1	.970	1.002
	vic2r	.000	.003	.028	1	.866	1.000
	insecure	.004	.003	2.059	1	.151	1.004
	aoj17	-.137	.071	3.656	1	.056	.872
	n10	.205	.037	30.226	1	.000	1.228
	Constant	-2.351	.463	25.833	1	.000	.095

a Variable(s) entered on step 1: size, q1, q2, ed, q10, vic2r, insecure, aoj17, n10.
b country country = 2 Guatemala

Table X.A.2: El Salvador. Variables in the Equation (b)

		B	S.E.	Wald	df	Sig.	Exp(B)
Step 1(a)	size	.014	.045	.102	1	.750	1.014
	q1	-.518	.125	17.176	1	.000	.596
	q2	-.002	.004	.236	1	.627	.998
	ed	.012	.017	.463	1	.496	1.012
	q10	.011	.034	.097	1	.756	1.011
	vic2r	.000	.002	.024	1	.877	1.000
	insecure	.002	.002	1.490	1	.222	1.002
	aoj17	-.028	.064	.190	1	.663	.973
	n10	.288	.035	66.741	1	.000	1.334
	Constant	-1.269	.464	7.489	1	.006	.281

a Variable(s) entered on step 1: size, q1, q2, ed, q10, vic2r, insecure, aoj17, n10.
b country Country = 3 El Salvador

Table X.A.3: Honduras. Variables in the Equation(b)

		B	S.E.	Wald	df	Sig.	Exp(B)
Step 1(a)	size	-.070	.056	1.563	1	.211	.933
	q1	-.087	.136	.412	1	.521	.916
	q2	.004	.005	.571	1	.450	1.004
	ed	.021	.020	1.063	1	.303	1.021
	q10	.053	.041	1.707	1	.191	1.055
	vic2r	-.002	.003	.763	1	.382	.998
	insecure	.008	.002	10.824	1	.001	1.008
	aoj17	.226	.092	6.026	1	.014	1.253
	n10	.321	.044	54.327	1	.000	1.379
	Constant	-3.658	.554	43.552	1	.000	.026

a Variable(s) entered on step 1: size, q1, q2, ed, q10, vic2r, insecure, aoj17, n10.
b country Country = 4 Honduras

Table X.A.4: Nicaragua. Variables in the Equation(b)

		B	S.E.	Wald	df	Sig.	Exp(B)
Step 1(a)	size	-.089	.051	3.029	1	.082	.915
	q1	-.027	.136	.040	1	.841	.973
	q2	-.001	.005	.044	1	.834	.999
	ed	-.004	.020	.031	1	.860	.996
	q10	.063	.037	2.867	1	.090	1.065
	vic2r	-.003	.003	1.635	1	.201	.997
	insecure	.004	.002	2.729	1	.099	1.004
	aoj17	.025	.072	.121	1	.728	1.025
	n10	.258	.037	48.926	1	.000	1.295
	Constant	-2.076	.481	18.653	1	.000	.125

a Variable(s) entered on step 1: size, q1, q2, ed, q10, vic2r, insecure, aoj17, n10.
b country Country = 5 Nicaragua.

Table X.A.5: Costa Rica. Variables in the Equation(b)

		B	S.E.	Wald	df	Sig.	Exp(B)
Step 1(a)	size	.043	.037	1.304	1	.254	1.044
	q1	-.093	.115	.649	1	.421	.911
	q2	.008	.004	4.926	1	.026	1.008
	ed	.034	.016	4.591	1	.032	1.035
	q10	.054	.027	3.954	1	.047	1.056
	vic2r	.001	.002	.115	1	.735	1.001
	insecure	.002	.002	1.960	1	.162	1.002
	aoj17	.059	.055	1.165	1	.280	1.061
	n10	.199	.033	36.367	1	.000	1.220
	Constant	-2.079	.406	26.163	1	.000	.125

a Variable(s) entered on step 1: size, q1, q2, ed, q10, vic2r, insecure, aoj17, n10.
b country Country = 6 Costa Rica.

Table X.A.6: Panama. Variables in the Equation(b)

		B	S.E.	Wald	df	Sig.	Exp(B)
Step 1(a)	size	-.064	.044	2.062	1	.151	.938
	q1	-.023	.135	.029	1	.864	.977
	q2	.005	.005	1.035	1	.309	1.005
	ed	.002	.019	.016	1	.899	1.002
	q10	.069	.056	1.515	1	.218	1.072
	vic2r	.000	.004	.000	1	.988	1.000
	insecure	.006	.002	5.435	1	.020	1.006
	n10	.544	.051	114.054	1	.000	1.723
	Constant	-3.844	.473	66.119	1	.000	.021

a Variable(s) entered on step 1: size, q1, q2, ed, q10, vic2r, insecure, n10.
b country Country= 7 Panama.

249

XI. Corruption and its Impact on Latin American Democratic Stability*

Dominique Zéphyr**

Abstract

The objective of this chapter is to analyze the impact of corruption on citizen attitudes towards democracy. To this end, the corruption measure developed by LAPOP is used in this study, which, as will be shown, overcomes many of the weaknesses of the indicators of perception of corruption. Additionally, there is an assessment of the impact that corruption victimization has on support for the political system and support for democracy. This is measured by the level of citizen satisfaction with the way in which democracy functions in practice and support for democracy as an ideal form of government. The inclusion of most of the Latin American countries in the AmericasBarometer allows for robust conclusions regarding the impact of corruption in the region.

Is corruption a challenge for democratization in Latin America and the Caribbean? Traditionally, studies on corruption have focused on assessing its impact on macroeconomic development and socioeconomic welfare of developing nations. It has been argued that corruption affects trade negatively, diminishes incentives for investment, and slows the development and economic growth (World Bank 1997). However, the impact of corruption on political development has only recently emerged as a topic for debate in the social sciences. For some authors, corruption can contribute to political stability (Huntington 1968; Waterbury 1976; Becquart-Leclercq 1989), given that it can may make state bureaucracies function more effectively. For example, Becquart-Leclerq (1989) argues that "corruption functions like grease in the gears; it has an important redistributive effect, it is a functional substitute for direct participation in power, it constitutes the cement between elites and parties, and it affects the effectiveness with which power is exercised" (192). Other scholars have pointed out that corruption has a negative effect on citizen attitudes towards the legitimacy of the political system, and it ultimately represents a threat to the consolidation of democratic regimes (Shin 1999; Camp, *et al.* 2000; Della Porta 2000; Pharr 2000).[1]

The study of the consequences of corruption on democratic stability in the Latin American context is particularly relevant given that global indicators on corruption show that most of the countries in the region reveal evidence of high levels of corruption. Former Organization of American States (OAS) Secretary General Cesar Gaviria emphasizes the harmful effects of corruption and the importance of this issue in the region, pointing out that "corruption is a terrible cancer that threatens the legitimacy of the institutions and the rule of law, and in this

---

*The author thanks Mitchell Seligson for his suggestions and comments. The errors and omissions are solely the author's.

** Research Coordinator for the Latin American Public Opinion Project.

[1] For a more exhaustive review of literature, see (Seligson 2002; Seligson 2006)

sense there is still a long way to go in the Americas."[2] Recent data gathering by means of surveys on political culture which have included items on citizen perception of and/or experience with corruption have made it possible to provide empirical evidence of the existence of a negative relationship between corruption and the legitimacy of the political system. Using data from the World Values Survey (1995-1997) together with those from Transparency International (1997), Canache and Allison (2005) found that citizen *perception* of high levels of corruption entails a lower level of support for the incumbent government and the political institutions in six Latin American countries. However, they found no evidence that the perception of corruption has any impact on citizen support for democracy as the best form of government.

Additionally, Seligson (2002, 2006) has developed an innovative methodology to measure corruption using the surveys of the Latin American Public Opinion Project (LAPOP) as a database. This new methodology measures levels of corruption based on day-to-day citizen *experiences* with bribery instead of perceptions of corruption. Seligson shows that, at the individual level, experience with corruption translates to less support for the political system in the six Latin American countries analyzed: Bolivia, Ecuador, El Salvador, Honduras, Nicaragua and Paraguay.

The objective of the present study is to analyze the impact of corruption on citizen attitudes towards democracy at a broader level. To this end, the corruption measure developed by LAPOP is used in this study, which, as will be shown, overcomes the weaknesses of the indicators of perception of corruption. Additionally, there is an assessment of the impact that corruption victimization has on support for the political system and support for democracy. This is measured by the level of citizen satisfaction with the way in which democracy functions in practice and support for democracy as an ideal form of government. It must be said that the inclusion of most of the Latin American countries in the AmericasBarometer allows for more robust conclusions regarding the impact of corruption in the region.

The empirical analysis in this work is based on the 2006-07 AmericasBarometer surveys. These were carried out person-to-person in twenty-two countries throughout Latin America and the Caribbean. For these surveys, a stratified, multi-staged, cluster sample was used. Furthermore, for the purposes of comparison, data from phone surveys in Canada and the United States gathered by LAPOP were also taken into account. In total, the data base comprises over 30,000 observations.

The principal hypothesis in this chapter is that experience with corruption negatively affects citizen opinions of democracy and their support for the political system. In other words, taking into account the idea that the existence of a democratic political culture entails stronger and more long lasting democracies, this part of the study argues that corruption poses a challenge for democracy in that it causes citizens to have a less positive view of the performance of democratic regimes. In the first section of this chapter an appraisal is made of the levels of corruption in the countries of Latin America and the Caribbean contrasting Transparency

---

[2] Message of the OAS General Secretary, Cesar Gaviria, to a conference on "Adjustment of Dominican Penal Legislation to the Convention Against Corruption" Santo Domingo, Dominican Republic, August 30, 2002

International's Corruption Perception Index with LAPOP's Corruption Victimization Index. The second section presents a study of the most common forms of victimization by corruption in Latin America and the Caribbean, that is to say, the places in which citizens are most likely to become victims of corruption. The third section offers a profile of persons who are the most likely to become victims of corruption, taking into account individual characteristics. In the final section the chapter's main hypothesis is tested, followed by conclusions.

The Level of Corruption in the Region

How much corruption exists in Latin America and the Caribbean? In order to take a first look at corruption in the region, Transparency International's Corruption Perception Index (CPI), developed in 1995 is used. The CPI is the oldest and best-known large scale measure of corruption.[3] It is an index scaled from one to ten, in which the value of one indicates a maximum level of corruption and ten a minimal level of corruption. The 2006 CPI shows that the corruption average for Latin America and the Caribbean was 3.5. The region presented, on average, higher levels of corruption than the European Union and Asia, but lower than those for Africa and Eastern Europe. Nevertheless, according to this index, the Latin American region is home some of the most corrupt countries in the world, among them Haiti, Venezuela and Ecuador. Furthermore, twenty-five of the thirty countries in the region for which the CPI was calculated in 2006, show levels of corruption lower than 5, with a third of the countries' scores below 3. These low scores are troublesome when taking into account that Transparency International considers corruption a serious problem in countries with scores lower than 5, and a rampant problem in countries with scores of under 3 (2006b).

Table XI-1 shows the levels of perception of corruption according to the CPI for the countries of the Americas that were included in the 2006-07 AmericasBarometer. As can be seen, there are substantial differences in the perceived levels of corruption among the countries analyzed here. Chile is the Latin American country with the lowest level of perception of corruption with a score of 7.3, which places it second, alongside the United States, among the countries with the least perceived corruption in the Americas. Canada is the country with the lowest perceived level of corruption in the Americas according to the CPI. On the other hand, Haiti received the lowest score in the region, (1.8), which places it not only as the most corrupt country in the Americas, but amazingly, the most corrupt country in the world. According to Transparency International's data, Haiti is in last position among the 163 countries where data regarding the perception of corruption was collected. Nevertheless, the levels of corruption are alarming not only in Haiti, but also in another nine of the countries analyzed by the AmericasBarometer, which show evidence of "generalized" levels of perception of corruption.

---

[3] The other global index on perception of corruption, which competes with the CPI in popularity, is the Corruption Control Indicator (CCI), part of the database on governability developed at the World Bank by the Kaufmann team. See (Kaufmann, *et al.* 2006).

Table XI-1. Perception of Corruption in Seventeen Latin American countries

Country	World Ranking	Regional Ranking	CPI Score (2006)	Surveys used	Range of confidence
Canada	14	1	8.5	7	8.0 - 8.9
Chile	20	2	7.3	7	6.6 - 7.6
United States	20	2	7.3	8	6.6 - 7.8
Uruguay	28	5	6.4	5	5.9 - 7.0
Costa Rica	55	7	4.1	5	3.3 - 4.8
El Salvador	57	8	4	5	3.2 - 4.8
Colombia	59	9	3.9	7	3.5 - 4.7
Jamaica	61	10	3.7	5	3.4 - 4.0
Brazil	70	14	3.3	7	3.1 - 3.6
Mexico	70	14	3.3	7	3.1 - 3.4
Peru	70	14	3.3	5	2.8 - 3.8
Panama	84	18	3.1	5	2.8 - 3.3
Dominican Republic	99	21	2.8	5	2.4 - 3.2
Bolivia	105	22	2.7	6	2.4 - 3.0
Guatemala	111	23	2.6	5	2.3 - 3.0
Nicaragua	111	23	2.6	6	2.4 - 2.9
Paraguay	111	23	2.6	5	2.2 - 3.3
Guyana	121	26	2.5	5	2.2 - 2.6
Honduras	121	26	2.5	6	2.4 - 2.7
Ecuador	138	28	2.3	5	2.2 - 2.5
Venezuela	138	28	2.3	7	2.2 – 2.4
Haiti	163	30	1.8	3	1.7 - 1.8
Source: (Transparency International 2006a)					

The CPI has been one of the best-known indexes available for making comparative studies on corruption at a global level. However, it has also received criticism from different sources, which has lead to a revision of its methodology. Part of the criticism concerns elements inherent to the index, and, to a certain extent, question its validity. For instance, Seligson (2002, 2006) pointed out three weaknesses in the CPI and other measures of perception of corruption. First, the index is based on *perceptions* about corruption and not the *experience* of corruption. Second, the index is based on the opinions of national and international experts, which makes it difficult to separate stereotypes from reality. Third, the measures of perception suffer from endogenous problems, and therefore are not to be trusted as they can easily be influenced by the media. Additionally, Luna (2006) argues that "perceptions may be conditioned by the circumstantial impact of specific scandals eventually becoming more volatile and becoming strongly dependent of the moment in which the measure is taken" (93).

Taking into account the weaknesses of the measurements of perceived corruption, the Latin American Public Opinion Project (LAPOP) has developed a methodology that allows for

corruption measurement starting with direct citizen experiences of corrupt acts. The AmericasBarometer included a battery of questions on corruption victimization that has traditionally been used in LAPOP surveys. Respondents were asked about their personal experience with corruption in different contexts: whether the police requested bribes; whether they were asked to pay bribes to public employees; and whether they had to pay a bribe at work or when they had dealings at the municipality, hospitals, schools and the courts. The following table presents the LAPOP survey questions that are used to measure the degree of citizen victimization by corruption.

Now we want to talk about your personal experience with things that happen in life...
EXC2. Did any police official ask you for bribe during the past year?
EXC6. During the past year did any public official ask you for a bribe?
EXC11. During the past year did you have any official dealings in the municipality? During the past year, to process any kind of document (like a license, for example), did you have to pay any money above that required by law?
EXC13. Are you currently employed? At your workplace, did anyone ask you for an inappropriate payment during the past year?
EXC14. During the past year, did you have any business in the courts? Did you have to pay a bribe at the courts during the past year?
EXC15. Did you use the public health services during the past year? In order to receive attention in a hospital or a clinic during the past year, did you have to pay a bribe?
EXC16. Did you have a child in school during the past year? Did you have to pay a bribe at school during the past year?

Based on these items, LAPOP has created two corruption victimization indices. One takes into account the total number of ways people have been victims of corruption over the past year; the other one reflects whether the person has been a victim of corruption or not. Taking into account the latter indicator, Figure XI-1 shows the percentage of persons that have been victims of at least one act of corruption over the past year, per country.

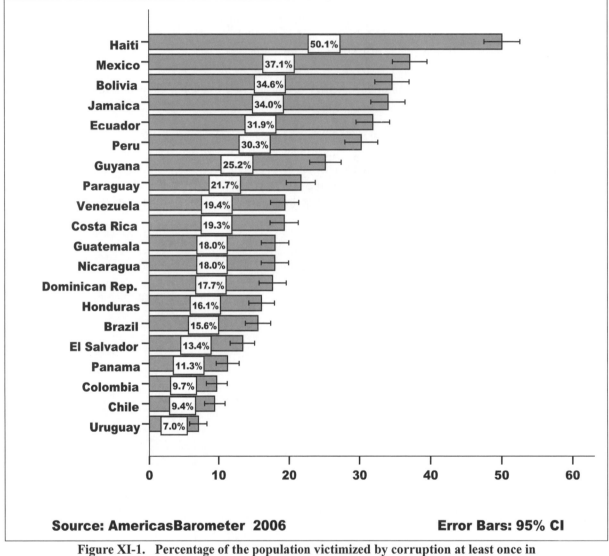

Source: AmericasBarometer 2006   Error Bars: 95% CI

Figure XI-1. Percentage of the population victimized by corruption at least once in
past year

As can be seen in Figure XI-1, the LAPOP Corruption Victimization Index shows Chile as having the lowest level of corruption among the countries studied. On the other hand, Haiti has the worst indices of corruption victimization, which also seems to confirm Transparency International's results. One out of every two Haitians has declared having been a victim of an act of corruption, that is to say 50% of Haitians have had to pay bribes; this percentage is more than

double the regional average (22%).[4] Although it may seem that the results of the Corruption Victimization Index developed by LAPOP are similar to those of Transparency International's CPI, there are substantial differences in the indicators. In fact, the correlation between the CPI and the Corruption Victimization Index is relatively low (r=0.47). Whereas in Table XI-1 Costa Rica appears to have one of the lowest perceived levels of corruption, according to LAPOP's Corruption Victimization Index, this country has a level of corruption similar to Guatemala In fact, in Central America, Guatemala, Honduras and Nicaragua had been placed among the countries with "generalized" or alarming perceived levels of corruption but exhibit intermediate levels of victimization. Moreover, Jamaica and Mexico at intermediate levels on the CPI become part of the six countries where the magnitude of the corruption problem is serious, with a third of their populations having been victims. Taking into account the aforementioned limitations of corruption perception indexes, and the discrepancies between the results presented by the two methodologies evaluated here, it can be concluded that LAPOP's Victimization by Corruption Index allows for the measurement of the magnitude of corruption in Latin American countries in a manner that is more in touch with reality, given that it measures people's day to day experience with acts of corruption.

Modes of Victimization by Corruption in Latin America and the Caribbean

An added strength of the methodology for measuring corruption developed by LAPOP is that it not only allows for comparisons between countries but also reveals the contexts in which acts of corruption take place. This is an important characteristic as it provides information that is valuable for the design of national anti-corruption strategies since the places where acts of corruption most frequently take place are identified. LAPOP's methodology focuses primarily on measuring the levels of corruption victimization among public service users. In other words, to calculate the percentage of persons who have been victims of corruption, only those who use these services were taken into account. Figure XI-2 presents the percentage of persons in Latin America and the Caribbean who have been victims of corruption, taking into account the place where the person declares having been a victim. As can be seen, the levels of victimization by corruption are greater in municipalities (15.2%) and at the courts (13%). Likewise, the data indicates that, on average, only 6.8% of the people in the region reported having been a bribe-victim of a public employee.

---

[4] For more information on corruption in Haiti, see (Zéphyr, *et al.* 2007).

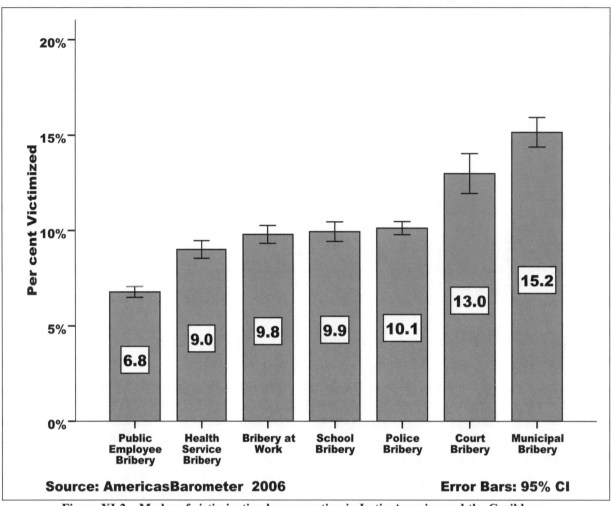

Figure XI-2. Modes of victimization by corruption in Latin America and the Caribbean

These regional results hide substantial differences among countries. For instance, results per country for the question *"Have you been asked to pay a bribe by a public official in the past year?"* are presented in Figure XI-3. This is the only item in the battery of questions on corruption victimization that was included in the questionnaires used in Canada and the United States. This allows for the comparison of levels of victimization by public employees in Latin America with those in the two countries mentioned. As can be seen, Ecuador, Bolivia, Mexico and Paraguay appear at the top of the graph with relatively homogenous levels of corruption victimization. Citizens in these countries are 40 times more likely to be asked for a bribe by a public official than people in the U.S. On the other hand, Chile, which has the lowest level of victimization among Latin American countries, has twice the percentage of people who reported having paid a bribe to a public employee than Canada does.

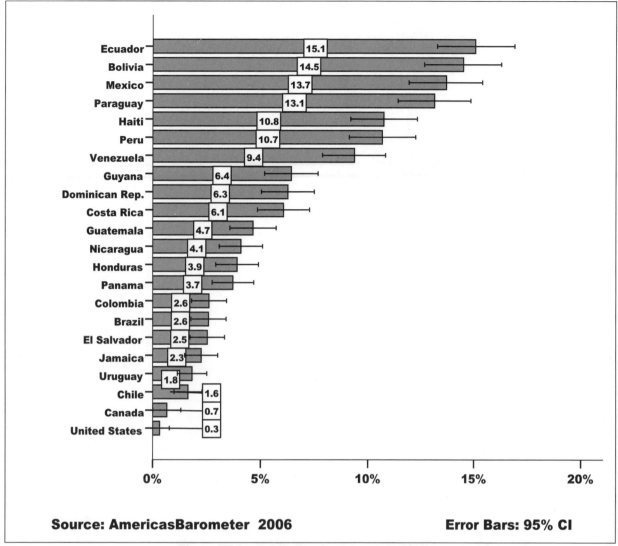

Source: AmericasBarometer 2006   Error Bars: 95% CI

Figure XI-3.   Public Employee requested bribe

In Latin America and the Caribbean, the highest levels of victimization by corruption can be found in the municipalities. Some 15.2% of people have been victims of corruption when they had dealings with these institutions. This shows the importance local government has in the life of the Latin American citizen, but it also demonstrates that corruption is a serious problem for local governments. As shown in Figure XI-4, the problem of corruption in municipalities is very serious, particularly in Haiti and also in Bolivia, Mexico, Brazil, Dominican Republic, Jamaica and Panama where percentages of people who have had to pay bribes are higher than the regional average (16%). Corruption in municipalities has been mentioned as one of the three most frequent modes in all the countries in the region that were included in the AmericasBarometer.

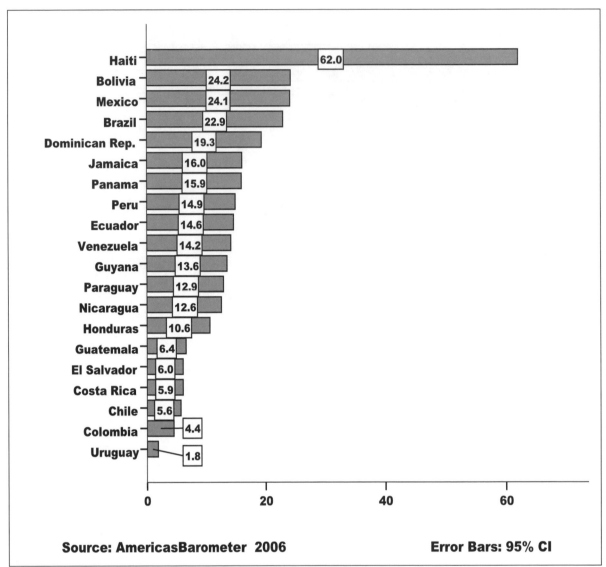

Source: AmericasBarometer 2006   Error Bars: 95% CI

Figure XI-4. Bribes in municipalities

This result turns out to be of particular relevance in the Latin American context given that decentralization of the central government's resources towards municipalities is being promoted as a strategy to foster democratic governance, as it is believed that this will lead to greater citizen participation and therefore more accountability of public officials. However, as shown in Chapter V of this book "*Decentralize or Centralize? Challenges for Reform of the State and Democracy in Latin America and the Caribbean*", decentralization does not have general citizen approval. Actually, only one of every two Latin American citizens supports decentralization. A hypothesis that emerges when taking into account the results in this chapter is that the divided opinion on decentralization in Latin America may be related to the high rates of corruption experienced at the municipal level. Figure XI-5 shows evidence in favor of this hypothesis, given that those who have had to pay bribes to municipal government officials show a lower level of support for decentralization of resources and powers toward local governments. The results of the AmericasBarometer suggest that decentralization must go hand-in-hand with efforts to fight corruption in municipalities so that decentralization will be supported by the majority of the population and also in order to avoid an increase in the levels of victimization by corruption provoked by transferences of power and resources to the municipalities.

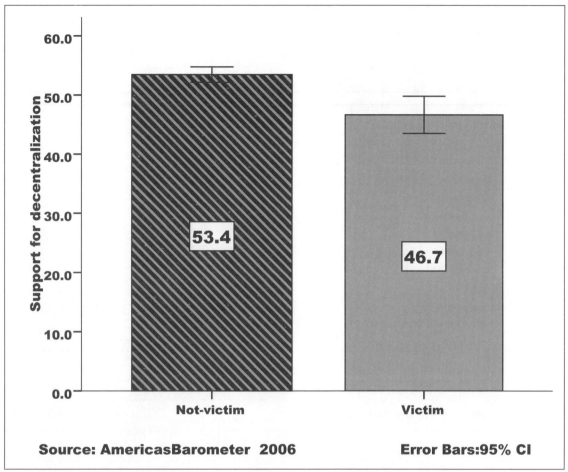

Figure XI-5.   Impact of victimization by corruption at municipalities on support for decentralization

The second highest level of victimization takes place at the courts. On average, some 13% of respondents claimed to have been victims of corruption when they had dealings at the courts. Figure XI-6 indicates that approximately 3% of people who had some business at the courts were asked to pay bribes in El Salvador, Costa Rica and Colombia whereas one out of every two Haitians and one out of every four Mexicans had an experience of bribe payment at the courts.

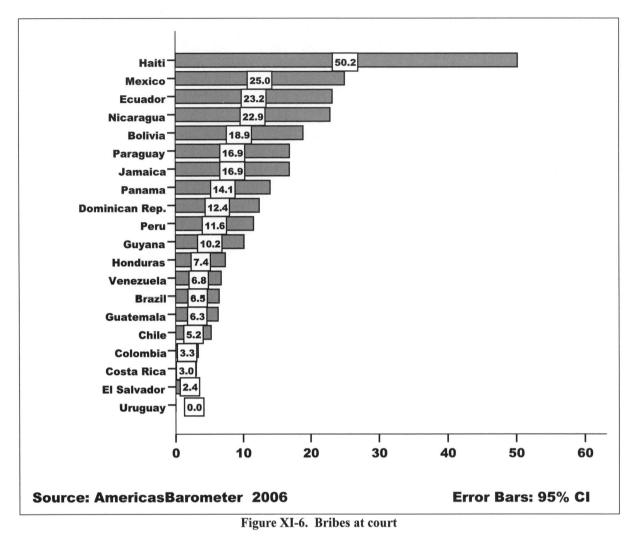

Figure XI-6. Bribes at court

As shown in Chapter XII of this book, being a victim of corruption has a negative impact on trust in the institutions that guarantee the rule of law in democratic Latin American societies, and the high level of corruption in the courts seems to partially explain this result. As shown in Figure XI-7, in fact, persons that have been victims of corruption at the courts have a lower level of trust in the justice system.

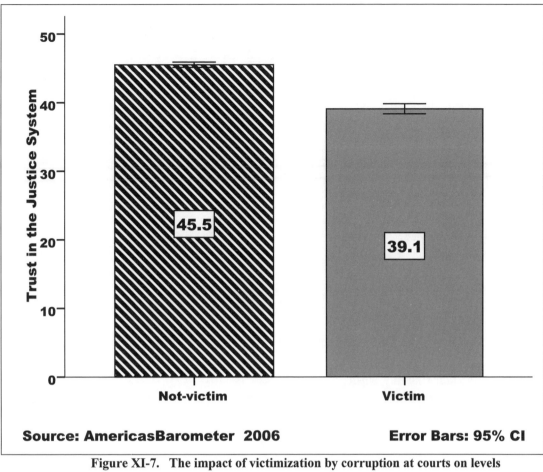

Figure XI-7. The impact of victimization by corruption at courts on levels of confidence in the justice system

Who are the most likely to become victims of corruption?

In an effort to identify potential victims, a logistic regression model was made. In this model the dependent variable indicates whether or not the respondent was a victim of at least one act of corruption over the past year. The independent variables are gender, age, educational level, income level, marital status and the size of the city of residence. These variables have been taken into account given that previous analyses have consistently shown that corruption does not affect all citizens equally.[5] The regression results are shown in Table XI-2. It can be seen that with the exception of marital status, the majority of variables that were included are statistically relevant factors ($p < 0.05$). Based on the coefficients estimated in the regression, the probability of becoming a victim was calculated taking into account the interviewee's gender and maintaining other variables constant at their average value. Furthermore, the probability of becoming a victim was calculated taking into account the individual effect of age, income and educational level.

---

[5] See studies of the results from the LAPOP national surveys at www.lapopsurveys.org

263

Table XI-2. Determinants of victimization by corruption in Latin America and the Caribbean
(Results of the logistic regression)

	Coefficient	Standard Dev.	t	Sig.
Gender	0.490	0.033	15.040	0.000
Age	-0.012	0.001	-8.290	0.000
Education	0.059	0.006	10.680	0.000
Income	0.019	0.010	1.830	0.067
Marital status (married)	0.085	0.037	2.300	0.022
Number of children	0.070	0.010	6.950	0.000
Size of city of residence	-0.017	0.019	-0.900	0.369
Constant	-1.880	0.111	-16.870	0.000

Dependent Variable: 0= Not victim; 1= Victim of corruption
Number of observations: 25,289
Effect of design = 1581
F(7, 1575) = 71.68

Figure XI-8 shows that women have a lower probability of becoming victims of corruption than men. On average, women are 8% less probable to become victims of corruption. This is due to the fact that, in Latin America, there is still a gap in the level of participation in public affairs between men and women, to the detriment of the latter. This reduces the number of situations in which women could be victimized.

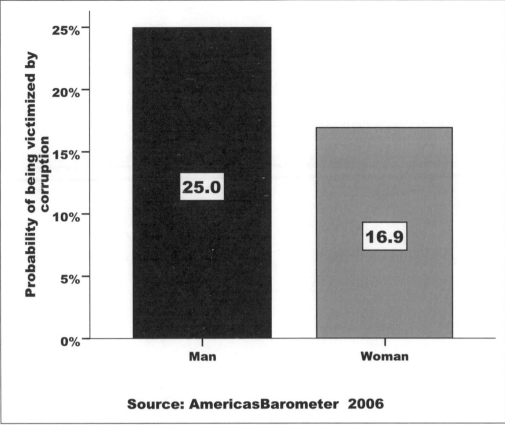

Source: AmericasBarometer 2006

Figure XI-8. Probability of becoming a victim of corruption by gender

As shown in Figure XI-9, young people are more prone to becoming victims of corruption. Considering that municipalities are the institutions where there are higher levels of corruption, it can be inferred that young people have a greater tendency to go to these institutions to do tasks such as request birth certificates or permits, which increases the opportunities of being exposed to a greater level of victimization by corruption as compared to older people.

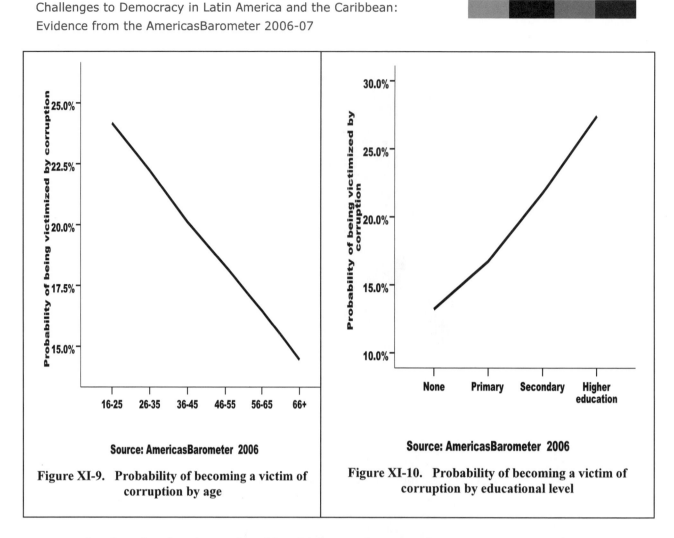

Source: AmericasBarometer 2006

Figure XI-9.   Probability of becoming a victim of corruption by age

Source: AmericasBarometer 2006

Figure XI-10.   Probability of becoming a victim of corruption by educational level

On the other hand, people with a higher socioeconomic status are expected to have the highest tendency to become victims of corruption, given that they have greater economic resources and are therefore more prepared to pay a bribe. They also participate more in public affairs. Figure XI-10 shows that education is a factor that is associated with victimization; the greater the level of education, the greater the probability of becoming a victim of corruption. Furthermore, the regression results indicate that there exists a positive, statistically significant relationship between income and corruption victimization. These results confirm the notion that persons with a higher socioeconomic level have greater probabilities of becoming victims of officials demanding bribes.

Corruption and its Impact on Democracy

This section examines the impact corruption has on democratic stability. The development of a democratic culture among citizens, and in particular the level of support or preference for democracy, is recognized in the literature as an important element for achieving durable and stable democracies (Almond and Verba 1963; Diamond 1999). This section analyzes the degree to which incidence of demands for bribes by public employees affects the opinions of

citizens regarding democracy. The study specifically focuses on whether being a victim of corruption affects support for democracy as it exists, measured by the degree of individual satisfaction with the way in which democracy functions in the countries studied and the support for democracy as an ideal form of government, that is--normative support for democracy.

Likewise, this section analyzes the effect of victimization by corruption on citizen opinions regarding the legitimacy of the political system. Easton (1965; Easton 1975) defined "political legitimacy" as "the conviction that it is right and proper...to obey the authorities and to abide by the requirements of the regime" (1975, 451). Similarly, Lipset (1994) states that "legitimacy involves the capacity of a political system to engender and maintain the belief that existing political institutions are the most appropriate or proper ones for the society" and considers legitimacy as a prerequisite for the maintenance and the stability of democracy. The argument is that a political system that is legitimate in the citizens' view will obtain a high level of support for its institutions. That is why, aside from examining the effect of being a victim of corruption on the satisfaction and support for democracy, its effect on political legitimacy is also studied. It is assumed that corruption victimization in Latin American countries will decrease the political system's legitimacy and that at the same time it may lead to less support for democracy, given that corruption causes citizens to lose trust in the political system's institutions and the performance of democratic regimes.

Victimization by Corruption and Satisfaction with Democracy

The first dependent variable analyzed is satisfaction with "the way democracy works." In the AmericasBarometer, this variable is measured using the following question: *In general, would you say you are very satisfied, satisfied, dissatisfied or very dissatisfied with the way in which democracy functions in [country]?* Satisfaction with democracy reflects citizen perception of the way the democratic regime actually works in their country. That is to say, satisfaction refers to the way democracy actually functions, not democracy as a form of ideal government in itself (Bratton, *et al.* 2004).

Figure XI-12 shows that the level of satisfaction with the way democracy works in Latin America is relatively low. The regional average for satisfaction with democracy is 46.8 on a scale of zero to one hundred points. Nevertheless, satisfaction with democracy varies from country to country. As can be seen in the Figure, countries with the lowest levels of satisfaction with democracy are Paraguay (27.6) and Ecuador (36.5). On the other hand, Uruguay exhibits the highest level of satisfaction with democracy (62.2), followed by Bolivia (54.1).

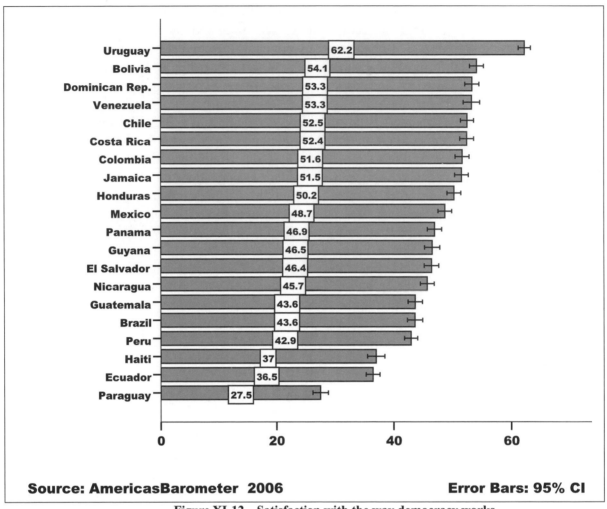

Source: AmericasBarometer 2006   **Error Bars: 95% CI**

Figure XI-12. Satisfaction with the way democracy works

In order to determine the impact of victimization by corruption on satisfaction with the way democracy works, a regression model was constructed. The predictors included in the regression are the following: (a) the total number of ways that people have been victims of corruption over the past year; (b) the usual sociodemographic variables: gender, age, education, wealth, and place of residence; and (c) dummy variables or dichotomic variables for each country which take into account the differences in the levels of satisfaction with democracy from country to country. In addition, variables have been included to measure the level of satisfaction with the performance of the incumbent government, the perception of the country's economic situation, and victimization by crime. The results of the regression are presented in Table XI-3. These indicate that the experience of corruption influences people negatively when assessing the way democracy functions.

Table XI-3. Determinants of satisfaction with the way democracy works

	Coefficient.	Stand.Dev.	T	Sig.
Total number of ways they have been victims of corruption over the past year	-0.534	0.165	-3.240	0.001
Satisfaction with the performance of the current president	0.297	0.006	49.720	0.000
Victimization by crime	-0.023	0.003	-6.610	0.000
Perception of the country's economic situation	0.155	0.006	25.090	0.000
Gender	0.158	0.255	0.620	0.535
Age	0.024	0.009	2.710	0.007
Education	-0.772	0.192	-4.020	0.000
Wealth	-0.254	0.080	-3.160	0.002
Urban	-1.249	0.300	-4.160	0.000
Constant	29.988	0.882	33.990	0.000

Number of obs =29469
F(28, 29440) = 278.01
Adj R-Squared. = 0.2084
Dependent Variable: Satisfaction with the way democracy works.
Dummy for countries (Reference country: Mexico).

Victimization by Corruption and Support for Democracy as an Ideal Form of Government

As mentioned earlier, one of the prerequisites for the consolidation of democracy in the country is generalized citizen support for democracy as an ideal form of government. In the AmericasBarometer, the level of support for democracy is measured with the following question, using a scale from one to seven: *Democracy may have problems but it is better than any other form of government. To what extent do you agree or disagree with this statement?*

According to Figure XI-13 the level of support for democracy as the best form of government is high in all the countries of the region. The regional average for support of democracy is 69.9. In fact, Peru and Panama, countries with the lowest levels of support for democracy, have a level of over 50 points on the scale from zero to 100. These figures suggest that the demand for democracy is greater than the supply, this is to say, the citizens in the region have a high level of support for democracy as the ideal form of government, whereas they have low levels of satisfaction on how democracy actually works in their countries.

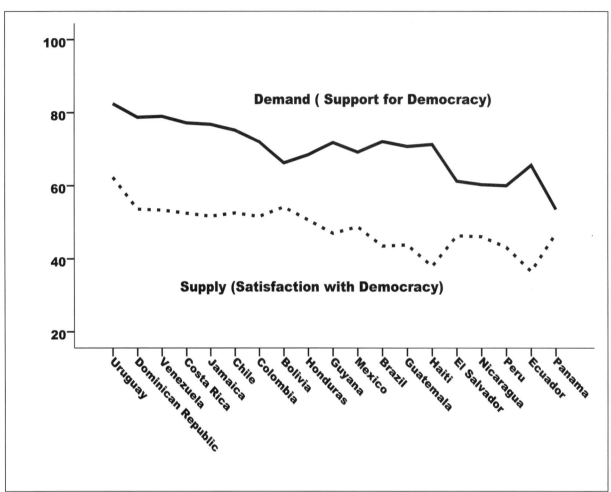

Figure XI-13. Supply and demand for democracy in Latin America and the Caribbean

Does victimization by corruption affect support for democracy as the ideal form of government? In order to answer this question, the previous regression model was estimated, this time with support for democracy as the dependent variable. The results (see Table XI-4) showed that corruption victimization has a statistically significant negative effect on Latin American citizens' propensity for expressing support for democracy as a form of government. This result contradicts Canache and Allison's conclusions (2003), which were based on measures of perception of corruption. They had found no empirical evidence that corruption affects citizens' opinions regarding democracy as a form of government.

Table XI-4. Determinants of support for democracy as a form of government

	Coefficient	Stand. Dev.	T	Sig.
Total number of ways they have been victims of corruption over the past year	-1.101	0.216	-5.090	0.000
Satisfaction with the performance of the current president	0.148	0.008	18.890	0.000
Victimization by crime	-0.013	0.004	-3.010	0.003
Perception of the country's economic situation	0.047	0.008	5.820	0.000
Gender	0.896	0.330	2.710	0.007
Age	0.148	0.012	12.830	0.000
Education	2.703	0.248	10.910	0.000
Wealth	0.430	0.104	4.150	0.000
Urban	-0.831	0.389	-2.130	0.033
Constant	48.234	1.136	42.470	0.000

Number of obs =28261
$F_{(27, 28233)}$ = 105.12
Adj. R- Squared = 0.0905
Dependent Variable: Support for democracy as a form of government
Dummy for countries (Reference country: Mexico)

Victimization by Corruption and Support for the Political System

The AmericasBarometer includes a battery of five questions that use a scale from one to seven to measure the political system's legitimacy among citizens[6]. The results of the regression on support for the system are presented in the Appendixes. The variable for the study, victimization by corruption, has a negative relation to legitimacy for the system, even after the control variables are taken into account, as can be seen in Figure XI-14. The figure shows that interviewees who were not victims of corruption have a significantly greater level of confidence in the system. As the number of acts of corruption increase, their support for the system diminishes. Furthermore, this result is supported when using LAPOP's index of victimization by corruption. In conclusion, these results confirm the empirical evidence from previous studies which found that corruption erodes support for the political system and therefore decreases citizen perception of its legitimacy (Seligson 2002, 2006; Canache y Allison 2005).

---

[6] B1. To what extent do you think the courts of justice guarantee a fair trial?
B2. To what extent do you respect the political institutions of (country)?
B3. To what extent do you think that citizens' basic rights are well protected by the political system of (country)?
B4. To what extent do you feel proud of living under the political system of (country)?
B6. To what extent do you think that one should support the political system of (country)?

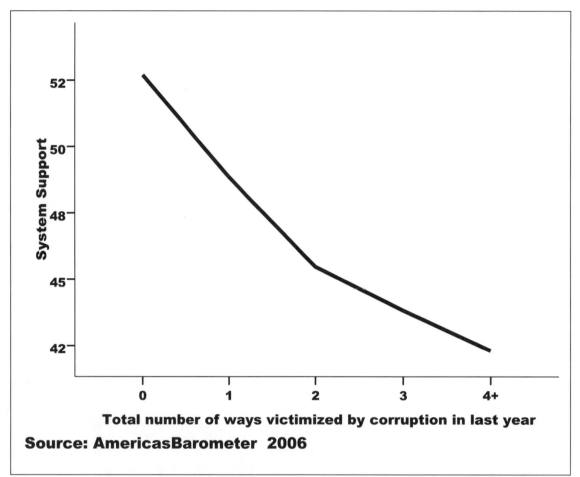

Figure XI-14. The Impact of Victimization by Corruption on Support for the System

Conclusions

This study used the methodology developed by the Latin American Public Opinion Project to determine the magnitude of the problem of corruption in Latin America and the Caribbean. This methodology measures the level of corruption based on actual citizen experience with bribery, instead of their perception of corruption. One of the advantages of this method is that it shows who are most likely to become victims of corruption and where acts of corruption occur. In general, the results of the analysis, which was based on AmericasBarometer data, confirm the fact that corruption is a serious problem in the region.

The data show that municipalities and the courts are the principal sites for corrupt practices. Furthermore, it was found that becoming a victim of corruption negatively affects citizen trust in the justice system and citizen support for the decentralization of resources from the central government to local governments. This suggests that success for programs of decentralization and the strengthening the rule of law in Latin America and the Caribbean depends to a great extent on inroads made in the fight against corruption in municipalities and in

the justice system. Additionally, it was found that, just as previous LAPOP studies suggest, corruption does not affect everyone equally. It has been seen that men, people of higher economic status, and the young are the most likely to be the victims of corrupt acts.

This study has found that corruption constitutes an obstacle for the consolidation of democracy in the region, given that empirical evidence has found that victimization by corruption reduces the level of support for democracy as an ideal form of government and decreases citizen satisfaction with the democratic regimes' performance. Furthermore, evidence indicates that corruption degrades the level of confidence in state institutions, therefore diminishing the political system's legitimacy.

A positive note is that this chapter highlights the fact that Latin American citizens see democracy as an ideal form of government, in spite of their dissatisfaction with the manner in which it functions in their respective countries. However, it was also shown that corruption can have harmful effects on the supply and demand of democracy. Should the current patterns continue, in the long run, democratic stability in the region may be undermined, principally in countries with higher levels of corruption.

References

Almond, Gabriel A., and Sidney Verba. *The Civic Culture: Political Attitudes and Democracy in Five Nations*. Princeton: Princeton University Press, 1963.

Becquart-Leclercq, Jeanne. "Paradoxes of Political Corruption: A French View." In *Political Corruption: A Handbook*, edited by Arnold J. Heidenheimer, Michael Johnston, Victor T. LeVine, 191-210. New Brunswick, NJ, 1989.

Bratton, Michael, Robert B. Mattes, and Emmanuel Gyimah-Boadi. *Public opinion, democracy, and market reform in Africa, Cambridge studies in comparative politics*. New York: Cambridge University Press, 2004.

Camp, Roderic Ai, Kenneth M. Coleman, and Charles L. Davis. "Public Opinion About Corruption: An Exploratory Study in Chile, Costa Rica and Mexico." Portland, Oregon, 2000.

Canache, Damarys, and Michael E. Allison. "Perceptions of Political Corruption in Latin American Democracies." *Latin American Politics and Society* 47, no. 3 (2005): 91.

Della Porta, Donatella. "Social Capital, Beliefs in Government, and Political Corruption." In *Disaffected Democracies: What's Troubling the Trilateral Countries?*, edited by Susan J. Pharr and Robert D. Putnam, 202-28. Princeton: Princeton University Press, 2000.

Diamond, Larry. *Developing Democracy: Toward Consolidation*. Baltimore: Johns Hopkins University Press, 1999.

Easton, David. *A Systems Analysis of Political Life*. New York,: Wiley, 1965.

———. "A Re-Assessment of the Concept of Political Support." *British Journal of Political Science* 5 (1975): 435-57.

Huntington, Samuel P. *Political Order in Changing Societies*. New Haven: Yale University Press, 1968.

Kaufmann, Daniel, Aart Kraay, and Massimo Mastruzzi. "Governance Matters V: Aggregate and Individual Governance Indicators for 1996-2005." (2006).

Lipset, Seymour Martin. "The Social Requisites of Democracy Revisited." *American Sociological Review* 59 (1994): 1-22.

Luna, Juan Pablo. *Cultura política de la democracia en Chile: 2006*. Edited by Latin American Public Opinion Project. Nashville, TN: Vanderbilt University, 2006.

Pharr, Susan J. "Officials' Misconduct and Public Distrust: Japan and the Trilateral Democracies." In *Dissaffected Democracies: What's Troubling the Trilateral Countries?*, edited by Susan J. Pharr and Robert D. Putnam. Princeton: Princeton University Press, 2000.

Seligson, Mitchell A. "The Impact of Corruption on Regime Legitimacy: A Comparative Study of Four Latin American Countries." *Journal of Politics* 64 (2002): 408-33.

———. "The Measurement and Impact of Corruption Victimization: Survey Evidence from Latin America." *World Development* 34, no. 2 (2006): 381-404.

Shin, Doh C. *Mass Politics and Culture in Democratizing Korea*. Cambridge: Cambridge University Press, 1999.

Transparency International. "The Corruption Perception Index." Transparency International, 2006a.

———. "CPI 2006 Regional Results: Americas ": Transparency International, 2006b.

274

Waterbury, John. "Corruption, Political Stability, and Development: Comparative Evidence from Egypt and Morocco." *Government and Opposition* 11 (1976): 426-45.

World Bank. *World Development Report, 1997.* Washington, D. C.: Oxford University Press, 1997.

Zéphyr, Dominique, Yves-François Pierre, and Abby Córdova. *Culture politique de la démocratie en Haïti: 2006.* Edited by Latin American Public Opinion Project. Nashville, TN: Vanderbilt University, 2007.

Appendix

Table XI-5. Determinants of support for the system

	Coefficient.	Stand. Dev.	t	Sig.
Total number of ways they have been victims of corruption over the past year	-1.408	0.155	-9.070	0.000
Satisfaction with the performance of the current president	0.258	0.006	45.830	0.000
Victimization by crime	-0.021	0.003	-6.590	0.000
Perception of the country's economic situation	0.125	0.006	21.580	0.000
Gender	-0.488	0.240	-2.040	0.041
Age	0.042	0.008	4.940	0.000
Education	-0.187	0.181	-1.040	0.299
Wealth	-0.076	0.075	-1.010	0.314
Urban	-1.475	0.282	-5.240	0.000
Constant	-1.408	0.155	-9.070	0.000

Number of observations = 30225
$F_{(28, 30196)} = 285.71$
Adj. R-squared = 0.2087
Dependent Variable: Index of support for the political system.
Dummy for countries (Reference country: Mexico).

XII. Justice and democracy: the Rule of Law in the Americas

Juan Carlos Donoso[1]

Abstract

The administration of justice is based on the ability of the judicial system to give the citizens what they are entitled to. Judicial independence is an indispensable requisite for the proper functioning of judicial power in the Americas. This chapter explores the effects that structural variables, such as the autonomy of the justice system have on personal attitudes of citizens towards that system and the consequences of those attitudes in the possibilities for the consolidation of liberal democracy in the continent.

Judicial reform and the consolidation of the autonomy of the justice system have been at the top of the list in Latin America when it came time to design new public policies. These reforms have been aimed to strengthen the judicial power with respect to the Executive and the Legislature, but also to improve the way the case load is managed, the competence of the judges and the overall mechanisms of conflict resolution. The relevance of justice reform, however, may seem diminished when the system overall lacks legitimacy among the population. The present chapter takes on the subject of the legitimacy of the justice system and citizen support for the institutions that make out the rule of law, especially in Latin American countries, as well as the consequences that these attitudes may come to have on the region's democratic consolidation. The first section of the chapter will focus on the effects that judicial strength has on individual attitudes towards the judicial system. A second segment will look at individual level variables that act as predictors of citizen support for the judiciary. Finally, I will examine the consequences that a low degree of support for the institutions of the rule of law can have on the process of democratic consolidation in Latin America, as well as on the raise of new "hybrid" democracies in the region.

Judicial "Power"

The strength of the justice system in a country is a key factor for the legitimacy of a democratic regime. The consolidation of democracy can only take place once a series of requisites have been fulfilled, one of which is the formation of an autonomous justice system that can generate in its citizens a feeling of trust in the rule of law (Becker 1999, Carothers 2006). A democracy with a weak judicial system may have serious problems in securing popular support for the rule of law (Prillaman 2000, Verner 1984). Holston and Caldeira (1998) observe that the concept of citizenship, indispensable in a democracy, includes as a minimum the notion of justice, legality, access and universality of the law. When the majority of the population perceives the justice system as inaccessible and inefficient, this may foster a feeling of

---

[1] I would like to thank USAID for the funding provided to LAPOP and the AmericasBarometer 2006. My thanks especially to the USAID mission in Ecuador, which has funded my studies at Vanderbilt University and has supported my academic career at all times.

"incomplete citizenship", which makes their commitment to the regime decrease in intensity or disappear all together (O'Donell 1994).

The strength of the justice system in a country can be interpreted in different ways. Some of the existing literature which deals with the subject identifies three main characteristics of a healthy judiciary. The first one is the free access of the citizenry, meaning that everyone should have the same opportunity to utilize the services of the justice administration system. For this to happen, two conditions must be fulfilled; physical presence of the judicial institutions throughout the territory and reasonable costs to those who demand the services of the justice system, so that everyone can use it. The latter condition is linked to the second characteristic of a healthy judiciary, which is efficiency. An effective judiciary must comply with two basic requisites. First, to process all cases within the time frames established by law and second, to execute the sentences dictated by the appropriate judges. The third and most important characteristic of a strong judiciary is the autonomy of the judicial system with respect to the executive and the legislature and the independence to rule against them (Cappelletti 1985). Although the terms "autonomy" and "independence" are similar, one must separate one from the other theoretically. Autonomy is an institutional trait that allows the judicial system to build its own institutional structure (Rios-Figueroa 2006). Independence, on the other hand, stems from the principle of conflict resolution by a neutral party (Larkins 1996). An independent judiciary, then, is one that can freely decide, based on the law and the facts and without taking into consideration the preferences of the parties involved (Fiss 1993).

Even though the constitutions of every Latin American country guarantee the autonomy of the judicial system, these provisions are not always applied in practice due to several reasons, such as power grabbing by the executive, the constant interference of political interest groups or pressure from public opinion in certain matters. In this study, judicial strength will be determined based on the annual reports from the U.S. State Department (www.state.gov). These reports, which begun in 1977, are published annually and their goal is to describe the efforts that every country makes to put in practice their commitment to protect the human rights of its citizens. The reports are individual and contain a detailed description of human rights violations that were reported in each country by affected individuals or by national or international media outlets. These violations are then analyzed in different contexts, on e of which is due process. Within this analysis, the reports evaluate the strength of the judicial system of every country and the main problems that they face. Although these chronicles are subject to the criteria of their authors, this is one of the few systematic sources of information about judiciaries in Latin America. Various academic studies written about the judicial system in the region ratify the validity of these reports (Cross 1999, Dakolias 1994, Howard and Carey 2004, Yamanashi 2002).

The Data

This section will attempt to demonstrate the importance of the strength of a judiciary has on the trust that the citizens of a country have in it. Confidence in the justice system in the Americas is measured based on the data from the 2006-2007 AmericasBarometer, gathered in 19 countries in the region. In Latin America and the Caribbean, the interviews were conducted face to face, while in the United States and Canada phone surveys were carried out and a shorter version of the questionnaire was used due to budget constraints. The questionnaire was produced by the Latin American Public Opinion Project –LAPOP- which is based at Vanderbilt University. To measure the legitimacy of the justice system, the AmericasBarometer utilizes the following question.

> **B10A.** To what extent do you trust the justice system?

In order to answer this question, the respondent is shown a scale from 1 to 7 in which 1 means 'not al all' and seven means 'a lot'. However, to facilitate the reader's comprehension, every scale has been turned into a 0 to 100 interval. Figure XI.1 illustrates how the countries in the Americas are distributed according to their level of confidence in the justice system. It is notable that the mean of the whole region is below the midpoint of the scale, at a score of only 42. Canada is the country where citizens trust the judiciary the most with a score of 64 in the scale from 0 to 100. The United States and Costa Rica follow closely, which is not a surprise, if one considers that those are thought to be the three strongest democracies in the region. The presence of Guyana, a small and relatively unknown country among the nations with the highest scores is unexpected. It could be speculated that the British influence in Guyana is at least partially responsible for the high level of support for the judiciary; however this is not a tendency that repeats itself in other countries that share that heritage, such as Jamaica, which finds itself just below the mean of the region, as the Figure shows. At the lower end of the scale is Ecuador, with a score of 28, less than half than Canada and well below the average for the Americas. Considering this country's recent political history, however, its levels of trust with compared to the other countries of the region is not all that surprising.

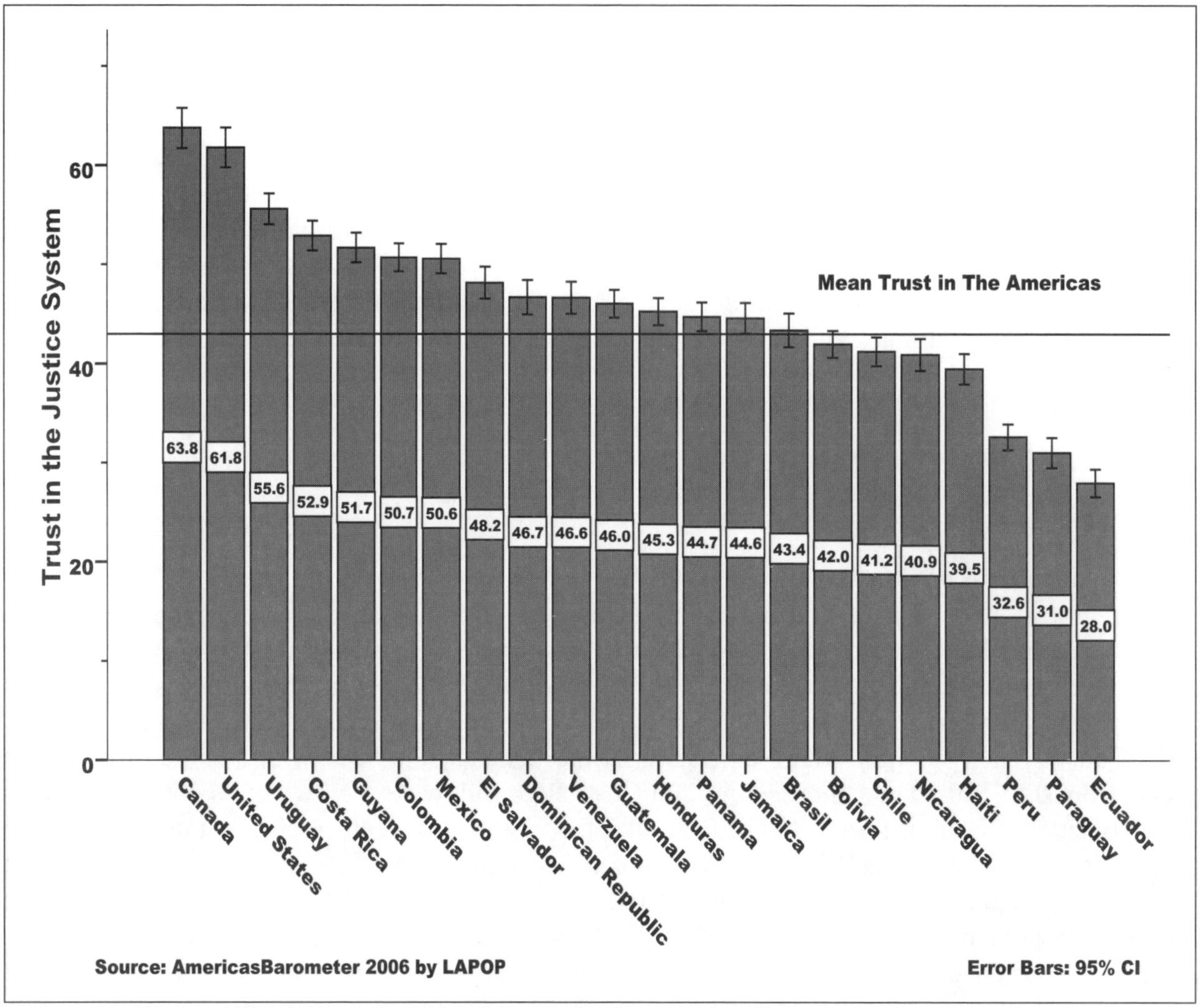

Figure XII-1. Level of Confidence in the Justice System in the Americas

Which factors explain the large differences that exist between countries? A fraction of the answer lies in the experiences, circumstances and attitudes of the citizens of each country. The rest of it, however, goes beyond individual differences. Each bar of Figure XII-1 shows the level of confidence of an average citizen in a given country. An analysis of variance suggests, however, that at least 15% of the variation in the dependent variable –level of confidence in the justice system- can be explained by difference between countries and not between individuals. This means that structural characteristics, like judicial strength in this case, can mold the attitudes of individuals (Seligson and Muller 1994).

As I mentioned above, the strength of the judicial system in the countries of the region was measured by looking at the individual Human Rights Country Reports published yearly by the U.S. State Department. Since these reports only give a descriptive narration of the strengths and weaknesses of the judicial system in each country, it was necessary to devise a coding scheme in order to systematize the information. To this order, a three point scale was built, in which a score of one would be assigned to countries with low levels of autonomy and judicial independence. Countries with mid and high levels of autonomy and independence received a score of two and three respectively. I based the scoring criteria on the one used previously by Cingranelli and Richards as well as the one used by Tate, Poe and Keith to measure the degree of human rights protection in a country (Tate, et al. 1999, www.humanrightsdata.org). This was the criteria used for assigning individual scores to each country:

1.- Low: The judiciary is not autonomous or independent. The interference from the executive is constant and judges can be removed without warning.
2.- Medium: The judiciary is described as partially independent. Executive influence is less notorious but judges do not enjoy full protections.
3.- High: The judiciary is generally independent. The courts can rule against the executive without fear of repercussions and judges enjoy full constitutional protections.

Figure XII-2 shows the scores that each country in the sample was assigned. Only four countries, Canada, The United States, Costa Rica and Chile, received a score of three, while eight countries, nearly half the sample, received a score of one. The values assigned to the countries according to this scale mostly coincide with the levels of confidence shown by the citizens of those countries in their justice systems, as shown in the previous graph.

To capture the impact that a structural trait such as the strength the judiciary of a country can have in the individual level of confidence that a citizen has on his justice system I have developed a hierarchical lineal regression model, which measures the effect that judicial strength has on individual confidence, controlling for other individual predictors that may also influence the dependent variable. These predictors include the level of education, the perception of corruption in the public sector, satisfaction with democracy and victimization by violence and crime during the year previous to the survey. Table XII-1 shows the result of the regression equation.

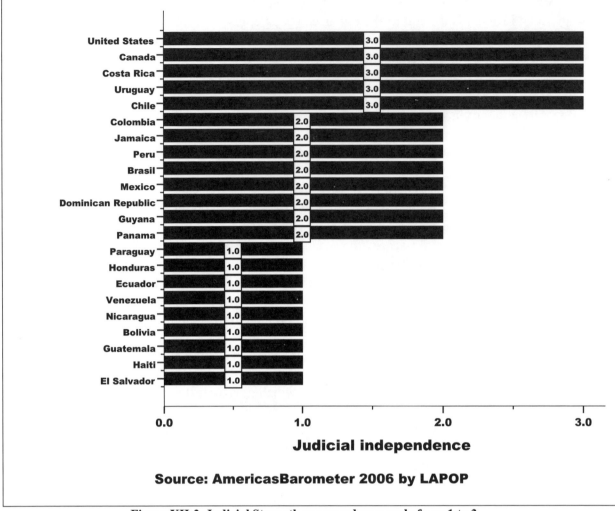

Figure XII-2. Judicial Strength measured on a scale from 1 to 3.

Table XII-1. Effect of Judicial Strength on Confidence on Judicial System

	Coef.	Std. Err.	P>z
Judicial Strength	0.242	0.110	**0.028**
Education	-0.048	0.016	**0.002**
Perception of corruption	0.181	0.013	**0.000**
Crime victimization	0.212	0.029	**0.000**
Satisfaction with democracy	0.530	0.016	**0.000**
Income	-0.005	0.006	0.382
Constant	4.068	0.232	0.000

As is shown in the table, the effect of judicial strength on individual trust in the judiciary is positive and significant. This means that the more autonomous and independent the judiciary of a country is, the more the citizens of that country will trust it, as is illustrated on Figure XII-3. Other variables that were also significant are perception of corruption and having been victimized by violent crime. The regression equation shows that people who perceive a high degree of corruption among public officials as well as citizens who were victimized by crime show lower levels of trust in their justice systems. Finally, education is another factor that has an important effect, although the relationship between this variable and trust in the judiciary is negative, meaning that people with higher levels of education tend to have lower levels of trust in the justice system than those with low levels of education.

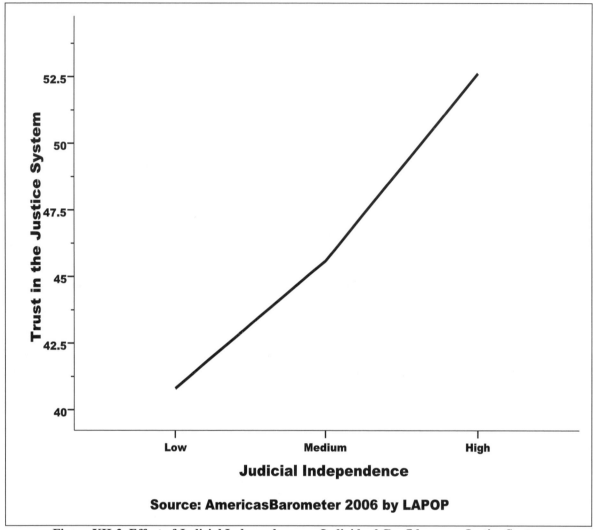

Figure XII-3. Effect of Judicial Independence on Individual Confidence on Justice System

It is important to note that the effect of judicial strength on individual confidence on the justice system could be attenuated by other predictors that were not included on the regression equation. The reason behind this omission is that some questions were not included in the questionnaires used in the United States and Canada, since brevity has to be prioritized when conducting a survey via telephone. The results shown in this model, whoever, show that even controlling for other individual level variables, such as personal experiences and perceptions; structural factors do create personal attitudes.

The following section will focus on uncovering the predictors of individual support for the institutions of the rule of law in Latin America. Now that I have shown that structural variables can have consequences in the generation of individual attitudes, the next pages will emphasize some of the individual level predictors that shape those attitudes. It is important to mention that Canada and the United States will not be included in that analysis due to the limitations that I have already addressed.

Support for the Institution of the Rule of Law

While most nations in Latin America have undergone a transition process to electoral democracy, many of the legal institutions in these countries still maintain authoritarian traits. This is a problem which is not exclusive to Latin America, but to the majority of democracies born from what is now known as the third wave of democratization (Huntington 1991, O'Donnell and Schmitter 1986). The path that these democratic regimes have walked clearly shows that the institutionalization of an electoral process is achieved more easily than that of the rule of law (Pereira 2000, Schedler, et al. 1999). But what is the rule of law? It is generally understood that the rule of law is intimately connected to the capacity of a legal system to apply the law efficiently and equally (Seligson 2004), but the formulation of a precise definition is a complicated job due mostly to the multiple dimensions of the concept (Goertz 2006). Many theoretical discussions have taken place about what constitutes a definition of the rule of law and what are its necessary and sufficient conditions (Collier, et al. 2006)

The current section has the goal of finding the variables that determine individual citizen support for the institutions that make up the rule of law in Latin America and the Caribbean. To this effect, I have chosen a battery of questions that attempt to capture some of the dimensions of the rule of law. It is important to note that the group of questions selected by no means covers every dimension of this essentially contested and complex concept. However, it is a good practical approximation to the effect of the analysis that will be done in this chapter. The questions in the AmericasBarometer that measure support for the institutions of the rule of law are:

B1. To what extent do you believe that you can get a fair trial under this country's legal system?
B10A. To what extent do you trust the justice system?
B18. To what extent do you trust the police?
B31. To what extent do you trust this country's Supreme Court?

As I stated above, these questions contain some of the dimensions of the concept of rule of law, such as the necessity for due process, the institutionalization of the justice system and the state's duty to provide security for its citizens (Schor 2003). The questions have been combined to create an index of citizen support for the institutions of the rule of law. A reliability test indicates that the index's Cronbach's Alpha is of .756, which means that the questions selected for the index of citizen support for the institutions of the rule of law are highly correlated and do not measure different concepts. A factor analysis also shows that the four variables create a single dimension. Figure XII-4 shows how the countries of Latin America and the Caribbean are distributed according to the level of their citizen's trust for the institutions that make up the rule of law. As the graph shows, there is an average score of 45 on a scale from 0 to 100 for the whole region, which again is worrisome, since it does not reach the midpoint of the scale. Again there are big differences visible between countries. Those countries at the top of the scale, such

as Guyana, Colombia and Costa Rica, score over 20 points higher that the countries at the bottom of the scale, like Ecuador and Paraguay.

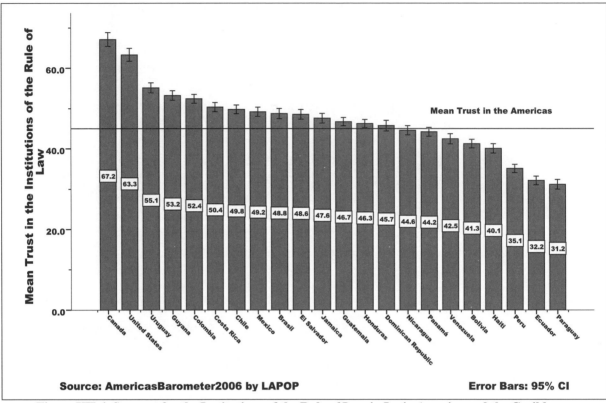

Figure XII-4. Support for the Institutions of the Rule of Law in Latin America and the Caribbean

What factors create popular support for the institutions that make up the rule of law? Socio-demographic variables such as education, age and geographic location inside a country are usually powerful explanatory variables for the generation of individual attitudes. For this study I have designed a regression model which attempts to uncover the predictors for individual support for the institutions of the rule of law in Latin America and the Caribbean. Table XI-2 contains the result of the regression equation. It is surprising that variables such as the geographic location of the citizens turn out not to be significantly related to the dependent variable. Institutions such as the Police and lower courts usually lack a strong presence in rural settings, which causes citizens in these areas to have a lower level of trust than citizens in urban areas. The difference, however, turned out not to be significant. This does not mean, however, that this tendency does not present itself in some countries; it just means that at the regional level, when one combines it with other factors, geographic location inside a country turns out to be statistically insignificant as a predictor of individual support for the institutions of the rule of law.

Table XII-2. Predictors for Individual Support of Institutions of the Rule of Law

	B	Std. Error	Sig.
(Constant)	44.251	8.950	0.000
Urban-Rural	3.049	2.545	0.232
Satisfaction with democracy	2.217	0.629	**0.000**
Corruption Victimization	-0.055	0.025	**0.028**
Corruption in Courts	-0.262	3.220	0.935
Perception of corruption	-0.114	0.042	**0.007**
Crime Victimization	-0.055	0.035	**0.028**
Education	0.121	0.310	0.696
Wealth measured by material possesions	-0.021	0.724	0.977
Income	-0.000	0.000	0.515
Mexico	0.833	8.004	0.917
Guatemala	-2.894	6.765	0.669
Salvador	-0.901	6.199	0.884
Honduras	-17.65	8.789	**0.048**
Nicaragua	2.733	6.855	0.690
Panama	1.104	16.12	0.945
Colombia	8.657	17.49	0.621
Ecuador	-19.19	7.115	**0.007**
Peru	-8.721	6.666	0.128
Chile	0.935	15.87	0.975
Dominican Republic	-12.49	6.000	**0.038**
Haiti	0.608	5.994	0.919
Jamaica	-4.008	5.734	0.485
Guyana	2.679	5.436	0.622
Uruguay	15.99	14.31	0.264
Venezuela	18.31	15.85	0.248
R Squared			0.177

Other variables which do not have a significant effect of the levels of individual trust for the institutions of the rule of law are economic factors, such as income and wealth measured in ownership of material goods, such as household appliances, cell phones, functioning bathrooms inside the house, etc. The data show that these variables have a positive but not significant effect on individual levels of confidence in legal institutions.

Education turned out to be another insignificant factor in predicting individual support for the institutions of the rule of law. Prior studies conducted by the Latin American Public Opinion Project have shown that the relationship between education and institutional legitimacy is usually negative. This means that those people with higher levels of education usually present lower levels of institutional trust than those that are less educated. A correlation analysis between the education and our index of individual trust for the institutions of the rule of law indeed shows that when these two variables are the only ones included in the mix, the relationship is negative. However, when one adds more ingredients to it, the effect of education is attenuated by personal experiences, especially with corruption and crime.

Corruption is a problem that has plagued all Latin American democracies since their rebirth in the late 70s and early 80s. In the last decade, several elected and appointed officials in Latin America, including Presidents, as in the cases of Mexico, Costa Rica and Ecuador, have faced criminal charges for acts of corruption committed during the exercise of their public mandate. Corruption can be defined as the utilization of public goods for private benefits (Weyland 1998) and it is a disease that has quickly proliferated and attracted the attention of the academic and political communities as well as the International Organizations. Due to its nature, corruption is extremely hard to measure (Buscaglia 2001, Seligson 2006) and that is why academics have used various strategies to do so. One of the more widely used measures is Transparency International's Corruption Perception Index, which is based in surveys carried out to businessmen in different countries all over the world. In this chapter I will use two different measures of corruption. One is similar to CPI and is based on a question from the questionnaire of the AmericasBarometer.

> **EXC7**. Keeping in mind your experience and what you've heard, is corruption among public officials:
> (1) Completely generalized   (2) Somewhat extensive
> (3) A little extensive   (4) Not generalized at all

The second way to measure corruption has is to capture the experiences of people with it. Citizens in Latin America and the Caribbean are often victims of corruption by public officials, such as police officers and judges and also by private entities, such as schools and even at the workplace. The AmericasBarometer has developed a battery of questions that is aimed at measuring the respondents' experiences with corruption at various settings, like the courts, public hospitals, schools and other public offices. Based on those questions we have created an index of corruption victimization which measures the frequency with which our respondents were victimized by corruption on the year prior to them answering our survey. For analytical purposes, I have separated the question that measures corruption in the judiciary and inserted it into the regression model separately, because of the relevance that corruption in the judicial system should have on the generation of individual attitudes towards the institutions of the rule of law. What the regression analysis shows is that not only those who have been victimized by corruption in the courts, but those people who had to pay bribes in different settings have much lower levels of trust than those who did not have to pay a bribe in the year prior to our survey, as shown in Figure XII-5.

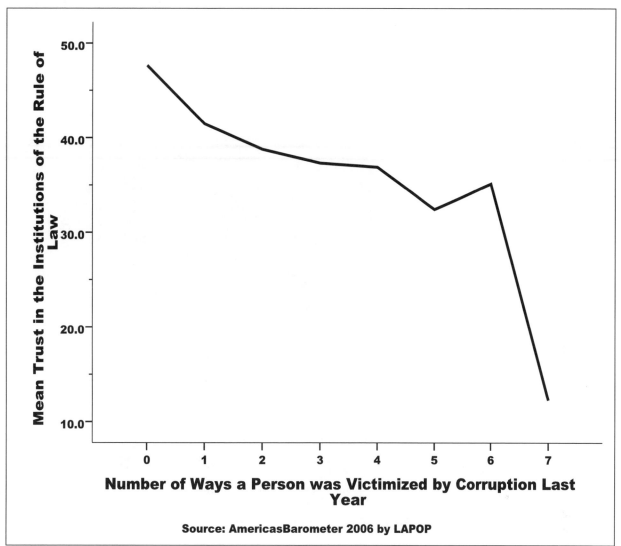

Figure XII-5. Corruption Victimization and Individual Trust for the Institutions of the Rule of Law

The respondents' perception of corruption also turned out to be a determinant factor in their support for the institutions that make out the rule of law. Just like with victimization, those people who perceive a high level of corruption in the public sector show lower levels of institutional support than their counterpart, which believe that corruption in the public sector is not at all generalized. Figure XII-6 illustrates the results of the relationship between these two variables. Two things should jump to the reader's attention. First, the difference between the groups with high and low levels of support for the institutions of the rule of law is not as drastic as when we asked them about their personal experiences with corruption. Second, apparently people who consider that corruption is not generalized at all in the public sector have lower levels of confidence in the institutions of the rule of law than those who perceive that it is somewhat generalized. The error bars at the top of the bars, however, show that the difference between one and the other is not statistically significant, but just a product of the low number of people who chose that option. Figure XII-6, then, brings us to the conclusion that the best way to measure

corruption is to look at it through the citizens personal experiences with it , because the results this measure produces are more reliable.

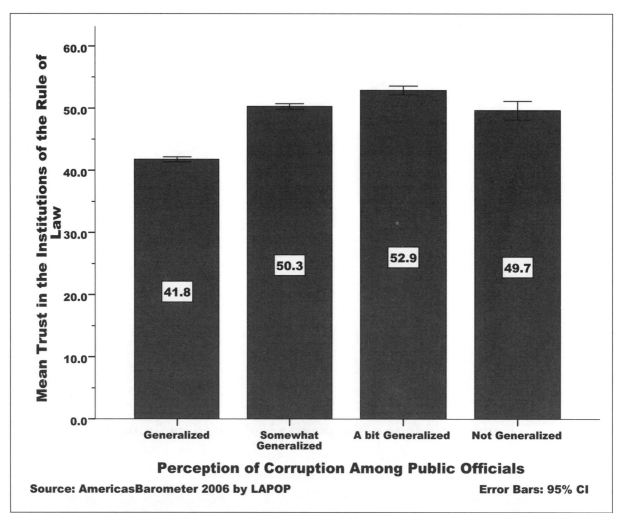

Figure XII-6. Perception of Corruption and Confidence in the Institutions of the Rule of Law

Personal experiences with crime also have an important effect in personal levels of institutional support. For the rule of law to be in place, effective democratic institutions are necessary but not sufficient. The rule of law also needs a collective understanding that the regime type and the institutions are better than the ones in place before the transition to democracy, even with all the problems faced by the new regimes (Cruz 2005). Violence and crime in Central American countries have generated exclusion and diminished social interaction as well as trust in the institutions of the rule of law in that part of the continent (Cruz 2004, Wielandt 2005). The same is happening in the southern hemisphere, where crime victimization has been raising steadily in the last decade. The AmericasBarometer questionnaire addresses the issue of crime in a battery of questions, among which we have selected one to analyze in the present chapter.

VIC1. Have you been the victim of a crime in the last 12 months?
(1) Yes   (2) No   (8) NS/NR

Figure XII-7 ratifies the results presented in the linear regression model. Those respondents who were victimized by a criminal act at least once in the year prior to the survey show significantly lower levels of institutional trust than those who were not victims of a violent crime in the last year.

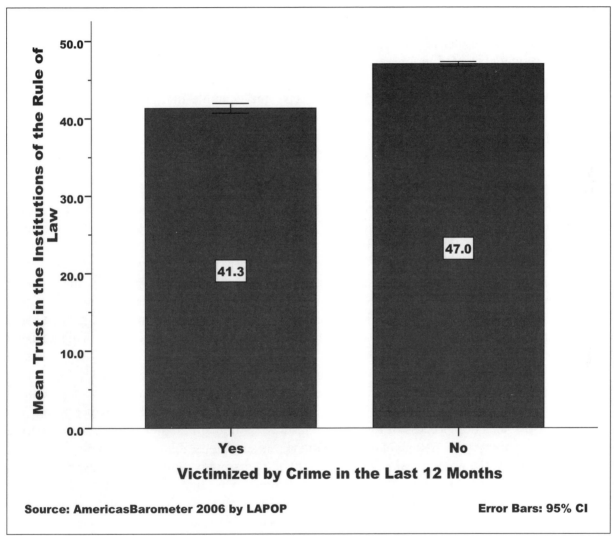

Figure XII-7. Crime Victimization and Confidence in the Institutions of the Rule of Law

Throughout this section I have enumerated some of the factors that contribute to explain the attitudes of citizens towards the institutions of the rule of law in their countries. With the exception of education, most of the socio-demographic variables did not produce a significant impact in the dependent variable. Neither family income and personal wealth measured in the ownership of material goods nor geographical location inside a country have a statistically

significant effect individual attitudes towards the institutions that make up the rule of law. The experiences of citizens with corruption and crime also play an important role in the formation of individual attitudes towards the legal institutions, as is displayed in previous pages. There is one part of the answer missing, however, and that part has to do with context. The regression model presented in this section uses dichotomous variables for each country, with the objective of analyzing the impact of context on individual support for the institutions for the rule of law, taking Costa Rica as a reference. The results indicate that while the effect is not significant for every country, it is in some of them, such as Ecuador, Peru, Chile and the Dominican Republic.

What does this means? How is it possible that a variable with the name of a country can significantly affect the formation of individual attitudes towards the rule of law? The answer is simple. What the results reveal is that the context in which one lives is important. For the regression model presented in this section, dichotomous variables were devised for every country in the sample except for Costa Rica. This is done so that the results can be compared to the country that is omitted from the model. Let's take the example of Ecuador. The regression coefficient for Ecuador is negative and statistically significant. This means that, ceteris paribus, the average Ecuadorian reports a lower level of institutional trust than the average Costa Rican. In simple terms, living in Ecuador has a negative impact on individual support for the institutions that make up the rule of law.

This can be explained in a simple way. Ecuador's political environment in the last decade has been characterized by instability and judicial insecurity, especially due to the events that have taken place the last couple years with the judicial sector (Inclán 2006, Mejía Acosta, et al. 2006). At the end of 2004, the legislature, with a simple majority, came up with a resolution that expelled 27 of the 31 Supreme Court Justices. The reason given by Congress was that through that resolution they were purging a court that only certain political interest groups. However, Congress made the mistake of building a new Supreme Court packed with judges that were linked with all of the political parties which made up the congressional majority. This decision was rejected by the majority of the population; and intense popular pressure forced then President Lucio Gutierrez to disqualify the new Supreme Court Justices. The mechanism to elect a new Supreme Court was never devised, since Gutierrez was overthrown five days later. The judicial system was shut down for a year, since its main institution did not function throughout the duration of the selection process of the 31 new justices. Although the new judges were selected under heavy scrutiny from national and international organizations, it has failed to obtain popular trust and support (Donoso, et al. 2006). The situation has only gotten worse by a series of irregularities committed by the National Chief of Police. Four Chiefs of Police were replaced in only two weeks due to incompetence and allegations of corruption. These events, compared to the relative political stability that has reigned in Costa Rica, exemplify the importance of context in the generation of individual attitudes in Latin America and the Caribbean.

Democracy and the Rule of Law

In the section leading up to this one, the discussion focused on the structural and individual predictors of citizen support for the institutions of the rule of law in Latin America and the Caribbean. We know that variables such as the strength of the judicial system, the experience of our respondents with crime and corruption, the level of education and the socio-political context are important in the generation of individual attitude towards the institutions of the rule of law. But is this relevant for the democratic consolidation of the region? The answer is definitely yes. The last few paragraphs of this chapter will be dedicated to demonstrate the importance of citizen support for the institutions of the rule of law in the survival of representative democracy.

The third wave of democratization begun in Latin America over 25 years ago and still democratic consolidation continues to be perhaps the greatest challenge of the region's nations. The many flaws in the administration of justice systems in the continent and the lack of security faced by citizens play a key role in this problem(Binder 1991, Buscaglia, et al. 2000). To better illustrate the relationship between popular support for the institutions of the rule of law and democratic consolidation I will again turn to the data gathered by the 2006-2007 AmericasBarometer. There are many ways to measure support for democracy in a country. One of them is to see if the general population thinks of democracy as the only game in town. This means that they prefer democracy to any other form of government, even with the problems that come with a democratic regime. The question formulated in our questionnaire is:

ING4. Democracy may have its problems but it is still better than any other form of government. To what extent do you agree with this phrase?

The respondents were shown a scale from 1 to 7 where one equals 'fully disagree' and seven represents 'fully agree'. Figure XII-8 shows the effect that support for the institutions of the rule of law has on the legitimacy of democracy as a form of government. The relationship between the two variables is as expected, with those reporting high levels of institutional trust also presenting high levels of acceptance for democracy as the best form of government. The graph also gives us some encouraging news. Even those people with extremely low levels of trust for the institutions that make up the rule of law are in the higher end of the scale of democratic desirability. This means that even citizens who completely distrust legal institutions believe in democracy. But what kind of democracy do they want?

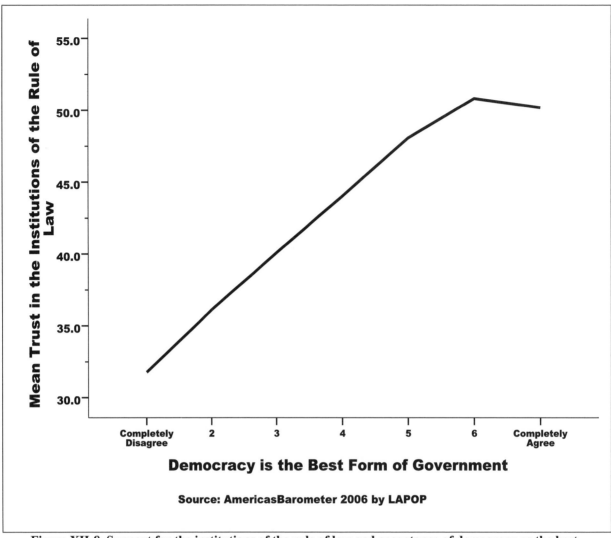

Figure XII-8. Support for the institutions of the rule of law and acceptance of democracy as the best form of government

In the last few years, observers and academics have been witnesses to the rise of what some now call "hybrid" democracies in the region. These democracies hold free and fair elections, but ignore some of the basic principles of liberal and representative democracies, such as the separation of powers, the right to private property and the guarantee of civil liberties. While many people question these kinds of democracies, some of these restrictions are supported by some people, who, tired of unfulfilled promises, are willing to give something up in exchange for some stability and personal economic growth.

A lot has been said in recent years about the rebirth of populism in Latin America. Populist regimes are characterized by strong and charismatic leaders who tend to woo the crowds by generating in them a feeling of identity. People who vote for populist leaders feel that they understand their needs and problems better than anyone and that they will work tirelessly to solve

them. This includes dodging legal 'obstacles' to get things done faster. The legal systems of many Latin American and Caribbean countries are slow and inefficient. Many countries in the region still have not resorted to oral trials, which makes legal processes long and tedious. Figure XII-9 illustrates the result of asking people about the usefulness of judges in a democratic regime.

> **POP3**.
> 1.Judges frequently get in the way of our presidents and they should be ignored.
> 2. Even when judges sometimos impede the labor of our presidents, their decisions must always be respected.

As the graph shows, there is a significant difference both statistically and substantively between those who believe that judges are a necessity and those who think they are not indispensable, with regards to their levels of trust in the institutions of the rule of law.

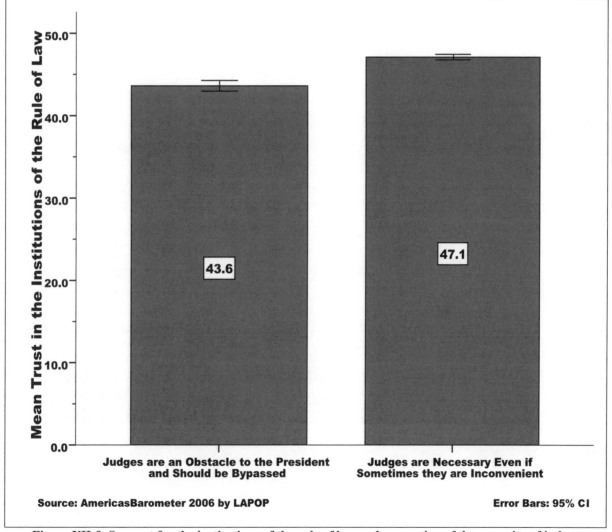

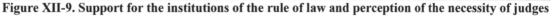

Figure XII-9. Support for the institutions of the rule of law and perception of the necessity of judges

Finally, there are people willing to justify extreme measures to improve the administration of justice in their countries. The Supreme Court is not the most trusted institution in Latin America and the Caribbean. In a scale from 0 to 100, the mean of support for this institution barely breaks 40. This makes the Supreme Court one of the least trusted institutions in the region, outperforming only Congress and the political parties. A battery of questions designed by the AmericasBarometer attempts to capture the people's tolerance for authoritarian and antidemocratic measures, such as shutting down a country's Supreme Court.

JC16. Do you think that there could ever be a reason to justify the closing of the Supreme Court by the President? (1) Yes (2) No

Figure XII-10 shows that people who would justify an eventual closing of the Supreme Court by the president have lower levels of trust for the institutions of the rule of law that their counterparts.

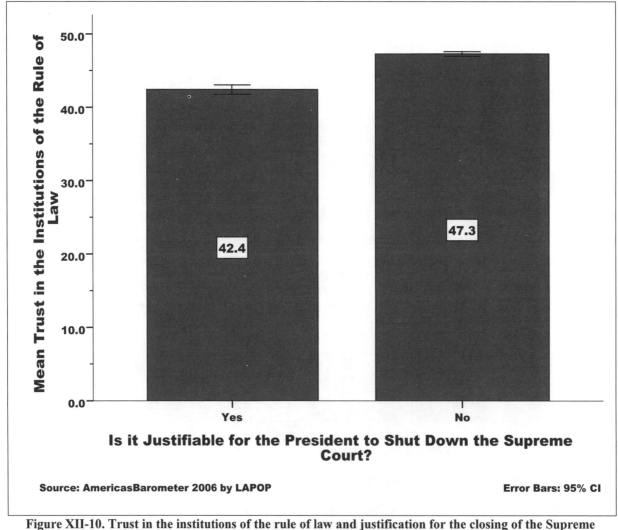

Figure XII-10. Trust in the institutions of the rule of law and justification for the closing of the Supreme Court

Conclusion

This chapter has attempted to uncover the factors that determine individual support for the institutions of the rule of law in Latin America and the Caribbean. I started by underlining the importance of structural variables, such as the need for a strong judiciary, capable of ruling against the government without fear of repercussions. I also reviewed some of the individual predictors of institutional support, from which corruption and crime victimization as well as context stand out. Finally, I observed the dangerous consequences that the lack of trust in the institutions of the rule of law can bring to liberal democracy in the region. Citizens who are disappointed with the way their governments provide justice and security are willing to tolerate drastic and authoritarian measures in order to fell safer. It is important that the governments in the continent work to control the raising levels of crime and corruption and to build solid and autonomous institutions with efficient mechanisms of accountability that can generate trust and support.

References

Becker, David. "Latin America: Beyond Democratic Consolidation." *Journal of Democracy* 10, no. 2 (1999): 138-51.

Binder, Alberto. "Reform of the Penal System in Latin America." Arlington, VA: Council of State Courts, 1991.

Buscaglia, Edgardo. "Judicial Corruption in Developing Countries: Its Causes and Economic Consequences." In *Essays in Public Policy*. Washington, DC: Hoover Institute, 2001.

Buscaglia, Edgardo, Valeria Merino, and Ana Lucia Jaramillo. "Estudio Sobre La Correlacion Entre La Existencia De Justicia Y La Consolidacion De La Democracia En Ecuador. Quito: Corporacion Latinoamericana para el Desarrollo, 2000.

Cappelletti, Mauro. "Who Watches the Watchmen? A Comparative Study on Judicial Responsability." In *Judicial Independence: The Contemporary Debate*, edited by S. Shetreet and J. Deschenes. Dordrecht: martinus Nijhoff Publishers, 1985.

Carothers, Thomas. *Promoting the Rule of Law Abroad: In Search of Knowledge.* Washington D.C.: Carnegie Endowment for International Peace, 2006.

Collier, David, Fernando Hidalgo, and Andra Maciuceanu. "Essentially Contested Concepts: Debates and Applications." *Journal of Political Ideolofies* 11, no. 3 (2006): 211-46.

Cross, Frank B. "The Relevance of Law in Human Rights Protection." *International Review of Law and Economics* 19 (1999): 87-98.

Cruz, Jose Miguel. "Pandillas Y Capital Social En Centroamerica." In *Maras Y Pandillas De Centroamerica*: UCA Editores, 2004.

———. "Violencia Y Democratizacion En Centro America: El Impacto Del Crimen En Los Regimenes De La Post Guerra." PNUD, 2005.

Dakolias, Maria. "Ecuador: Judicial Sector Assesment." Washington D.C: The World Bank, 1994.

Donoso, Juan Carlos, Daniel Moreno, Diana Maria Orces, Vivian Schwartz-Blum, and Mitchell A. Seligson. "Democracy Audit: Ecuador 2006." Quito: Latin American Public Opinion Project, 2006.

Fiss, Owen. "The Limits of Judicial Independence." *University of Miami Inter-American Law Review* 25 (1993).

Goertz, Gary. *Social Science Concepts: A User's Guide*: Princeton University Press, 2006.

Holston, James, and Teresa P.R. Caldeira. "Democracy, Law and Violence: Disjunctions of Brazilian Citizenship." In *Fault Lines of Democracy in Post-Transition Latin America*, edited by Felipe Aguero. Coral Gables: North-South Center Press, 1998.

Howard, Robert, and Henry Carey. "Is an Independent Judiciary Necessary for Democracy?" *Judicature* 87, no. 6 (2004): 284-91.

Huntington, Samuel. *The Third Wave: Democratization in the Late Twentieth Century* Norman: University of Oklahoma Press, 1991.

Inclán, Silvia. "Fragile Judicial Independence in Latin America: A Decade after Judicial Reform." In *Annual Meeting of the Midwest Political Science Association*. Chigago, 2006.

Larkins, Christopher. "Judicial Independence and Democratization: A Theoretical and Conceptual Analysis." *The American Journal of Comparative Law* 44, no. 4 (1996): 605-26.

Mejía Acosta, Andres, Maria Caridad Araujo, Anibal Perez-Linan, and Sebastian Saiegh. "Veto Players, Fickle Institutions and Low Quality Policies: The Policy Making Process in Ecuador (1979-2005)." Inter-American Development Bank, 2006.

O'Donell, Guillermo. "Delegative Democracy." *Journal of Democracy* 5 (1994): 55-69.

O'Donnell, Guillermo, and Philippe Schmitter. *Transitions from Authoritarian Rule: Tentative Conclusions About Uncertain Democracies*. Baltimore: John Hopkins University Press, 1986.

Pereira, Anthony. "An Ugly Democracy? State Violence and the Rule of Law in Post-Authoritarian Brazil." In *Democratic Brazil: Actors, Institutions and Processes.*, edited by Peter Kingstone Jr and Thimoty J. Powers. Pittsburgh: University of Pittsburgh's Press, 2000.

Prillaman, William. *The Judiciary and Democratic Decay in Latin America: Declining Confidence in the Rule of Law*. Westport: Praeger, 2000.

Rios-Figueroa, Julio. "Judicial Independence: Definition, Measurement and Its Effects on Corruption: An Analysis of Latin America." Doctoral Dissertation, New York University, 2006.

Schedler, Andreas, Larry Diamond, and Marc F. Plattner. *The Self Restraining State: Power and Accountability in New Democracies*. Boulder: Lynne Riener, 1999.

Schor, Miguel. "The Rule of Law and Democratic Consolidation in Latin America." In *Latin American Studies Association*. Dallas, Texas, 2003.

Seligson, Mitchell. "Auditoria De La Democracia: Ecuador 2004." edited by CEDATOS. Quito, 2004.

———. "The Measurement and Impact of Corruptiuon Victimization: Survey Evidence in Latin America." *World Development* 34, no. 2 (2006): 381-404.

Seligson, Mitchell, and Edward N. Muller. "Civic Culture and Democracy: The Question of the Causal Relationship." *American Political Science Review* 88 (1994): 635-54.

Tate, Neal, Linda Camp Keith, and Steven Poe. "Repression of the Human Right to Personal Integrity Revisited: A Global Cross-National Study Covering the Years 1976-1993." *International Studies Quarterly* 43 (1999): 291-315.

Verner, Joel G. "The Independence of Supreme Courts in Latin America: A Review of the Literature." *Journal of Latin American Studies* 16, no. 2 (1984): 463-506.

Weyland, Kurt. "The Politics of Corruption in Latin America." *Journal of Democracy* 9, no. 2 (1998): 108-21.

Wielandt, Gonzalo. "Hacia La Construccion De Lecciones Del Posconflicto En America Latina Y El Caribe. Una Mirada a La Violencia Juvenil En Centroamerica." Santiago de Chile: CEPAL, 2005.

www.humanrightsdata.org. "The Cingranelli and Richards Human Rights Dataset." (2004).

www.state.gov. *U.S. State Department's Annual Human Rights Country Reports* 2005 [cited].

Yamanashi, David Scott. "Judicial Independence and Human Rights." In *American Political Science Association Annual Meeting*, 2002.